Operation
Desert Shield/
Desert Storm

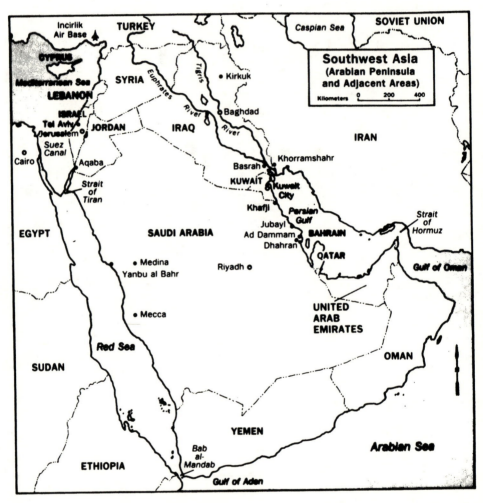

Southwest Asia (Arabian Peninsula and Adjacent Areas). Source: History and Museums Division, U.S. Marine Corps.

OPERATION DESERT SHIELD/ DESERT STORM

Chronology and Fact Book

Kevin Don Hutchison

Foreword by Major General John H. Admire, USMC

GREENWOOD PRESS
Westport, Connecticut • London

Library of Congress Cataloging-in-Publication Data

Hutchison, Kevin Don.
    Operation Desert Shield/Desert Storm : chronology and fact book /
Kevin Don Hutchison : foreword by John H. Admire.
       p. cm.
    Includes bibliographical references (p.) and index.
    ISBN 0–313–29606–5 (alk. paper)
    1. Persian Gulf War, 1991. I. Title.
DS79.72.H88 1995
956.7044′2—dc20   95–21530

British Library Cataloguing in Publication Data is available.

Library of Congress Catalog Card Number: 95–21530
ISBN: 0–313–29606–5

First published in 1995

Greenwood Press, 88 Post Road West, Westport, CT 06881
An imprint of Greenwood Publishing Group, Inc.

Printed in the United States of America

The paper used in this book complies with the
Permanent Paper Standard issued by the National
Information Standards Organization (Z39.48–1984).

10 9 8 7 6 5 4

This book is dedicated to my Uncle Lollie—T/5 Louis Szatmary,
Company K, 3rd Battalion, 101st Infantry Regiment,
3rd Army—Survivor of the Battle of the Bulge.

CONTENTS

ILLUSTRATIONS

FOREWORD

In the 1991 Gulf War the United States and Coalition Forces combined in an unprecedented demonstration of commitment and unity. An Iraqi Army of aggression was defeated and Kuwait liberated. In a harsh and barren desert American and Coalition Forces persevered and achieved an astounding victory. The success of Desert Storm, however, was much more than a military one. The Gulf War was the revitalization of American resolve and confidence.

The mission of our nation's armed forces was relatively simple, rather tangible, somewhat physical. It was to defeat the Iraqi Army and to liberate Kuwait. But the mission of the American citizen was relatively complex, rather intangible, somewhat psychological. In accomplishing their tasks the American people healed our nation of scars it had borne since the Vietnam conflict. Vietnam was a war in which our nation became fragmented by protest and divided by dissent. In the aftermath of the conflict America appeared to become hostage to its military power and to its national prestige. America seemed to doubt or to question its resolve and its resiliency.

As a consequence of this lingering perception, Saddam Hussein probably doubted he could defeat the American military on the battlefield. But the Iraqi leader may have been convinced he could defeat the American people on the home front as had happened in Vietnam. Saddam Hussein, however, committed the cardinal sin, a crucial mistake. He underestimated the American people. It was a fatal error.

The American people forged a national consensus that defied division and fragmentation. In the process the American citizen returned and restored to our nation a most precious gift--the gift of pride in America and in ourselves.

The American people created a special closeness, a unique bond, between its armed forces and its citizens. This was accomplished by letters and cards from school children across our nation. By the care packages from civic groups and organizations. By the bright yellow ribbons and majestic red, white, and blue of our national flag that adorned so many homes and businesses throughout our land. By the parades in major cities and small towns. By, most important, the prayers. The compassion of the American people sustained and inspired its armed forces during difficult and demanding and often dangerous times in the desolate desert.

In the process, it was the American people who became the heroes. It was the American citizen who defied and who defeated Saddam Hussein. It was the conviction of the American people that inspired the courage of the American service member. Across the plains and mountains, on farms and in factories, on main streets and country back roads, Americans embraced their military and a military embraced the people it represents.

Kevin Hutchison's book is a tribute to the courage and the compassion, the struggle and sacrifices, of the American armed forces in the Gulf War. But to the soldiers, Marines, Sailors, and Airmen who served on the battlefield, the true heroes were the American people on the home front. It was the support of the American citizen that was crucial to success. As the American military and citizen shared the challenges and sacrifices of war, so did they share the glory of peace. Kevin Hutchison understands that peace is the ultimate objective and purpose of war. His book is a testament to America's crusade to protect, preserve, and perpetuate the values of democracy.

Major General John H. Admire, USMC

ACKNOWLEDGMENTS

Special thanks to:
All Desert Storm veterans.
All military unit historians.
Master Bruce Lee and his *Tao of Jeet Kune Do*.
Harold Lamb and his works, especially *The March of the Barbarians*.

Grateful acknowledgments to:
Maj. Gen. John Admire, USMC; V. Adm. Stanley Arther, USN; Lt. Gen. Walt Boomer, USMC; Maj. Gen. William Keyes, USMC; R. Adm. Riley Mixson, USN; Maj. Gen. James Myatt, USMC; Gen. Colin Powell, USA (Ret.); Paul Bryant (computer consultant); Pat Antonelli, The Library Network (Wayne, Michigan); 1st Sgt. Maj. R. Lamote, Belgian Ministry of Defense; Felix Muradas, Biblioteca Nacional, Madrid; Capt. Luis Pons, Biblioteca Central de la Armada Argentina; Maria Corke, State Library of New South Wales; Prof. Panayotis Nicolopoulos, National Library of Greece; Danny Crawford, Reference Head, USMC History and Museums, Washington Navy Yard; Pierre Waksman, Marine Nationale, Paris; Elwood White, Reference Librarian, USAF Academy Library; Frederick J. Graboske, Head, USMC Archives; Hannah Zeidlik, Chief, Historical Resources Branch, USA Center for Military History; Office of Information, Navy Department; Director General History National Defence HQ, Ottawa.

INTRODUCTION

At 0200 2 August 1990, the Iraqi Hammurabi Armored and Tawakalna Mechanized Divisions supported by Iraqi Special Forces and the Medina Armored Division invaded their neighbor to the southeast, the sovereign nation of Kuwait. Commanded by Lt. Gen. Ayad Futayih Al-Rawi, the Hammurabi and Tawakalna quickly overran the Kuwaiti brigade positioned on Kuwait's border and drove toward the capital of Kuwait City. The Medina Armored Division screened the west from attack from any countering actions of the Gulf Cooperation Council's Peninsula Shield Brigade. Meanwhile the Iraqi Special Forces vertically enveloped Kuwait City by helicopter and Sea Commandos interdicted the southern coastal road. Six Iraqi helicopters, two fighter aircraft, and numbers of armored vehicles were claimed destroyed by the Kuwaiti Air Force before the Kuwaitis fled the Iraqi onslaught. At 0530 the battle for Kuwait City began. By 1400, the Iraqis had captured the capital.

This battle was due to a major miscalculation on the part of Iraqi President Saddam Hussein, who hoped to seize the abundant oil wealth of his neighbor, pay his foreign debts, obtain the country's long desired free access to the Gulf, and become the dominant power in the region. Not a strategist, he did not anticipate the world's reaction and resolve. On the day of the invasion, the United Nations passed Resolution 660 which demanded an immediate withdrawal from Kuwait. It was followed shortly by Resolution 660, calling for economic sanctions against Iraq on 6 August, and on 9 August Resolution 662, unanimously declaring the invasion illegal.

Responding to the Iraqi invasion, the United States began a five and a half month operation titled Desert Shield. Nine million tons of equipment and supplies and 527,000 troops were transported 6,000 miles to the Middle East. The United States united 540,000 ground troops from 31 diverse nations, including recent Cold War enemies. What followed was one of the most operationally successful wars in history. Operation Desert Storm, the United Nations Coalition's attack on Iraq, commenced on the morning of 17 January 1991 and ended with the Iraqi surrender at Safwan airfield 45 days later. Operation Desert Storm brilliantly achieved its mission ejecting the Iraqi army from Kuwait, in the process destroying most of the army's ability to make war. According to the *Gulf War Air Power Survey*, Iraqi troop strength plunged from 1,100,000 on 1 February 1991 to 400,000 by 1 April. Divisions during this period declined from 66 to 30 and tanks suffered attrition from 7,000 to 2,300 by the war's end.

Operation Desert Shield/Desert Storm: Chronology and Fact Book is a succinct consolidation of records and information that are now available to the public. Due to the doubtful declassification and release of additional information for the foreseeable future, what you hold in your hand is the most complete history of the war that will be available for years to come. The information here comes from four major official sources: *The Gulf War Air Power Survey*, *Certain Victory: The U.S. Army in the Gulf War*, *The United States Navy in Desert Shield/Desert Storm*, and the five volume *The U.S. Marines in the Persian Gulf, 1990-1991*. Carefully added to this foundation is verified information from newspapers, magazines, military journals, books, data bases and veteran interviews. Many agencies worldwide have provided official records. Coalition information and records from foreign archivists, information clerks, and reference librarians were graciously provided. The efforts and assistance of these information professionals are greatly appreciated. They are identified in the book's acknowledgments.

I have chosen to title the book *Operation Desert Shield and Desert Storm*, rather than refer to the conflict as the often-cited Persian Gulf War, to avoid confusion with the Iran-Iraq War, also referred to as the Gulf War. That war occurred in the same geographic area. Operation Desert Shield and Desert Storm is the unique title of a military operation, not to be repeated.

The history of the region and the recent story of the eight-year Iran-Iraq War is omitted. Iraq's relationship with the west, the establishment of the countries' southern boundaries and access to the Persian Gulf are fully explored in other sources. Likewise, the topic of the bloody Iran-Iraq conflict, its yearly offenses, retreats, and resulting estimated 750,000 Iraqi dead and wounded is not discussed. The purpose of this text is to relate the daily military events from July 1990-April 1991. Attempts to prevent the conflict, deeds of political figures, and diplomatic events affecting the war, except for the most important, are as a rule, not included. The direction and reason for this book are the recording of fact, the activities of the Coalition fighting Soldiers, Marines, Sailors, and Airmen. It is concerned with, in short, military chronology.

Thus the book focuses on when the movements and activities of the principals take place. Units deploy, the buildup occurs, and, like a well released arrow, the outcome is unswervingly and rapidly concluded. At the end of the war, as a response to U.S. President George Bush's call for Iraqis to overthrow their government, rebellion in the Kurdish north and Shi'ite south resulted in a crackdown by Saddam Hussein. Operation Provide Comfort, the U.S. operation to send humanitarian and security assistance to Northern Iraq began 7 April 1991 but, due to the operation being humanitarian in nature and not military, its story is not included here.

There is no speculation about motive, no attempt to surmise and divine the unknown and unclassified. The text keeps to known fact and record, and, in the very few cases where there is no verification of truth (most notably the attempted assassination of Saddam Hussein), the source is provided. Lessons learned, conclusions, the significance of Operation Desert Shield/Desert Storm, all of these subjects are ignored.

Instead this is a record of the many accomplishments, units and numbers, missions, weapon system results, when and where events occurred, and who was involved (Coalition Order of Battle). Unfortunately, National Guard and Reserve units, though important, are scarcely mentioned. Sheer numbers and thereby lack of space precludes including these warriors. Likewise, the Iraqi Order of Battle is far from complete. In my previous book *World War II in The North Pacific: Chronology and Fact Book* I included nearly every Japanese North Pacific commander, and I would have liked to provide as thorough information (i.e., the identity of all Iraqi commanders) in this volume. Due to the sudden and rapid conclusion of the war, however, this information is not available. Sadly, this important information must be left for future editions.

As a chronology, the book is laid out day-by-day with its information according to a definite system. I have established a hierarchy of information in order that the reader can quickly identify information desired, if available, for a particular date. First listed, if applicable, are activities of major figures, crucial events, and grand strategy. As a rule, U.S. forces are always given priority, and combat arms (i.e., infantry, artillery, armor) are given precedence. Naval and air force activities follow, with Coalition forces coming after according to the same order. The last citation for every date, if available, is the activity of the Iraqi armed forces.

For the date of 24 February 1991, the day the ground war began, and continuing until the ground offensive was completed 100 hours later, there were so many major forces maneuvering and accomplishing crucial tasks that it was a challenge to place the information in easily accessible form. So that information can be found readily, I have used **bold** letters to immediately draw the reader's eye to the unit discussed in a particular paragraph.

Operation
Desert Shield/
Desert Storm

Chapter 1

OPERATION DESERT SHIELD

Mid-July 1990 Lt. Gen. Ayad Futayih al-Rawi, Commander, Republican Guard Forces Command and the hero of the April and July 1988 attacks on Iran in the Iran-Iraq War is ordered by Iraqi President Saddam Hussein to prepare to invade the country of Kuwait.

17 July Saddam Hussein angrily threatens war with Kuwait and the United Arab Emirates for driving down the price of oil by exceeding OPEC production quotas.

Kuwait places its armed forces on high alert.

19 July The first intelligence of Iraqi movement at the Kuwaiti border arrives at U.S. Central Command.

21 July U.S. Central Command is alerted by intelligence that approximately 3,000 military vehicles are moving south from Baghdad, and an Iraqi armor division has advanced to an area just north of Kuwait.

25 July Kuwait's 20,000-man armed forces are mobilized. Commander is Maj. Gen. Jaber al-Sabah.

26 July U.S. Central Command is informed by intelligence that 120,000 Iraqi forces are in southeastern Iraqi staging areas.

31 July U.S. Central Command informs Washington that Iraq appears prepared to invade Kuwait.

2 August At 0200 the Iraqi Hammurabi Armored and Tawakalna Mechanized Divisions (Republican Guard) easily overrun a Kuwaiti brigade guarding the border and invade Kuwait. Republican Guard Special Forces brigades assault Kuwait City by helicopter and Sea Commandos cut the southern coastal road. To the west, the Medina Armored Division screens any possible counterattack from the Gulf Cooperation Council's Peninsula Shield Brigade. At 0530 the battle for Kuwait City begins, and by 1400 is over.

0230 Gen. Colin Powell in Washington orders Joint Chiefs of Staff operations director Lt. Gen. Thomas Kelly to find Gen. H. Norman Schwarzkopf and order him to Washington. Central Command, Tactical Air Command, Military Airlift Command, and Strategic Air Command are issued a Warning Order by Powell to prepare to deploy, with the U.S. Navy receiving a Partial Deployment Order. At 0800 President George Bush, Gen. Powell and Gen. Schwarzkopf meet in the White House. Military options are presented to President Bush by Gen. Schwarzkopf.

At CIA headquarters at Langley, Virginia, Gen. Carl Stiner, head of U.S. Special Operations Command learns of the Iraqi invasion. He flies on his USAF Learjet to the Special Operations Command headquarters at MacDill AFB, Tampa, Florida. Meeting with senior Israeli special operations officers at Pope Air Force Base, Maj. Gen. Wayne Downing, Commander, Joint Special Operations Command, also learns of the invasion, and is briefed by the Israelis on their established contingencies (including Scud hunting in the Iraqi desert). In the deserts of Texas and New Mexico, Delta Force, U.S. Army Rangers, and the 160th Special Operations Aviation Regiment have just completed a desert exercise. By the war's end 7,705 special operations soldiers will serve (with another 1,049 in Turkey to quickly rescue downed pilots).

A U.S. mobile operations center (Operation *Ivory Justice*) is deployed to Abu Dhabi.

The Kuwaiti Air Force claim to destroy six Iraqi helicopters, two fighters, and numerous armored vehicles, and then flee south from Ali Al Salem Air Base with 15 KAF F-1 fighters (source: Col. Saber Al-Suwaidan).

4th Battalion, 2nd Brigade, 325th Parachute Infantry, 82nd Airborne Division (Division Ready Brigade) is alerted. The Ready Brigade is commanded by Col. Ronald Rokosz and Maj. Gen. James Johnston is the 82nd Airborne's commander.

At Ansbach, Germany, 1st Armored Division headquarters intelligence officer Keith Alexander (G-2) and Lt. Col. Thomas Strauss (G-3) begin compiling intelligence on Iraqi Forces.

Due to a continuous Middle Eastern presence since 1949, eight U.S. Navy ships are on station in the Persian Gulf (Middle East Force). The USS ROBERT G. BRADLEY (FFG-49) less than 50 miles off Kuwait receive repeated pleas for assistance on bridge-to-bridge radio. The frigate's commander Cdr. Kevin J. Cosgriff orders the ship to man battle stations. USS INDEPENDENCE Carrier Battle Group cruises the Indian Ocean near Diego Garcia, as the DWIGHT D. EISENHOWER cruises the central Mediterranean.

Off the Philippines is the U.S. 13th Marine Expeditionary Unit (Battalion Landing Team 1/4, Medium Helicopter Squadron 164 and Marine Service Support Group 13) commanded by Col. John E. Rhodes, USMC. At Subic Bay is approximately 2,000 U.S. Marines of the 3rd Battalion, 7th Marines (Air-Ground Task Force 4-90). Off Monrovia, Liberia is the 22nd Marine Expeditionary Unit commanded by Col. Granville R. Amos on the USS SAIPAN (LHA-2), PONCE (LPD-15) and SUMTER (LST-1181) (Amphibious Squadron Four).

At Seymour Johnson AFB, North Carolina, the 335th TFS (Lt. Col. Steve Pingel), and the 336th TFS of the 4th TFW are informed of Iraq's invasion of Kuwait. The squadron's fly the F-15E Eagle and the 4th TFW is commanded by Col. Hal Hornburg.

The USAF 384th and 407th Air Refueling Squadron (AREFS) with three KC-135R, is at Diego Garcia and the 99th and 905th AREFS with two KC-135R aircraft are at Al Dhafra, UAE Deployed at Incirlik, Turkey are the 14 F-111Es of the 77th Tactical Fighter Squadron.

British Royal Navy "Armilla Patrol" present in the Persian Gulf are: BATCH III TYPE-42 destroyer HMS YORK (D-98) commanded by Capt. A. G. McEwen, BATCH I BROADSWORD-Class frigate HMS BATTLEAXE (F-89) commanded by Cdr. A. C. Gordon-Lennox, BATCH IIA LEANDER-Class frigate HMS JUPITER (F-60) commanded by Cdr. J. W. T. Wright and the APPLELEAF-Class support tanker HMS ORANGELEAF (A-110) commanded by Capt. M. S. J. Farley. Only HMS YORK and HMS ORANGELEAF are in their operational area with the other ships in port. In Britain HUNT-Class coastal minehunters HM ships CATTISTOCK (M-31) commanded by Lt. Cdr. M. P. Shrives, ATHERSTONE (M-38) commanded by Lt. Cdr. P. N. M Davies and HURWORTH (M-34) commanded by Lt. Cdr. R. J. Ibbotson are alerted and will be deployed with the improved HECLA-Class survey ship HMS HERALD (A-138) commanded by Cdr. P. H. Jones. TYPE-42 destroyer HMS GLOUCESTER (D-96) commanded by Cdr. P. L. Wilcocks, BATCH I BROADSWORD-Class frigate HMS BRAZEN (F-91) commanded by Cdr. J. C. Rapp, HMS LONDON (F-95) commanded by Capt. I. R. Henderson, large fuel tanker RFA OLNA (A-123) commanded by Capt. A. F. Pitt, DSC, fleet replenishment ship RFA FORT GRANGE (A-385) commanded by Capt. P. L. Nelson, and STENA-TYPE repair ship RFA DILIGENCE (A-132) commanded by Capt. A. Mitchell are deployed to the Middle East during the following weeks.

The Iraqi III Corps begins constructing a double row of barriers, minefields and defensive fortifications circling southeastern Kuwait approximately 5-15 kilometers parallel to the Saudi Arabian border. Five infantry divisions will finally face the U.S. Marines from Manaqish to Wafrah. Respectively these are: the 7th 14th, 29th, 42nd, and 8th Infantry Divisions with the 5th Mechanized Division in reserve at the Burqan oil field and the 3rd Armored Division approximately 20 kilometers north of Al Jaber Air Base. At the important Al Jahra road intersection and the Mutla Ridge will be the IV Corps' 1st Mechanized Division and 6th Armored Division.

3 August At a National Security meeting initial options are presented to President George Bush, with the president agreeing that force may be required. Gen. Colin Powell informs the president that Gen. Schwarzkopf and Lt. Gen. Thomas Kelly are working on further options, and will brief him soon.

Baghdad announces it will withdraw from Kuwait on 5 August. U.S. intelligence, however, reports that reinforcements are pouring into Kuwait, and Iraqi armored divisions are deploying on the Saudi Arabian border. The world fears an Iraqi invasion of Saudi Arabia.

The USS LASALLE (AGF-3) commanded by Capt. John B. Nathman is deployed. The USS INDEPENDENCE Carrier Battle Group commanded by V.Adm. Jerry L. Unruh, USN moves toward the Gulf of Oman.

F-15C Eagles of the 1st Tactical Fighter Wing (commanded by Col. John McBroom) at Langley AFB add fuel tanks in preparation for flying to Saudi Arabia. From Hickam and Andersen AFB two KC-10s and one KC-135R deploy to Diego Garcia.

4 August At a National Security Council meeting Gen. H. Norman Schwarzkopf USA and Gen. Charles A. Horner USAF brief President George Bush on all military options available. Land and carrier-based air power can arrive in days; 12 fighter squadrons, a bomber squadron to support an Airborne division and a Marine brigade. It will be 17 weeks until sufficient ground forces will be deployed to be able to attack. Several weeks time will be required to establish a ground defense. Contingency plans are also presented for use if Iraq uses chemical weapons. King Fahd of Saudi Arabia requests a situation briefing shortly after the meeting, and National Security Advisor Brent Scowcroft gathers a briefing team to travel to Saudi Arabia.

At approximately 2200 at Fort McPherson, Georgia Lt. Gen. John Yeosock, (Commander of Army Central Command or ARCENT) Maj. Gen. William G. Pagonis, (Director of Logistics) and assorted military experts meet in Yeosock's living room. Pagonis's group works on what is needed logistically to deploy forces to Saudi Arabia.

USS INDEPENDENCE Carrier Battle Group (V.Adm. Jerry L. Unruh, USN, Carrier Battle Group commander) is steaming en route to the North Arabian Sea area.

From Al Jaber Air Base 19 Kuwaiti A-4Qs aircraft are evacuated to Dhahran Air Base, Saudi Arabia and Bahrain International Airport, Bahrain.

5 August Approximately 0030 Yeosock's planning group is ordered to Central Command's (CENTCOM) headquarters at McDill Air Force Base, Tampa, Florida. After arriving and continuing to work, Gen. Yeosock boards a jet for Washington to pick up Secretary of Defense Cheney, and fly with a list of requirements to Riyadh and a meeting with King Fahd.

USS INDEPENDENCE (CV-42) commanded by Robert L. Ellis, Jr., ANTIETAM (CG-54) commanded by Capt. Lawrence E. Eddingfield, JOUETT (CG-29) commanded by Capt. Floyston A. Weeks, GOLDSBOROUGH (DDG-20) commanded by Cdr. James A. Reid, BREWTON (FF-1086) commanded by Cdr. Charlie A. Jones, REASONER (FF-1063) commanded by Cdr. Richard B. Marvin, CIMMARON (AO-177) commanded by Cdr. Eric B. Shaver, DURHAM (LKA-114) commanded by Capt. Charles M. Kraft, FORT MCHENRY (LSD-43) commanded by Cdr. James A. Hayes, and FLINT (AE-32) commanded by Cdr. Alan D. Thomson begins participation in Operation Desert Shield. If needed, aircraft of the carrier INDEPENDENCE are in position to launch long-range air strikes.

U.S. Navy air units HC-11 (DET 11), HS-8, HSL-33 (DET 9), VA-196, VAQ-139, VAW-113, VF-154, VF-21, VFA-25, and VS-37 begin participation in Operation Desert Shield.

6 August The United Nations condemns the Iraqi invasion in United Nations Security Council Resolution 660 and imposes world-wide economic sanctions against Iraq in United Nations Security Resolution 661.

Secretary of Defense Dick Cheney, Gen. H. Norman Schwarzkopf USA and Lt. Gen. Charles A. Horner USAF discusses the deployment of United States forces in Saudi Arabia. Later in the day, Cheney travels to Egypt to request permission for U.S. war ships to pass through the Suez Canal.

At the home of Gen. Edwin H. Burba, Jr. Maj. Gen. Pagonis receives a call from U.S. Army Chief of Staff Gen. Carl E. Vuono to go to Saudi Arabia. Gen. Burba will eventually mobilize U.S. Army Reserves and the National Guard for deployment to Saudi Arabia. Pagonis begins selecting his logistics team (including Col. Jim Ireland, Col. Jack Tier, Col. Steven Koons). Pagonis meets with Gen. Schwarzkopf at McDill Air Force Base after arriving.

The U.S. 82nd Airborne Division (Maj. Gen. Jim Johnson) receives its "execute" order. At 2100 at Fort Bragg, North Carolina Sergeant First Class Elijah Payne, receives a phone call from Staff Sergeant John Ferguson, the division watch NCO. Four days of waiting ends as paratroopers within two hours gather on Ardennes Street with rucksacks and duffle bags. Reaching Saudi Arabia they will first assume defensive positions around the airports.

U.S. Army 24th Infantry Division (Mechanized) commanded by Maj. Gen. Barry McCaffrey is ordered to move one armored brigade to Savannah, Georgia within 18 hours. The division is ordered by Lt. Gen. Gary Luck to be prepared to fight as soon as they arrive in Dhahran.

The U.S. 26th Marine Expeditionary Unit commanded by Col. William C. Fite III loads at Morehead City, North Carolina onto Amphibious Squadron Two. Amphibious Squadron Two consists of: INCHON (LPH-12) commanded by Capt. Harold J. Tickle, NASHVILLE (LPD-13), WHIDBEY ISLAND (LSD-41 commanded by Cdr. Thomas L. Breitinger, FAIRFAX COUNTY (LST-1193) commanded by Cdr. Mark A. Hoke, and NEWPORT (LST-1179) commanded by Cdr. Timothy A. Kok.

R.Adm. William M. Fogarty, U.S. Navy commander, Middle East Force, prepares plans with staff to prevent seatrade with Iraq and Kuwait.

Israel offers to assist in the defense of Saudi Arabia if requested. Throughout the war the United States does its utmost to maintain a "low profile" for Israel to prevent the expansion of the war.

7 August C-Day, Commencement of deployment of American troops.

Deployment order for Southwest Asia is issued. Lt. Gen. Richard Graves, III Corps commander alerts the US Army 1st Cavalry Division at Fort Hood. The intial defense plan for the Ready Brigade, 82nd Airborne Division is being finalized. The Ready Brigade is the first U.S. combat ground forces that have ever been deployed to Saudi Arabia. Brig. Gen. Richard Timmons is in charge of the first U.S. ground forces in Saudi Arabia.

At 0300 hours the 24th Infantry Division (Mech) is alerted.

The U.S. 101st Air Assault Division is alerted. The division is commanded by Maj. Gen. J.H. Binford Peay III. Its strength is 18,000 personnel (including 700 women), 400 helicopters and 500 vehicles.

Sailing for the Red Sea, the USS DWIGHT D. EISENHOWER (CVN-69) Carrier Battle Group passes through the Suez Canal. In the Gulf of Oman the USS INDEPENDENCE (CV-62) Carrier Battle Group arrives on station (both carriers combined possess in excess of 100 fighter and attack aircraft). The USS SARATOGA Carrier Battle Group (including the USS WISCONSIN) departs the east coast of the United States. Fast Sealift squadrons are activated.

At Langley Air Force Base, Virginia the U.S. Air Force 1st Tactical Fighter Wing prepares to fly to Dhahran, Saudi Arabia (27th Tactical Fighter Squadron commanded by Lt. Col. Don Kline and 71st Tactical Fighter Squadron). The 71st with 24 F-15 Eagles depart today with six to seven inflight refuelings during the 14 to 17 hour flights. This is the longest operational fighter deployment in history.

8 August President George Bush orders U.S. armed forces to Saudi Arabia.

At Pope Air Force Base next to Fort Bragg, paratroopers of the 2nd Brigade, 82nd Airborne Division (Col. Ronald Rokosz) begin to take off for Saudi Arabia.

The first elements of the 101st Air Assault Division, the 1st Battalion, 101st Aviation Regiment (1-101) commanded by Lt. Col. Dick Cody depart with the 82nd Airborne.

The 2nd Brigade of the 24th Infantry Division (Mech) arrives fully stocked with fuel and ammunition at Savannah in preparation for transportation to Saudi Arabia.

Marine Maj. Gen. Walter E. Boomer is promoted to lieutenant general and appointed Commanding General, I Marine Expeditionary Force.

The USS DWIGHT D. EISENHOWER in the Red Sea and USS INDEPENDENCE in the Gulf of Oman are in position to conduct air strikes. TICONDEROGA (CG-47), SCOTT (DDG-995), and SURIBACHI (AE-21) begin participation in Operation Desert Shield.

Lt. Gen. Pagonis arrives in Riyadh and reports to Gen. Yeosock. They fly to the King Abdul Aziz Airbase at Dhahran. Pagonis described the scene in his book *Moving Mountains* as resembling the hospital scene in the movie *Gone With the Wind*. Thousands of American troops, most notably the 82nd Airborne mill about. Transport planes continue to land every few minutes in the 140 degrees, bringing hundreds more. Pagonis along with Lt. Col. Ed Lindbloom and Saudi Col. Khalif al-Shahari begin to move the service people to shelter--for the most part, primitive facilities.

U.S. Air Force 77th Tactical Fighter Squadron (TFS) of the 1st Tactical Fighter Wing (TFW) commanded by Lt. Col. Don Kline flies 24 F-15Cs to Dhahran over 14 hours. They begin landing every ten minutes. Dhahran Air Base is commanded by Saudi Arabian Royal Air Force Brig. Gen. Prince Turki Bin Nasser Abdul Aziz. At Riyadh the 552nd Airborne Warning and Command Wing (AWACW) land five E-3s.

At Seymour Johnson AFB the 335th TFS ('Chiefs') and their sister squadron the 336th TFS ('Rocketeers') of the 4th TFW receive their "execute" order.

USAF B-52 heavy bombers begin deploying to Diego Garcia.

In a Radio Baghdad broadcast Saddam Hussein declares Kuwait the nineteenth province of Iraq.

U.S. Maritime Prepositioning Ships (MPS) Squadron 2 departs Diego Garcia. Other maritime pre-positioned ships steam from Guam (Maritime Prepositioning Squadron 3) and Saipan for the Middle East. They carry among other supplies: cranes, refrigerated vans, forklifts, 6,000 sleeping bags, 124,000 Class-1 rations (MREs), medical supplies, 450,000 board feet of lumber, 1,800 sheets of plywood, 32,550 hand grenades, 3,000 land mines, 16 bread ovens, 5.5 million gallons of aviation fuel. Crewed by civilians the Maritime Pre-Positioning Force is named posthumously after Marine holders of the Medal of Honor. Ships of MPSRon-2 are MV CPL LOUIS J. HAUGE JR. (T-AK3000), MV PFC WILLIAM B. BAUGH JR. (T-AK3001), MV 1ST LT. ALEXANDER BONNYMAN JR. (T-AK3003), MV PVT. HARRY FISHER (T-AK3004), and MV PFC. JAMES ANDERSON JR. (T-AK3002).

USS DWIGHT D. EISENHOWER (CVN-69), JOHN L. HALL (FFG-32), GUAM (LPH-9) and NEOSHA (TAO-143) begin participation in Operation Desert Shield.

The British Operation *Granby I* deployment begins. Royal Air Force Tornado F-3 fighters land at Dhahran, Saudi Arabia and are commanded by Air Vice Marshal "Sandy" Wilson, RAF.

9 August The first U.S. Army paratroopers have arrived in Saudi Arabia. Commanded by Brig. Gen. Edison Scholes, 76 soldiers and staff officers of the XVIII Airborne Corps are located at the Dhahran Airport.

At Riyadh, Commander, U.S. Navy Central Command, Forward R.Adm. G.A. Sharp arrives.

U.S. Navy SEAL teams 2, 4, and 8 begin participation in Operation Desert Shield along with Commander, Naval Special Warfare Unit 2, and Commander, Special Boat Squadron 2.

A.J. HIGGINS (TAO-190) begins participating in Operation Desert Shield.

At 1130 six F-15E Eagles of the 4th TFW lift off for Seeb, Oman.

A USAF RC-135 Rivet Joint aircraft begins supporting Operation Desert Shield. Three more will be added by 19 August. At Dhahran 24 F-15Cs of the 27th TFS, 1st TFW arrive.

Saudi Arabia is maintaining 24 hour Combat Air Patrols. AWACS time is shared evenly between the U.S. and Saudis to maintain a 24 hour watch.

Turkey agrees to an expanded U.S. presence in their country. The Americans will primarily use air base facilities. The Turkish Air Force commander is Gen. Cemil Cuha.

Britain and France agree to deploy air forces to the Persian Gulf.

U.S. intelligence indicates that the Iraqis are developing an integrated air defense network.

10 August Gen. Schwarzkopf is briefed by Col. John A. Warden, USAF, of the air campaign plan to eject Iraq forces from Kuwait (plan *Instant Thunder*). CINCCENT calls for the participation of the 1st, 4th and 7th Marine Expeditionary Brigades.

Logistics expert Maj. Gen. Pagonis commandeers a four-door sedan and begins operating out of it as his headquarters. He also secures 10,000 Bedouin tents to keep the American soldiers out of the sun.

The U.S. 3rd Air Cavalry Regiment and the 11th Air Defense Brigade are alerted for Saudi Arabian deployment.

Combat air patrols are begun over Saudi Arabia by fighters of the 71st TFS, 1st Tactical Air Wing, USAF. At Al Dhafra, UAE, 24 F-16C Falcons arrive of the 17th TFS, 336th TFW, and at Al Kharj 24 F-15Es of the 336 TFS, 4th TFW arrive.

Hospital ships USNS MERCY and USNS COMFORT prepare to deploy from the United States.

French GEORGES LEYGUES-Class destroyers DUPLEIX (DD-641) commanded by Cdr. Gilles Combarieu and MONTCALM (DD-642) commanded by Cdr. Jean-Loup Bariller sail for the Middle East. The *5th Combat Helicopter Regiment* assigned to the French Rapid Deployment Force (30 Gazelles, and 12 Pumas) begin to be loaded on the carrier CLEMENCEAU (R-98) commanded by Capt. Jean Wild.

At Dhahran a British squadron of 12 F-3 Royal Air Force Tornado F.Mk 3 interceptors land. All RAF detachments will be comprised of aircraft and personnel from multiple units, so the British air unit is christened No. 5 (Composite) Squadron. RAF commander is Air Vice-Marshal William J. Wratten (Commander HQ No.11 Group).

Coalition forces from the Royal Saudi Air Force, USAF, and the U.S. Navy begin **Exercise Arabian Gulf** to practice coordinating air operations over the Persian Gulf.

11 August At Sana'a, Yemen and Khartoum, Sudan demonstrations of support for Saddam Hussein take place. Some Yemenis volunteer to fight for Iraq, but post-war records leave it unclear how many actually fight (probably only a few hundred). On 3 March at the Iraqi surrender at Safwan, senior Iraqi generals will disavow any knowledge of these troops. Also, all PLO member organizations support Saddam except for the Popular Front for the Liberation of Palestine-General Command. Saudi Arabia will remain concerned about threats to their southern and western flank from Sudan and Yemen throughout Operations Desert Shield and Desert Storm.

Gen. Powell is briefed on plan "*Instant Thunder*" by Col. John A. Warden.

Almost overwhelmed by the volume of supplies, men and equipment, Maj. Gen. Pagonis is reinforced by the 7th Transportation Group (Col. David Whaley). Whaley's men are quickly divided into transportation, military police, engineering, contracting, and port and airport management. They immediately get to work.

First Fast Sealift ships arrive for loading at Savannah.

At Masirah AB, the first of 16 USAF C-130 Hercules of the 40th Tactical Airlift Squadron (TAS), 317th TAW lands. At Jeddah 16 KC-135s of the 190th AREFG arrive. At Riyadh four RC-135s of the 55th Surveillance and Reconnaissance Wing (SRW) arrive and at Al Dhafra 24 F-16Cs of the 33rd TFS, 363rd TFW arrive. RC-135s begin 24 hour operations.

First elements of Egyptian and Moroccan troops arrive in Saudi Arabia. The Egyptian unit contains 500 men. The commander of the Egyptian 2nd Field Army is Maj. Gen. Hussein Tantawi and the commander of the 3rd Field Army Maj. Gen. Muhammad'Adil Ibrahim al-Qadi.

12 August The 2nd Brigade, 82nd Airborne Division begins *Desert Dragon II*. The brigade begins to defend the port of al-Jubayl (Falcon Base) with the 4-325th Airborne while awaiting the arrival of the U.S. Marines and the establishment of Forward Operating Base Essex at an-Nuayriyah. FOB Essex is at the convergence of five roads, which if held, will greatly disrupt any Iraqi attack. A brigade of the 101st Airborne Division embarks for Saudi Arabia. The last of the 2nd Brigade, 82nd Airborne Division arrives in Saudi Arabia.

The 7th Marine Expeditionary Brigade (MEB) begins moving from Twentynine Palms, California (about 17,000 personnel). Approximately 250 C-141 sorties will be required to deploy the brigade.

U.S. Navy SEAL teams 1, 3, and 5 begin participation in Operation Desert Shield along with Commander, Special Warfare Group 1, Commander Special Boat Squadron 1, and Special Boat Units 11, 12, and 13.

At Diego Garcia, seven B-52s "Buffs" of the 69th Bombardment Squadron (BMS), 42nd BMW arrive. F-15 Eagles support AWACS with Combat Air Patrols and other F-15s are on alert for ground attack or air-to-air missions.

At Thumrait, Oman, 12 RAF Jaguars arrive.

13 August Elements of the 1st and the 3rd Brigades (Col. Glynn Hale) of the 82nd Airborne Division begin to depart the United States to join the 2nd Brigade in Saudi Arabia (though throughout the war they remain physically separated). They will occupy an area halfway between Dhahran and al-Jubayl. Though first named the All American Base, to avoid Saudi hard feelings it is later named Champion Main.

Equipment of the 24th Mechanized Division embarks for Saudi Arabia on the FSS CAPELLA from Savannah, Georgia. During Operation Desert Shield 1,600 armored, 3,500 wheeled vehicles and 90 helicopters of the division will be transported to Saudi Arabia on 10 ships. Transit time will average 15-25 days.

USS O'BRIEN (DD-975) begins participation in Operation Desert Shield. USS WISCONSIN commanded by Capt. Jerry M. Blesch passes through the Straits of Gibraltar as it steams for the Persian Gulf.

Four USAF special operations MH-53s of the 20th Special Operations Squadron (SOS), 1st SOW arrive at Al Jouf. At Diego Garcia seven B-52s of the 69th BMS, 42nd BMW land. At King Fahd ten KC-135Rs of the 11th and 306th AREFS, 340th AREFW, 16 C-130Es of the 41st TAS, 317th TAW, and ten KC-135Rs of the 305th and 70th AREFS, 305th AREFW arrive.

A RAF Nimrod aircraft arrives at Seeb.

Lead elements of the Egyptian 4th and 23rd Armored Divisions begin ferrying across the Red Sea to the Saudi Arabia.

HMS CATTISTOCK (M-31) commanded by Lt. Cdr. M. P. Shrives, ATHERSTONE (M-38) commanded by Lt. Cdr. P. N. M. Davies, and HMS HURWORTH (M-39) commanded by Lt. Cdr. R. J. Ibbotson, depart Rosyth for the Middle East.

French carrier CLEMENCEAU (R-98) commanded by Capt. Jean Wild departs Toulon with the cruiser COLBERT (C-611) and DURANCE-Class replenishment tanker VAR (A-608) for Djibouti. The carrier carries 48 helicopters of the 5th Regiment d'Helicoptere de Combat. French naval elements will include before the war's end: KERSAINT-Class guided missile destroyer DU CHAYLA (DDG-630), commanded by Cdr. Hebrard, anti-submarine destroyer LA MOTTE-PICQUET (D-645), commanded by Cdr. Paul Marie Charles Varaut, COMMANDANT RIVIERE-Class frigates DOUDART DE LAGREE (F-728), commanded by Cdr. Rossignol, COMMANDANT BORY (F-726) commanded by Cdr. Pierre-Yves Beau, DUPLEIX commanded by Cdr. Giles Combarieu, MONTCALM commanded by Cdr. Jean-Loup Bariller, COMMANDANT DUCUING commanded by Cdr. Jean-Michel L'Henaff, PROTET commanded by Cdr. Maurice De Moisson, JEAN DE VIENNE commanded by Cdr. Jean-Luc Delaunay, PREMIER MAITRE L'HER commanded by Cdr. Benoit Chomel de Jarnieu, mine countermeasure ships ERIDAN-Class PEGASE (M-644), L'AIGLE (M-647), SAGITTAIRE (M-650), and DURANCE-Class replenishment tanker DURANCE (A-629). This initiates *Operation Salamandre*. Its mission is to have force available to rescue French citizens in Kuwait.

14 August Gen. Schwarzkopf's Combat Analysis Group concludes that fifty percent of Iraq's ground forces must suffer attrition before a successful ground campaign can be waged.

The 2nd Brigade, 82nd Airborne Division (Col. Ronald Rokosz) prepare to defend Dhahran and ad-Dammam airfields and port facilities (*Desert Dragon I*). Strength is 4,575 paratroopers and equipment and the brigade is supported by an Apache helicopter battalion, a Sheridan light tank company, a battalion of 105mm howitzers, and a platoon of MLRS (Multiple Launch Rocket System). If the Iraqis attack, the 82nd Airborne plans to fight the Iraqis along the coast road bordered by the sabhas (coastal salt flats). The 82nd's light vehicles could cross these coastal salt flats but they would not support the Iraqi tanks. The 82nd will engage at long range with attack helicopters and Air Force close air support, and at closer distance with artillery, Sheridan tanks and TOW antitank missiles.

The I Marine Expeditionary Force (Lt. Gen. Walt Boomer USMC) and the 7th Marine Expeditionary Brigade (MEB) commanded by Maj. Gen. John I. Hopkins USMC begin to arrive at Al Jubail and Dhahran.

First Fast Sealift Squadron departs Savannah for Saudi Arabia. USNS COMFORT (T-AH-20) deploys for the Middle East.

Lt. Col. Rick Shatzel, USAF, Commander of 353rd Tactical Fighter Squadron (Panthers) informs his men that they will be departing for Saudi Arabia tomorrow. The Panthers fly A-10 Warthogs which specialize in tank killing with their General Electric GAU-8/A nosemounted Gatling gun. The gun is 19 feet, 10 inches long and fully loaded weighs 4,029 pounds. It fires 3,000-4,000 of its foot long, two pound rounds per minute.

At Jeddah, ten USAF KC-135Rs of the 99th AREFS, 19th AREFW arrive.

An Army Space Programs Office satellite and a Navy navigation satellite begins transmitting images for the U.S. Army XVIII Airborne Corps.

U.S. intelligence indicates that Iraqi ground forces have assumed a "clearly defensive posture" in Kuwait.

At Thumrait, Oman, twelve RAF Jaguars arrive.

U.S. intelligence indicates that Iraq flies 47 air sorties today.

15 August Iraq orders all westerners in Kuwait to report to three hotels. Saddam Hussein offers Iran the return of land gained during the Iran-Iraq War in order to obtain forces which fortify Shatt-al-Arab.

U.S. Marine Headquarters announces the deployment of 45,000 Marines and sailors to the Persian Gulf region. The 7th Marine Expeditionary Brigade commander Maj. Gen. John I. Hopkins arrives at Al Jubayl. Lt. Gen. Boomer assigns defense of the northernmost Gulf, and Bahrain Island to the 3rd Marine Aircraft Wing and the two-squadron air force of the Bahrain Amiri Defense Force.

The entire U.S. 82nd Airborne has now arrived in Saudi Arabia. The division is commanded by Maj. Gen. Jim Johnson. Unlike other U.S. units, troopers are to wear their kevlar helmets at all times.

The first ships of Maritime Prepositioning Shipping Squadron 2 arrive at Al Jubayl. Ships hold tanks, howitzers, amphibious assault vehicles, light armored vehicles as well as supplies and other equipment. The three major ports of Saudi Arabia (Ad Dammam, Al Jubayl and Jidda on the west coast) are some of the largest and best-equipped port facilities in the world. Logistics expert Maj. Gen. Pagonis's number one rule is *nothing* sits on the dock. A great effort is begun to move supplies and equipment to storage areas quickly upon arrival.

The USS SARATOGA Carrier Battle Group passes through the Strait of Gibraltar for the Middle East. USS JOHN F. KENNEDY Carrier Battle Group departs Norfolk, Virginia for the Mediterranean Sea. USS JOHN F. KENNEDY (CV-67) is commanded by Capt. John P. Gay USN and USS SARATOGA (CV-60) is commanded by Capt. Joseph S. Mobley USN.

Arriving at Diego Garcia six USAF B-52Gs of the 69th and 328th BMS, 42nd BMW bring the force to full strength.

French COMMANDANT RIVIERE-Class frigate PROTET (F-748) commanded by Capt. Maurice De Moisson and D'ESTIENNE D'ORVES-Class frigate COMMANDANT DUCUING (F-795) commanded by Jean-Michel L'Henaff join up off the Gulf of Oman. French Navy Chief of Staff is Adm. Bernard Louzeau.

Iraq flies 19 air sorties today.

16 August USNS MERCY (T-AH-19) heads for the Middle East. Maritime Prepositioning Ships Squadron 2 arrives in Saudi Arabia from Diego Garcia.

Due to U.N. Security Council Resolution 661 the Multinational maritime interception operation begins. USS JOHN L. HALL (FFG-32) is the first U.S. warship to intercept a ship sailing from Iraq to Kuwait.

Maj. Gen. Royal N. Moore, Jr. Commanding General of the 3rd Marine Aircraft Wing arrives.

OLNA (A-123) commanded by Capt. A. F. Pitt departs Devonport and is the first British vessel to deploy to the Persian Gulf.

The following ships depart Wilhelmshave for Crete to strengthen the eastern Mediterranean: German LINDAU-Class minesweepers FGS KOBLENZ (M-1071), FGS WETZLAR (M-1075) and FGS MARBURG (M-1080), HAMELN-Class fast mine warfare boats FGS UBERHERRN and FGS LABOE, RHEIN-Class depot ship FGS WERRA (A-68), Type-760 ammunition transport FGS WESTERWALD (A-1435). The government increases patrolling Europe's territorial waters for NATO while so many coalition ships are in the Middle East. The German Navy is commanded by V.Adm. Klaus Rehder.

Italian MINERVA-Class corvettes SFINGE (F-554) and MINERVA (F-551) depart Italy to strengthen the eastern Mediterranean, south of Cyprus. The Italian Navy is commanded by Adm. Filoppo Ruggero. Italian naval commanders in Operation Desert Shield/Desert Storm will be: R.Adm. Mario Buracchia, R.Adm. Enrico Martinotti, Capt. Paolo Belfiore, Capt. Mario Host, Capt. Giorgio Imbimbo, Capt. Alfredo Liberi, Capt. Orlando Nana, Capt. Sirio Pianigiani, Cdr. Andrea Campregher, Cdr. Paolo D'Arrigo, Cdr. Franco Eccher, Cdr. Ferdinando Manera, Cdr. Giuseppe Piro, Lt. Diego Martini, Lt. Giovanni Messina, Lt. Giuseppe Perrelli, and Lt. Francesco Scarpetta.

17 August Air campaign plan "*Instant Thunder*" is received by Gen. Schwarzkopf. It now includes the use of Navy and Marine Corps aircraft and identifies ten target categories for the offensive air campaign. They are: (1) national leadership facilities, (2) national telecommunications, (3) oil distribution and storage, (4) electric power, (5) railways (bridges are later added), (6) nuclear/chemical/biological capabilities, (7) military research/production/storage, (8) strategic air defense, (9) airfields (especially those holding interceptors and bombers), and (10) ballistic missile capabilities. With minor modifications these target categories are retained throughout Desert Storm.

U.S. intelligence have identified eight Iraqi divisions which seem to control eleven heavy and twelve light brigades.

The 24th Infantry Division (Mechanized), commanded by Maj. Gen. Barry McCaffrey departs Savannah, Georgia on MSC Fast Sealift Cargo Ships ALTAIR and CAPELLA. The first U.S. Army prepositioned ship arrives in Saudi Arabia.

Main elements of the 101st Airborne Division (Air Assault), commanded by Maj. Gen. J.H. Binford Peay begin to deploy to Saudi Arabia. The deployment continues for the next 13 days utilizing 56 C-141s and 49 C-5s to move 117 helicopters, 487 vehicles, 123 equipment pallets and 2,742 soldiers. The other two brigades of the 101st will move by ready-reserve ship from Jacksonville, Florida.

Lt. Gen. Walter E. Boomer, USMC, Commanding General, I Marine Expeditionary Force arrives at Riyadh, Saudi Arabia.

Transit Group 1 (USS SHREVEPORT (LPD-12) commanded by Capt. David J. Montgomery, TRENTON (LPD-14) commanded by Capt. James A. Curtis, PORTLAND (LSD-37) commanded by Cdr. Mark S. Falkey and GUNSTON HALL (LSD-44) commanded by Cdr. William J. Marshall sails from Morehead City, N.C. for the Persian Gulf. The group contains elements of the 4th Marine Expeditionary Brigade commanded by Maj. Gen. Harry W. Jenkins, Jr. The brigade (about 8,000 personnel) includes two battalions of the 2nd Marines, 2nd Marine Division. The division at Camp Lejeune, North Carolina prepares to support the 4th MEB.

En route to the Persian Gulf the battleship USS WISCONSIN transits the Suez Canal. WHITE PLAINS (AFS-4) commanded by Capt. Bernard W. Patton begins participation in Operation Desert Shield.

At Shaikh Isa, Bahrain, the first of F-4G "Wild Weasel" squadron arrives (561st TFS, 35th TFW) with 24 F-4Gs. Two U-2s of the Surveillance and Reconnaissance Wing (SRW) begin participating in Operation Desert Shield. At Bateen, UAE, 16 C-130Es of the 50th TAS, 314th TAW arrive.

The Belgium Navy deploys two Tripartite minehunters. BNS IRIS (M-920) is commanded by Cdr. Lucarelli and BNS-MYOSOTIS (M-922) is commanded by Cdr. Ectors. A support vessel BNS ZINNIA (A-961) commanded by Cdr. Van Dyck is also deployed. Built as a co-operative effort between France, Belgium, and The Netherlands, the minehunters are designated ERIDAN-Class in France and ALKMAAR-Class in The Netherlands. The IRIS will eventually clear 117 mines off Mina Saud.

18 August President George Bush authorizes the first-ever activation of the first stage of the Civil Reserve Air Fleet. This will facilitate the tremendous airlift task demanded to bring equipment and supplies 8,000 miles to Southwest Asia.

Iraqi troops begin to dismantle their field fortifications at Shatt-al-Arab (see: 15 August).

Logistics expert Maj. Gen. Pagonis is appointed Commanding General, Army Central Command, Support Command (Provisional).

USS ENGLAND (CG-22) commanded by Capt. Conrad C. Van der Schroeff stops and boards the first vessel of the multinational intercept operation in the Persian Gulf. It is the Chinese flagged HENG CHUNG HAI en route from Iraq to Qing Dao, China. USS ROBERT G. BRADLEY (FFG-49) commanded by Cdr. Kevin J. Cosgriff and REID (FFG-30) commanded by Cdr. Craig H. Murray fire warning shots across the bows of two Iraqi oil tankers in separate incidents. USS SCOTT (DDG-995) diverts the Cyprus flagged DONGOLA en route from Sudan to Aqaba in the northern Red Sea, but does not board it. The battleship WISCONSIN (BB-64) commanded by Capt. Jerry M. Blesch begins participation in Operation Desert Shield.

F/A-18 Hornets of Marine Group 70 begin 24 hour combat air patrols over the northern Gulf. The Marines will remain the most forward defense for Coalition vessels until hostilities begin. No Iraqi aircraft ever penetrates the Marine's air barrier for 152 days, though the Marines patience is tested with a number of near engagements.

The first MAC C-5 and C-141s deploying the 415th TFS to Saudi Arbaia are prepared.

At King Fahd International Airport the first USAF A-10 squadron arrives (353rd TFS, 354th TFW) with 24 A-10s. At Al Dhafra, UAE, two KC-135Rs of the 99th and 905th AREFS, 9th AREFW.

Iraqi Air Force fighters simuulate air-to-air missile attacks, ground-controlled intercepts and attacking ground forces. The Iraqi Army begins to withdraw from Iranian soil occupied since the end of the Iran-Iraq War.

19 August Secretary of Defense Dick Cheney announces that V.Adm. Henry H. Mauz, Jr. USN (Commander, U.S. Seventh Fleet) is appointed Commander, U.S. Naval Forces Central Command (COMUSNAVCENT).

From the three 755-foot maritime pre-positioning ships U.S. Navy cargo handlers at Jubail, Saudi Arabia, average 100 lift-hours per day. The ships contain more equipment and supplies than 3,000 C-141 cargo flights could have transported; enough to support 16,800 Marines for 30 days of combat.

USS TATTNALL (DDG-19), and JOHN RODGERS (DD-983) begin participation in Operation Desert Shield.

Col. Alton C. Whitley (commander, 37th TFW) and Lt. Col. Ralph Getchell (commander, 415th TFS) fly to Saudi Arabia in a C-5 Galaxy to lead the arrival of 18 of the squadron's F-117 Stealth Fighters.

Two USAF B-52s fly coordination training missions with AWACS.

Italian MAESTRALE-Class frigate LIBECCIO (F-572) sails for operational waters off Muscat in the Gulf of Oman.

20 August Iraq announces that adult male hostages are now in place at vulnerable targets as human shields.

First aircraft deploying soldiers of the 24th Infantry Division (Mech) departs the United States for Saudia Arabia.

Marines of the 7th Marine Expeditionary Brigade is in its combat position on the Saudi border, prepared to fight. The 16,800 Marines are the first Coalition heavy ground combat unit available in the war. The 26th Marine Expeditionary Unit, Special Operations Capable (SOC) arrives off Monrovia from the South Atlantic to relieve the 22nd Marine Expeditionary Unit.

Transit Group 2 sails for the Persian Gulf from Morehead City, N.C. It consists of USS NASSAU (LHA-4) commanded by Capt. John I. Dow, RALEIGH (LPD-1) commanded by

Capt. Richard J. McCarthy, PENSACOLA (LSD-38) commanded by Cdr. Danny C. Nelms, and SAGINAW (LST-1188) commanded by Cdr. Paul K. Kessler.

At Shaikh Isa, Bahrain, 18 USMC AV-8B Harriers of the Third Marine Air Wing arrive. These are the first Marine aircraft to arrive in the theater.

At King Fahd Airport 24 USAF A-10 Warthogs of the 356th TFS, 354th TFW arrive and two of four HC-130s of 9th SOS, 1st SOW arrive at Al Jouf. At Al Dhafra, UAE, one KC-135R of the 41st AREFS, 416th BMW arrives and at Diego Garcia three KC-135Rs of the 384th AREFS, 384th BMW arrives. B-52s begin to fly 16 training sorties over Saudi Arabia and 11 sorties over Diego Garcia which will be completed 6 September.

Royal Netherlands Navy JACOB VAN HEEMSKERCK-Class air defense frigate HrMs WITTE DE WITH (F-813), KORTENAER-Class frigate HrMs PIETER FLORISZ (F-826), and fast combat support ship HrMs POOLSTER (A-835) depart Dan Helder for the eastern Mediterranean.

Italian LUPO-Class frigate ORSA (F-567) joins LIBECCIO (F-572) in the Ionian Sea for duties in the Gulf of Oman. Italian vessels by the war's end will include: STROMBOLI (A-5327), MAESTRALE-Class frigate LEFFIRO (F-577), AUDACE (DDG-551), two LUPO-Class frigates LUPO (F-564) and SAGITTARIO (F-565), LERICI-Class minehunters MILAZZO (M-5552) and VIESTE (M-5553), ex-U.S. Navy ADJUTANT-Class coastal minesweeper PLATANO (M-5516), STROMBOLI-Class replenishment tanker VESUVIO (A-5329), MTS-1011-Class ramped transport ship TREMITI, and SAN GIORGIO-Class amphibious transport dock SAN MARCO (L-9893).

21 August The 2nd Brigade, 82nd Airborne (Col. Ronald F. Rokosz) has many units attached to it at Falcon Base including much of the 3/73 Armor and a company of attack helicopters.

The 26th Marine Expeditionary Unit (SOC) is to proceed from Monrovia for the Mediterranean.

At King Khalid AB, Saudi Arabia, (commanded by Brig. Gen. Abdulaziz Bin Khalid Al-Sudairi) the first 18 USAF F-117A "Stealth Fighters" of the 415th TFS, 37th TFW USAF arrive. At Riyadh AB, three EC-130 Compass Call and nine of ten KC-135Qs of the 349th and 350th AREFS, 9th AREFW arrive.

On the southern Kuwait border, well-equipped Iraqi armored and mechanized units are moving to the rear and being replaced by less well-equipped infantry forces. Iraq has now completed sea mining of Kuwait's harbors.

22 August President George Bush signs Executive Order 12727 authorizing the call-up of 200,000 reservists for up to 180 days.

U.S. Army pre-positioned ship GREEN HARBOR arrives at Ad-Dammam from Diego Garcia.

Transit Group 3 (USS IWO JIMA (LPH-2) commanded by Capt. Michael S. O'Hearn, GUAM (LPH-9) commanded by Capt. Charles R. Saffell, Jr., MANITOWOC (LST-1180) commanded by Cdr. Dale A. Rauch and LAMOURE COUNTY (LST-1194) commanded by Capt. Raymond A. Duffy departs Morehead City, N.C. for the Persian Gulf. The ships contain the last elements of the 4th Marine Expeditionary Brigade.

USS SARATOGA (CV-60) Carrier Battle Group passes through the Suez Canal for the Red Sea. BIDDLE (CG-34) commanded by Capt. Louis F. Harlow and the PHILIPPINE SEA (CG-58) commanded by Capt. Patrick A. Callahan begin participation in Operation Desert Shield. SURIBACHI (AE-21) ceases participation in Operation Desert Shield.

At Shaikh Isa, 24 USMC F/A-18 Hornets land.

U.S. Navy air units HS-3, HS-7, HSL-34 (DET 1), and HSL-46 (DET 7) begins participation in Operation Desert Shield.

At Riyadh, four USAF C-21s arrive.

French aircraft carrier CLEMENCEAU (R 98) arrives at Djibouti.

By this date the Coalition ship count participating in Desert Shield is: three Belgium ships, three Canadian, seven French, six German, two Italian, two Netherlands, three Spanish, and seven British, and 45 U.S.

Iraqi air transports increasingly land on Kuwaiti airfields. Republican Guard units continue to move northward.

23 August U.S. intelligence reports Iraqi tanks with decontamination materials, indicating that they may be preparing a chemical attack.

The 2nd Brigade of the 82nd Airborne makes its first deployment to the desert to establish battle positions (BP) for any Iraqi attack. During the 24 hour deployment the heat is intense but heat casualties few due the insistence of Lt. Gen. Gary Luck that the paratroopers force-hydrate (drink fluids regularly until it hurts).

NEOSHA (TAO-143) ceases participation in Operation Desert Shield.

The first USAF TR-1 arrives. Two of the aircraft of the 17th Reconnaissance Wing (RW) arrive at an unknown destination in the theater. At Thumrait, Oman four MC-130s of the 8th SOS, 1st SOW arrive and at Riyadh one C-20 of the 608th Marine Air Group (MAG) arrives.

Stealth fighter pilots at King Khalid AB begin orientation sorties.

Royal Australian Navy's DAMASK Task Group departs Western Australia for the Gulf of Oman. The Task Group consists of two OLIVER HAZARD PERRY-Class frigates HMAS ADELAIDE (F-01) commanded by Capt. W.A. Dovers and HMAS DARWIN (F-04) commanded by Capt. R.E. Shalders and a DURANCE-Class replenishment tanker HMAS SUCCESS (AOR-304) commanded by Commo. G.V. Sloper. HMAS BRISBANE commanded by Commo. C.A. Ritchie and HMAS SYDNEY (F-03) commanded by Capt. L.G. Cordner, will eventually deploy for the Middle East.

The Spanish Group consisting of SANTA MARIA (Capt. Zarco Navarro), DESCUBIERTA (Capt. Munoz-Delgado Diaz Del Rio), and CAZADORA (Capt. Mayo Consentino) begins participation in Operation Desert Shield. The Group is commanded is Capt. Rapallo Comendador.

Royal Saudi Air Force maintains continous combat air patrols.

Iraqi aircraft fly their first night missions over Kuwait. Defensive patrols by MiG-29s and MiG-23s increase.

24 August   Gen. H. Norman Schwarzkopf, Commander, U.S. Central Command (CENTCOM) briefs Gen. Colin L. Powell, Chairman of the Joint Chiefs of Staff on a four-phased plan to eject the Iraqis from Kuwait. The structure of the air campaign remains unchanged throughout the war: a strategic air campaign into Iraq, air supremacy over the Kuwait theatre, preparation of the battlefield attriting the Iraqi Army and finally air support for the ground campaign. In the words of Gen. Schwarzkopf, " . . .*We will initially attack into the Iraqi homeland using air power to decapitate his leadership, command and control, and eliminate his ability to reinforce Iraqi ground forces in Kuwait and Southern Iraq. We will then gain undisputed air superiority over Kuwait so that we can subsequently and selectively attack Iraqi ground forces with air power in order to reduce his combat power and destroy reinforcing units . . .*"

The U.S. Embassy in Kuwait is ordered closed. Approximately 100 U.S. officials (including U.S. Marine guards) and civilians are moved to Baghdad by the Iraqi government. Approximately 1,000 Americans will now be hostages in Iraq.

Strength of 82nd Airborne Division in Saudi Arabia is more than 12,000 paratroopers.

Most of the 24th Infantry Division (Mech) soldiers have now arrived in Saudi Arabia.

The battleship USS WISCONSIN (BB-64) commanded by Capt. Jerry M. Blesch passes through the Strait of Hormuz and into the Persian Gulf. SAMPSON (DDG-10) commanded by Cdr. William D. Sullivan, MONTGOMERY (FF-1082) commanded by Cdr. Robert A. Higgins, DETROIT (AOE-4) commanded by Capt. Michael B. Edwards, and THOMAS C. HART (FF-1092) commanded by Cdr. David C. Rollins begins participation in Operation Desert Shield.   EISENHOWER (CVN-69), TICONDEROGA (CG-47), TATTNALL (DDG-19), SCOTT (DDG-995), JOHN RODGERS (DD-983) and JOHN L. HALL (FFG-32) cease participation in Operation Desert Shield.

The USS DETROIT (AOE-4) is the first U.S. warship to arrive in Jeddah, Saudi Arabia, to assist in establishing the neccessary logisics center that will support Operation Desert Shield and Desert Storm. She will support SARATOGA (CV-60), JOHN F. KENNEDY (CV-67) and AMERICA (CV-66) during the war as well as units of the Greek, Turkish, Saudi, Spanish and Italian navies (in excess of 265 ships).

U.S. Navy air units HC-8 (DET 2), and HSL-32 (DET 7) begins participation in Operation Desert Shield.

U.S. Air Force now has 222 A-10, F-4G, F-15C, F-15E, F-16, F-111, F-117, and B-52 aircraft in Saudi Arabia and the surrounding region. At Taif, Saudi Arabia, eight EF-111

Raven electronic warfare aircraft arrive, and at Shaikh Isa, six A-6E all-weather attack and 12 EA-6Bs electronic warfare aircraft arrive.

Canadian Task Group 302.3, including IROQUIS-Class destroyer HMCS ATHABASKAN (DD-282), ST. LAURENT-Class frigate HMCS FRASER (FF-233), RESTIGOUCHE-Class frigate HMCS TERA NOVA (DD-259) and operational support ship HMCS PROTECTEUR (AOR-509) depart Halifax with soldiers of the Canadian # 119 Air Defense Battery. The three ships--with a combined age of 70 years--are able to sail only after being outfitted with weaponry cannibalized from half-finished frigates. They begin *Operation Friction*.

The British Royal Air Force begin flying orientation and training flights.

Iraqi defensive air patrols over Kuwait and southern and central Iraq increase. Two Iraqi Mirage F-1s shadow Coalition fighters south of the Kuwaiti border. The Iraqi Air Force commander is Lt. Gen. Hamid Sha'ban al-Takriti.

25 August In United Nations Security Council Resolution 665 a maritime embargo is instituted against Iraq.

Gen. Schwarzkopf briefs Gen. Powell on the four-phase plan to eject Iraqi forces from Iraq code-named *Desert Storm*. The earliest Schwarzkopf believes he can initiate a ground offensive is December.

More than 40,000 XVIII Airborne Corps troops have arrived since 10 August.

The 7th Marine Expeditionary Brigade, due to 259 Military Airlift Command (MAC) sorties and five Maritime Prepositioning Ships is now at the following strength: 15,248 Marines, 425 artillery pieces, 123 tanks, and 124 aircraft. Maj. Gen. Hopkins reports to Gen. Schwarzkopf that he is prepared to defend the approaches of the vital seaport of Al Jubayl. The Ground Combat Element is Regimental Landing Team 7 (RLT-7) of four infantry battalions and a light armored infantry battalion. The 1st Marine Expeditionary Brigade from Hawaii begins to fly for Saudi Arabia and Maj. Gen. J.M. Myatt, USMC arrives in Saudi Arabia.

At Taif, the first of 18 USAF F-111Fs of the 492nd TFS, 48th TFW arrive, and at Al Dhafra (or Shaikh Isa?) the first six RF-4Cs of the 152nd Tactical Reconnaissance Group (TRG) arrive.

The use of military force to maintain the trade embargo against Iraq is approved by the U.N. Security Council.

Iraq flies over 25 sorties today.

26 August Water is cut off by Iraq to foreign embassies in Kuwait, and electricity is cut off to the American Embassy. The embassies are surrounded by Iraqi soldiers.

At 0700 Schwarzkopf's Chief of Staff Maj. Gen. Robert B. Johnston, USMC, arrives at Riyadh.

In anticipation of their sea-embarked equipment, personnel of the U.S. Army 24th Infantry Division (Mech) are arriving.

Maritime Prepositioning Shipping Squadron 3 arrives at Al Jubayl from Guam. The deploying elements join the 1st Marine Expeditionary Brigade which has already arrived.

At Bateen, UAE, two USAF EC-130Hs of the 41st Electronic Combat Squadron (ECS), 28th Air Division (AD) arrives. The F-117 Stealth Fighters of the 415th TFS at King Khalid AB assume alert duty, and are now ready to fight.

Coalition troop strength is: 5,000 Egyptian troops, 8,500 French, 3,000 Gulf Cooperation Council, 7,000 Kuwaiti, 1,000 Moroccan, 45,000 Saudi, 1,200 Syrian, 70,000 Turkey (positioned on the Iraqi border), and 40,000 U.S. for total of 180,700.

Iraq flies over 70 sorties today.

27 August Headquarters, U.S. Central Command transfers from Florida to Riyadh.

First U.S. Army Reserve units are activated.

The first two Fast Sealift ships (USNS ALTAIR (T-AKR-291) and USNS CAPELLA (T-AKR-293) arrive in Saudi Arabia from Savannah. Averaging 27 knots, they have crossed 8,700 nautical miles carrying elements of the U.S. 24th Infantry (Mechanized) Division. Also, the Saudi Arabian deployment of Fleet Hospital 5 is announced. The first heavy tanks of the 24th Mechanized Division begin to be unloaded in Saudi Arabia.

A British Tornado GR. Mk 1 squadron departs Germany, landing in Bahrain.

Iraqi combat air patrols over southern Iraq and central Kuwait are nearly continous in company with airborne warning aircraft.

28 August Iraq counts Kuwait as part of its country, broadcasting the "re-establishment" of the 19th province of Iraq.

USS BLUE RIDGE (LCC-19) begins participating in Operation Desert Shield.

U.S. Navy air units HC-1 (DET 6), and VP-19 begin participation in Operation Desert Shield.

At Seeb, Oman, six USAF KC-135Rs of the 41st AREFS, 416th BMW, and one KC-135R of the 301st AREFS, 301st AREFW arrive. At Al Ain, UAE, 16 C-130Es of the 37th TAS, 435th TAW arrive.

French aircraft carrier CLEMENCEAU (R 98) departs Djibouti for port calls at Fujairah and Abu Dhabi. They will then head for Yanbu, Saudi Arabia.

29 August Departing Norfolk en route to the Persian Gulf are three minesweepers. They are IMPERVIOUS (MSO-449), commanded by Lt. Cdr. David M. Jackson, LEADER (MSO-490), commanded by Lt. Cdr. Steven E. Lehr and ADROIT (MSO-509), commanded by Lt. Cdr. Steven E. Thorton and Mine Counter Measures Ship USS AVENGER commanded by Cdr. James D. Cope. USS ADROIT and USS IMPERVIOUS are Naval Reserve ships.

At Ramstein AB, Germany, 13 U.S. airmen are killed after a Galaxy cargo plane (C-5A 68-0228) of the 60th MAW crashes taking off for Saudi Arabia. This is the first aircraft loss of the Persian Gulf War.

At Seeb, Oman, three USAF KC-135Rs of the 905th AREFS, 319th BMW arrive, at Doha, Qatar, 24 F-16Cs of the 614th TFS, 401st TFW arrive, and at Tabuk, ten F-15Cs of the 58th TFS, 33rd TFW arrive.

A British Jaguar squadron moves from Thumrait, Oman to Seeb, Oman.

Iraqi sorties increase to the highest rate since the Kuwait invasion (171 sorties).

30 August General Order #1 is issued by U.S. Central Command. It concerns Saudi Arabian religious and cultural sensitivities.

U.S. Army and Marine Corps weapons strength is now: 84 attack helicopters, 169 TOW missile systems, 118 M1 and 82 M-60A1 tanks, and 109 artillery pieces.

The U.S. Army's 197th Infantry Brigade arrives in Saudi Arabia.

USS JOHN F. KENNEDY Carrier Battle Group transits the Strait of Gibraltar for the Middle East. USS SAMPSON (DDG-10) commanded by Cdr. William D. Sullivan diverts the Bahamian flagged KOTA WIRAMA en route from Jeddah to Iraq, in the northern Arabian Sea (cargo is porcelain). COMFORT (TAH-20) passes through the Suez Canal.

At Al Minhad, UAE, 24 F-16Cs of the 4th USAF TFS, 388th TFW arrive, as well as three EC-130Hs of the 41st ECS, 28th AD.

British Replenishment ships RFA OLNA commanded by Capt. A. F. Pitt, and RFA FORT GRANGE commanded by Capt. P. L. Nelson begin participation in Operation Desert Shield.

United States regional strength by this date is: 14 tactical fighter squadrons, three carrier battle groups, a B-52 heavy bomber squadron, four tactical airlift squadrons, seven Army and Marine Corps brigades with attack helicopters, and a Patriot air defense system.

By this date elements of the British 22nd Special Air Service Regiment and Special Boat Squadron have arrived in Saudi Arabia.

Concentrating on air-to-ground training and combat air patrols, the Iraqi Air Force has launched 360 sorties over the past two days, with 197 today.

31 August A Fort Campbell, Kentucky, Special Forces Group (Col. Jesse Johnson) is the first Army Special Forces to arrive in Saudi Arabia. Its initial mission is to support the Saudi Arabian ground forces, as well as the Saudi Army National Guard.

The first Iraqi merchant vessel AL KARAMAH is boarded by a team from the USS BIDDLE (CG-34) commanded by Capt. Louis F. Harlow. Seaman David Lee Handshoe takes the ZANOOBIA's helm.

Arriving at Rota en route to the Mediterranean Sea is MARG 3-90. It consists of USS INCHON commanded by Capt. Harold J. Tickle, NASHVILLE, FAIRFAX COUNTY commanded by Cdr. Mark A. Hoke, and NEWPORT commanded by Cdr. Timothy A. Kok transporting the 26th MEU.

At King Fahd the first two USAF EC-130 aircraft of the 193rd Special Operations Group (SOG) arrive. At King Fahd 24 A-10s of the 74th TFS, 388th TFW (Lt. Col. Jim Green). At Tabuk 12 F-15Cs of the 58th TFS, 33rd TFW arrive. At Riyadh a E-3 of the 552nd AWACS, 552nd AWACW arrives, and at Incirlik, Turkey eight F-111Es of the 55th TFS, 20 TFW arrive.

Iraq flies 173 sorties today.

1 September The 101st Airborne Division (Air Assault) is ordered to relieve the 82nd Airborne Division at FOB Essex. With their arrival, the 101st renames the base FOB Bastogne.

USS BLUE RIDGE (commanded by Capt. Joseph K. Henderson), flagship of Commander, Seventh Fleet, arrives for duty in the Persian Gulf.

At Sharjah, UAE, six USAF EC-130 Airborne Battlefield Command and Control Center aircraft of the 7th Airborne Command and Control Squadron (ACCS), 28th Air Division arrive. At Al Jouf, two MH-53s of the 20th SOS, 1st SOW, arrive and at Al Minhad, UAE, 24 F-16Cs of the 421st TFS, 388th TFW arrive.

Greece approves the stationing of a Strategic Air Command tanker force at Hellenikon Air Base. Hellenic Air Force commander is Air Marshal Nikolaos Stappas.

Iraqi Army forces continue to strengthen their defenses. They are capable of launching a ground attack in approximately 18 to 24 hours of issuing the attack order. People's Army Commander is Taha Yasin Ramadan al-Jazrawi.

2 September At Al Jubayl, Saudi Arabia, elements of the I Marine Expeditionary Force unload their supplies from maritime prepositioning ships that have arrived from Diego Garcia. The I Marine Expeditionary Force assumes operational control of all Marine forces in the theater.

At Taif, Saudi Arabia, 18 USAF F-111F aircraft of the 493rd TFS, 48th TFW arrive bringing the total to 32 aircraft. At Al Minhad, F-16s arrive bringing the strength to 120 aircraft, at Tabuk, two F-15Cs of the 58th TFS, 33rd TFW arrive and at King Fahd, 24 A-10s of the 76th TFS, 23rd TFW (Col. David Sawyer) arrive bringing the base strength to 96 aircraft.

Iraq flies 68 sorties today.

3 September   Gen. Schwarzkopf is briefed on the Black Hole's (the special air power planning group) plan for Phase I of the air campaign against Iraq.

Cross training between U.S. and Saudi Special Forces begin in preparation for the creation of special reconnaissance teams. The teams will later deploy along the Saudi-Kuwait border in the region of the Eastern Provincial Area Command.

Desert Dragon III begins. With the 101st Airborne Division relieving the 82nd Airborne at FOB Bastogne, the 101st establishes two areas of operations to the north and west (Normandy and Carentan, respectively). If the Iraqi Army invades, the 101st helicopters will first destroy the enemy light reconnaissance vehicles, its air defense and artillery vehicles, then atrite the Iraqis until the 24th Infantry Division (Mech) takes over.

South of the Kuwait-Saudi border, the Eastern Area Command (Saudi Maj. Gen. Saleh Bin Ali Almohoyya) a provisional Arab mechanized division of 267 M60A3 and AMX-10 tanks, 800 fighting vehicles and 140 artillery pieces is in position to be the first to fight any Iraqi invasion of Saudi Arabia.

The USS DWIGHT D. EISENHOWER and USS TICONDEROGA pass through the Strait of Gibraltar for the eastern United States. GUNSTON HALL (LSD-44) commanded by Cdr. William J. Marshall, KILAUEA (TAE-26), PORTLAND (LSD-37) commanded by Cdr. Mark S. Falkey, SHREVEPORT (LPD-12) commanded by Capt. David J. Montgomery, SPARTANBURG COUNTY (LST-1192) commanded by Cdr. James J. Adams, and TRENTON (LPD-14) commanded by Capt. James A. Curtis begin participation in Operation Desert Shield.

U.S. Marine Corps Maj. Gen. Royal N. Moore establishes the 3rd Marine Aircraft Wing in the area, positioning his headquarters at Shaikh Isa Air Base, Bahrain. This will remain wing headquarters until it moves to Jubayl in January 1991.

U.S. Marine Corps Brig. Gen. James A. Brabham assumes command of the 1st Force Service Support Group. Col. Michael V. Brock begins commanding the 1st Surveillance, Reconnaissance and Intelligence Group, and Lt. Col. Thomas A. Flaherty assumes command of the 1st Radio Battalion.

Capt. Michael R. Johnson, USN, assumes command of the 3rd Naval Construction Regiment, I Marine Expeditionary Force.

At Al Jouf, two USAF MH-53s of the 20th SOS, 1st SOW arrive.

Strength of U.S. military personnel is 104,304.

A USAF F-16C flown by Capt. Richard Setzer crashes near Sharjah, UAE, with Setzer escaping injury (33rd TFS/363RD TFW). He is rescued by a UAE search and rescue helicopter.

Iraqi air activity is at a low level, flying 37 sorties today.

4 September   Elements of the 24th (Mechanized) Infantry Division arrives in Saudi Arabia.

The first Iraqi freighter ZANOOBIA is boarded in the northern Arabian Sea. The boarding team is led by Coast Guard Lt.(jg) John Gallagher of the USS GOLDSBOROUGH (DDG-20) commanded by Cdr. James A. Reid. The master and crew are detained, and the ZANOOBIA containing tea is sailed to Muscat, Oman. This is the first Iraqi vessel seized.

SHREVEPORT, TRENTON, GUNSTON HALL, PORTLAND and SPARTANBURG COUNTY transporting elements of the 4th MEB (Maj. Gen. Harry W. Jenkins, Jr. USMC) transit the Suez Canal.

The first Kuwaiti Boeing 747 air mission is flown. The Kuwaiti Air Force commander is Brig. Gen. Daud al-Ghanim.

5 September The 1st Marine Division (Brig. Gen. James M. Myatt) is in place in Saudi Arabia and is ready to assume control of the Ground Combat Element of the I Marine Expeditionary Force. It will consist of three infantry regiments (1st, 3rd, and 7th Marines) and an artillery regiment (11th Marines) the 1st Light Armored Infantry, 1st Combat Engineers, 1st Reconnaissance, 3rd Assault Amphibian, and the 1st and 3rd Tanks.

Firing suspension of the battleship WISCONSIN's 16-inch guns is lifted by the U.S. Navy. USS SAMUEL B. ROBERTS (FFG-58) commanded by Cdr. John W. Townes, OGDEN (LPD-5) commanded by Capt. Braden J. Phillips, OKINAWA (LPH-3) commanded by Capt. Mack A. Thomas, and CAYUGA (LST-1186) commanded by Cdr. David W. Hagstrom begin participation in Operation Desert Shield.

With 360 women among the 1,260 crew aboard the USS ACADIA (AD-42) (Capt. Larry L. King) the ship departs San Diego. This is the first test of a war-time combined male-female crew.

At Shaikh Isa, the final F-4G "Wild Weasels" of the USAF 52nd TFW arrive, bringing the strength to 12 aircraft. Theater strength for the aircraft is now 36.

An American in Kuwait is wounded by Iraqi troops while attempting to avoid capture.

Approximately fifty percent of Iraqi air sorties are for transportation. Three combat air patrols and night ground controlled intercept training sorties are flown today. Iraq flies a total of 79 sorties today.

6 September Headquarters Company, 2nd Brigade, 82nd Airborne (Capt. Dominic J. Caraccilo) establishes its firing range against a berm by the naval port of al-Jubayl. The troopers are harassed by the large size of the flies in the area.

Air movement of the U.S. Army 24th Infantry Division (Mech) is completed.

The three major subordinate headquarters of I Marine Expeditionary Force are in place in Saudi Arabia (1st Marine Division, 3rd Marine Aircraft Wing, 1st Force Service Support Group).

USS JOHN F. KENNEDY Carrier Battle Group enters its area of responsibility. USS NASSAU (LHA-4) commanded by Capt. John I. Dow, PENSACOLA (LSD-38) commanded by Cdr. Danny C. Nelms, and SAGINAW (LST-1188) commanded by Cdr. Paul K. Kessler begins participation in Operation Desert Shield.

At Taif three USAF EF-111s arrive, at Riyadh, a E-3A AWACS arrive and at Jeddah, two KC-135Rs of the 19th AREFW arrive.

In London, England, Parliament meets in emergency session and overwhelmingly supports Western military deployment.

The French 6th Light Armor Brigade begins its deployment to its Area of Responsibility.

The Iraqi Army continues to strengthen its defensive positions. Approximately 79 Iraqi Air Force sorties are flown today, including combat air patrols.

7 September Two brigades of the 24th Infantry Division (Mech) are deployed to the desert. The 12th Aviation Brigade begins to deploy, and the first U.S. Army Reserves arrive in Saudi Arabia.

Amphibious Ready Group (ARG) ALPHA arrives in the Gulf of Oman. ALPHA transporting the 13th Marine Expeditionary Unit (MEU) consists of USS DURHAM (LKA-114), USS OGDEN (LPD-5), USS OKINAWA (LPH-3), USS FORT MCHENRY (LSD-43), and USS CAYUGA (LST-1186). Amphibious Ready Group BRAVO commanded by Col. Ross A. Brown is on their way to Saudi Arabia on USS DUBUQUE (LPD-8), SAN BERNARDINO (LST-1189) and SCHENECTADY (LST-1195).

HUNT-Class Minehunters HMS CATTISTOCK commanded by Lt. Cdr. M. P. Shrives, HMS ATHERSTONE commanded by Lt. Cdr. P. N. M. Davies, HMS HURWORTH, commanded by Lt. Cdr. R. J. Ibbotson and Ocean Survey Ship HMS HERALD commanded by Cdr. P. H. Jones (Improved HECLA-Class) begins participation in Operation Desert Shield.

At Jeddah, one USAF KC-135R of the 384th BMW, three KC-135s of the 416th BMW, and four KC-135Rs of the 42th BMW arrive.

Nine Iraqi divisions form their forward defensive positions from the Persian Gulf, to the northwestern corner of Kuwait. A counterattack force of two armor, one mechanized and two infantry divisons backs up the forward line.

8 September Last elements of the 1st and 3rd Brigades of the 82nd Airborne Division arrive in Saudi Arabia, after being transported by 582 C-141 sorties.

Hospital ship USNS COMFORT (T-AH-20) arrives in the Persian Gulf. RALEIGH (LPD-1) commanded by Capt. Richard J. McCarthy, IWO JIMA (LPH-7) commanded by Capt. Michael S. O'Hearn, LA MOURE COUNTY (LST-1194) commanded by Capt. Raymond A. Duffy, MANITOWAC (LST-1180) commanded by Cdr. Dale A. Rauch, and HASSAYAMPA (TAO-145) transporting the 4th MEB begin participation in Operation Desert Shield.

At King Fahd four USAF AC-130 gunships of the 16th SOS, 1st SOW arrive. At Sharjah and Al Ain the last of two C-130 squadrons brings the theater strength to 96. RF-4Cs fly long-range optical reconnaissance missions.

9 September USS DUBUQUE (LPD-8), SAN BERNADINO (LST-1189) and SCHENECTADY (LST-1185) begin participating in Operation Desert Shield. REID (FFG-30) commanded by Cdr. Craig H. Murray and VANDERGRIFT (FFG-48) commanded by Cdr. Christopher H. Johnson cease participation in Operation Desert Shield. They have been in the area since 27 April.

Reconnaissance missions along the Saudi-Kuwait border are flown by USAF U-2, TR-1, RF-4, and RSAF RF-5 aircraft. U.S. Strategic Air Command awaits approval to bring B-52 strength to 28.

First French Aviation helicopters arrive in Saudi Arabia. They are two AS 330B Pumas and four SA 342M Gazelles of the *3 Regiment d'helicopters de combat* flying off of the CLEMENCEAU.

10 September Iran and Iraq resume diplomatic relations. Free oil is offered by Saddam Hussein to any Third World country able to arrange shipping to Iraq.

Imminent danger/hostile fire pay is now retroactive to 1 August for U.S. personnel.

The U.S. 82nd Airborne Division's 2nd Brigade for the third and final time deploys from the field from al-Jubayl.

CURTISS (TAVB-4) begins participation in Operation Desert Shield.

On board the French destroyer DUPLEIX, the British, Dutch, French and Italians begin a meeting to establish five patrol areas. At Djibouti, French Adm. Bonneau is the acting coordinator.

Iraq flies 90 air sorties today.

11 September In an address to a joint session of Congress President George Bush states "We will not let this aggression stand." He reiterates four objectives: 1) the complete, immediate and unconditional Iraqi withdrawal from Kuwait, 2) the restoration of Kuwait's legitimate government, 3) assurance of security and stability in the Persian Gulf, and 4) the safety of American citizens abroad.

The deployment of the U.S. Army 1st Cavalry Divison begins.

The 4th Marine Expeditionary Brigade arrives in the Gulf of Oman. They land from the amphibious ships USS GUNSTON HALL (LSD-44) commanded by Cdr. William J. Marshall, USS PORTLAND (LSD-37) commanded by Cdr. Mark S. Falkey, USS SHREVEPORT (LPD-12) commanded by Capt. David J. Montgomery, and USS SPARTANBURG COUNTY (LST-1192) commanded by Cdr. James J. Adams.

At Al Jouf eight USAF MH-60s of the 55th SOS, 1st SOW arrive.

Iraq flies 82 sorties today.

12 September Gen. Colin Powell arrives in Saudi Arabia.

Major combat elements of the 24th Infantry Division (Mechanized) finish arriving in Saudi Arabia. Five Patriot missile batteries are now deployed in concert with 32 PAC II missiles.

USS BIDDLE commanded by Capt. Louis F. Harlow diverts the Liberian flagged ship ARI in the northern Red Sea. She is en route from Jeddah to Aqaba carring wood and steel.

At King Khalid AB USAF Gen. Michael J. Dugan visits the Stealth Fighter pilots of the 415th TFS. At King Fahd five USAF AC-130 gunships arrive completing Phase I. Theater strength is 962 fixed wing aircraft (600 combat) and approximately 1100 rotary wing aircraft.

13 September Amphibious Ready Group BRAVO arrives off Saudi Arabia transporting the 1st Battalion, 2nd Marines. BRAVO consists of USS SAN BERNARDINO (LST-1189), USS DUBUQUE (LPD-8) and USS SCHENECTADY (LST-1185).

At Al Dhafra, UAE, a KC-135R of the 384th BMW arrives.

British Defense Secretary Thomas King announces the movement of the 7th Armoured Brigade (commanded by Brig. Patrick Cordingley) from its base at Fallingbostel, Germany to Saudi Arabia.

Approximately 80 Iraqi air sorties are flown per day. Approximately one-half of supply flights land at Kuwait International Airport. US intelligence discovers that high readiness is not being maintained by Republican Guard units.

Egypt approves the beddown of Strategic Air Command air refueling aircraft at Cairo West AB. The Egyptian Air Force commander is Air Vice Marshal Said Kamel.

Iraq flies 80 sorties today.

14 September The 2nd Battalion, 325 AIR, 82nd Airborne Division is the first 2nd Brigade unit to move to Ab Qaiq. Col. Rokosz will establish three separate infantry battalion base camps. They will be Camp Red (1-325), Camp Gold (4-325), and Camp White (2-325). The airborne troopers nickname Ab Qaiq, Butt Cake.

The 197th Infantry (Mech) of the 24th Infantry Division (Mech) from Fort Benning, Georgia, completes its movement into the Saudi desert.

Cruisers MISSISSIPPI (CGN-40) commanded by an unknown commander, and SAN JACINTO (CG-56) commanded by Capt. Paul W. Ecker begin participation in Operation Desert Shield.

USAF flies close air support and tactical air control system exercises. Of 20 B-52s at Diego Garcia, 14 are on alert, armed with Cluster Bomb Units (CBU) or M-177 bombs. Strategic Air Command has 186 tankers commited to Operation Desert Shield (94 in theater, 13 in the Pacific, and 79 in the Atlantic or Europe), with 47 held in reserve. The Command's reconnaissance aircraft have flown 74 sorties/892 hours in RC-135 aircraft, 32 sorties/251 hours in U-2 aircraft, and 15 sorties/117 hours in TR-1 aircraft.

The meeting of British, Dutch, French and Italians on board DUPLEIX is completed. Five patrol areas of responsibility in the Persian Gulf and the Straits of Hormuz are established. Each area is to be patrolled continuously by two ships. Bab el Mandeb is assigned to the Belgians and French; the Straits of Tiran to the French and Spanish; and the Straits of Oman by the French, Italians, and Spanish.

USS JOHN F. KENNEDY (CV-67) carrier battle group passes through the Suez Canal, and into the Red Sea.

Elements of the 4th Marine Expeditionary Brigade arrives in the Gulf of Oman on the amphibious ships USS NASSAU (LHA-4) commanded by Capt. John I. Dow, USS PENSACOLA (LSD-38) commanded by Cdr. Danny C. Nelms and USS SAGINAW (LST-1188) commanded by Cdr. Paul K. Kessler. NASSAU is flagship for the largest amphibious task force (ATF) in recent history and will become the first LHA-class ship in history to fly strike missions with her AV-8B Harrier jump jets. Her Harriers will fly 252 sorties and deliver in excess of 500,000 pounds of bombs on the enemy, directed by her air boss, Cdr. William Stewart.

The first multinational boarding of an Iraqi vessel occurs, when after 24 hours of radio negotiations with the master of tanker AL FAO, the Australian frigate HMAS DARWIN (F-04) and USS BREWTON (FF-1086) commanded by Cdr. Charlie A. Jones fire across her bow. The Australian boarding party is led by Quartermaster 2nd Class James Lecomte and the Americans are again led by Coast Guard Lt.(jg) John Gallagher.

USS THOMAS S. GATES (CG-51) commanded by Capt. Henry C. Giffin III, and SEATTLE (AOE-3) commanded by Capt. Wilber C. Trafton begins participation in Operation Desert Shield. SEATTLE, as part of the JOHN F. KENNEDY Carrier Battle Group has Helicopter Combat Support Squadron 8, DET 3 and EODMU 2 DET 10 aboard. She will serve as the only combat logistics support platform in the Red Sea during the beginning of Desert Shield, eventually making 282 connected replenishments, 700 vertical replenishments, and serving 53 Coalition ships (nearly 5,553 tons of cargo).
U.S. Navy air units HC-8 (DET 5), HSL-42 (DET 1), HSL-44 (DET 9), VA-46, VA-72, VA-75, VAQ-130, VAW-126, VF-14, VF-32, and VS-22 begin participation in Operation Desert Shield.

The British 7th Armoured Brigade (commanded by Brig. Patrick Cordingley) are committed to Operation Granby. Quartermaster Maj. Glyn Ireland has the awesome responsibility for supplying the Brigade.

The Italian government announces that in accordance with Operation Locusta they are deploying a squadron of Tornado aircraft to Abu Dhabi. The Italian Air Force commander is Gen. Stelio Nardini.

Saudi Royal Air Force pilots are being trained as forward air controllers. The Saudi Air Force commander is Lt. Gen. Abdullah Hamdan.

Iraqi forces in Kuwait now consist of ten divisions (155,000 troops) equipped with approximately 1,350 tanks, 900 armored personnel carriers and 650 artillery pieces. In neighboring areas of Iraq, twelve additional divisions of reinforcements and reserves await orders from Saddam Hussein.

15 September MERCY (TAH-19) begins participation in Operation Desert Shield.

At Taif, 14 USAF EF-111s of the 390th ECS, 366th TFW arrive.

Coalition ground Order of Battle is 589 TOW missile systems, 385 tanks, 276 artillery pieces, and 38 Multiple Launch Rocket Systems.

Strength of total fixed wing aircraft in theater is 1,043, with 117 attack helicopters.

France announces that it will be sending 4,000 troops to Saudi Arabia, one armored division with the following theoretical organization: 6th Light Armored Division General Staff; 2nd Foreign Infantry Regiment (Nimes); Armored Reconnaissance; 1st Regiment de Spahis (Valence); Elements of the 6th Regiment Foreign Engineers (Camp de l'Ardoise, Gard); Logistics: 6th Regiment Support Command; 5th Orange Fighter Squadron; 33th Strasbourg Tactical Reconnaissance Squadron.

HMS GLOUCESTER (MANCHESTER-Class Type 42C) commanded by Cdr. P. L. Wilcocks begins participation in Operation Desert Shield.

16 September Two large Coalition air interdiction exercises are flown. One is a package of 40 F-16s, and a second package is of eight F-16s and two F-4G Wild Weasels.

17 September The 4th Marine Expeditionary Brigade is in the Gulf of Oman, just outside the Persian Gulf aboard its four ships USS IWO JIMA, GUAM, RALEIGH and LAMOURE COUNTY. They prepare for landing rehearsals.

At 0230, the LM-2500 engines of USS ROBERT G. BRADLEY (FFG-49) pass their 10,000th hour of operation as she supports Operation Desert Shield.

At Al Dhafra, a USAF KC-135R of the 384th BMW arrives.

18 September Ground forces are familiarized with A-10 "Warthog" missions.

USS CONCORD (AFS-5) begins participation in Operation Desert Shield. USS DAVID R. RAY (DD-971) commanded by Cdr. Wesley A. Bergazzi ceases participation in Operation Desert Shield. She has been in the area since 9 June.

In the Red Sea, the USS KENNEDY and SARATOGA launches coordination exercises with 63 aircraft, using KC-135 refueling support.

Twenty F-16s from the USAF 401st Tactical Fighter Wing join 14 F-111s of the 20th TFW on a weapons training deployment. Joint USAF AWACS and RC-135 missions provide continuous surveillance of Kuwait and southern Iraq.

Two Spanish DESCUBIERTA-Class corvettes DESCUBIERTA (F-31) commanded by Capt. Munoz-Delgado Diaz Del Rio and CAZADORA (F-35) commanded by Capt. Mayo Consentino with ex-USS PAUL REVERE-Class supply ship ARAGON (L-22) are to be relieved. They are to be relieved by the FFG-7-Class frigate NUMANCIA (F-83) commanded by Capt. Marco Franco and two additional DESCUBIERTA-Class corvettes DIANA (F-32) commanded by Capt. Curiel Pina and INFANTA CRISTINA (F-34) commanded by Capt. Palencia Luaces. They are operating in the Gulf of Oman.

The first Royal Saudi Air Force liaison officers complete training to provide tactical air control, for forward Saudi ground forces.

Coalition troop strength by country is 5,000 Egyptian, 13,100 French, 3,000 Gulf Cooperation Council, 7,000 Kuwaiti, 1,200 Moroccoan, 2,000 Pakistan, 45,000 Saudi, 4,000 Syrian, 100,000 Turkey (positioned on the Iraqi border), 6,000 British, and 140,000 U.S., for a total of 326,300.

Today Coalition ship count is three Belgium, three Canadian, one Denmark, 14 French, one Greek, three Italian, two Netherlands, one Norway, three Spanish, 45 U.S., two USSR for a total of 78.

19 September USS JOHN F. KENNEDY and SARATOGA launch two large packages using KC-135 refueling support.

French chain of command for *Operation Daguet* is: Col. Barro, Corps Commander; 1st Cavalry Regiment (Maj. Ayot); Operations, (Maj. de Camas); Nuclear, Biological, Chemical, (Capt. Rosains); Technical Service (Capt. Henric Sante); Medicine, (N'Guyen), Commissioner, (Commandant Chollet); 1st Squadron, 1st Foreign Cavalry Regiment, (Capt. Dumont Saint-Priest); 2nd Squadron, 1st Regiment de Spahis, (Capt. Roman-Amat); 3rd Squadron, 1st Foreign Cavalry Regiment, (Capt. Winckler); 4th Squadron, 1st Regiment de Spahis, (Capt. Mandon). Total strength is 800 personnel, 200 vehicles.

The USAF flies 287 sorties including joint and combined packages.

The first element of a British Tornado GR.Mk 1 squadron arrives in Bahrain.

The Egyptian 3rd Mechanized Division begins deployment. Commander of Egyptian forces is Maj. Gen. Salah Halabi.

20 September The U.S. Army 197th Infantry Brigade complete deployment in the theater.

USS ELMER MONTGOMERY (FF-1082) commanded by Cdr. Robert A. Higgins diverts the Philippine flagged HAUL TRIBUTE in the northern Red Sea. It is en route from Pireaeus to Aqaba carrying military equipment.

At Dhahran six new F-15s of the Royal Saudi Air Force land.

21 September The Turkish Foreign Ministry states that it will extend the use of military bases to the United States for action against Iraq.

USS SARATOGA (CV-60) commanded by Capt. Joseph S. Mobley, BIDDLE (CG-34) commanded by Capt. Louis F. Harlow, PHILIPPINE SEA (CG-58) commanded by Capt. Patrick A. Callahan, SAMPSON (DDG-10) commanded by Cdr. William D. Sullivan, and DETROIT (AOE-4) commanded by Capt. Michael B. Edwards cease participation in Desert Shield. They reduce the strength of Central Command to 606 combat and 968 aircraft.

U.S. Navy air units HC-8 (DET 2), HS-3, HS-7, HSL-34 (DET 1), and HSL-46 (DET 7) cease participation in Operation Desert Shield.

At Yanbu on the Red Sea, Egyptian armored forces begin to arrive.

At Dover AFB, Delaware, the first Japanese chartered Evergreen International Airline flight flies for Dhahran with sustainment cargo.

The Iraqi Air Force continues to rotate aircraft as it has for four days.

22 September All U.S. Army 101st Airborne Division personnel are now in country, and await additional equipment.

French aircraft carrier CLEMENCEAU begins unloading at Yanbu, Saudi Arabia.

French Order of Battle *La Force d'Action Rapide*: 28th Regiment (Orleans); 18th Regiment (Epinal). Reinforcements: 41st Regiment (Senlis); 40th Regiment d'Armee (Thionville); 42nd Regiment (Rastatt); 53rd Regiment (Fribourg); 58th Regiment (Laon).

French air commander is Col. LeGuen, later relieved by Lt. Col. Giordan.

23 September Hospital ships USNS COMFORT (T-AH-20) and USNS MERCY (T-AH-19) sail for the first time together in the Persian Gulf.

At Seeb, two USAF KC-10s of the 2nd BMW arrive, and at Diego Garcia, two KC-10s of the 22nd AREFW arrive.

USAF training operations continue including a five B-52 low-level strike mission defended by F-4Gs.

24 September The U.S. Army 24th Infantry Division recieves the last of its equipment and closes in theater. The 82nd Airborne's base at Ab Qaiq is now referred to as Falcon Base or "Butt Cake" and the base at al-Jubayl "Falcon Forward."

SAN JOSE (AFS-7) commanded by Capt. Walter D. Bird begins participation in Operation Desert Shield.

At Jeddah, two USAF KC-10s of the 68th AREFW arrive.

At Al Dhafra, UAE, the first eight of ten Italian Air Force Tornados arrive.

25 September United Nations Security Resolution 670 establishes an air blockade of Iraq.

At King Fahd Airport, Col. Jesse Johnson, commander of the 5th Special Forces, has meeting with Lt. Col. Dick Cody about the destruction of two Iraqi radars with his 1-101st Apaches which cover the approach to Baghdad. The motto of the 1-101st is *'Expect No Mercy'*.

USS YELLOWSTONE (AD-41) commanded by Capt. Edmund L. Pratt, Jr. begins participation in Operation Desert Shield. CONCORD (AFS-5) ceases participation in Operation Desert Shield.

French aircraft carrier CLEMENCEAU completes unloading at Yanbu, Saudi Arabia.

26 September U.S. Marine Corps Commandant Alfred M. Gray addresses a Marine detachment in Saudi Arabia. He is accompanied by Sergeant Major of the Marine Corps, David W. Sommers.

Four USAF B-52 low-level sorties are flown. By this date, support equipment vans of the 415th TFS (Elvira I and Elvira II) have arrived at King Khalid AB.

The Argentine MEKO-360-Class destroyer ARA ALMIRANTE BROWN (DD-10) and the MEKO-140-Class frigate ARA SPIRO FF-12 depart Punta Alta Naval Base for the Gulf of Oman. The Commander-in-Chief of the Navy is Adm. Ramon A. Arosa.

The second element of a British Tornado GR.Mk 1 squadron arrives at Bahrain.

At King Khalid Military City 48 French helicopters arrive.

Coalition air forces fly combined-package training operations.

27 September Gen. Schwarzkopf tours the northern Saudi border. He encounters two Iraqi soldiers seeking food and water. Schwarzkopf examines the Iraqis' truck and equipment, finding the truck in disrepair and the soldiers' gas masks still containing their internal packing material. This indicates to the general that the soldiers have never had their gas masks fitted.

The first U.S. warning shot during a merchant interception is fired by the crew of the USS ELMER MONTGOMERY (FF-1082). They then board the Iraqi tanker TADMUR.

At Riyadh, four C-21s arrive (unit is classified).

U.S. Central Command air forces fly surveillance and combat air patrol sorties at near wartime levels. This rehearses the proposed D-Day Air Tasking Order.

Canadian supply ship PROTECTEUR arrives for duty in the Persian Gulf with the destroyers TERRA NOVA commanded by Cdr. Stuart D. Andrews and ATHABASKAN commanded by Cdr. K. John Pickford. Canadian forces will consist of the supply ship, two destroyers and 36 CF-18 Jet Fighters. Gen. John de Chastelain is the Canadian Forces Chief of Staff.

28 September To defend against possible airspace intrusion over Masirah Island, four USAF F-15Cs are deplyed to Masirah, Oman at the Government of Oman's request. At Cairo West, Egypt, three KC-135Rs of the 319th BMW arrive.

Fifty-six-year-old General Sir Peter de la Billiere is selected as the top British commander. The British call their response to American and Saudi requests for help Operation Granby after the eighteenth-century commander Marquess of Granby.

29 September USS ELMER MONTGOMERY (FF-1082) commanded by Robert A. Higgins diverts the German flagged RED SEA ENSIGN in the northern Red Sea, en route from Jeddah to Aqaba. She is carrying chemicals and steel.

Sixteen USAF and RAF aircraft train in opposition to RSAF F-15s. Formation night tactical operations and helicopter aerial refueling exercises are conducted by three HC-130s.

Gen. de la Billiere meets with his Joint Commander, Air Chief Marshal Sir Patrick Hine and is briefed on the Kuwaiti occupation. In the evening, the Queen and the Prime Minister approve de la Billiere's appointment as commander of Operation Granby.

Canadian Navy # 409 Squadron ("the Desert Cats") depart from Baden-Sollingen, Germany, with 18 CF-18A Hornets for Qatar. In early January they will be joined by an additional six Hornets and a CC-137 (Boeing 707).

The Iraqi Air Force flies 115 sorties over Kuwait (including regular fighter sorties).

30 September The Soviet Union announces that its troops will participate in supporting the Coalition, but only under UN auspices. In fact, their troops never assist in Desert Shield/Desert Storm.

HMS BRAZEN commanded by Cdr. J. C. Rapp (BROADSWORD-Class Type 22 ASW frigate) and HMS LONDON commanded by Capt. I. R. Henderson (BOXER-Class Type 22 ASW Frigate) begin participation in Operation Desert Shield.

A F-15E flown by Maj. Peter S. Hook and Capt. James B. "Boo Boo" Poulet crashes in Oman, killing both (336th TFS/4th TFW). The aircraft was training in low altitude intercept training with British Jaguars. This is the first F-15E Eagle loss in Operation Desert Shield, and will lead to the appointment of Lt. Col. Steve "Steep" Turner as the commander of the 336th TFS (The "Rocketeers").

By 3,541 strategic airlifts, 127,739 passengers and 115,826 short tons of cargo has been transported to the theater by the U.S. Transportation Command by this date.

Elements of the French Foreign Legion arrive in Saudi Arabia (2nd Mechanized Battalion, 21st Marine Battalion). They join other elements already incountry. French troops will number 10,000 along with 40 fighters and 14 naval vessels.

Iraqi forces in the KTO number 22 divisions (13 light and 9 heavy with approximate strength of 433,000 soldiers, 3,350 tanks, 2,340 APCs and 2,140 artillery).

The Iraqi Air Force flies 123 sorties.

1 October ARG ALFA and CTG 150.6 conduct *Operation Camel Sand*, the first major amphibious rehearsal in Operation Desert Shield off Ras Madrakah, Oman. It includes most U.S. Navy ships in the area.

USS INDEPENDENCE (CV-62) commanded by Capt. Robert L. Ellis, Jr. transits the Strait of Hormuz for the Persian Gulf. This is an historic entrance of a carrier battle group into the Persian Gulf, the last being the CONSTELLATION in 1974. Their mission is to discover if it is possible to carry out carrier operations in the Gulf. At Bahrain, SUPER SEVANT II arrives with U.S. minesweepers USS IMPERVIOUS (MSO-449), USS ADROIT (MSO-509), and USS LEADER (MSO-490). Also included is the new mine countermeasures ship USS AVENGER (MCM-1) commanded by Cdr. James D. Cope.

Coalition combined air package training missions are flown.

The Iraqi Air Force flies 92 sorties today.

2 October Carrier Battle Group MIDWAY (CV-41) commanded by Capt. Arthur K. Cebrowski deploys from Yokosuka, Japan.

French frigate DOUDART DE LAGREE (F-728) commanded by Cdr. Rossignol intercepts the North Korean merchant vessel SAM IL PO transporting plywood panels. After repeatedly hailing the ship by bridge-to-bridge radio, the frigate fires warning shots across its bow. The French are allowed to board, the North Korean master claiming that he had not monitored the radio. After verifying the cargo and the ship's destination, the vessel is allowed to proceed.

Iraq flies 105 sorties.

3 October Gen. Schwarzkopf visits the USS INDEPENDENCE commanded by Capt. Robert L. Ellis, Jr.

The USS MOOSBRUGGER (DD-980) commanded by Cdr. Frank B. Guest III begins participation in Operation Desert Shield.

U.S. Navy air unit HSL-42 (DET 6) begins participation in Operation Desert Shield.

Eight French Mirage fighters depart BA 125 Istres-Le Tube for Al Ahsa, Saudi Arabia, for *Operation Daguet*. They are commanded by Col. Jean-Pierre Job.

Danish corvette OLFERT FISCHER (Cdr.(s.g.) Henrik Michael Elbro) begins deployment in Persian Gulf. It will continue its deployment until 22 August 1991 with two additional commanders (Cdr.(s.g.) Henrik Muusfeldt and Cdr.(s.g.) Thor Bogesgaard Nielsen).

The Iraqi Air Force flies 127 sorties. Four MiG-23 Floggers perform combat maneuvers out of Qasr Amij South dispersal airfield.

4 October USS INDEPENDENCE (CV-62) departs the Persian Gulf after accomplishing its mission. USS SAMUEL B. BOBERTS (FFG-58) commanded by Cdr. John W. Townes III diverts the Sudanian flagged BLUE NILE in the northern Red Sea. She is en route from the United Kingdom to Aqaba with chemicals and steel.

U.S. Navy amphibious rehearsal *Camel Sand* on the Arabian Peninsula is completed.

Central Command conducts a D-Day-type air tasking coordination exercise (eight F-16s, four F-4Gs, two EF-111s, and four Saudi F-15s, and 12 F/A-18s) They also conduct a Close Air Support (CAS) exercise of 34 A-10s, two AC-130s, one MC-130, five OV-10s, ten F/A-18s, and 14 AV-8s.

West of Hafr Al-Batin, the 6th French Light Armored Division defends the Coalition's desert flank.

A Syrian Special Forces regiment patrols the Iraqi/Neutral Zone area north of Hafr Al-Batin. They are supported by the still arriving 9th Syrian Armored Division. The Special Forces top commander is Maj. Gen. 'Ali Haydar and overall commander is Maj. Gen. Ali Habib.

East of Wadi Al-Batin an Egyptian Ranger battalion supports the right of the 9th Syrian Armored Division. To the Ranger's rear is the 3rd Egyptian Mechanized Infantry Division.

USSR SLAVA-Class missile cruiser CHERVONA UKRAINA and SOVREMENNY-Class destroyer BYSTRY passes through the Suez Canal. In early August the UDALOY-Class destroyer ADMIRAL TRIBUTS and another destroyer had assisted a British Royal Air Force patrol craft. The world speculates if the Soviet ships will assist the Coalition, but the ships continue on to join the Soviet Pacific Fleet.

The Belgium Navy deploys the WIELINGEN-Class frigate BNS WANDELAAR (F-912) commanded by Capt. Eugene Alleman. She will rendezvous with RFA SIR GALAHAD and RFA SIR PERCIVALE and will operate with the French in the Bab el Mandab straits.

Iraq flies 120 sorties.

5 October French aircraft carrier CLEMENCEAU returns to Toulon. She will not serve in Desert Shield/Storm again.

The Iraqi Air Force flies 117 sorties (mostly navigation and ground attack training).

6 October Final elements of 101st Airborne Division (Air Assault) arrive in Saudi Arabia. Col. James T. Hill commands the 1st Brigade.

Training air exercise packages are flown by Coalition air forces.

General Peter de la Billiere, commander of all British forces in *Operation Granby* departs Britain for Saudi Arabia.

British logistic landing ship RFA SIR GALAHAD (L-3005) commanded by Capt. D. A. Reynolds departs Portsmouth to load at Marchwood.

The French 6th Light Armored Division has arrived in Saudi Arabia, but is not deployed.

The Egyptian 3rd Mechanized Division has arrived in Saudi Arabia, but is only half deployed (some records state the division is deployed). The Egyptian 4th Armored Division awaits permission from Saudi Arabia to travel to their kingdom.

The Iraqi Air Force flies 127 sorties. A reconnaissance flight crosses the Saudi border for approximately two minutes.

7 October A U-2R of the USAF 9th SRW arrives at a classified location.

British logistic landing ship RFA SIR GALAHAD departs Marchwood for the Middle East. RFA Logistics Landing Ship SIR TRISTRAM (SIR BEDIVERE-Class) commanded by Capt. S. Hodgson, begins participation in Operation Desert Shield.

Coalition air strike training continues. A new record of 1,186 tons of sustainment cargo is airlifted today.

From Germany, 12 CF-18 Hornets of Canadian No. 409 Squadron arrive in Qatar in support of *Operation Scimitar*.

The Iraqi Air Force flies 112 sorties.

8 October Two UH-1N Huey helicopters of Marine Medium Helicopter Squadron 164 crash killing eight Marines. It is a night training mission, and is the first fatal U.S. Marine accident of *Operation Desert Shield*.

In the Gulf of Oman USS REASONER (FF-1063) commanded by Cdr. Richard B. Marvin, HMS BATTLEAXE (F-89) commanded by Cdr. A.C. Gordon-Lennox, and HMAS ADELAIDE (F-01) (unknown commander) intercept the Iraqi merchant ship ALWASITTI. ALWASITTI refuses to stop even after all three Coalition ships fire warning shots. The Iraqi vessel is secured by four Royal Marines inserted by helicopter from the HMS BATTLEAXE. USS GOLDSBOROUGH (Cdr. James A. Reid), HMS BRAZEN (Cdr. J. C. Rapp) and HMAS DARWIN (Capt. R.E. Shalders) divert the Iraqi flagged TADMUR in the northern Arabian Sea as she is en route from Aqaba to Iraq with cooking oil, rice and flour. SAVANNAH (AOE-4) and SYLVANIA (AFS-2) commanded by Capt. Edward J. Simmons begins participation in Operation Desert Shield.

U.S. Navy air units HC-6 (DET 4), and HC-8 (DET 1) begin participation in Operation Desert Shield.

Near Abu Dhabi an RF-4C #64-1044 of the 106th Tactical Reconnaissance Squadron crashes killing Maj. Barry K. Henderson and Maj. Stephen G. Schramm.

Gen. de la Billiere visits the port of Jubail, Saudi Arabia. The 7th Armoured Brigade is just beginning to arrive.

British Tornado GR.Mk 1 squadron transfers from Bahrain to Tabuk, Saudi Arabia. The British base commander at Bahrain is Group Capt. David Henderson.

Four French Mirage 2000Cs and four Mirage F1CRs arrive at Al Ahsa.

Additional Coalition combat air patrols are flown in the western and central Iraqi-Saudi border areas due to Iraqi air activity.

Iraq flies 107 sorties today.

9 October   Saddam Hussein states that he will attack Saudi Arabia and Israel with long-range missiles in the event of war.

At Al Ain, UAE, 16 USAF C-130s of the 130th Tactical Airlift Group (TAG) arrive. At Sharjah, UAE, 16 C-130s of the 63rd TAS AFRES, 440th TAW arrive.

British logistic landing ship RFA SIR PERCIVALE (L-3036) commanded by Capt. I. F. Heslop departs Marchwood for the Middle East. She later joins with RFA SIR GALAHAD and the Belgian frigate WANDELAAR for the journey to the Persian Gulf. BATCH-I-TYPE-42 destroyer HMS CARDIFF (D-108) commanded by Cdr. A. R. Nance and RFA ARGUS (A-135) commanded by Capt. D. E. W. Lench are deployed.

Canadian No. 409 Tactical Fighter Squadron flies its first combat air patrol.

The last of the Egyptian 3rd Armored Division arrives.

10 October   1st Armored Division commander Maj. Gen. Ron Griffith returns to division headquarters, Ansbach, Germany from the Pentagon. He has been told to prepare his division to deploy to Saudi Arabia if orders arrive.

The first unit-sized activation of Marine reservists occurs at Marine Corps Air Station, Kaneohe, Hawaii. Combat Service Support Detachment 40 is to maintain and repair equipment of the 1 Marine Expeditionary Brigade that had departed for Saudi Arabia to obtain its pre-positioned equipment aboard Maritime Prepositioning Ship 3.

SCHENECTADY (LST-1185) ceases participation in Operation Desert Shield.

British SIR BEDIVERE (SIR BEDIVERE-Class RFA Logistics Landing Ship) commanded by (unknown captain) begins participation in Operation Desert Shield.

Iraq flies 140 sorties.

11 October   President George Bush is briefed on *Operation Desert Storm*. The President is very confident with the air plan (the first phase or *Operation Instant Thunder*).

Tanks of the 3rd Armored Cavalry Regiment, 2nd Armored Division and the 1st Cavalry Division continue to be unloaded in Saudi Arabia.

SPICA (TAFS-9) begins participation in Operation Desert Shield.

An USAF F-111F flown by Capt. Thomas R. Caldwell and Capt. Frederick A. Reid crashes killing both (45th TFS/48th TFW).

The U.S. Air Force reports its aircraft have an 89% mission-capable rate.

The advance party of the British Staffordshire Regiment (commanded by Lt. Col. Charles Rogers) arrives at Al Jubail.

The Iraqi Air Force flies 148 sorties, with a majority of the sorties training flights.

12 October USS SAMUEL B. ROBERTS (FFG-58) commanded by Cdr. John W. Townes, III, diverts the Qatar-flagged BAR'ZAN in the northern Red Sea. The BAR'ZAN is en route from Port Suez to Aqaba carrying rice and flour. Later she diverts the Honduras flagged LEPANTO in the northern Red Sea. LEPANTO is en route from Jeddah to Aqaba carrying beans, nuts and seeds.

At Taif a second USAF U-2 arrives.

Iraq flies 52 sorties today.

13 October DUBUQUE (LPD-8), SAN BERNADINO (LST-1189), SAVANNAH (AOE-4), SYLVANIA (AFS-2), and YELLOWSTONE (AD-41) cease participation in Operation Desert Shield.

U.S. Navy units HC-6 (DET 4) and HC-8 (DET 1) cease participation in Operation Desert Shield.

Composition of French reinforcements are: 4th Squadron (Huet) of the 1st Foreign Cavalry Regiment; 4th Squadron of 1st Hussars Parachute Regiment; elements of the 13th Parachute Dragon Regiment (*Regiment de Dragons parachutistes* or CRAP); antitank elements of the 21st Marine Infantry Regiment (Cne. Delhoume); one section of ground to air missiles of the 35th Parachute Artillery Regiment; one section ground radar of the 35th Ground Radar; 6th Service Regiment mobile bakery; heavy vehicle transport of the 511th Regiment Train. Total strength is 152 vehicles, 480 personnel.

The Iraqi Air Force flies 130 sorties today.

14 October Iraq announces again that it will withdraw from Kuwait if allowed to retain the islands of Bubiyan and Warba. The islands prevent free access from Iraq to the Persian Gulf.

The first five of 40 USAF KC-135As arrive at King Khalid. Three KC-135Qs and five KC-135A of the 380th BMW arrive there today. At a classified location, a U-2 of the 9th SRW arrives.

Iraq flies 123 sorties today.

15 October U.S. ground forces weaponry strength is: 261 attack helicopters, 668 support helicopters, 559 main battle tanks, 456 artillery pieces, 48 Multiple-Launch Rocket System and nine tactical missile systems.

The 2,500th maritime intercept is made by USS ELMER MONTGOMERY (FF-1082) commanded by Cdr. Robert A. Higgins. It hails the Indian-registered cargo vessel JAY GAYATRI in the Northern Red Sea.

ACADIA (AD-42) commanded by Capt. Larry L. King and WHITE PLAINS (AFS-4) commanded by Capt. Bernard W. Patton begins participation in Operation Desert Shield.

At Masirah, two USAF KC-135Rs of the 41st AREFS, 416th BMW arrive.

U.S. aircraft strength is 110 air-to-air, 286 air-to-ground, and 210 dual-purpose combat aircraft (supported by 410 support aircraft).

Four French Jaguars from BA 136 Toul-Rosieres land in Al Ahsa.

Iraq flies 114 sorties.

16 October The Iraqi Air Force flies 173 sorties. This is the highest since 30 August and most are air combat maneuvers.

17 October A negotiating team from the Department of Defense leaves for Saudi Arabia to meet with the Saudi government over the cost of Desert Shield. The Saudi government will agree to pay for all American contracts as well as 4,800 tents, 1,073,500 gallons of packaged petroleum products, 333 heavy equipment transporters, 20 million meals and 20.5 million gallons of fuel per day.

Goal of U.S. Central Command is fielding eight Patriot missiles systems in the theater.

USS MACDONOUGH (DDG-39) commanded by Cdr. Grey A. Glover, NICHOLAS (FFG-47) commanded by Cdr. Dennis G. Morral, and DENEBOLA (TAKR-289) begins participation in Operation Desert Shield.

U.S. Navy air unit HSL-44 (DET 8) begins participation in Desert Shield.

HMS CARDIFF commanded by Cdr. A. R. Nance (SHEFFIELD-Class-Type-42 Destroyer) begins participation in Operation Desert Shield.

At Hafar Al Batin French forces have closed.

Four French Jaguars arrive at Al Ahsa from BA 136 Toul-Rosieres.

Iraq flies 112 sorties.

18 October All U.S. Army 1st Cavalry Division personnel have arrived in theater and await their equipment to arrive by sea.

British Tornado GR.Mk1 ZA466/FH, No. 16 Squadron flown by Squadron Leaders Ivor Walker and Bobby Anderson crashes due to accident at Tabuk. Both eject safely.

Iraq flies 153 sorties.

19 October British RFA Logistics Landing Ships SIR GALAHAD (SIR GALAHAD-Class), and SIR PERCIVALE (SIR BEDIVERE-Class) begins participation in Operation Desert Shield.

Iraq flies 93 sorties.

20 October Gen. Schwarzkopf meets with Kuwaiti Maj. Gen. Jaber. General Jaber requests training assistance to form three light infantry brigades. If they are not formed,

Jaber is afraid they may attack on their own and begin the war prematurely. CINC Schwarzkopf agrees to the request enthusiastically.

USS SAMUEL B. ROBERTS commanded by Cdr. John W. Townes, III, diverts the United Arab Emirates flagged AL WATTYAH in the northern Red Sea. She was en route from Jeddah to Aqaba carrying chemicals and electrical materials.

The main body of the British Staffordshire Regiment begins to arrive at Al Jubail. They will be quartered in what they quickly dubbed "The Pig Pens", a large fly-ridden shed near the harbor. Only four toilets serve 2,000 soldiers.

Iraq flies 93 sorties.

21 October Fifteen additional morgue sets arrive in Saudi Arabia.

The Iraqi merchant ship AL BAHAR AL ARABI has shots fired across its bow by the USS O'BRIEN (DD-975).

At King Khalid nine USAF KC-135As arrive from a classified bomber wing.

Coalition troop strength by country is 2,000 Bangladesh, 14,000 Egyptian, 8,000 French, 3,000 Gulf Cooperation Council, 7,000 Kuwaiti, 2,000 Moroccan, 5,000 Pakistani, 45,000 Saudi, 19,000 Syrian, 95,000 Turkey (positioned on the Iraqi border), 6,000 British, 200,000 U.S., for 406,200 total.

Coalition ship count is three Belgium, three Canadian, one Denmark, 14 French, one Greek, four Italian, three Netherlands, one Norway, one Poland, one Portugal, three Spanish, 55 U.S. 12 British, two USSR for a 104 total.

Iraq flies 75 sorties.

22 October Gen. Colin Powell arrives in Riyadh. He is shown the plan to force Iraqi out of Kuwait. He is concerned over the obvious factor of sufficient supply to sustain the attack.

Final elements of the 1st Cavalry Division (Brig. Gen. John H. Tilelli, Jr. USA) arrives in Saudi Arabia.

The Iraqi merchant ship AL BAHAR AL ARABI is cleared to proceed after a multi-national boarding team led by personnel from the USS REASONER (FF-1063) commanded by Cdr. Richard B. Marvin investigates.

HMS JUPITER (LEANDER-Class Frigate) commanded by Cdr. J. W. T. Wright, and HMS BATTLEAXE (BROADSWORD-Class Type 22 ASW Frigate) completes their participation in Operation Desert Shield. BATTLEAXE has been in the area since 4 June.

Iraq flies 112 sorties.

23 October Aircraft carrier USS SARATOGA (CV-60) commanded by Capt. Joseph S. Mobley, SOUTH CAROLINA (CGN-37), and BIDDLE (CG-34) commanded by Capt. Louis F. Harlow begins participation in Operation Desert Shield.

U.S. Navy air units VA-35, VAQ-132, VAW-125, VFA-81, VFA-83, HS-3, HS-7, HSL-34, and VS-30 begin participation in Operation Desert Shield.

In northeast Saudi Arabia the USAF conducts a large-scale, joint Close Air Support exercise.

Iraq flies 106 sorties.

24 October Brig. Gen. Buster Glosson, USAF, meets with Col. Dave Sawyer (76th TFS) and Col. Sandy Sharpe (355th TFS) for lunch. The A-10s Warthogs are tasked with destroying radar sites on the Iraqi border the first night of Desert Storm. The deadliest AAA Iraqi fire the A-10 will confront in the war will be the ZSU-23-4 (four-barrel 23mm machine gun).

ALGOL (TAKR-287) begins participation in Operation Desert Shield.

Exercise *Initial Hack* begins. During the 36-hour exercise Coalition air forces will practice pre- and post-strike air refueling, airfield attacks and defense, CAS, and command and control procedures against a D-Day Air Tasking Order.

The Iraqi Air Force flies 90 sorties.

25 October Aircraft carriers USS JOHN F. KENNEDY (CV-67) commanded by Capt. John P. Gay and SARATOGA (CV-60) commanded by Capt. Joseph S. Mobley conduct dual carrier operations. USS PHILIPPINE SEA (CG-58) commanded by Capt. Patrick A. Callahan renews participation in Operation Desert Shield.

Al Dhafra, Taif, and Al Ahso airfields are "targeted" in Coalition air exercise *Initial Hack*.

Iraq flies 150 sorties today.

26 October In the *London Financial Times* a senior engineer of the Kuwait Oil Company reports that Iraq has prepared 300 of 1,000 oil wells for destruction with explosives.

Coalition air exercise *Initial Hack* ends after 48 hours. More than 300 simulated combat and 200 other sorties were flown. They supported 18 packages utilizing approximately 40 Coalition air units.

British commander Lt. Gen. de la Billiere meets with Lt. Col. Arthur Denaro, commander of the Queen's Royal Irish Hussars at Jubail.

The Iraqi Air Force flies 176 sorties today.

27 October All eight Patriot missile systems are now operational.

Iraq flies 67 sorties today.

28 October USS PHILIPPINE SEA commanded by Capt. Patrick A. Callahan diverts the German flagged OLANDIA in the northern Red Sea. She is en route from Italy to Aqaba carrying spare parts. Later, the USS MOOSBRUGGER commanded by Cdr. Frank B. Guest, III, diverts the Sudanian flagged BLUE NILE en route from Port Sudan to Aqaba. U.S. Navy SEALs and a 21-man USMC boarding team are inserted on the Iraqi merchant ship AMURIYAH after the USS REASONER (commanded by Cdr. Richard B. Marvin) and HMAS DARWIN (Capt. R.E. Shalders) fire warning shots. F-14s and F/A-18s from the carrier INDEPENDENCE (Capt. Robert L. Ellis, Jr.) make six low subsonic passes in an effort to stop the ship. Not carrying prohibited cargo, the vessel is finally allowed to proceed. USS WORDEN (CG-18) commanded by Capt. William B. Hunt, and BUNKER HILL (CG-52) commanded by Capt. Thomas F. Marfiak begin participation in Operation Desert Shield.

At King Khalid, three USAF KC-135As arrive from an unknown bomber wing.

Iraq flies 130 sorties today.

29 October Last elements of 17,000-man US Army 1st Cavalry Division depart the ad-Dammam Pegasus Complex for Assembly Area Horse.

The USAF begins a daily exercise designated *"Desert Triangle."* It is to challenge Iraqi air defenses through aggressive Coalition air operations.

The Iraqi Air Force flies 94 sorties today.

30 October The U.S. 4th Marine Expeditionary Brigade begins military exercises off Ras al-Madrakah, Oman. ARG ALFA and CTG 150.6 begins amphibious rehearsal *Sea Soldier II*.

Ten crew members are killed on board the USS IWO JIMA (Capt. Michael S. O'Hearn) from a massive steam leak in the engine room. Sailors are: BTFR Tyrone Michael Brooks, BT3 David Alan Gilliland, BT2 Mark Edward Hutchison, EM2 Daniel Lupatsky, FN Michael Nunnally Manns, Jr., BTFA Daniel Clayton, BT2 Fred Russell Parker, Jr., MM3 James Arthur Smith, Jr., Lt. John Mather Snyder, BT1 Robert Lee Volden. USS MOBILE BAY (CG-53) commanded by Capt. Stephen R. Woodall, FIFE (DD-991) commanded by Cdr. Curtis A. Kemp, MARVIN SHIELDS (FF-1066) commanded by Cdr. M. D. Simpson, and W.S. DIEHL (TAO-193) begins participation in Operation Desert Shield.

Stealth F-117 pilots now participating in Operation Desert Shield are: Clarence Whitescarver, Phil Mahon, Brian Foley, Joe Bouley, John Savage, Bill Behymer, Dave Francis, Kevin Tarrant, Paul Dolson, Lou McDonald, Robert Bledsoe, George Kelman, Joe Salata, Mike Riehl, Greg Feest, Robert Donaldson, Lee Gustin, Jerry Leatherman, Wes Wyrick, Ralph Getchell, Barry Horne, Blake Bourland, Robert Warren, Mark Lindstrom, Dan Backus, and Marcel Kerdavid.

HMS YORK (MANCHESTER-Class-Type-42C) commanded by Capt. A. G. McEwen completes participation in Operation Desert Shield.

Four Saudi Tornados make a high-speed approach to within 15 miles of the Saudi-Kuwaiti border as part of Exercise *Desert Triangle*. No observable Iraqi response is noted.

Iraq flies 163 sorties today.

31 October Special Forces Team 595 commanded by Master Sergeant Joseph Lloyd has joined the Kuwaiti 35th Armored Brigade (Col. Salam al-Masoud) near Hafar al-Batin, (approximately 50 miles from the Kuwaiti border). When the 35th finally receives its mission from the Muthannah Task Force it will discover that it will be leading the Joint Forces Command-North to liberate Kuwait City. The Muthannah Task Force consists of the Royal Saudi Land Force's 20th Mechanized Brigade, and the Kuwaiti 35th Armored Brigade.

Quarters for most troops serving in Operation Desert Shield are Spartan, with conditions for infantry trying. Capt. Grant Holcomb of the 2nd Marine Division described his living conditions in a letter to elementary school students. With daily temperatures 115-120 degrees, men are forced to drink vast quantities of water until the stomach hurts. Work is in the often freezing night to avoid the day's sun. Marine infantry sleep on the sand, enduring dew, scorpions, voracious giant beetles and six types of vipers.

USS LASALLE (AGF-3) commanded by Capt. John B. Nathman is on duty in Operation Desert Storm. The LASALLE is the command ship of R.Adm. William Fogarty, USN, and includes Capt. Richard R. Clark, USCG, Director of Maritime Interception Force Operations, the commander of all Coast Guard Forces in the Middle East. Capt. Clark relieved Capt. Paul J. Prokop in October and will be relieved in March 1991 by Capt. Fred Wilder.

By this date British repair ship RFA DILIGENCE commanded by Capt. A. Mitchell has begun participation in Operation Desert Shield.

Portuguese logistic support ship NRP SAO MIGUEL (A-5208) loads supplies at Marchwood for British forces in Saudi Arabia.

Two Spanish DESCUBIERTA-Class corvettes DIANA (F-32) commanded by Capt. Marco Franco and INFANTA CRISTINA (F-34) commanded by Capt. Palencia Luaces, accompanied with the FFG-7-Class frigate NUMANCIA (F-83) commanded by Cdr. Marco Franco depart Spain for the Gulf of Oman. They are to relieve Spanish ships patrolling the Gulf of Oman (SANTA MARIA, DESCUBIERTA, CAZADORA) and will arrive 23 November.

French commanders are: At Riyad International airport, Col. Bassan and at Al Ahsa, Col. Amberg, (Col. Voynnet is second in command).

Iraq flies 158 sorties today.

1 November USS INDEPENDENCE (CV-62) Carrier Battle Group is relieved by the USS MIDWAY (CV-41) Carrier Battle Group.

The USS BIDDLE (CG-34) commanded by Capt. Louis F. Harlow diverts the Polish flagged WLADYSLAW JAGIELLO in the northern Red Sea as she is en route from Sweden to Aqaba. SAMPSON (DDG-10) commanded by Cdr. William D. Sullivan renews participation in Desert Shield.

U.S. air strength is 109 air-to-air, 277 air-to-ground, and 258 dual-mission aircraft (supported by 450 support aircraft).

C Company, Staffordshire Regiment, is the last company of the regiment to move to the desert region around Al Fadili (approximately 40 kilometres west of Al Jubail).

At Riyadh, a British Hercules detachment is formed which by mid-January number nine aircraft, including two from the Royal New Zealand Air Force. For entertainment they listen to propaganda on Radio Baghdad, 'The Voice of Peace'.

The Syrian 9th Armored Division begins to deploy in the theater.

Two Iraqi F-1s violate the Saudi airspace by 9 nautical miles. They are chased away by two USAF F-15s directed by AWACS.

2 November USS BIDDLE diverts the German flagged RED SEA EUROPA en route from Greece to Aqaba. USS MIDWAY (CV-41) commanded by Capt. Arthur K. Cebrowski, OLDENDORF (DD-972) commanded by Cdr. Cyrus H. Butt, IV, CURTS (FFG-38) commanded by Cdr. Glenn H. Montgomery, and KISKA (AE-35) commanded by Cdr. Ronald E. Hewitt begin participation in Operation Desert Shield.

U.S. Navy air units HC-11 (DET 4), HS-12, HSL-37 (DET 6), VA-115, VA-185, VAQ-136, VAW-115, VFA-151, VFA-192, and VFA-195 begin participation in Operation Desert Shield.

The Iraqi Air Force flies 98 sorties with two Mikoyan MiG-25s making high speed runs at the Saudi Arabian border.

3 November U.S. Army VII Corps commander Lt. Gen. Frederick Franks informs Maj. Gen. Ron Griffith, 1st Armored Division commander that he has been told by his superiors to prepare the VII Corps to deploy to Saudi Arabia if orders arrive.

USS ANTIETAM (CG-54) commanded by Capt. Lawrence E. Eddingfield, ENGLAND (CG-22) commanded by Capt James W. Orvis, and BARBEY (FF-1088) commanded by Thomas J. Wilson cease participation in Operation Desert Shield.

U.S. Navy air unit HSL-35 (DET 7) ceases participation in Operation Desert Shield. The unit has been in the area since 31 July.

At Masirah, three USAF KC-135Rs arrive from Seeb to reduce aircraft crowding, and two KC-135Rs of the 301st AREFS, 301st AREFW arrive as rotational replacements.

Lt. Gen. de la Billiere transfers the 7th Armoured Brigade to American command.

The British Staffordshire Regiment begins training at Al Fadili with a short battalion exercise.

The Iraqi Air Force flies reconnaissance flights along the Saudi border. They fly a total of 138 sorties today.

4 November Secretary of State James Baker visits the desert base of the 1st Cavalry Division.

USS INDEPENDENCE (CV-42) commanded by Capt. Robert L. Ellis, Jr., JOUETT (CG-29) commanded by Capt. Floyston A. Weeks, GOLDSBOROUGH (DDG-20) commanded by Cdr. James A. Reid, BREWTON (FF-1086) commanded by Cdr. Charlie A. Jones, REASONER (FF-1063) commanded by Cdr. Richard B. Marvin, CIMMARON (AO-177) commanded by Cdr. Eric B. Shaver, and FLINT (AE-32) commanded by Cdr. Alan D. Thomson cease participation in Operation Desert Shield.

As part of *"Desert Triangle,"* four F-16s and two F-4Gs make high speed approaches to within 10 nautical miles of the Iraqi border but observe no result.

Supporting Operation Desert Storm by this date 7,865 SAC tanker sorties have been flown, offloading 195,893,000 pounds of fuel for 12,178 aircraft.

Syrian T-62 tanks and crews arrive in Saudi Arabia.

Iraq flies 133 sorties.

5 November Strength of XVIII Airborne Corps is: 763 tanks, 444 howitzers, 63 Multiple-Launch Rocket Systems (MLRS), 18 Army Tactical Missile Systems launchers (ATACMS), 1,494 Armored fighting vehicles, 24 Patriot launchers, 24 Hawk launchers, 117 Vulcans, 320 Stingers, 227 attack helicopters, 741 support helicopters, 18 infantry battalions, 368 Tube-launched, Optically Tracked, Wire-guided antitank missiles (TOW).

British RFA RESOURCE commanded by an unknown captain (RESOURCE-Class Replenishment Ship) begins participation in Operation Desert Shield.

Coalition air forces fly four strike/close air support packages consisting of 20 or more aircraft.

Iraq flies 129 sorties.

6 November The M1A1 tank rollover program begins. By the end of the war 1,032 Abrams tanks will be upgraded with heavier armor.

Iraq flies 186 sorties today.

7 November Gen. Schwarzkopf is briefed by his intelligence staff and the 513th Military Intelligence Brigade on the trafficability of Kuwait and southeastern Iraq. Schwarzkopf's conclusion after learning of terrain factors, avenues of approach, and effects of weather is that mid-February is an ideal time for attack.

Orders for the deployment of the U.S. Army VII Corps to Saudi Arabia arrives. Troops are told to watch late night television news.

DETROIT (AOE-4) commanded by Capt. Michael B. Edwards renews participation in Operation Desert Shield.

U.S. Navy air units HC-8 (DET 2) renews its participation in Operation Desert Shield.

The British Staffordshire Regiment begins intensive realistic live-fire training at Al Fadili. WOI Steve Huyton is wounded above the knee by a grenade but will recover.

British RFA ARGUS commanded by Capt. D. E. W. Lench (aviation support ship) with 4 Sea King 4 helicopters begins participation in Operation Desert Shield.

The Iraqi Air Force flies 170 sorties including border reconnaissance and defensive sorties.

8 November The second phase of the Saudi Arabian build-up is ordered by President George Bush when he orders more than 150,000 additional air, sea, and ground troops to the Persian Gulf.

U.S. Army VII Corps the "Jayhawk Corps" is alerted for deployment at its German home base. The VII Corps includes more than 6,000 tracked combat vehicles and 59,000 wheeled vehicles. Over the next two months, 220,000 troops and 769,000 short tons of equipment will arrive.

The U.S. Army 1st Armored Division (Maj. Gen. Ronald Griffith, USA) prepares to deploy to Saudi Arabia from Ansbach, Germany. The 17,000 man division (growing to 24,000 with auxiliaries and support elements) must be packed and convoyed to seaports. Seven thousand wheeled vehicles must be driven to the ports, and two thousand tracked vehicles must be sent by rail.

The U.S. Army 1st Infantry Division (Maj. Gen. Thomas G. Rhame) is alerted and over the next two months will deploy over 12,000 soldiers and 7,000 pieces of equipment to the war zone. Major non-divisional units deployed in support of the 1st Infantry Division are the 937th Engineer Group, the 541st Maintenance Battalion and the 716th Military Police Battalion.

Due to President Bush's orders, Marine numbers in the Persian Gulf area double (deployment includes II Marine Expeditionary Force units from the Marine Corps east coast bases, and the 5th Expeditionary Brigade from California). Marine Commandant Gray states, *"There are four kinds of Marines: those in Saudi Arabia, those going to Saudi Arabia, those who want to go to Saudi Arabia, and those who don't want to go to Saudi Arabia but are going anyway."*

The U.S. Army 11th Air Defense Artillery Brigade strength is 12 operational Patriot missile systems.

CAYUGA (LST-1186), and ships of Amphibious Ready Group Alpha (commanded by COMPHIBRON 5 Capt. T.L. McClelland) DURHAM (LKA-114, Capt. Charles M. Kraft, Jr.), FORT MCHENRY (LSD-43, Cdr. James A. Hays), OGDEN (LPD-5, Capt. Braden J. Phillips), and OKINAWA (LPH-3, Capt. Mack A. Thomas) cease participation in Operation Desert Shield.

Iraq flies 96 sorties today.

10 November Lt. Gen. de la Billiere has a phone conversation with Tom King requesting a British division as reinforcement.

The Iraqi Air Force flies 76 sorties.

11 November The British Staffordshire Regiment pauses before *Exercise Ferozeshah* for Remembrance Day.

Iraq flies 94 sorties today.

12 November Maj. Gen. Ron Griffith, 1st Armored Division Commander, departs Ansbach, Germany, for Saudi Arabia and a Dhahran meeting with Gen. Schwarzkopf.

USS ROBERT G. BRADLEY (FFG-49), and TAYLOR (FFG-50) commanded by Cdr. Kevin P. Green cease participation in Operation Desert Shield. They have been in the area since 28 July.

U.S. Navy air unit HSL-42 (DET 7, DET 9) ceases participation in Operation Desert Shield.

Exercise Sneaky Sultan II begins to test the Stealth Fighter pilots ability and the F-117's ability to generate sorties on short notice to support a D-Day senario.

Tom King, British Secretary of State for Defense tours the Gulf region until 14 November.

Coalition troop strength is as follows: 2,000 Bangladesh (Lt. Gen. Muhammad Nurreddin Khan), 200 Czechoslovakian, 29,000 Egyptian (Maj. Gen. Salah Halabi), 5,000 French, 3,000 Gulf Cooperation Council, 7,000 Kuwaiti (Maj. Gen. Jaber al-Sabah), 2,000 Moroccan (Col. Ahmad Binyas), 2,000 Pakistani, 45,000 Saudi, 19,000 Syrian, 95,000 Turkey (positioned at border), 11,000 British, 210,000 U.S., for a total of 430,200.

Coalition ship strength today is: two Argentinan, three Belgium, three Canadian, one Denmark, 15 French, seven German, one Greek, three Italian, three Netherlands, one Portugal, three Spanish, 65 U.S., 16 British, and four USSR for a 127 ship total.

Coalition air forces fly a 108-aircraft close air support exercise. This exercise includes the participation of Kuwaiti A-4s for the first time.

The Iraqi Air Force flies 130 sorties (this includes two MiG-25 intercept sorties targeting simulated high-value air assets).

13 November Reserve call-up is extended to 180 days by Presidential Executive Order #12733.

Gen. Schwarzkopf meets with his seven division and two corps commanders at Dhahran, Saudi Arabia. He describes three Iraqi centers of gravity: (1) Saddam Hussein; (2) the Iraqi Nuclear, Biological, Chemical threat; and (3) the Republican Guard. These will be the key targets in the coming war.

Twenty units of the 4th Marine Division and the 4th Marine Aircraft Wing report to the 5th Marine Expeditionary Brigade, Camp Pendleton, California. This is the second involuntary Marine Corps Reserve call-up.

USS MISSOURI (BB-63) commanded by Capt. Albert L. Kaiss departs Long Beach, California for the Persian Gulf.

In *Exercise Sandy Beach*, airspace defended by French and Qatar Mirage F-1s is attacked by 20 U.S. planes. Additionally, a close air support exercise is flown by 120 Coalition aircraft.

British Jaguar GR.Mk 1AXX754, No. 54 Squadron, flown by Flight Lieutenant Keith Collister, crashes over Qatar. Collister is killed.

The Iraqi Air Force flies 160 sorties today.

14 November Richard B. Cheney, Secretary of Defense authorizes the U.S. Army call-up authority to 80,000, call-up of Reserve combat units and U.S. Marine Corps call-up 15,000 Reservists. In excess of 70 percent of personnel used in the U.S. Army Persian Gulf build-up will come from U.S. Army National Guard and Reserve.

Maritime Prepositioning Shipping Squadron 1 departs the East Coast for Al Jubayl carrying part of the logistic support of II Marine Expeditionary Force.

The British Staffordshire Regiment participates in the first brigade level exercise named *Exercise Jubail Rat.*

Iraq flies 170 sorties.

15 November Exercise *Imminent Thunder* begins approximately 100 miles south of the Kuwaiti border. American and Saudi Arabian forces exercise including an amphibious landing of the 4th Marine Expeditionary Brigade (1,000 Marines). Simultaneously, approximately 25 miles south of Kuwait, another 1,000 Marines of the 1st Marine Expeditionary Brigade exercises. The exercise includes 16 ships, and 1,100 aircraft.

Armed Forces radio "Wizard 106" now reaches the U.S. 1st Cavalry Division at Assembly Area Horse.

Marine Maj. Gen. Jeremiah W. Pearson, III, flying a combat air patrol nearly engages an Iraqi fighter near the Kuwait coast. He will fly combat missions over Iraq 17 January.

USS MOOSBRUGGER (DD-980) commanded by Cdr. Frank B. Guest, III, diverts the Russian flagged NIKOLAY SABITSKIY in the northern Red Sea, en route from Russia to Aqaba. The NIKOLAY SABITSKIY is carrying household goods.

Participating in Exercise *Imminent Thunder* Coalition air forces launch nine combined strike packages and a 700-aircraft CAS package. F-117s of the 37th TFW fly 32 sorties during the exercise against a "mirror image" of southeastern Iraq and Kuwait.

U.S. ground forces weapon systems strength: 270 attack helicopters, 770 support helicopters, 857 main battle tanks, 538 artillery pieces, 63 Multiple-Launch Rocket Systems, and 18 tactical missile systems (this does not include British 7th Armoured Brigade assets).

U.S. air strength in the theater is: 91 air-to-air, 264 air-to-ground, 240 dual-role combat aircraft (supported by 440 support aircraft).

British *Exercise Jubail Rat* is completed at 0930.

The Iraqi Air Force flies 40 sorties today.

16 November Maj. Gen. Ron Griffith, 1st Armored Division commander returns to Ansbach, Germany after meeting with Gen. Schwarzkopf at Dhahran, Saudi Arabia.

Admiral Frank B. Kelso, Chief of Naval Operations, announces that U.S. ships would not be rotated every six months as was previous policy.

The British 7th Armoured Brigade is now operationally effective. Cycles of 15 day training periods begin to maintain effectiveness followed by three day rests at Camp 4 at Al Jubail. Camp 4 provides a gym, telephones, showers, flush toilets, and air-conditioned rooms.

British Lt. Gen. de la Billiere visits HMS BRAZEN commanded by Cdr. James C Rapp. HMS LONDON commanded by Capt. I. R. Henderson is the British flagship for *Operation Granby*.

The Iraqi Air Force flies 128 sorties today.

17 November SIRIUS (TAFS-8) begins participation in Operation Desert Shield.

U.S. Navy air unit HC-6 (DET 7) begins participation in Operation Desert Shield.

British Royal Air Force is now commanded by AVM W.J. "Bill" Wratten replacing AVM "Sandy" Wilson.

18 November The 2nd Marine Division (Maj. Gen. William M. Keyes) is ordered to deploy to the Persian Gulf.

USAF B-52s fly eleven sorties in support of Exercise *Imminent Thunder*.

Iraq flies 172 sorties today.

19 November Lt. Gen. de la Billiere has a conference with British medical advisers on casualty care.

Netherlands air defense frigate HrMs JACOB VAN HEEMSKERCK (F-812) and KORTENAER-Class frigate HrMs PHILIPS VAN ALMONDE (F-823) depart Holland to relieve HrMs WITTE DE WITH (F-813) and HrMs PIETER FLORISZ (F-826). The Dutch vessels will join the USS MIDWAY (CV-41) Carrier Battle Group.

Exercise Imminent Thunder involves a 296-sortie CAS exercise.

Iraq flies 135 sorties today.

20 November CHARLES F. ADAMS-Class destroyer HMAS BRISBANE (DDG-41) departs Stirling, Australia and HMAS SYDNEY (FF-04). They are to replace Australian vessels deployed in the Middle East.

Final elements of the British 7th Armoured Division arrive. The deployment of the brigade's equipment has taken 42 ships.

Iraq flies 129 sorties today.

21 November Exercise *Imminent Thunder* ends.

U.S. Army VII Corps begins deploying to Saudi Arabia.

The Iraqi Air Force flies 147 sorties (including 32 helicopter flights) today.

22 November President George Bush arrives in Saudi Arabia to spend thanksgiving with the U.S. troops.

A ship departs Bremerhaven, Germany carrying elements of the U.S. 2nd Armored Cavalry Regiment.

USS BIDDLE (CG-34) commanded by Capt. Louis F. Harlow diverts the German flagged PREMIER in the northern Red Sea en route from Cyprus to Aqaba.

British Defense Secretary Thomas King announces a large increase in British force strength deployed to the Middle East. This increase will include the 1st Armoured Division commanded by Maj. Gen. Rupert Smith, and the 4th Armoured Brigade.

Iraq flies 117 sorties today.

23 November Gen. Schwarzkopf relates his plan to eject Iraq from Kuwait to Lt. Gen. Sir Peter de la Billiere, the British forces commander.

SIRIUS (TAFS-8) ceases participation in Operation Desert Shield.

U.S. Navy air unit HC-6 (DET 7) ceases participation in Operation Desert Shield.

Lt. Gen. Billiere meets with Maj. Gen. Rupert Smith, the British Division commander for the first time in Riyadh.

Spanish Navy ships SANTA MARIA, DESCUBIERTA, and CAZADORA complete particpation in Operation Desert Shield.

Iraq flies 90 sorties today.

24 November Iraq flies 152 sorties today.

25 November A U.S. Navy 12-plane package involved in Exercise *Desert Triangle* provokes no observable response from the Iraqi air defense system.

The Iraqi Air Force flies 117 sorties today.

26 November The first U.S. Marine Reservists arrive at Camp Lejeune.

USS PHILIPPINE SEA (CG-58) commanded by Capt. Patrick A. Callahan, fires shots across the bow of the Iraqi-flagged cargo ship KHAWLA BINT AL ZAWRA in the Northern Red Sea. Boarding parties from the PHILIPPINE SEA, THOMAS C. HART (FF-1092) commanded by Cdr. David C. Rollins and two multinationals then board the Iraqi vessel. The rescue and salvage ship OPPORTUNE (ARS-41) commanded by Lt. Cmdr. Edgar Jones begins participation in Operation Desert Shield. In December Lt. Cmdr. Darlene Iskra will relieve Lt. Cdr. Jones, becoming the first female to ever command a U.S. Navy ship.

Coalition air forces fly a 117-plane CAS exercise.

Iraq flies 105 sorties today.

27 November USS MOOSBRUGGER (DD-980) commanded by Cdr. Frank B. Guest, III, ceases participation in Operation Desert Shield.

U.S. Navy air unit HSL-42 (DET 6) ceases participation in Operation Desert Shield.

By this date the Coalition has made 4,162 ship challenges, 500 boardings, and 19 diversions.

A Coalition 167-aircraft CAS exercise is flown.

The Iraqi Air Force flies 45 sorties (including 37 transport and helicopter flights).

28 November Iraq flies six reconnaissance flights today. It flies a total of 117 sorties today.

29 November Military force is authorized by the United Nations Security Council, if Iraq does not vacate Kuwait by 15 January 1991.

At Taif 20 F-111Fs of the 494th TFS, 48th TFW arrive.

A 125-aircraft CAS exercise is flown by Coalition air forces. Also, four combined strikes packages of 16-54 aircraft are flown. 24 hour operations are flown by RC-135s. TR-1 air missions are extended by two hours.

The Iraqi Air Force flies 148 sorties (U.S. intelligence records also state a total of 129 flown today).

30 November First roundout brigades of Army National Guard are called to active duty.

By this date British repair ship RFA DILIGENCE (Capt. A. Mitchell) has completed her participation in Operation Desert Shield.

Iraq flies 122 sorties today.

1 December Secretary of Defense Dick Cheney increases U.S. Army selected Reserve call-up authority to 115,000 personnel.

U.S. Army XVIII Airborne Corps completes arrival in theater. U.S. ground forces strength is: 273 attack helicopters, 777 support helicopters, 867 main battle tanks, 546 artillery pieces, 63 MLRS, and 18 tactical missile systems (this does not include the British 7th Armoured Division).

The 5th Marine Expeditionary Brigade (about 7,500 personnel) sails from San Diego for Saudi Arabia on Amphibious Group 3. PhibGru3 consists of USS TARAWA (LHA-1), NEW ORLEANS (LPH-11), TRIPOLI (LPH-10), DENVER (LPD-9), JUNEAU (LPD-10), VANCOUVER (LPD-2), ANCHORAGE (LSD-36), GERMANTOWN (LSD-42), MOUNT VERNON (LSD-39), PEORIA (LST-1183), BARBOUR COUNTY (LST-1184), FREDERICK (LST-1184 and MOBILE (LKA-115).

Strength of I MEF is 41,374 (1st Marine Division is 14,183 personnel, 7,889 3rd Marine Air Wing). Tank strength is 126 M60A1/A3s, and seven M60 W/M9s.

V.Adm. Henry H. Mauz, Jr. is relieved by V.Adm. Stanley R. Arthur as Commander, Navy Central Command and Commander, 7th Fleet.

At King Fahd six OA-10s of the 602nd Tactical Air Control Wing (TAIRCW), 602nd TAIRCW arrive.

U.S. aircraft strength is: 91 air-to-air, 284 air-to-ground, and 240 dual-purpose combat aircraft (supported by 452 support aircraft). A Coalition air defense exercise is performed over central and eastern Saudi Arabia.

Tank strength of the British 7th Armoured Brigade is 170 Challenger tanks, 15 helicopters, 139 armoured fighting vehicles and 24 artillery pieces. The unit is serving with the I MEF.

British Navy Commodore Christopher Craig arrives in Saudi Arabia. Lt. Gen. de la Billiere relates to him his desire for him to create plans for an offensive campaign high up into the Gulf.

French *Armee de l'air* commander Col. Jean-Pierre Job is promoted to Brigadier General.

Iraq flies 161 sorties today.

2 December By this date USAF reports the following sortie totals: 2,326 combat air patrols; 3,426 air-to-air training; 14,621 air-to-ground training; 469 tactical reconnaissance; 421 strategic reconnaissance; 2,800 electronic reconnaissance; 253 AWACS; 4,831 air refueling; 17,536 theater airlift. Sortie total is 46,683.

British forces begin their first Battle Group exercise which will include a night march and a dismounted night attack while wearing NBC suits and combat body armor.

Iraqi forces conduct test firing of surface-to-surface missiles within Iraq, (from Al Amarah to Wadi Amij) targeted away from Coalition forces.

The Iraqi Air Force flies 209 sorties (one airborne early warning aircraft invading Jordanian airspace).

3 December U.S. Marine Corps is granted a higher call-up number of 23,000 reservists by Defense Secretary Richard Cheney. An additional 63,000 National Guard and Reserves are also approved.

USS JOHN F. KENNEDY Carrier Battle Group enters its area of responsibility (AOR).

USAF receives 4,100 body bags of planned 5,000 shipment.

British Commodore Christopher Craig, Senior Naval Officer, the Middle East assumes command of the British Task Group.

Iraq flies 137 sorties today.

4 December From Tonopah AB, 18 USAF F-117 Stealth Fighters of the 37th TFW arrive at a classified location.

Lt. Gen. Billiere spends a night at the desert camp of A Squadron, Queen's Dragoon Guards commanded by Maj. Hamish MacDonald.

The U.S. Marine 2nd Division's advance party heads for Saudi Arabia.

USS LEFTWICH (DD-984) commanded by Cdr. Patrick M. Garrett begins participation in Operation Desert Shield. She becomes a member of Middle East Force and Battle Force ZULU with Commander, Destroyer Squadron 35 (Capt. William L. Putman).

At King Khalid AB 20 F-117 Stealth Fighters of the 416th TFS (commanded by Lt. Col. Gregory T. Gonyea) arrive. With the arrival of the 'Ghost Riders' both combat squadrons of the 37th TFW (Col. Alton C. Whitley) have arrived in Saudi Arabia.

British Battle Group exercise is completed.

5 December Ready Reserve Force (RRF) of 173 ships has now completed their original deployment.

The 14th (Brig. Gen. Buster C. Glosson) and 15th Air Divisions (Provisional) (Brig. Gen. Glenn A. Profitt II) are formed.

Exercise *Desert Force* begins (10 strike training packages of 243 USAF, Saudi, British, and French aircraft).

The Iraqi Air Force flies 100 sorties.

6 December Equipment of VII Corps begins arriving in Saudi Arabia.

At Al Jubayl, Saudi Arabia the 2nd Marine Division's advance party arrives, and begins to offload ships of the Maritime Prepositioning Squadron.

U.S. Navy ship strength is 15 in the Mediterranean Sea, nine in the Red Sea, 21 in Northern Arabian Sea and Gulf of Oman, and 19 in the Arabian Sea.

At Incirlik, Turkey, a USAF EP-3 aircraft arrives.

7 December USS HORNE (CG-30) commanded by Capt. Thomas J. Barnett deploys from San Diego and the USS JARRETT (FFG-33) commanded by Cdr. William L. Snyder deploys from Long Beach, California for Operation Desert Shield.

Exercise Desert Force concludes. Results are 74 aircraft in two strike packages attacked simulated targets.

South of Dhahran, a French Air Force Mirage crashes, killing the pilot.

Iraq flies 134 sorties today.

8 December Gen. Schwarzkopf briefs senior Egyptian commanders on his plan in Cairo.

4th Marine Expeditionary Brigade begins amphibious exercise with Amphibious Task Group 2 off the coast of Oman (*Sea Soldier III*).

9 December First elements of the II Marine Expeditionary Force begin to land in Saudi Arabia. They arrive at a rate of about 1,000 per day.

USS SARATOGA (CV-60), BIDDLE (CG-34), PHILIPPINE SEA (CG-58), and O'BRIEN (DD-975) cease participation in Operation Desert Shield.

U.S. Navy air units HS-3, HS-7, HSL-34 (DET 1), HSL-46 (DET 7), VA-35, VAQ-132, VAW-125, VF-103, VF-74, VFA-81, VFA-83, VS-30, and VP-11 cease participation in Operation Desert Shield.

First elements of the British 1st Armoured Division commanded by Maj. Gen. Rupert Smith begin arriving at Jubail.

The Iraqi Air Force flies 186 sorties.

10 December Elements of the II Marine Expeditionary Force (Lt. Gen. Carl E. Mundy, Jr.) participate in a review on W.P.T. Hill Field at Camp Lejeune, North Carolina. After being reviewed and addressed by Gen. Alfred M. Gray, Jr., the Commandant of the U.S. Marine Corps and Commander in Chief, U.S. Atlantic Fleet, Admiral Powell F. Carter, Gen. Mundy orders commanders to deploy to Southwest Asia. Many Marines deploy immediately to Cherry Point and then Saudi Arabia.

Sea Soldier III includes a USMC amphibious assault followed by a heliborne assault.

Lt. Gen. de la Billiere meets with Cdr. Philip Wilcocks on his destroyer HMS GLOUCESTER. The British Navy plan now covers three tasks: 1) British Type-42 destroyers with American destroyers far in the northern Gulf waters guard the southern Coalition ships from Iraqi air power 2) Hunt-Class mine countermeasure ships conduct anti-mine warfare, and 3) Forward logistic and operational support of the Coalition with Britain's Fleet Auxiliaries.

11 December Participating in Exercise *Sea Soldier III* 2,600 4th MEB troops conduct an amphibious assault.

USS SOUTH CAROLINA (CGN-37) commanded by Capt. Edward B. Hontz, and THOMAS C. HART (FF-1092) commanded by Cdr. David C. Rollins cease participation in Operation Desert Shield.

At Taif, 12 F-111 of the 495th TFS, 48th TFW arrive. Headquarters, USAF orders call-up of 14 Reserve Component KC-135E units. Call-up affects 12 of 13 Air Guard units and two of three USAF Reserve units.

HMS LEDBURY (M-30) commanded by Lt. Cdr. D. H. L. MacDonald, and HMS DULVERTON (M-35) commanded by Lt. Cdr. C. G. Welborn depart Rosyth for the Middle East.

Deployment of a Czechoslovakian chemical decontamination battalion begins.

12 December The Main Body of the 2nd Marine Division begins to depart for Saudi Arabia.

AWACS provide continuous coverage of southern Iraq and Kuwait. During a CAS exercise, 129 aircraft participate with 141 supporting four strike packages.

British forces begin to bolt Chobham armor on their Challenger tanks and Warrior armoured fighting vehicles.

French Mirage 2000Cs fly their first combat air patrols.

The Iraqi Air Force flies 213 sorties (139 fighter, 40 transport, three reconnaissance).

13 December Cruisers USS THOMAS S. GATES, commanded by Capt. Henry C. Giffin III, and the USS MISSISSIPPI, commanded by Capt. Don P. Pollard, divert the Cyprus flagged TILIA. It is back en route from Al-Aqaba to Hodeida carrying stolen Kuwaiti automobiles. Later, the USS SAMPSON (DDG-10) commanded by Cdr. William D. Sullivan diverts the Cyprus flagged DONGOLA en route from Al-Aqaba to Port Sudan (also carrying stolen cars). Both are ordered back to Al-Aqaba.

Iraqi fire trenches have been completed by the tri-border area.

The Iraqi Air Force flies 188 sorties.

14 December Maj. Gen. William M. Keyes, 2nd Marine Division arrives in Saudi Arabia. The 2nd Marine Division has attached to it the United Kingdom's 7th Armored Brigade (Brig. Patrick Cordingley). Composed of two armoured regiments (the Royal Scots Dragoon Guards and the Queen's Royal Irish Hussars) and the armoured infantry battalion the 1st Staffordshire Regiment, it contains 114 Challenger tanks, 45 Warrior infantry fighting vehicles, and 16 Scimitar medium reconnaissance vehicles. The 7th Armoured Brigade is manned by 9,466 soldiers.

As part of *Sea Soldier III*, 3,400 Marines have now landed.

The advance party of the USAF 4th TFW arrives at Al Kharj, Saudi Arabia.

The Iraqi Air Force flies 98 sorties today.

15 December The USS JOHN F. KENNEDY (Capt. John P. Gay) launches 12 aircraft as the *Desert Triangle* mission of the day. There is no response. The United States Navy now has 98 warships on station, en route, or dedicated to Operation Desert Shield.

In the northern Red Sea the USS MISSISSIPPI (Capt. Don P. Pollard) diverts the Cyprus flagged TILIA en route from Aqaba to Hodeida.

U.S. ground forces weapons systems available include: 274 attack helicopters, 789 support helicopters, 939 main battle tanks, 542 artillery pieces, 63 MLRS, and 18 tactical missile systems (this does not include strength of British 7th Armoured Brigade).

At Masirah two USAF KC-135Rs of the 301st AREFS, 301st AREFW arrive as rotational replacements.

U.S. Air Order of Battle strength: 92 air-to-air, 337 air-to-ground, 222 dual-purpose combat aircraft (supported by 464 support aircraft).

The Iraqi Air Force flies 174 sorties.

16 December The Desert Storm Campaign Plan envisions four-phases. The phases are: Phase I (the Strategic Air Campaign), Phase II (achieving air supremacy in the Kuwaiti theatre of operations), Phase III (Battlefield Preparation), and Phase IV (the ground offensive).

USS MISSISSIPPI (Capt. Don P. Pollard) and the SNS DIANA (Captain of Corvettes Curiel Pina) divert the Cyprus TILIA in the northern Red Sea en route from Aqaba to Hodeida.

Maj. Gen. Pagonis's 22nd Support Command is designated.

USS SAMPSON (DDG-10), and DETROIT (AOE-4) cease participation in Operation Desert Shield.

U.S. Navy air unit HC-8 (DET 2) ceases participation in Operation Desert Shield.

At Incirlik, Turkey 24 USAF F-15Cs of the 525th TFS, 36th TFW arrive.

17 December USAF aircraft call signs are changed to increase security.

The British 7th Armoured Brigade (Brig. Patrick Cordingley) is transferred by Gen. H. Norman Schwarzkopf from the 2nd Marine Division to the U.S. Army Central Command.

Coalition air forces begin Operation *Border Look*. Numerous AWACS and combat air patrols are flown near the border to prepare the Iraqis for the presence of large numbers of aircraft.

The Iraqi Air Force flies 154 sorties.

18 December In Warren, Michigan, the U.S. Marine Corps new M1A1 tank is displayed by the General Dynamics Land Systems Division. The 2nd Tank Battalion of Camp Lejeune, North Carolina will use the tank in the Persian Gulf War while other Marine units will use the old M60A1.

In the northern Red Sea the USS MISSISSIPPI (Capt. Don P. Pollard) diverts the Cyprus flagged TILIA en route from Aqaba to Hodeida.

Al Kharji AB, Saudi Arabia is completed by the extraordinary efforts of USAF Red Horse Engineers as well as help by Greek and Saudi workers. A complete weight lifting/exercise facility is donated by Arnold Schwarzenegger. Al Kharji (better known as "Al's Garage") will be utilized by the 335th TFS and 336th TFS, 4th TFW.

The Iraqi Air Force flies 208 sorties today (156 fighter sorties).

19 December Secretary of Defense Dick Cheney and Gen. Colin Powell arrive in Riyadh to judge the Coalition's status and report it to President Bush.

The USS MISSISSIPPI (Capt. Don P. Pollard) and the SNS DIANA divert the German flagged RED SEA EUROPA in the northern Red Sea. She is en route from Rotterdam to Aqaba.

In Qatar Exercise *Sandy Beach* involves 16 U.S. fighters and six allied fighters.

The Iraqi Air Force flies 191 sorties today.

20 December By this date 280,000 American troops are in the Middle East.

USS INDEPENDENCE (CV-62) commanded by Capt. Robert L. Ellis, Jr. arrives in San Diego from the Persian Gulf.

At Al Kharj, 24 USAF F-15Cs of the 36th TFW arrive, and at Riyadh a E-3 of the 552nd AWACW arrives. To standardize and stabilize its organizational structure the F-117s Stealth Fighters of the 37th TFW are redesignated a provisional unit by CENTAF (37th TFW-P).

The Iraqi Air Force flies 210 sorties (170 fighter sorties).

21 December Returning from liberty, 21 sailors from the USS SARATOGA die when a ferry capsizes off Haifa, Israel.

USS MOOSBRUGGER (DD-980) commanded by Cdr. Frank B. Guest III returns and MARS (AFS-1) commanded by Capt. William W. Pickavance begins participation in Operation Desert Shield. An anti-ship mine is discovered in the Persian Gulf.

At Al Kharj, 24 USAF F-15Cs of the 36th TFW arrive. At King Fahd 18 A-10s of the 10th TFW arrive.

British Prince Charles arrives in Saudi Arabia.

British Staffordshire Regiment celebrates Ferezoshah Day with a parade led by the regimental flag and Union Jack. The parade is attended by the USMC 1/7 Battalion.

The French Chain of Command of the 4th Dragoon Regiment is: Corps Commander, Lt. Col. Michel Bourret; Assistant Corps Commander, Lt. Col. Bart; Operations officer, Squadron Commander Decock; Assistant Operations Commander Capt. Fritsch. Order of Battle is 1st Squadron (13 AMX 30 B.2), Capt. Allavena; 2nd Squadron (13 AMX, 30 B.2), Capt. de Fontenilles; 3rd Squadron (13 AMX 30 B2), Capt. Jouannic.

The Iraqi Air Force flies 174 sorties today.

22 December The U.S. Army 2nd Armored Cavalry Regiment has now arrived in theater.

The Iraqi Air Force flies 138 sorties.

23 December Two American sailors are killed and five injured when a truck they are riding on overturns at Abu Dhabi, United Arab Emirates.

USAF F-15s and Kuwaiti F-1s conduct air-to-air training for the first time. At Shaik Isa 12 F-4Gs of the 52nd TFW arrive.

24 December USAF A-10s of the 74th Tactical Fighter Squadron (the Flying Tigers), direct descendants of Chennault's World War II unit, begin night attack training.

The USS JOHN F. KENNEDY commanded by Capt. John P. Gay launches 15 aircraft in a simulated attack against northwestern Saudi Arabia.

Iraq flies 98 sorties today.

25 December The 4th Battalion, 7th Infantry, 1st Armored Division lifts off for the long flight to their Initial Staging Area "Andersonville" in Saudi Arabia. Named after the Civil War Confederate prison, the 1st Armored Division will eat strange tasting local food, sleep at close quarters, and have no room for recreation or training. They will wait and wait and wait to be called to port and pick up their vehicles. After being painted desert sand color they will drive their vehicles onto a transport to take them 400 kilometers into the desert to Tactical Assembly Area Thompson.

The first order of Operation Desert Shield is issued by the 2nd Marine Division.

The people of Staffordshire, England present members of the Staffordshire Regiment mugs for Christmas. Still, the day is probably the lowest for morale during the war despite a visit from Lt. Gen. Peter de la Billiere.

The Iraqi Air Force flies 176 sorties (124 fighter sorties). From six bases Iraqi fighters conduct night ground control intercept training.

26 December In the Northern Arabian Sea the USS OLDENDORF (Cdr. Cyrus H. Butt, IV), USS FIFE (Cdr. Curtis A. Kemp), USS TRENTON (Capt. James A. Curtis), HMS BRAZEN, and HMAS SYDNEY (Capt. L.G. Cordner) divert the IBN KAHLDOON ("Peace Ship") en route from Aden to Umm Qasar with 60 peace activists. Crewmembers resist Navy boarding crew (SEALs and U.S. Marines of the 4th MEB) attempting to grab their weapons, which results in warning shots being fired, and smoke and noise grenades being thrown for crowd control. A multinational team from HMAS SYDNEY (F-03), USS OLDENDORF (DD-972) and USS FIFE (DD-991) board the vessel. Unflagged, she is diverted to Muscat.

At Shaikh Isa Airport, 11 USAF F-4Gs arrive. This brings the total to 47.

After staying overnight with the Staffords Lt.Gen. de la Billiere runs with them on their morning run. A highlight of his experience in the Gulf War he met with them last night in the dark, under the stars.

The Iraqi Air Force flies 156 sorties today.

27 December Saudi King Fahd addresses Coalition troops.

Gen. Schwarzkopf describes to Gen. Powell, Dick Cheney and other commanders his tactical flanking maneuver in Riyadh. Gen. Schwarzkopf is shown the Maj. Gen. Pagonis's logistics plan for his far western flanking "end run." Pagonis's doctrine is based on one of Alexander the Great.

The U.S. 1st Cavalry Division (Brig. Gen. John H. Tilelli, Jr. USA) begins to move to new positions to be able to guard Hafar al-Batin (KKMC) from Iraqi attacks down the Wadi al-Batin.

The U.S. 2nd Marine Division's forward command post (CP) makes its first displacement forward. From a three-day wargame simulating an aggressor force in September, Maj. Gen. Keyes has concluded that the division will have four CPs (main, rear, forward and a mobile CP) The mobile CP consisting of four light armored vehicles (LAV) includes Gen. Keyes and it is from his LAV he will direct his division in Desert Storm.

At Marine Barracks, Washington, D.C. Company A departs for the 2nd Marine Division. This is the first deployment of the unit since 1906 when a detachment was sent to Cuba for pacification duty.

At King Fahd 18 USAF A-10s of the 10th TFW arrive.

French "Daquet" unit, named after a small energetic deer is placed under tactical control of the XVIII Airborne Corps. French 6th Light Armored Division is its major unit. Chain of

Command of 11th Marine Artillery Regiment is: Commander Col. Novack; Second in Command, Lt. Col. Gouirand; 1st Battery, Capt. Chauvet; 2nd Battery, Capt. Baillot; 4th Battery, Capt. Boutroy.

The Iraqi Air Force flies 191 sorties (151 fighter sorties).

28 December The Department of Defense announces that for the first time in history U.S. forces are to be vaccinated for chemical/biological weapons.

USS AMERICA (CV-66 commanded by Capt. John J. Mazach) and THEODORE ROOSEVELT (CVN-71 commanded by Capt. Charles S. Abbot) Carrier Battle Groups depart Norfolk. Final ships carrying the 3rd Armored Division are late departing Germany due to the Christmas holidays.

Most of the Marine 2nd Division has deployed to the "Triangle" a 600-square-kilometer area north of Abu Hadriyah and An Nuayrihah.

The main strength of the 2nd Marine Aircraft Wing (Maj. Gen. Richard D. Hearney) has arrived. They have 32 aircraft squadrons.

At Al Kharj 20 USAF F-15Es arrive.

A fifth surface-to-surface missile test is fired within Iraq.

The Iraqi Air Force flies 115 sorties.

29 December Maj. Gen. Pagonis meets with Gen. Schwarzkopf about his plan to establish logbases (supply cache) to support the Coalition forces.

At Al Kharj, 23 USAF F-15Es of the 335th TFS, 4th TFW arrive.

Two New Zealand C-130s begin participation in Operation Desert Shield.

The Iraqi Air Force flies the most sorties since the Kuwait invasion (231 sorties, 175 fighter sorties).

30 December At Al Kharj, 24 USAF F-16s of the 157th TFS, 4th TFW arrive and at Cairo West, Egypt, ten KC-135Es of the 126th AREFS, 128th AREFG arrive.

The Iraqi Air Force flies 219 sorties.

31 December Gen. Schwarzkopf is informed that the Syrians will not fight.

Maj. Gen. Keyes states in Operation Order 2-90 that he wants the 2nd Marine Division to focus on training that prepares it for mechanized operations and obstacle breaching. Most training will take place on the "Thunderbolt" range of 250 square kilometers.

The USS MISSISSIPPI (Capt. Don P. Pollard) diverts the Yugoslavian flagged LEDENICE in the northern Red Sea. She is en route from Sudan to Aqaba. Presenting no original manifest and the document presented having whiteout changes, the LEDENICE is sent to Djibouti.

From Hahn AB, 24 USAF F-16s of the 50th TFW arrive. At Cairo West, Egypt, five KC-135Es of the 116th AREFS, 141st AREFW arrives, at Masirah a KC-135R of the 301st AREFS, 301st AREFW arrives and at Jeddah three KC-135Es of the 116th AREFS, 141st AREFW arrives.

French Mirage 2000s are exercised by two U.S.-Saudi strike packages.

French Order of Battle of 1st Foreign Cavalry Regiment (Garrison Orange) is: Commander Col. Ivanoff; Second in Command, Lt. Col. Duronsoy; Operations, Lt. Col. Clement-Bollee; 1st Squadron Capt. Dumont-Saint-Priest; 2nd Squadron, Capt. Yakovlev; 3rd Squadron, Capt. Winckler; 4th Squadron, Capt. Faure.

Twelve Italian Tornados participate in air refueling practice with a KC-135.

The Syrian 9th Armored Division closes in theater.

For the first time Iraq orders 17-year-olds to report for military training.

The Iraqis fly 107 sorties (records also list 129 sorties as total).

1 January 1991 Schwarzkopf presents Lt. Gen. Khalid Bin Sultan al-Saud commander of the Multinational Joint Combat Group a plan to make the Syrian troops the Egyptian reserves. They agree.

U.S. ground weapons systems strength: 344 attack helicopter, 1016 support helicopters, 1046 main battle tanks, 650 artillery pieces, 90 MLRS, and 18 tactical missile system (does not include strength of British 7th Armoured Brigade).

Infantry of the 1st Armored Division begin to arrive at Tactical Assembly Area Thompson, northeast of the King Khalid Military City (KKMC). As all U.S. Tactical Assembly Areas in Saudi Arabia, it is named after a Medal of Honor winner. KKMC is at the southern end of the Wadi Al-Batin.

Strength of the I Marine Expeditionary Force is 60,534 (1st Marine Division is 14,692 personnel, 2nd Marine Division 10,575, 3rd Marine Air Wing 10,937 with 28 AH1J/Ws, 18 UH-1Ns, 24 CH-46Es, 20 CH-53Ds, 6 RH-53Ds, 15 CH-53Es, 40 AV-8Bs, 20 A-6Es, 12 EA-6Bs, 72 FA-18A/Cs, 12 KC-130F/R/Ts, 8 OV-10/D, and a UC-12B).

The battleship USS MISSOURI (Capt. Albert L. Kaiss) arrives in the Gulf of Oman. SACRAMENTO (AOE-1) commanded by Capt. Dennis W. Irelan begins participation in Operation Desert Shield.

U.S. Navy air unit HC-11 (DET 7) begins participation in Operation Desert Shield.

At Al Dhafra, 24 USAF F-16s of the 50th TFW arrive and at Jeddah three KC-135Es of the 145th AREFS, 160th AREFG arrive.

U.S. air strength is: 116 air-to-air, 385 air-to-ground, 318 dual-purpose aircraft (supported 549 support aircraft).

Iraq launches only 36 sorties due to poor weather.

2 January Lt. Gen. de la Billiere learns of Wing Commander David Farquhar losing secret documents and a lap-top computer in London. Though shocking, it is later discovered that nothing of importance was compromised.

Rain begins and continues intermittently through 14 January.

USNS ANDREW J. HIGGINS (T-AO-190) runs aground off Oman, rupturing its hull. There are no injuries.

By this date 325,000 U.S. troops are in the Middle East. These include 55,000 Marines and 35,000 American sailors.

U.S. Navy Middle East ship strength is 55 (Red Sea=10, North Arabian Sea/Gulf of Oman=20, Persian Gulf=25).

By this date the Coalition has made 6,221 maritime challenges, 749 boardings and 32 diversions.

A NCO of the British 16 Tank Transporter Squadron is killed when a Warrier tank traps him against the winch of a tank transporter.

Oiler HMAS WESTRALIA (AO-195) commanded by Capt. J.S. Moore departs Stirling, Australia for the Middle East. She will relieve HMAS SUCCESS commanded by Commo. G.V. Sloper. By late January, Australian warships begin operating with the USS MIDWAY Carrier Battle Group. The Australian Chief of Naval Staff is V.Adm. Michael W. Hudson.

At Al Kharj, 18 USAF F-16s land and 8 C-130s of the 773rd TAS, 463rd TAW arrive. At Riyadh, a E-3 of the 552nd AWACS, 552nd AWACW arrives. USAF sorties today total 567.

At Dhahran a third British Tornado GR.Mk 1 squadron begins to arrive at Dhahran.

Iraq flies 37 sorties.

3 January USAF Central Command sorties numbers 93.

Arriving at Jeddah: ten USAF KC-135Es of the 108th AREFS, 126th AREFW, ten KC-135Es of the 117th AREFS, 190th AREFG, eight KC-135Es of the 171st AREFW, and four KC-135Es of the 134th AREFG. At Thumrait, Oman, eight C-130s of the 345th TAS arrive, and at Al Khari 18 F/A-18s of the 138th TFS, 4th TFW arrive.

Iraqi air sorties number 93.

4 January In the North Red Sea the USS MISSISSIPPI (Capt. Don P. Pollard) and the Spanish frigate SNS INFANTA-CHRISTINA (Captain of Corvettes Palencia Luaces) divert the Russian-flagged DMITRIY-FURMANOV en route from the Soviet Union to Aqaba. She does not have a manifest and is carrying detonators, tank parts and rocket launchers. Near Dubai, the battleship USS MISSOURI aids Saudi-flagged tanker TABUK, which has two small fires and an inoperative pump.

At Jeddah, three USAF KC-135Es of the 145th AREFS, 160th AREFG, and two KC-135Es of the 72nd AREFS, 434th AREFW arrive.

USAF Central Command sortie count is 762.

Coalition air forces fly 144 CAS sorties today.

At Dhahran the last elements of a third British Tornado GR.Mk 1 squadron arrives.

Iraq flies 48 sorties today, most being transport missions into Kuwait.

5 January From Moody AFB, Georgia, 24 F-16 Fighting Falcons of the 69th USAF Tactical Fighter Squadron (the "Werewolves") begin deploying. At King Fahd 16 A-10s and six OA-10s arrive.

At Jeddah two USAF KC-135Es of the 336th AREFS, 452nd AREFW and four KC-135Es of the 72nd AREFS, 434th AREFW arrives.

Total USAF sorties today number 771.

Iraq flies 60 sorties today. More than 50 percent of these sorties are transportation missions.

6 January After having dug trenches, made protective berms and strung barbed wire at TAA Thompson, the 1st Armored Division soldiers begin training. Map training is first and then over a period of days formations are practiced in a special "maneuver box" established on latitude-longitudinal lines (approximately 15 kilometers wide by 50 kilometers of depth). A gunnery range is laid out allowing tanks and Bradleys to use "service" ammunition for the first time instead of the "training" ammunition the tankers had hitherto used.

The "Sara", the USS SARATOGA (Capt. Joseph S. Mobley) makes her fifth transit of Suez Canal during this deployment. This is an U.S. Navy record for canal transit. In the Northern Red Sea the USS MISSISSIPPI (Capt. Don P. Pollard) diverts the Russian flagged PETR MASHEROV and PYOTR en route from Jeddah to Aqaba (the ships lay to, then proceed). DETROIT (AOE-4) commanded by Capt. Michael B. Edwards and PHILIPPINE SEA (CG-58) commanded by Capt. Patrick A. Callahan renews participation in Operation Desert Shield.

U.S. Navy air units HC-8 (DET 2), HS-3, HS-7, HSL-46, VA-35, VAQ-132, VAW-125, VF-103, VF-74, VFA-81, VFA-83, and VS-30 renew participation in Operation Desert Shield.

At Al Ain, UAE, eight USAF C-130s of the 180th TAS, 139th TAG arrive. At Jeddah, four KC-135Es of the 336th AREFS, 452nd AREFW arrive. At King Fahd, six OA-10s of the 602nd Tactical Air Command Wing (TACW) and 18 A-10s of the 706th TFS, 917th TFW arrive.

USAF sorties today number 551.

Iraq flies 88 sorties (64 fighter sorties).

7 January U.S. Intelligence estimates that 542,000 Iraqi troops (35 divisions) 4,300 tanks and 3,100 artillery pieces are positioned in the Kuwaiti theatre.

Strength of 1st Marine Division is 17,824 personnel.

At Thumrait, Oman eight C-130s of the 327th TAS, 459th MAW have arrived.

Exercise *Fish Barrel* begins. Coalition air forces fly 266 simulated close air support and air interdiction missions. B-52s finish a strike training mission over northeast Saudi Arabia.

At Yanbu on the Red Sea, ships carrying elements of the French 6th Armored Division (7,100 men) and the Egyptian 4th Armored Division (13,700 personnel) arrive. The last of the French 4th Dragoon's tanks have just arrived.

Iraq flies 59 sorties today (17 fighter sorties).

8 January In reponse to a terrorist threat in Riyadh, the entire 82nd Airborne Division is ordered to move to that location (*Operation Quick Silver*). After alerted, however, only the 3rd Brigade (Col. Glynn Hale) conducts the mission.

USS YELLOWSTONE (AD-41) commanded by Capt. Edmund L. Pratt renews participation in Operation Desert Shield. U.S. Navy sealift numbers 245 ships with 253 offloads having been completed, or 12 billion pounds of fuel and equipment.

At Al Minhad Air Base, UAE, 24 USAF F-16 Fighting Falcons of the 69th Tactical Fighter Squadron have now arrived from Moody AFB and at Riyadh two EC-130s arrive.

There are now more than 360,000 U.S. servicemen in the Middle East region.

There are now 63 U.S. Navy ships in the region (Eastern Mediterranean=12, Red Sea=12, North Arabian Sea/Gulf of Oman=21, Persian Gulf=18).

Coalition Exercise *Fish Barrel* includes 575 sorties today (285 CAS sorties).

Iraq flies 130 sorties (89 fighter sorties). Records also list 53 as the sortie total today.

9 January The U.S. Army 82nd Airborne Division's Ready Brigade transfers to Thumama Airfield.

USS BIDDLE (CG-34) commanded by Capt. Louis F. Harlow begins participation in Operation Desert Shield. The ELMER MONTGOMERY (FF-1082) commanded by Cdr. Robert A. Higgins ceases participation in Operation Desert Shield.

U.S. Navy air unit HSL-34 (DET 1) renews participation in Operation Desert Shield.

At Riyadh an E-3 AWACS and RC-135 arrives.

Coalition forces fly 575 sorties in *Exercise Fish Barrel* (211 CAS sorties).

The British 1st Armoured Division closes in theater. Training at 'Devil Dog Dragoon' range is completed for elements of the Staffordshire Regiment. The range by the coast includes infantry and tank fire ranges as well as a 'village' for FIBUA (fighting in built-up areas) training.

Iraq air sorties number 81.

10 January The U.S. Army's 101st Airborne Division (Air Assault) is flown to King Khalid Military City.

The U.S. Army's 1st Brigade, 2nd Armored Division (Col. John B. Sylvester) called the "Tiger Brigade" reports to the 2nd Marine Division from United States Army Central Command. The 2nd Marine Division now number more than 20,000 personnel and 196 M1A1 tanks, 59 Bradley Fighting Vehicles, 66 M60A1 tanks, 248 assault amphibious vehicles, and 159 light armored vehicles.

Led by USS NASSAU (LHA-4), commanded by Capt. John I. Dow, an eight-ship amphibious task force (nearly 10,000 Marines and sailors) arrives in the Persian Gulf.

In the Northern Red Sea the USS MISSISSIPPI (Capt. Don P. Pollard), and SNS DIANA commanded by Captain of Corvettes Curiel Pina diverts the DMITRIY-FURMANOV from the Red Sea through the Suez Canal.

At Riyadh, two USAF E-3s of the 552nd AWACS, 552nd AWACW and two RC-135s of the 55th Surveillance and Reconnaissance Wing (SRW) have arrived.

Iraq flies 130 sorties (89 fighter sorties).

11 January The 101st Airborne Division continues to be transported to King Khalid Military City.

At Taif two USAF TR-1s arrive. USAF sorties number 788.

The British 1st Armoured Division is ordered to to join the U.S. Army VII Corps.

Canadian destroyer HURON commanded by Cdr. Richard Melnick sails from Esquimalt, B.C. for Halifax. After reaching port its 315-member crew will fly to Saudi Arabia to relieve the crew of its sister ship ATHABASKAN (Cdr. K. John Pickford).

Order of Battle of the French 6th Foreign Engineer Regiment: Commander, Col. Manet; Second in Command, Lt. Col. Danigo; 1st Company, Capt. Breuille; 2nd Company, Capt. Rittimann; 3rd Company, Capt. Boullet.

Coalition air forces fly 250 CAS training sorties.

12 January The U.S. Congress votes to approve the use of force to eject Iraq from Kuwait. This is the first time since the 7 August 1964 Gulf of Tonkin Resolution that Congress has voted directly for offensive U.S. military action.

U.S. Central Command personnel number 408,876.

In the North Arabian Sea the USS RANGER (CV-61 commanded by Capt. Ernest E. Christenson) Carrier Battle Group and Amphibious Group Three (13 ships, 7,500 Marines) arrives in the Arabian Sea. This is the largest amphibious task force formed since the Korean War.

The USS MIDWAY (Capt. Arthur K. Cebrowski) again enters the Persian Gulf. The HARRY W. HILL (DD-986) begins participating in Operation Desert Shield. Amphibious Group 3 commanded by R.Adm. Stephen S. Clarey, USN, arrives. Ships are: ANCHORAGE (LSD-36) commanded by Cdr. Terrence P. Labrecque, DENVER (LPD-9) commanded by Capt. Nigel E. Parkhurst, JUNEAU (LPD-10) commanded by Capt. Thomas A. Fitzgibbons, BARBOUR COUNTY (LST-1195) commanded by Cdr. Joseph B. Wilkinson, Jr., CAYUGA (LST-1186) commanded by Cdr. David W. Hagstrom, DURHAM (LKA-114) commanded by Capt. Charles M. Kraft, MOBILE (LKA-115) commanded by Capt. Ronald V. Berg, FORT MCHENRY (LSD-43) commanded by Cdr. James A. Hayes, FREDERICK (LST-1184) commanded by Cdr. Thomas W. Thiesse, GERMANTOWN (LSD-42) commanded by Cdr. William J. Marshall, III, MOUNT VERNON (LSD-39) commanded by Cdr. David E. Myers, NEW ORLEANS (LPH-11) commanded by Capt. Douglas J. Bradt, PEORIA (LST-1183) commanded by Cdr. Terry W. Tilton, OGDEN (LPD-5) commanded by Capt. Braden J. Phillips, OKINAWA (LPH-3) commanded by Capt. Mack A. Thomas, JASON (AR-8) commanded by Capt. Roy W. Tobin, PONCHATOULA (TAO-148), SYLVANIA (AFS-2) commanded by Capt. Edward J. Simmons, TARAWA (LHA-1) commanded by Capt. Wirt R. Fladd, TRIPOLI (LPH-10) commanded by Capt. G. Bruce McEwen, and VANCOUVER (LPD-2) commanded by Capt. Clarence W. Burck begins participation in Desert Shield.

The repair ship USS JASON (AR-8), commissioned in 1944, will provide repair services to 73 U.S. Navy and nine ships of the Italian, French, Belgian and British navies during the war.

At Shaikh Isa, 12 USAF RF-4Cs of the 67th TRW arrives. At King Fahd International five HH-3Es of the 71st SOS, 939th ARW arrives. At Incirlik, four HC-130s of the 67th SOS, 39th SOW, two MC-130s and a C-130 of the 7th SOS, 39th SOW arrive.

Lt. Col. Jim Green (74th TFS, the "Flying Tigers) reports to deputy of operations Col. Tom Lyon that the Tigers are now trained in night operations and are mission ready.

There are now two JSTARS aircraft in the theater. The USAF flies 770 sorties today beginning to change over to a wartime posture flying load out (armed and ready).

The French 6th Armored Division closes at King Khalid Military City.

Joint Forces Command, Northern Area Commander is Maj. Gen. Abd al-Rahman al-Alkami, and Commander, JFC-North is Maj. Gen. Sulaiman al-Wuhayyib. Senegali troops are commanded by Col. Mohamadou Keita, Nigerian troops, by Col. Amadou Seyni.

Iraq flies 221 sorties.

13 January The Joint Chiefs of Staff alert units worldwide that hostilities are imminent issuing Defense Condition (Defcon) 2.

The U.S. Army XII Corps closes in theater and is now fully manned and equipped.

The USS RANGER (CV-61, commanded by Capt. Ernest E. Christenson), PRINCETON (CG-59, commanded by Capt. Edward B. Hontz), VALLEY FORGE (CG-50, commanded by Capt. Ernest F. Tedeschi), PAUL F. FOSTER (DD-964, commanded by Cdr. Timothy M. Ahern), KANSAS CITY (AOR-3, commanded by Capt William E. Franson), and SHASTA (AE-33, commanded by Cdr. Daniel E. Gabe) begin participation in Operation Desert Shield.

Marine All Weather Fighter Attack Squadron 121 begins arriving in Bahrain to provide battlefield intelligence and forward air control with its new F/A-18D Hornets.

U.S. Navy air units HC-11 (DET 8), HS-14, VA-145, VA-155, VAQ-131, VAW-116, VF-1, VF-2, VS-38, and VRC-30 begins participation in Desert Shield.

Brig. Gen. Buster Glosson addresses A-10 pilots "Hog drivers" at 1500 and informs them in detail what to expect in the early hours of Operation Desert Storm.

At Jeddah eight USAF KC-10s of the 68th Air Rescue Wing (ARW) arrive.

The USAF scheduled 721 sorties today, but flew only 288 due to poor weather. All air-to-ground and air-to-air units are loaded out and are ready for war.

British Tornado GR.Mk1 ZD718/BH, No. 14 Squadron flown by Flight Lieutenants Kieran Duffy and Norman Dent crash on a low-level training flight. Both Duffy and Dent are killed.

Iraq flies 142 sorties (61 fighter, 56 transport).

14 January Maj. Gen. Ron Griffith of the 1st Armored Division makes a visual reconnaissance west of the Iraqi defenses, and 20 kilometers south of the Iraqi border. He finds that the terrain is passable for both tanks and armored vehicles. Later, viewing U-2 imagery film with Lt. Gen. Franks it is certain that, with little exception, terrain 60 kilometers wide north to Al Bussayah is passable. This results in a western line of departure for the 1st and 3rd Armored Divisions that will prevent crowding with other units of the VII Corps.

The Command Post of the U.S. 2nd Marine Division arrives in the area of Al Kibrit.

USS THEODORE ROOSEVELT (CVN-71, Capt. Charles S. Abbot) Carrier Battle Group arrives on station in the Red Sea after transiting the Suez Canal. USS LEYTE GULF (CG-55) commanded by Capt. Bob R. Patton, Jr., RICHMOND K. TURNER (CG-20) commanded by Capt. James L. Burke, CARON (DD-970) commanded by Cdr. Brent B. Gooding, HAWES (FFG-53) commanded by Cdr. Robert D. Liggett, PLATTE (AO-186) commanded by Cdr. Roger K. Hope, and SAN DIEGO (AFS-6) commanded by Capt. Timothy R. Beard begins participation in Operation Desert Shield.

USS LEYTE GULF will embark LAMPS Mk II Helos of HSL-42 DET 3 in excess of 220 combat missions during the Persian Gulf War.

U.S. Navy air units HC-8 (DET 4), HS-9, HSL-42 (DET 3), HSL-44 (DET 5), HSL-48 (DET 2, DET 3), VA-36, VA-65, VAQ-141, VAW-124, VF-41, VF-84, VFA-15, VFA-87, VS-24, and VRC-40 begins participation in Operation Desert Shield.

At Shaikh Isa, six USAF RF-4Cs arrive and at Taif, a U-2 arrives. At Al Kharj, Saudi Arabia, 44 F-15E Strike Eagles of the 4th TFW are ready for war.

The Joint Surveillance Target Attack Radar System (JSTARS) flies over Saudi Arabia for the first time in its Boeing 707. The system provides revolutionary ability to detect all moving targets and many stationary objects over all of Kuwait and much of southern Iraq.

British BROADSWORD-Class frigates HMS BRILLIANT (F-90) commanded by Capt. T. D. Elliot, and HMS BRAVE (F-94) commanded by Capt. R. M. Williams depart Devonport, England for the Persian Gulf.

The Canadian CF-18 fighters of 416 and 439 Squadrons ("Desert Cats") are stationed at two Qatar bases. They are commanded by Col. Romeo Lalonde of Penetanguishene, Ontario and his deputy commander Lt. Col. Dennis Roberts of St. Catharines, Ontario. The bases nicknamed Canada Dry One and Canada Dry Two were originally manned by the 409 Tactical Fighter Squadron of BadenSollingen and infantry of the 3rd Battalion, the Royal Canadian Regiment of London, Ontario. Now the Canadian force is defended by the 100-man 1st Battalion, the Royal 22nd Regiment (Van Doos).

15 January The United Nations deadline for Iraqi forces to withdraw from Kuwait arrives and passes without compliance. Israel begins a 24-hour-a-day curfew on the occupied Gaza strip.

XVIII Airborne Corps goes to MOPP (Mission Oriented Protective Posture Level) I and begin ingesting anti-nerve agent pills. Col. Walter E. Mather is Chief of Staff of the XVIII Corps.

Nearly half of the active duty strength of the entire U.S. Marine Corps--84,000--is deployed in the Persian Gulf (66,000 ashore with MEF and 18,000 afloat). The V Marine Expeditionary Force is activated to assume missions assigned to the I Marine Expeditionary Force, previous to its Southwest Asia deployment. The last of the II Marine Expeditionary Force (nearly 30,000 Marines and sailors) arrives in Saudi Arabia. Some 17,000 Marine Corps Reserves are on active duty.

U.S. Central Command numbers 422,041 personnel. Weapons available are 383 attack helicopters, 1,120 support helicopters, 1,110 main battle tanks, 2,426 assorted armored and armored fighting vehicles, 711 artillery pieces, 121 MLRS, and 18 tactical missile systems (does not include strength of British 1st Armored Division).

USS AMERICA (CV-66, Capt. John J. Mazach) Carrier Battle Group passes through the Suez Canal arriving on station in the Red Sea. The USS RANGER (CV-61, Capt. Ernest E. Christenson) Carrier Battle Group arrives on station in the Persian Gulf.

The USS VIRGINIA (CGN-38) commanded by Capt. Gary M. Voorheis, NORMANDY (CG-60) commanded by Capt. Joseph W. Perrotta, Jr., WILLIAM V. PRATT (DDG-44) commanded by Cdr. Dennis R. Dean, PREBLE (DDG-46) commanded by Cdr. Thomas W. Frohlich, NIAGARA FALLS (AFS-3) commanded by Capt. Robert E. Houser, KALAMAZOO (AOR-6) commanded by Capt. Timothy P Winters, SANTA BARBARA (AE-28) commanded by Cdr. Michael Frimenko, Jr., J. HUMPHREYS (TAO-188), and THOMAS C. HART (FF-1092) commanded by Cdr. David C. Rollins begins participation in Operation Desert Shield.

U.S. Navy air units HC-6 (DET 1, DET 5), HS-11, HSL-44 (DET 7), VA-85, VAQ-137, VAW-123, VF-102, VF-33, VFA-82, VFA-86, and VS-32 begins participation in Operation Desert Shield.

At Al Kharj, Capt. Jeff Latatas is the first of the 4th TFW to learn the date of the beginning of Operation Desert Storm.

At a classified base, two USAF TR-1s of the 9th SRW has arrived. At Jeddah, three KC-10s of the 22nd ARW has arrived. At Seeb, eight KC-10s of the 2nd BMW arrives, and at Diego Garcia five KC-10s of the 22nd ARW has arrived.

U.S. Air Order of Battle strength is: 195 air-to-air, 477 air-to-ground, 426 dual-purpose combat aircraft (supported by 749 support aircraft). USAF flies 605 sorties with the Coalition flying a total of 1,200 today.

Since 21 December, 17 anti-ship mines have been found in the Persian Gulf, with 16 thought to be Iraqi.

The British 7th Armoured Brigade is withdrawn from the I Marine Expeditionary Force, to merge into the British 1st Armoured Division. It is replaced by the 1st Brigade of the U.S. 2nd Armored Division.

The USS AMERICA (CV-66, Capt. John J. Mazach) Carrier Battle Group arrives on station in the Red Sea. The USS RANGER (Capt. Ernest E. Christenson) carrier battle group begins duties in Persian Gulf.

Iraq flies 64 sorties today.

16 January   First Coalition missiles strike Iraqi early warning radar sites at 2339Z (Z or Z-time is Greenwich Mean time). They are fired by AH-64s led by MH-53s. Operation Desert Storm begins at 0200 (local time). By 0230 Baghdad is under heavy attack.

0636 At Barksdale AFB the first of seven B-52G Stratofortresses nicknamed "Buffs" of the Eighth Air Force take-off on a round-trip bombing mission to Iraq. The bombers carry AGM-86C Cruise missiles with 1,000-pound conventional blast-fragmentation warheads. The Stratofortresses will fly 1,624 sorties during the war from the U.S. U.K., Spain, Middle East and Diego Garcia and drop 25,700 tons of bombs--30 percent of all U.S. bombs. During the war 74 of the United States 122 B-52Gs are tasked (nearly 61 percent). Every three hours they will be bombing the Republican Guard.

There are 425,000 U.S. troops in the region (75,000 Marines, 60,000 Navy).

U.S. Navy ship strength totals 108 (Eastern Mediterranean=13, Red Sea=26, Persian Gulf=34, North Arabian Sea/Gulf of Oman=35).

Coalition ground forces strength is 19 countries, with 14 countries contributing naval forces. On Tapline Road, west of Hafar al-Batin, Saudi Arabia, a convoy of the U.S. XVIII Airborne Corps and VII Corps begins moving supplies and equipment to relocate west in preparation for ground warfare. By the end of the day the convoy is 120 miles long.

Ammunition ship NITRO (AE-32) commanded by Cdr. William H. Ward begins participation in Operation Desert Shield. Part of the THEODORE ROOSEVELT (CVN-71) Battle Group the NITRO will resupply three carrier and two battleship battle groups during the conflict and transfer in excess of 6,700 pallets of ammunition (13.3 million pounds).

Aircraft maintainers are the first USAF personel certain that the attack will come today as the load their planes with live munitions and ammunition repeatedly to the multiple playings of Lee Greenwood's "God Bless the USA."

A-10 Warthog pilots open their top secret packets and find that what Brig. Gen. Glosson had informed them of on 13 January is true. General Glosson's honesty about the opening targets of Operation Desert Storm is greatly appreciated.

At Moron, Spain, six USAF B-52Gs of the 2nd BMW from Barksdale arrive. At Incirlik five MH-53s of the 21st SOS, 39th SOW arrive. At Riyadh, a RC-135 of the 55th SRW arrives. At Jeddah, four KC-135E of the 101st AFRFW arrive. From Andersen, Guam, six B-52Gs arrive at a classified location.

British Special Forces are in their training camp in the Arabian peninsula. They deploy quickly to a holding base 900 kilometers northwest of Riyadh.

At Dhahran, final elements of six British reconnaissance Tornado GR.Mk 1As arrive at Dhahran, Saudi Arabia. British RAF offensive forces total approximately 50 Tornados and 12 Jaguars at three bases.

Chapter 2

OPERATION DESERT STORM

17 January 1991 Operation *Eager Anvil* begins when Task Force Normandy is launched from the Al Jouf airstrip. At 0200 six White Team helicopters, two Air Force MH-53j Pave Lows (White One and White Two flown by Capt. Mike Kingsley and Col. Robert Leonik) of the USAF 20th Special Operations Squadron and four Apaches (commanded by Lt. Col. Richard Cody) and led by White Three (Chief Warrant Officer Dave Jones and Chief Warrant Officer Tom O'Neal) cross the Iraqi Border. Twenty kilometers to the west, the six helicopter Red Team (led by Capt. Corby Martin and Capt. Ben Pulsifer) also prepares to attack an Iraqi radar station. At 0238 (2338Z) CWO Tom "Tip" O'Neal launches a Hellfire missile at White Team's radar station firing the first shot of Operation Desert Storm. At 0241 14 USAF F-15E Eagle attack fighters (415th and 416th TFS), an EF-111A Raven radar buster and four Navy F-14 Tomcats race across the corridor created by the USAF Pave Low-Apache radar attack. At 0300 F-117A Stealth Fighters strike key command and communications targets in Baghdad. At 0302 F-15Es hit fixed Scud missile positions at the H-2 oil pumping stations near the Jordanian border destroying nine armed Scud missiles.

At 1000 an A-10 Warthog attacks the Iraqi 52nd Armored Brigade. A-10s of the 355th TFS (Capt. Rob Givens, Capt. Mark Roling) the 511th TFS (Lt. Col. Mike O'Connor and Maj. John Condon) and the 76th Tactical Fighter Squadron (Capt. Blas Miyares and 1st Lt. Dave Ferguson) are tasked with attacking Early Warning Ground Control Intercept sites and flying Battlefield Air Interdiction missions. Attacks continue throughout the day destroying 13 vehicles and killing approximately 15 soldiers. Doomed for threatening Gen. Frank's right flank if it existed in the future ground war, the 52nd will lose an average of 3-4 tanks per day under never-ending aerial attack. The unit is nicknamed by the Americans the "go-away brigade."

At 1830 A Battery, 1-27th Field Artillery (Capt. Jeff Lieb) destroys the Al-Abraq SA-2 surface-to-air missile position 30 kilometers inside Kuwait with its MLRS launcher. For the first time the U.S. Air Force has to clear a path for the high flying missiles. Staff Sergeant Ronnie Wint launches the first long-range precision tactical missile strike in history.

Maj. Gen. Ron Griffith, Commander of the 1st Armored Division has selected the "Desert Wedge" formation for his three fighting brigades (1st, 2nd and 3rd). His 4th Brigade consists of two battalions of Apache tank-killer helicopters. While the U.S. Marines and

Arab forces fix the Iraqis in place south of Kuwait, and the XVIII Airborne Corps feints in the direction of Bagdad the VII Corps with the 1st Armored Division as its spearpoint (the 2nd Brigade is the heaviest in the U.S. Army) will stab deeply north then east and crush Saddam Hussain's most elite forces, the Republican Guard.

Three U.S. Marines and one Navy corpsman (HM Clarence Dean Conner) are hit near the Kuwaiti border by Iraqi artillery. These are the first ground casualties of Operation Desert Storm. At Al Jubayl the 2nd Tank Battalion of the Marine 2nd Division completes offloading its equipment. This is the last of the division's units to arrive.

Due to the air war, ever increasing line-crossers surrender. It is eventually discovered that the 2nd Marine Division's area of operations is controlled by the 7th and 14th Iraqi Divisions of the Iraqi III Corps. These divisions are composed of, respectively, the 19th, 38th, 39th, and 116th Infantry Brigades; and the 14th, 18th, 56th, and 426th Infantry Brigades. Behind them in depth are the III Iraqi Corps operational reserves, the 3rd Armored Division (6th, 12th Armored Brigades and 8th Mechanized Brigade). Included are also the 20th Mechanized Brigade (III Corps operational reserves) and the 5th Iraqi Mechanized Division.

Between 0100 and 0200 the USS SAN JACINTO (CG-56) fires the first Tomahawk cruise missile of the war from its position on the Red Sea. The USS BUNKER HILL (CG-52) fires a Tomahawk moments later from the Persian Gulf. Of the 52 fired, 51 Tomahawks are successfully launched. The USN launch 116 Tomahawk Land Attack Missiles (TLAMS) against Iraq today, with LEFTWICH being the farthest northern shooter in the Persian Gulf.

Six U.S. Navy aircraft carriers launch 228 combat sorties on the first day of Operation Desert Storm. The Persian Gulf Battle Force is USS MIDWAY (CV-41), RANGER (CV-61), THEODORE R. ROOSEVELT (CV-71) carrier battle groups with Commander, Carrier Group (COMCARGRU 5,) on MIDWAY. Red Sea Battle Force is USS JOHN F. KENNEDY (CV-67), SARATOGA (CV-60) and AMERICA (CV-66) with COMCARGRU 2, R.Adm. Riley D. Mixson) on the JOHN F. KENNEDY. Four Navy F/A-18 Hornets of the USS SARATOGA attack an Iraqi airfield when two Iraqi MiG-21s were detected. Lt. Cdr. Mark Fox and Lt. Nick Mongillo of Fighter/Attack Squadron 81 participate in the only U.S. Navy air-to-air kills in the Operation Desert Storm. There will be 548 U.S. Navy aircraft carrier fixed wing and combat support sorties today.

At 0400 approximately 48 U.S. Marine F/A-18A and -C Hornets and Grumman A-6E Intruders begin the Marine Corps offensive action by conducting a coordinated night air strike against airfields and Scud missile sites at Tallil and Qurna, the An Nasiriyah power plant and the Shaibah Air Base. Attacks are flown by the Marine Aircraft Group 11. At dawn Marine Aircraft Group 13 (Forward) with aircraft from the King Abdul Aziz Naval Base strike additional targets. The 3rd Marine Aircraft Wing will fly 144 combat sorties over Iraq and Kuwait today.

Strength of the 3rd Marine Air Wing is 34 AH-1J/Ws, 30 UH-1Ns, 60 CH-46Es, 26 CH-53Ds, six RH-53Ds, 22 CH-53Es, 60 AV-8Bs, 20 A-6Es, 12 EA-6Bs, 72 FA-18A/Cs, five FA-18Ds, 15 KC-130F/R/Ts, eight OV-10A/Ds, and two UC-12Bs.

Just after 0300 Capt. Jon K. Kelk, callsign "Pennzoil 63" in F-15C 85-0125 of the 58th TFS/33rd TFW succeeds with the first kill of the war--a MiG-29 destroyed by an AIM-7 missile. Kill number 2 and 3 is by USAF Capt. Robert E. "Citgo 65" Graeter of the 58th

TFS/33rd TFW flying F-15C 85-0105. He destroys a Mirage F-1 with an AIM-7 with another Mirage F-1 flying into the ground. Kill Number 4 is by Captain Steve W. Tate ("Quaker 11") of the USAF 71st TFS, 1st TFW flying F-15C Eagle # 83-0017 who fires a Fox one (AIM-7 Sparrow, radar-guided missile) and destroys a Iraqi Mirage F1EQ. Aerial kill number 5 is Capt. Charles J. "Sly" Magill USMC ("Zerex 71") flying F-15C 85-0107 of the 58th TFS/33rd TFW who destroys a MiG-29 with an AIM-7. Kill number 6 is credited to Capt. Rhory R. 'Hoser' Draeger ("Zerex 73") flying F-15C 85-0108 of the 58th TFS/33rd TFW who destroys a MiG-29 with an AIM-7. Finally, Kill Number 7 and 8 are by Lt. Cdr. Mark I. "MRT" Fox USN VFA-81 flying F/A-18C 163508 from the USS SARATOGA who destroys two F-7A MiG-21s with AIM-9s.

Capt. John Whitney, 353rd TFS (Panthers) is the first A-10 Warthog pilot in Operation Desert Storm to experience battle damage. An Iraqi bullet cuts through the leading edge of Whitney's right wing severing a hydraulic line. Perhaps catastraphic in another plane, in the tough A-10 Warthog he lands safely.

A "gorilla package" of 22 F-15E Strike Eagles of the 4th TFW, supported by two radar-jamming EF-111s, hit fixed Scud sites at Al Qaim and H-2 (an Iraqi AB). AAA fire is unbelievable.

U.S. Marine Capt. Charles J. Magill flying as an exchange pilot with the U.S. Air Force 33rd Tactical Fighter Wing shoots down an Iraqi MiG-29. This is the only U.S. Marine air-to-air kill of the war.

Arriving: at Athens, Greece, a RC-135 of the 55th SRW; at Incirlik, two E-3s of the 552nd AWACW; at Diego Garcia, six B-52Gs; two U-2Rs of the 9th SRW at an unknown theater location; at Moron, Spain, two B-52Gs of the 416th BMW; at Incirlik, Turkey, four F-111Es of the 79th TFS, 20th TFW, three EC-130s, six EF-111As of the 42nd ECS, five F-15Cs of the 32nd TFG, 11 F-16s and 13 F-4Gs of the 23rd TFS, 52nd TFW.

B-52 sorties today number a total of 31 (16 AI, 15 OCA). From Moron, Spain, three B-52s led by Capt. Mark Medvec bomb a missile factory near Mosul with approximately 60 tons of explosive.

USAF F-111 Aardvark Strike Aircraft fly two Leadership (L), four Nuclear/Biological/Chemical (C), 24 Airfield (A) and eight Scud (SC) strikes for a total of 38 Precision Guided Munitions (PGM) strikes. Eight C, nine A, eight military support (MS), and four SC strikes are flown for a total of 29 nonPGM strikes.

Today USAF F-117A Nighthawk Stealth Fighters fly 24 Strategic Air Defense (SAD), eight C3/Telecommunications (CCC), 16 Leadership (L), four Nuclear/Biological/Chemical (C), and nine military support (MS), for a total of 61 strikes against Iraqi targets.

Advance parties of the British 1st Armoured Division leave for their concentration center northeast of Hafar Al Batin codenamed *Keyes*. Due to this, Maj. Glyn Ireland, Quartermaster of the Staffordshire Regiment, has claim to being the most forward Stafford present when the war begins.

British Wing Commander Ian Travers Smith, RAF, leads the first operational mission from Tabuk attacking a heavily defended Iraqi airfield. By the end of the war he has flown 20 operational sorties and earned the Distinguished Service Order. Wing Commander Jeremy John Witts, RAF, leads the first low level air attack against Mudaysis airfield. By the war's end he has led 13 raids and also earned the Distinguished Service Order.

Canadian fighter pilots Capt. Christopher Sponder of Cambridge, Ontario and Capt. Robert Beardsley of Red Deer, Alberta are flying an aircover mission over the northern Gulf when they are alerted of the war's beginning by flashes of Tomahawk missiles being launched. Canada contributes 26 CF-18 fighters and a Boeing 707 air-to-air refueling plane to support Desert Storm. There are 36 pilots in the "Desert Cats" and the top Canadian Army commander is Gen. John de Chastelain.

Canada flies a total of 36 sorties today.

Twelve French Jaguars attack the Ahmed Al Jaber airfield with 250 kg bombs from under 100 ft. Heavy antiaircraft fire is encountered from AAA SAMs and small arms. Two Jaguars are hit and diverted to Jubail rather than returning to Al Ahsa. The French commander at Al Ahsa is Col. Marc Amberg.

Air sorties today number: USAF-1381, USN-415, USMC-169, Allied-423.

Six coalition aircraft are hit today, three destroyed. A A-4KU of the Kuwaiti Air Force is struck by antiaircraft fire just over the Kuwaiti-Iraqi border; a French Jaguar A is hit by SA-7s as it attacks Al Jaber (three struck but it is later repaired); and F/A-18C 163484 from the USS SARATOGA is shot down (Navy Lt. Cdr. Michael Scot 'Spike' Speicher of Strike Fighter Squadron 81 of Jacksonville, Florida). Speicherof is killed and if this F/A-18 Hornet was not hit by a surface-to-air missile it may the only air-to-air loss of the war. A-6E 158539 (AA 502) of VA-35, is damaged and later repaired; British Tornado GR.Mk1 ZD791/BG, No.15 Squadron flown by Flight Lieutenants John Peters, 28, and Adrian 'John' Nichol, 27, is shot down, both becoming POWs. Italian Tornado MM7074, of 50 Stormo/155 Gruppo flown by Flight Captain Mario Bichirloni is shot down with Bichirloni also becoming a POW--the only Italian POW of the war.

Total Saudi Arabia air sorties today number 181.

Total Kuwaiti sorties today number 24 air interdiction.

Four Iraqi MiG-29s, two MiG-21s, two Mirage F-1s and one MiG-25 are shot down. A Mirage F-1 unable to complete a turn flies into the ground. The Coalition achieves air superiority.

The Iraqi Army greatly increases its electronic warfare activity. This continues for the next three weeks.

Iraq flies 54 combat air patrols.

18 January The first Iraqi Scud missile impacts in Israel, injuring 12 civilians. U.S. Air Force F-15s scramble to bomb the launching sites.

Coalition forces must fight Iraq during Operation Desert Storm in the worst weather in at least 14 years. Approximately 15 percent of scheduled sorties during the first 10 days of the war are canceled due to poor visibility or low overcast sky conditions. During the ground war's last days, cloud ceilings of 5,000 to 7,000 feet will be common. Today, a frontal system moves into Iraq causing a F-16 strike against the At-Taji Rocket Production Facility north of Baghad to be diverted to the Ar-Rumaylah airfield.

Task Force 2-34th Armor, 1st Infantry Division conducts its first mounted rehearsal, concentrating on clearing enemy trenches quickly and with minimum casualties. On G-Day the 1st Infantry Division will mass 241 tanks and 100 Bradley Fighting vehicles on a frontage of 6 kilometers. As they assault, they will use tank plows and armored combat earth movers to crush the enemy and collapse his fortifications.

The 5th Battalion, 11th Marines, 1st Marine Division (commanded by Lt. Col. James L. Sachtleben) moves from its position 30 kilometers south of Safaniya, Saudi Arabia, to the area of Al Qaraah to conduct an artillery raid.

USS NICHOLAS (FFG-47) and a Kuwaiti patrol boat force Iraqis to abandon eleven oil platforms. The Iraqis have fired several small surface-to-air missiles from the platforms. Five Iraqis are killed and 23 prisoners of war are captured and taken aboard the NICHOLAS.

The U.S. nuclear submarine LOUISVILLE (SSN-724) is operating in the Red Sea. Submarines NEWPORT NEWS (SSN-750), PHILADELPHIA (SSN-690) and PITTSBURGH (SSN-720) are operating in the Mediterranean Sea. USS HALYBURTON (FFG-40) commanded by Cdr. Robert M. Hartling), and VREELAND (FF-1068) commanded by Cdr. Randall R. Brown begins participation in Operation Desert Storm.

U.S. Navy combat forces YANKEE (TF-155) in the Red Sea and ZULU (TF-154) in the Persian Gulf strike Iraqi targets with Tomahawk cruise missiles.

U.S. Navy air unit HSL-44 (DET 6) begins participation in Operation Desert Storm.

Eight Coalition aircraft are destroyed today (two A-6Es, one F-15E, one OV-10 Bronco and four Tornados). The U.S. has lost four aircraft, and counts five personnel as missing in action. U.S. Marine pilot Lt. Col. Clifford Acree, 39, of Oceanside, California and aerial observer Warrant Officer 4 Guy Hunter of VMO-2, Camp Pendleton, California are shot down by a SAM (the first of five U.S. Marine aviator POWs of the war). U.S. Navy Lt. Jeffrey N. Zaun, 28, and Lt. Robert Wetzel, 30, are shot down in their A-6E Intruder and captured. Lt. William T. Costen, 27, St. Louis, Missouri and Lt. Charles J. Turner, 29, Richfield, Minnesota of the USS RANGER are listed as killed in action after their A-6E Intruder is shot down. An F-15E flown by Majors Thomas F. Koritz, 39, of Rochelle, Illinois (pilot) and Donnie R. Holland, 42, of Bastrop, Louisiana (WSO) of the 4th TFW(P)/4th TFW are killed in action.

USCentCom sorties today are: USAF-1529, USN-233, USMC-122, Allied-316.

U.S. carriers launch 435 fixed-wing combat and combat support sorties today.

A 16-ship package of F-15E Strike Eagles hit Basrah (bridges, fuel storage tanks and an electric power plant). They are led by Capt. Mark "Chairman" Mouw who with Capt. Tom "Radar" O'Reilly planned the raid. Maj. Donnie Holland and Maj. Tom Koritz are killed.

At Incirlik, 24 USAF F-16s of the 612th TFS, 401st TFW arrive.

F-111s fly four C, 14 A, and one SC PGM strikes for total of 19. They fly 12 SAD, three C, for a total of 15 NonPGM strikes.

USAF F-117s fly 15 SAD, eight CCC, five L, three C, three MS, three Railroad/bridges (RR), and five Scud (SC) missions for a total of 40 strikes.

B-52 sorties today total 30 (27 AI, 3 OCA).

A British Tornado is shot down flown by Flight Lieutenant John Peters and his crewman Flight Lieutenant Adrian Nichol. Tornado GR.Mk1 ZA392/EK, No.15 Squadron flown by Wing Commander Nigel Elsdon, 39, (pilot) and Flight Lieutenant Robert 'Max' Collier, 42, is shot down by a SAM. Both men are killed with WC Elsdon the most senior Coalition officer killed in the Operation Desert Storm.

Twelve French Jaguars attack the Ras Al Qualayah munitions storage facility on Kuwait's east coast.

The U.S. Air Force begins flying strike missions from Incirlik, Turkey against northern Iraq (fifty to sixty strikes per day, each in three waves, until the war's end).

Canada flies a total of 28 air sorties today.

Italian Tornados fly a total of eight air interdiction sorties today for a total of eight air sorties.

Total Saudi Arabian air sorties today number 108.

Total Kuwaiti air sorties today number eight air interdiction.

The Iraqi Army has massed five armored divisions--more than one thousand tanks--near the Wadi al-Batin in Southern Kuwait since the air war has begun.

19 January President George Bush authorizes a National Guard/Reserves call-up extension for two years (1 million men).

U.S. Navy nuclear submarine USS LOUISVILLE (SSN-724) launches the first submarine-launched Tomahawk cruise missile in military history. The submarine is submerged in the Red Sea and will fire three more TLAMs before being relieved by the USS CHICAGO (SSN-721) 6 February. Launching the TLAM today is the first combat of a U.S. submarine since World War II.

U.S. Navy combat forces YANKEE (TF-155) in the Red Sea and ZULU (TF-154) in the Persian Gulf launch Tomahawk cruise missiles. By the war's end the following U.S. ships will launch at least one of the four types of Tomahawks in the Navy's inventory ((TLAM-N, TLAM-C, TLAM-DTASM): USS WISCONSIN, MISSOURI, VIRGINIA, MISSISSIPPI, BUNKER HILL, MOBILE BAY, LEYTE GULF, SAN JACINTO, PHILIPPINE SEA, PRINCETON, NORMANDY, SPRUANCE, CARON, DAVID R. RAY, PAUL F. FOSTER, and FIFE.

For the first time in history, U.S. Navy A-6s and A-7s launch a standoff land attack missile against Iraq. U.S. carriers launch a total of 341 sorties today.

Kill Number 9 is accomplished by Capt. Richard C. Tollini ("Citgo 21") flying F-15C 85-0101 (58th TFS/33rd TFW) when he destroys a MiG-25 with a AIM-7. Kill Number 10 is by Capt. Lawrence E. "Cherry" Pitts ("Citgo 22") flying F-15C 85-0099 (33rd TFW) shooting down a MiG-25 with an AIM-7. Kill Number 11 is by Capt. Cesar A. "Rico" Rodriguez ("Chevron 25") flying F-15C 85-0114 destroying a MiG-29 as it attempts to evade him and flies into the ground. Kill Number 12 is by Capt. Craig W. Underhill ("Chevron 26") flying F-15C 85-0122 (58th TFS/33rd TFW) destroys a MiG-29 with an AIM-7. Kill Number 13 is Capt. David S. Prather ("Rambo 03") flying F-15C 79-0069 (525th TFS/36th TFW) destroying a Mirage F1EQ with an AIM-7. Kill Number 14 is by Lt. David G. Sveden ("Rambo 04") flying F-15C 79-0021, (32nd TFS/32nd TFG), destroying a Mirage F1EQ with an AIM-7.

Seven additional B-52s of the 379th BMW arrive in theater at a classified location.

B-52 sorties today total 32.

F-111s fly three SAD, one C, five A, one MS, two SC for a total of 12 PGM strikes. They fly four SAD, one A, two MS, four SC, four E, and four O for 19 NonPGM strikes.

F-117s fly six SAD, five CCC, seven L, four C, one MS, two RR, and one SC mission for a total of 26 strikes.

The main body of the British Stafford Regiment moves to the 1st Armoured Division concentration area 60 kilometres from the border (codenamed *Keyes*). The area is an old Egyptian position which had been dug-in. Defensive positions are prepared utilizing the old positions as much as possible. Armor of the Warrior tanks continue to be upgraded by bolting on Chobham armor.

Flying Officer Malcolm David Rainer, RAF, attacks two surface-to-air missile sites while part of an eight aircraft formation. Coming under intense anti-aircraft fire he scores a direct hit on the missile site. During the war he will fly 27 missions and with Squadron Leader Nigel Leslie Risdale and Flight Lieutenant Brian Geoffrey Marcel Robinson, RAF, earn the Distinguished Flying Cross.

Canada flies a total of 31 air sorties today.

French Jaguars again attack the munitions storage facility at Ras Al Qulayah.

F-4G 'Wild Weasel' 69-7571, 81st TFS/52nd TFW flown by Capt. Tim Burke crashes (shot down?) over Saudi Arabia.

U.S. Central Command sorties today are: USAF-1275, USN-178, USMC-(fixed wing) 108, Allied-302.

Exercise *Sea Soldier IV* begins in Oman.

Total Saudi Arabian air sorties today number 131.

Total Kuwaiti sorties today number 20 air interdiction.

The 50th Armored Brigade, 12th Iraqi Armored Division, Jihad Corps, is attacked for the first time. It is commanded by Col. Mohammed Ashad.

Two Iraqi Mirage F-1s, a MiG-25 and a MiG-29 are shot down. A MiG-29 crashes on take-off (other records record 6 Iraqi aircraft shot down today).

20 January "Phase Bravo" the massive movement of U.S. troops, supplies, equipment, fuel, tanks and armored vehicles begins. For the next month, twenty-four hours a day, seven days a week, the movement continues. U.S. service personnel study their small booklets entitled *Identifying the Iraqi Threat* and *How They Fight.*

A and B Batteries of 2-7th Patriot, 11th Air Defense Artillery (Col. Joseph Garrett) destroy three of four Scud missiles launched at Dhahran. Israel quickly requests the Patriot missile defense system and the 10th Air Defense Brigade (Col. David Heebner) from Darmstadt, Germany, sets up air defense batteries within 27 hours.

U.S. Navy combat forces YANKEE (TF-155) in the Red Sea and ZULU (TF-154) in the Persian Gulf launch 34 Tomahawk cruise missiles. Nine oil platforms are attacked and neutralized by the U.S. Navy at Dorra. USS LEYTE GULF (CG-55) enters the Persian Gulf.

U.S. carriers today launch a total of 363 sorties.

U.S. Air Force A-10s and U.S. Navy A-6s destroy an Iraqi artillery battery.

F-111s fly four A PGM strikes. They fly four SAD, six C, 15 A, six MS for a total of 31 NonPGM strikes.

F-117s fly six SAD, four SAM, two CCC, one L, five C, seven MS, and three SC strikes for a total of 28.

B-52 sorties today total 27 all air interdiction (AI).

British SAS commandos of the 250-man 22nd SAS Regiment (Col. Andrew Massey) enter Iraq for the first time from their headquarters at Al Jouf. They travel by foot and Land-Rover and will ambush road patrols, cut communications, create diversions, and hunt Scud missiles. The Scud search concentrates in the southern 'Scud Box' along the Amman-Baghdad highway. By the war's end four of the unit's members will die and five will be captured.

Seven coalition aircraft are lost today. Two are noncombat losses (Tornado GR.Mk1 ZD893/AG, No. 20 Squadron flown by Squadron Leader Peter Batson and Wing Commander Mike Heath ejecting safely, and a UH-60 crashing killing Staff Sergeant Galand V. Haily). Two F-16s, a F-15E, a Tornado, and an A-6E are damaged or destroyed by enemy fire. F-16C 87-0257, 614th TFS/401st TFW(TJ) flown by Capt. Harry M. 'Mike' Roberts, 30, of Savannah, Georgia becomes a POW. Also, an F-16 flown by Jeffrey Scott Tice, and an F-15E 88-1692, 4th TFW(P) flown by Col. David W. Eberly, and Maj. Thomas E. Griffith, Jr., become POWs. An A-6E Intruder is extensively damaged but lands safely onboard its aircraft carrier.

Coalition sorties surpass 7,000.

The United States counts 11 personnel missing in action and eight aircraft lost by this date.

British Royal Air Force using JP-233 runway denial munitions have closed eight Iraqi airfields since the beginning of the air war. Tornado GR.Mk 1 ZA396 flown by Flight Lieutenant David Waddington, 24, (pilot) and Flight Lieutenant Robert Stewart, 44, (navigator) is shot down on a mission attacking the Tallil Airfield. Waddington and Stewart become POWs.

Poor weather grounds the French Jaguars today.

U.S. Central Command sorties number: USAF-1223, USN-1001, USMC-(fixed-wing)-517, Allied-1387. Over 1,000 HARM missiles have been fired at Iraqi SAM targets.

Canada flies a total of 14 air sorties today.

Italian Tornados fly a total of four air interdiction sorties today, for a total of four sorties.

Total Saudi Arabian air sorties today number 118.

Total Kuwaiti air sorties today number 12 air interdiction.

21 January Iraqi Scud launch sites and troop concentrations are the focus of Coalition air operations. The United States warns Iraq that it will be held accountable for the mistreatment of U.S. prisoners of war after it announces that POWs will be used as "human shields" at strategic targets. Five Americans, two Britons, an Italian and a Kuwaiti POW are displayed on Baghdad TV.

The USS THEODORE ROOSEVELT Carrier Battle Group arrives in the Persian Gulf. U.S. carriers today launch 327 sorties. Responsibility for antisurface warfare (ASUW) shifts to COMCARGRU 7, V.Adm. Ronald Zlatopter on the USS RANGER from Commander Destroyer Squadron 15 (COMDESRON 15) on the USS MIDWAY. He had appointed subordinate ASUW commanders (northern Persian Gulf=COMDESRON 35 on USS LEFTWICH (DD-984); South/Central Persian Gulf=Commanding Officer, USS WISCONSIN (BB-64); Underway replenishment area and Coalition combat logistics ships= Canadian Naval Commander). Command structure and operating area is now: Northern Persian Gulf=COMDESRON 7 on the USS PAUL F. FOSTER (DD-964); South/Central Persian Gulf=Commanding Officer of USS RANGER; Underway Replenishment Area=Canadian Naval Force Commander (Commo. Kenneth Summers).

Objectives for Antisurface Warfare (ASUW) is: *1) Destroy all Iraqi surface combatants and minelayers, 2) Deny Iraq the use of oil platforms for military purposes, 3) Move back Iraqi surface forces in the northern Persian Gulf from south to north; and 4) Prevent attacks or threats against Coalition forces and countries in the Gulf.*

F-14A 161430 (AA 212), VF-103, CV-60, is shot down over Wadi Amif. U.S. Navy Radar Intercept Officer Lt. Lawrence R. Slade is captured by the Iraqis (the last of three U.S. Navy

POWs in the war). Slade's pilot Lt. Devon Jones is later rescued by U.S. Air Force search and rescue (Super Jolly Green piloted by Capt. Tom Trask and A-10s of the 353rd TFS flown by Captains Paul Johnson and Randy Goff). One AH-64 is lost by accident. After the war Capt. Johnson was awarded the Air Force Cross (one of only two earned during the war) and Capt. Goff is awarded the Distinguished Flying Cross.

Coalition sorties number 8,000 by this date.

For the second day weather prevents French Jaguars from flying.

U.S. Central Command sorties count is: USAF-1394, USN-240, USMC-(fixed Wing)-213, Allied-246.

F-111s fly one SAD, three A, eight MS, and four SC strikes for a total of 16 PGM strikes. They fly 18 SAD, six CCC, seven A, NonPGM strikes for a total of 31.

F-117s fly nine SAD, four CCC, nine L, 11 C, and one airfield (A) strikes and a total of 34 strikes.

B-52 sorties total 37, all AI.

Coalition troop strength is 6,000 Bangladesh, 1,700 Canadian, 200 Czechoslovakia, 35,000 Egyptian, 10,000 French, 3,000 Gulf Cooperation Council, 200 Honduras, 100 Hungarian medics, 7,000 Kuwaiti, 2,000 Moroccan, 500 Nigerian, 5,000 Pakistani, 45,000 Saudi, 500 Senegal, 20,000 Syrian, 100,000 Turkey (positioned at Iraqi border), 35,000 British, 450,000 U.S., for a total of 721,000 troops.

Coalition ship strength today is: two Argentina, three Australia, six Belgium, three Canadian, one Denmark, 14 French, five Germany, one Greek, ten Italian, three Netherlands, one Norway, one Poland, one Portugal, four Spain, two Turkey, 100 U.S., 18 British, four USSR for a 179 total.

Canada flies a total of 14 air sorties today.

Total Saudi Arabian air sorties today number 122.

Total Kuwaiti air sorties today number eight air interdiction.

Iraq flies less than 25 sorties today.

22 January An Iraqi Scud missile hits Ramat Gan, Israel and kills two citizens. Oil tank fires are started by the Iraqis at Mina Abdullah, Ash Shuaiba, and Wafra, Kuwait.

The U.S. Army 82nd and 101st Airborne Divisions begin to be flown by C-130s to their attack positions near Rafha. The first elements of the 82nd Airborne arrive at Tactical Assembly Area (TAA) Hawk. The troopers dig in and attempt to acquaint themselves with the nearly continuous noise of aircraft. Up to ten times per day they assume an increased protective posture against chemical (NBC) attack. The Iraqi border to their north is defended by border posts manned by platoon-sized units.

The U.S. Army 1st Armored Division closes in theater.

A major I Marine Expeditionary Force sand-table exercise is held. Maj. Gen. William M. Keyes, Commanding General, 2nd Marine Division realizes that the area of the attack is not large enough for the 1st and 2nd Marine Divisions to maneuver, thus taking too much time to breach the Iraqi defenses and presenting too great a target. Lt. Gen. Walter E. Boomer, Marine Expeditionary Force Commander is to be consulted to agree to a separate breach.

U.S. Air Force special operations rescue forces recover one U.S. Navy crew member of a F-14 shot down 21 January (Lt. Devon Jones, USN).

U.S. Central Command sorties: USAF-1362, USN-189, USMC(fixed Wing)-149, Allied-282.

U.S. carriers today launch 354 sorties. Combat Logistic Force ships are divided into two task forces: Task Force 73 ships service the Persian Gulf and Indian Ocean and Task Force 63 service the Mediterranean and Red Sea.

On one of its 14-hour missions a E-8A JSTARS (Col. George Muellner) vectors two A-10s and an AC-130 gunship onto an Iraqi 71 vehicle convoy. 58 of the enemy vehicles are destroyed and an Iraqi armored division assembly area is detected.

F-111s fly one SAD, three CCC, 20 A, for a total of 24 PGM strikes. They fly two CCC, one L, five A, eight MS for a total of 16 NonPGM strikes.

F-117s fly four L, 24 A, five MS, seven RR, one electricity (E) for a total 41 total strikes.

B-52 sorties total 40 (36 AI and 4 OCA).

Spanish ships VICTORIA (Captain of Frigates Gonzalez Aller Suevos), VENCEDORA (Captain of Corvettes Nieto Manso) and INFANTA ELENA (Captain of Corvettes Perez Perez) begin participation in Operation Desert Storm.

German ships PADERBORN (M-1076) commanded by Cdr. Thoner, and SCHLESWIG (M-1073) commanded by Cdr. Heise begin participation in Operation Desert Storm.

RAF Tornado GR.Mk1 ZA467/FF, No. 16 Squadron flown by Squadron Leader Gary Lennox, 34, (pilot) and Squadron Leader Kevin Weeks, 37, is shot down while attacking the H-2 airfield--both flyers are killed. One AH-1 Cobra is a noncombat loss with the crew safe and an AV-8B crashes killing 1st Lt. Manuel Rivera, Jr., 31, of Bronx, NY.

British SAS Special Forces blow up a communications network cable that reached from Baghdad to Iraq's forward areas. At 2100 "Bravo Two Zero," an eight-man squad commanded by Sgt. Andy McNab is inserted by helicopter southwest of Al-Haqlaniyah, Iraq, to hunt Scud missiles.

Six French Jaguars attack a Kuwaiti naval base. They fire six AS 30Ls at three Iraqi ships.

Alpha jets of Qatar's 300-man, 24-Mirage F1EDA 7 Squadron make their first attack against Iraqi ground troops with their AM-39 air-to-ground missiles.

Canada flies a total of 28 air sorties today.

Italy flies a total of eight air sorties today.

Total Saudi Arabian air sorties today number 120.

The Kuwait Air Force does not fly today.

Four Iraqi ships (a T-43 and three patrol boats) are attacked by four A-6E Intruders and U.S. ships. By this date in excess of 10,000 Coalition sorties have been flown against Iraq.

23 January The elite 1-325, 82nd Airborne Scout platoon (SSG Al Akers, SPC William McIluride, PFC Everett Hayhurst, Sgt. Jeffrey Koenig, SPC David Cardenas, and SPC Jimmy Bullock) nightly recons the Iraqi positions at Objective Falcon. With many meeting engagements this is the most dangerous part of the war for the task force.

5th Battalion, 11th Marines, 1st Marine Division conduct an artillery raid on the police post at Qalamat al Manaqish, Kuwait. The raid is to deceive and disrupt the Iraqi forces on the Saudi-Kuwaiti border. Three vehicles are destroyed and two flee. One Iraqi drives into Marine machine gun fire. In the following weeks four raids will be conducted. The unit is commanded by Lt. Col. James L. Sachtleben, USMC.

USS HAMMOND (FF-1067) and VULCAN (AR-5) begins participation in Operation Desert Storm.

U.S. Central Command sorties: USAF-1679, USN-238, USMC (fixed-wing)-216, Allied-291.

U.S. carriers today launch 346 sorties (combat and support).

The airwar shifts from attacking Iraqi runways to destroying hardened aircraft shelters. For the next two weeks F-111Fs target approximately 60 percent of their missions on these shelters.

F-111s fly 19 A PGM strikes. They fly 12 A NonPGM strikes.

F-117s fly ten CCC, six RR and one SC mission for a total of 17 strikes today.

B-52 sorties total 41 (27 AI, 14 OCA).

Four coalition aircraft are lost today. A F-16 is shot down over Kuwait, a AV-8B is lost while training and an AH-64 is a noncombat loss. The U.S. Air Force pilot is rescued by Helicopter Anti-Sub Squadron (Light) 44 embarked on the USS NICHOLAS. Tornado GR.Mk1 ZA403/CO, No. 17 Squadron flown by Flying Officer Simon Burges, 23, (pilot) and Squadron Leader Robert Ankerson, 40, (navigator) is lost with both flyers becoming POWs.

B-52s, F-111s, and F-15Es attempt to kill Saddam Hussein. His location is plotted in a railyard bunker northwest of Basrah (Source: *Strike Eagle: Flying the F-15E in the Gulf War*).

Using 250-kg. bombs, artillery sites in Kuwait are hit by eight French Jaguars.

Three Iraqi ships (a AL QADDISIYAH-Class-tanker, a hovercraft and a Zhuk) are attacked by A-6Es. The WINCHESTER-Class hovercraft and Zhuk patrol boat are sunk and the tanker is disabled. At least three Iraqis are killed.

Saudi Arabia announces that one of their nine AL SIDDIQ-Class fast attack craft assisted in sinking an Iraqi minelayer. Their MSC-322-Class coastal minesweepers ADDIRYAH (412), AL QUYSUMAH (414), AL WADEEAH (416) and SAFWA (418) are active.

Canada flies a total of 28 air sorties today.

Italy Tornados today fly a total of nine air sorties.

Total Saudi Arabian air sorties today number 133.

Total Kuwaiti air sorties today number 12 air interdiction.

Total Qatar air sorties today number four air interdiction.

24 January Scud hunting diverts 40 percent of all air sorties. Air refueling tankers are allowed for the first time over Iraqi airspace. Due to this capability, Stealth fighters are able to strike hardened shelters at Kirkuk and Qayyara West airfields north of Baghdad, where many Iraqi aircraft are hiding from the heavy air attacks in the south. A key mission for F-117s becomes destroying Iraqi aircraft before they can flee to Iran.

Near Qurah Island a helicopter from the USS CURTS (FFG-38) rescues 22 Iraqis while under attack. Returning the enemy fire the U.S. Navy helicopter kills three Iraqis which results in 29 more surrendering. A helicopter from USS LEFTWICH (DD-984) carries ten SEALs joining the chopper from CURTS carrying seven SEALs that are taking the 51 enemy prisoners of war into custody. A SEAL Platoon of Naval Special Warfare Group 1 guards the prisoners. Eight SEALs embarked on NICHOLAS also participate. Qurah Island becomes the first liberated Kuwaiti territory.

U.S. Marine 4th, 5th MEB and 13th MEU on ships of Amphibious Task Groups 2 and 3 are conducting amphibious exercise Operation *Sea Soldier IV*. This is the *largest amphibious force assembled since the Korean War Inchon Landing*.

USS HORNE (CG-30) commanded by Capt. Thomas J. Barnett, JARRETT (FFG-33) commanded by Cdr. William L. Snyder, and PASSUMPSIC (TAO-107) begin participation in Operation Desert Storm.

U.S. Central Command sorties: USAF-1741, USN-455, USMC (fixed-wing)-278, Allied-337.

U.S. carriers today launch 434 sorties (combat and support). An F/A-18 of the USS THEODORE ROOSEVELT (CVN-71) is a non-combat loss.

F-111s fly 31 A, and four RR for a total of 35 PGM strikes. They fly 13 SAD, four CCC, five A, for a total of 22 NonPGM strikes.

F-117s fly one SAD, one L, 18 A, 14 RR, and eight SC strikes for a total of 42.

B-52 sorties total 35 (21 AI, 13 OCA, and an unknown).

A Tornado of 617 Squadron, RAF is shot down attacking Al Basrah. By this date 15,000 Coalition sorties have been flown (8,000 combat and 7,000 support). There have have been 220 Tomahawk cruise missiles launched.

French Jaguars fly their first mission into Iraq hitting gun and artillery positions. The French air base at Al Ahsa (in Eastern Saudi Arabia, south of Dhahran) has a total strength of 27 Jaguars, 12 Mirage 2000 air-superiority aircraft and four Dassault Mirage F1CR combat/reconnaissance aircraft. Approximately 1,200-1,300 French Air Force personnel are stationed at the base. The base commander is Col. Marc Amberg.

Canada flies a total 20 air sorties.

Total Saudi Arabian air sorties today number 132.

Total Kuwaiti air sorties today number 19 air interdiction.

Two Iraqi Mirage F-1EQs are shot down over the Persian Gulf by a Saudi F-15C (Capt. Ayedh al-Shamrani) of No. 13 Squadron, Royal Saudi Air Force. This is the only known offensive air strike against the Coalition during the Operation Desert Storm and is probably aimed at Coalition ships. Capt. Ayedh al-Shamrani becomes a national hero for Kills Numbers 15 and 16.

Four Iraqi ships are sunk (a Zhuk patrol boat, two minelayers and a minesweeper). While attacking the Umm Qasr Naval Base four Iraqi ships are attacked by A-6Es and F/A-18s. U.S. ships have located and destroyed 25 mines by this date.

Saudi Arabia claims sinking an Iraqi minelayer.

25 January An Iraqi Scud hits Tel Aviv killing one Israeli. During the war 40 Scuds are fired at Israel killing four civilians. During hostilities 289 Israelis were wounded and 11,727 apartments were damaged or destroyed.

"An act of environmental terrorism", Iraq begins releasing millions of barrels of oil into the Persian Gulf from the Kuwait's Sea Island oil tanker terminal. Five Iraqi tankers at Mina al Ahmadi, Kuwait, are also drained of oil attempting to foul Saudi Arabia's desalinization plants. The spill is approximately 20 miles long, 3 miles wide and 3 feet deep.

U.S. Central Command sorties: USAF-1526, USN-396, USMC (fixed-wing)-138, Allied-347.

U. S. carriers launch 395 combat and support sorties today.

By this date 17,500 Coalition sorties have flown. Today, a record 2,700 are flown.

F-111s fly 14 A PGM strikes. They fly eight RR and four classified NonPGM strikes for a total of 12.

F-117s fly one SAD, one CCC, seven A, seven RR, and 15 SC strikes for a total of 31.

B-52 sorties total 42 (34 AI, 8 OCA).

American now have 482,000 troops in the Middle East.

NATO's Standing Naval Force Channel is deployed to the central Mediterranean. The force includes: mine-hunting vessels from Germany, Belgium, England, Norway and Dutch ALKMAAR-Class minehunters HrMs ALKMAAR (M-850) and HrMs ZIERIKZEE (M-862).

Near the Sea Island oil terminal a minelayer is hit by U.S. ships. It ignites a portion of the oil terminal and the surrounding water on fire.

Canada flies 22 air sorties today.

Total Saudi Arabian air sorties today number 143.

Total Kuwaiti air sorties today number six air interdiction.

26 January U.S. Army's 1st Infantry Division closes in theater.

Due to mechanical problems, a F/A-18C Hornet is lost to the U.S. Navy, but the pilot is recovered safely. The air campaign's sorties now pass 20,000. *Air missions begin to focus on preparation of the battlefield, with targets ranging from military storage facilities to Republican Guard troop fortifications.*

The Sea Island oil slick is eight miles wide, contains approximately 120 million gallons, and extends 31 miles into the Persian Gulf. A special team of the U.S. Coast Guard, Environmental Protection Agency, and National Oceanographic and Atmosphere Administration personnel is sent to Saudi Arabia to assist the Saudis.

USS FORD (FFG-54) begins participation in Operation Desert Storm.

Three Iraqi MiG-23s are shot down by F-15Cs of the USAF 33rd Tactical Fighter Wing using AIM-7 missiles (Capt. Anthony E. 'Kimo' Schiavi ("Citgo 26") flying 85-0104, and the second kill of Capt. Rhory R. 'Hoser' Draeger ("Citgo 25") flying 85-0119. Draeger records kills number 17 and 19. At least 12 MiG-29s, F-1s and 12 transport aircraft have landed in Iran, fleeing the Coalition anti-aircraft shelter campaign. They have been prevented from maintaining their air forces as a strategic reserve as they had in the Iran-Iraq War.

U.S. Central Command sorties: USAF-1635, USN-403, USMC (fixed-wing)-266, Allied-368.

U.S. carriers launch 306 sorties (combat and support) today. An A-7E #158830 of VA-72 hits the barricade and is pushed over the side.

F-111s fly 18 A, four SC, two O, and two Republican Guard (RG/GOB) PGM strikes. They fly eight NonPGM strikes.

F-117s fly three SAD, four C, 26 A, one MS, one classified and 14 SC for a total of 49.

B-52 sorties today total 37 (33 AI, 4 OCA).

A battery of 155mm howitzers fire the largest artillery bombardment of the war to date. The United States Marines attack Iraqi troops six miles within Kuwait with their howitzer's fire.

The U.S. Army's UAV platoon arrives in theater.

Canada flies 24 air sorties today.

French aerial sorties today number four (two air interdiction, two training).

Total Saudi Arabian air sorties today number 161.

Total Kuwaiti air sorties today number 19 air interdiction.

Two Iraqi vessels (a patrol boat and a TNC-45) are left burning in a Kuwait harbor by A-6Es.

By this date there are 110 enemy prisoners of war (EPWs).

27 January U.S. Patriot missiles are fired to intercept six Iraqi Scud missiles targeted at Saudi Arabia.

Operation Desert Storm is the first war in history that makes comprehensive use of space systems support. Systems that aid Coalition forces are: Defense Meteorological Satellite Program (DMSP) weather satellites; US LANDSAT multi-spectral imagery satellites; Global Positioning System (GPS); Defense Support Program (DSP) early warning satellites; Tactical Information Broadcast Service and communications satellites.

The 2nd Marine Division conducts an artillery raid against Iraqi positions (a logistics site and truck park). This is the division's first offensive operation against Iraq and is primarily to measure Iraqi reactions.

As part of Operation *Sea Soldier IV* a rehearsal of an amphibious assault is conducted in Oman.

Attempting to stop the oilspill, U.S. Air Force F-111s attack manifold pipelines with GBU-15 laser-guided bombs which feed the Sea Island terminal. The oil slick is now 35 miles long and 10 miles wide.

U.S. Central Command sorties: USAF-1471, USN-502, USMC (fixed-wing)-169, Allied-331.

U.S. carriers launch 382 sorties today (combat and support).

A U-2R of the 9th SRW arrives at a classified location.

F-111s fly 44 A, three SC PGM strikes for a total of 47. They fly four SAD, six CCC, 11

A, for a total of NonPGM strikes.

F-117s fly two SAD, two CCC, three L, ten C, 28 A, nine MS, five RR, four SC for a total of 63 strikes.

B-52 sorties today total 36 (all AI).

By this date the total Iraqi naval losses reported by Central Command are: five patrol boats, four mining vessels, six unknown vessels, one hovercraft, one tanker, and one oil platform service ship.

Two Iraqi MiG-23s and two Mirage F-1s are shot down by two F-15Cs of the USAF 53rd Tactical Fighter Squadron, 36th TFW. The two MiG-23s are destroyed by Capt. Jay T. Denny "Opec 01" flying 84-0025 firing AIM-9s. A MiG-23 and Mirage F1EQ are destroyed by Capt. Benjamin D. Powell "Opec 02" flying 84-0027. Capt. Denny records Kills Numbers 20 and 21 and Capt. Powell killing numbers 22 and 23. Within the last 24 hours 23 Iraqi aircraft have fled to Iran. Iran announces that any warplanes landing within its borders will be confiscated (thus preserving the country's neutrality). *Coalition air supremacy is now achieved.*

An Iraqi ship is sunk by A-6Es.

Canada flies 20 air sorties today.

Italy today flies a total of seven air sorties.

Total Saudi Arabian air sorties today number 155.

Total Kuwaiti air sorties today number 12 air interdiction.

28 January The Sea Island oil terminal slick seems to stop flowing. It is estimated to now contain 460 million gallons of oil.

United States ground forces continue to receive weak artillery fire from across the Kuwaiti border. Counterbattery missions are fired to wipe out the sporadic fire.

U.S. Special Operations Forces commander Gen. Wayne Downing is briefed in Riyadh by SAS commanders about the Iraqi theatre and British special operations.

U.S. Central Command sorties: USAF-1670, USN-300, USMC (fixed-wing)-223, Allied-430.

U.S. carriers launch 452 sorties today (combat and support).

USS SAMUEL B. ROBERTS (FFG-58) in the North Red Sea finds 160 railroad cars on the German-flagged freighter RED SEA ENERGY that are inaccessible. En route from Greece to Aqaba, Jordan, the freighter is diverted.

Capt. Donald S. Watrous ("Bite 04") flying F-15C 79-0022, 53rd TFS/36th TFW shoots down a MiG-23 for Kill Number 24.

F-111s fly five CCC, 20 A, four MS, seven RR, and two SC PGM strikes for a total of 38. They fly three A, three MS, two RR, and a RG/GOB for a total of nine NonPGM strikes.

F-117s fly four CCC, four L, 14 C, three A, 13 MS, five RR, two SC three Republican Guard (RG) for a total of 48.

B-52 sorties today total 36 (all AI).

Lt. Gen. Billiere meets with RAF personnel at Dhahran. The RAF flies two Buccaneer training sorties today for a total of two sorties.

After attacking Faylakah Island repeatedly, a AV-8B Harrier is shot down (Marine Capt. Michael C. Berryman of VMA-311 becomes a POW). A U.S. Army AH-1S is a noncombat loss. The status of seven U.S. aircrewmen is changed from missing in action to prisoner of war (POW).

Coalition aircraft attack an Iraqi convoy inside Kuwait destroying 24 tanks, armored personnel vehicles, and trucks.

Canadian air sorties today number 20.

French aerial sorties today number two (both air interdiction).

Italy flies a total of seven air sorties today.

Total Saudi Arabian air sorties today number 178.

Total Kuwaiti air sorties today number 20 air interdiction.

Iraqi aircraft ferrying to Iran continues. Due to Coalition air superiority it is speculated that the aircraft relocation is actually defections. Only three of Iraq's 66 airfields have conducted flight operations, and of the 30 sorties, 25 are sorties heading for Iran.

Due to his heavy responsibilities, Maj. Gen. Gus Pagonis (Chief of Logistics) is promoted to Lt. Gen. when the promotion is approved by President Bush.

The Adnan Republican Guard is pounded by nine B-52 strikes today. Hundreds of ground-attack sorties also hit them.

29 January The Iraqi 5th Mechanized Division and the 15th Mechanized Regiment attacks the coastal road junction of Al Khafji. This and other attacks are ordered by Saddam Hussein to force the Coalition into ground war, increase his troops' morale, and obtain prisoners for intelligence purposes. North of Ras Al Khafji the Iraqi 5th Mech crosses into Saudi Arabia with their turrets turned seeming to surrender. When they attack, U.S. AC-130s and Cobra gunships destroy four of the tanks and 13 other Iraqi vehicles.

Two USMC reconnaissance teams (one led by Team Leader Chuck Ingraham) is cut off in Khafji. Located on the roof of a building, Ingraham calls "danger close" fire support and close air support for the next two days. He and his sister team's fire blunts, then destroys the Iraqi attack.

Elements of the U.S. 1st and 2nd Marine Divisions as well as Saudis and Qataris units fight the battle of Khafji for two days. The 2nd Light Armored Infantry Battalion, 2nd Marine Division (Lt. Col. Keith T. Holcomb) is engaged along the berm near the Kuwaiti border. In the 2nd Division's first direct Iraqi engagement, TOW gunner Corporal Edmond Willis destroys an enemy tank. Thirteen Marines are killed, seven by a U.S. Maverick missile that hits their vehicle. Four more are killed by fellow Marines firing a TOW missile at their vehicle. These Marines are LCpl Frank C. Allen, Cpl Stephen E. Bentzlin, Cpl Ismael Cotto, LCpl Thomas A. Jenkins, LCpl Michael E. Linderman, Jr., LCpl James H. Lumplins, Sgt. Garrett A. Mongrella, PFC Scott A. Schroeder, LCpl David T. Snyder, LCpl Dion J. Stephenson, and LCpl Daniel B. Walker.

Umm Al Maradim Island, 12 miles off Kuwait's coast is captured by U.S. Marines. They are from 13th Marine Expeditionary Unit deploying from the USS OKINAWA (LPH-3). Marines raise the Kuwaiti flag, this being the second island reclaimed for Kuwait.

BEAUFORT (ATS-2) begins participation in Desert Storm. Over 256 Tomahawk cruise missiles have been launched by today.

Army Specialists Melissa Rathbun-Nealy and David Lockett are captured, Specialist Nealy being the is first woman POW.

An Iraqi MiG-23 is shot down fired by a F-15C flown by Capt. David G. Rose ("Chevron 17") flying 85-0102, 58th TFS/33rd TFW. This is kill Number 25.

U.S. Central Command sorties: USAF-1670, USN-300, USMC (fixed-wing)-233, Allied-430.

U.S. carriers today launch 331 sorties (combat and support).

F-111s fly four C, seven A, 14 RR, four SC PGM strikes for a total of 29. They also fly one C, 12 A, four MS NonPGM strikes for a total of 17.

F-117s fly three CCC, two L, three C, ten MS, nine RR, two SC and one RG for a total of 30 strikes.

B-52 sorties total 42 (all AI).

At Thumrait, eight C-130s of the 166th TAG and eight C-130s of the 907th TAG, 459th MAW arrive.

A helicopter of HMS BRAZEN flown by Lt. Cdr. Michael Scott Pearey RN, and a Lynx of HMS GLOUCESTER attack 17 Iraqi ships. Twelve are damaged and four sunk. Lt. Philip David Needham RN flying a Sea Skua from HMS CARDIFF sinks a large patrol boat. It appears the ships are trying to flee to Iran. Though the Iraqi Navy is small, the missile-firing boats present a threat to Coalition ships, and Silkworm missiles are never removed as a threat the entire war. Also, Iraqi aircraft with air-to-surface capability present a Coalition anti-ship threat.

RAF Buccaneers fly six training sorties, today for a total of six aerial sorties.

Canadian Maj. David Kendall of Calgary and Capt. Steve Hill strafe an Iraqi patrol boat (31 January is also given for this date). *These are the first shots fired by Canadians since the Korean War.* Canada flies a total of 22 air sorties today.

Today alone 28 B-52 bombers drop 470 tons of bombs on the Republican Guard. Before attacks on the Iraqi 20th Infantry Division "personalized" propaganda leaflets are dropped advising the troops that, *"If you want to live, leave now. Do not allow anyone to stop you. Save yourself by fleeing south. If you choose to stay, you choose death."*

French aerial sorties today number six (four air interdiction and two training).

Italy flies a total of seven air sorties today.

Total Saudi Arabian air sorties today number 188.

Total Kuwaiti air sorties today number 19 air interdiction.

Coalition military strength now numbers 700,000 personnel. U.S. personnel number 490,000.

30 January Oil flowing from the Sea Island terminal has ceased.

A massive rehersal demonstrating requirements for breaching and passing through the Iraqi defenses is given. Representatives of every U.S. Army VII Corps and British 1st Armoured Division unit participate.

Elements of the 6th Marines, 2nd Marine Division (Col. Lawrence H. Livingston) are maneuvered to prevent any Iraqi attacks on the division area. The enemy continues to probe the Saudi border.

In the Northern Persian Gulf, the USS CURTS and LEFTWICH rescue 20 Iraqi soldiers from a POLNOCHNY-Class landing craft sunk by a U.S. Navy A-6 and British Lynx. The landing craft has been laying mines. The USS LEFTWICH is the primary combat search and rescue platform in the Persian Gulf, and embarks her ten SEALs.

U.S. nuclear submarine LOUISVILLE (SNN-724) ceases participation in Desert Storm.

By this date 46 Iraqi Naval vessels have been sunk or damaged. Today during the so-called "Bubiyan Turkey Shoot" eight patrol boats are attacked by A-6Es and F/A-18s. Four are sunk and three damaged by the Shatt al-Arab Channel and off Bubiyan Island. Flying four sorties in nine hours, Lt. Cdr. David Lionel Harold Livingstone of HMS GLOUCESTER attacks a T-43 minesweeper and two TNC-45 patrol craft. Three LSMs are sunk by A-6Es and Jaguars near Shatt-al-Arab.

U.S. Central Command sorties: USAF-1421, USN-273, USMC (fixed-wing)-262, Allied-401.

By this date the U.S. Navy has flown in excess of 3,500 sorties from its six aircraft carriers. Today they launch 382 sorties (combat and support). All 18 F/A-18s of the USS SARATOGA drop 100,000 pounds of 1,000 pound bombs on Iraqi fortifications in Kuwait.

This has been the most bomb tonnage of any single U.S. Navy mission.

The Republican Guard troops are the target of approximately 300 air sorties daily. Five B-52 strikes hit them today.

B-52 sorties today total 48 (42 AI, 6 OCA).

F-111s fly one CCC, seven L, five C, 56 A, one E, and two RG/GOB PGM strikes for a total of 72. They fly four MS, and eight E NonPGM strikes for a total of 12.

F-117s fly four SAD, four CCC, six C, nine MS, 22 RR, one SC, two oil (O) and one RG missions, for a total of 49 strikes.

RAF Buccaneers' fly three training sorties today, for a total of three sorties.

Canada flies 18 air sorties today.

French aerial sorties number two (both air interdiction).

Italian Tornados fly a total of six air sorties today.

Total Saudi Arabian air sorties today number 180.

The Kuwaiti Air Force does not fly today.

31 January A Scud missile lands harmlessly in the West Bank.

Maj. Gen. Wayne Downing, Commander, Special Operations Task Force arrives in Saudi Arabia in direct response for the need to prevent Scud launches. The Task Force consists of one squadron of Delta Force commandos and a contingent of helicopters from the 160th Special Operations Aviation Regiment. The 'Night Stalkers' have their headquarters at Ar Ar, Saudi Arabia. They will operate in "Scud alley" northwest of Highway 10 near the Syrian border. British SAS commandos will operate south of Highway 10 to the Saudi border.

Three American special operations contingents are now participating in the Operation Desert Storm: 1) In Turkey, a special operations unit commanded by Gen. Richard Potter is ready to rescue downed pilots over northern Iraq; 2) 7,000 Air Force, Army, and Navy special operations forces of "White SOF" (commanded by Col. Jesse Johnson) rescue pilots in southern Iraq and Kuwait, perform recon missions, attack special targets, and act as liaisons with foreign units; and 3) "Black SOF" commanded by Maj. Gen. Wayne Downing is never publicly recognized.

Two USMC reconnaissance teams of the 1st Reconnaissance Battalion return safely from Khafji after being cut off for two days.

With the severe failure of the 29 January attack, Iraqi forces fortify their positions and helplessly await their fate.

Alerted by the Kuwaiti Resistance, at 1925 a A-6E Intruder of Marine Aircraft Group 11 drops a laser-guided 2,000-pound bomb on a small building about 11 kilometers south of Ash Shuaybah. A high-level meeting of Iraqi military officers is supposed to be taking place. It is believed the Iraqi III Corps commander, Lt. Gen. Boomer's counterpart is killed.

Fourteen Americans are killed in a AC-130H over Kuwait. They remained in the target area too long supporting a 5th Special Forces operation. The helicopter crashes into the Persian Gulf and is *the greatest single personnel loss of the air campaign. The crash is also the second-largest contributor of American combat deaths in the war.*

USAF F-111s fly two C, 54 A PGM strikes for a total of 56 and fly seven A, eight MS, four RR NonPGM strikes for a total of 19.

F-117s fly seven CCC, one C, two A, six MS, 15 RR, one SC, two RG for a total of 34 strikes.

B-52 sorties today total 41 (all AI).

Off of the Khawar al Amaya oil platform the USS LEFTWICH captures 15 EPWs.

Four CF-18 Hornet pilots of the "Desert Cats" (Capt. Scott Whitley, 29, of Ottawa, Capt. Arnold Tate, 29 of Toronto, Capt. Jeffrey Tait, 26, of Richmond, B.C. and Lt. Col. Donald Matthews) take off from their base near Doha, Qatar to sweep the Kuwaiti sky for U.S. F-16 ground-attack fighters of the U.S. 401st Tactical Fighter Wing.

Canada flies 20 air sorties today.

At Doha, Qatar, eight Mirage F-1s of the French Air Force are based. Due to the Iraqis also flying the fighter, the French pilots are not allowed in the combat zone, and must only fly defensive patrols over Qatar.

U.S. Central Command sorties: USAF-1520, USN-449, USMC (fixed-wing)-237, Allied-403.

U.S. carriers launch 422 sorties today (combat and support). Coalition forces have flown 32,000 sorties by this date (2,600 today).

Over ten B-52 strikes and over 350 tactical fighter strikes have hit Republican Guard troops. Seventeen packages hit them concentrating on the Hammurabi Division. The Iraqi 20th Infantry Division have leaflets dropped on them following previous leaflets and a B-52 attack. The leaflets state: *"We told you that you were to be bombed and you were. We are telling you again that you will be bombed tomorrow, leave now/flee south or die."*

The British 1st Armoured Division completes arriving in its forward tactical assembly areas.

The confidence and morale of Col. Turki's Arab Coalition Forces are immeasurably strengthened by the Battle of Khafji.

RAF Buccaneer's fly four training sorties today, for a total of four sorties.

Italy Tornados fly a total of seven air sorties today.

French aerial sorties today number two (both air interdiction).

Total Saudi Arabian air sorties today number 175.

Total Kuwaiti air sorties today number 24 air interdiction.

Coalition personnel numbers pass 705,000.

1 February At 2200 on the escarpment of PL Blue the 4-325 AIR (Lt. Col. John Vine) engages Iraqis setting up an ambush position. Veterans of Operation Just Cause the 'Gold Falcons' fight for 15 minutes, forcing the Iraqis to flee.

I Marine Expeditionary Force Commander Lt. Gen. Walter E. Boomer is briefed by 2nd Marine Division Commander Maj. Gen. William M. Keyes on separate breaches in the Iraqi defenses for the 1st and 2nd Divisions. At the meeting's end, Lt. Gen. Boomer provides Maj. Gen. Keyes an oral warning order to prepare a new Marine plan.

By this date, the I Marine Expeditionary Force has captured 137 EPW, most from forward observation posts. Col. John H. Admire, Commander, Task Force Taro, advises Gen. Myatt that he has learned from the Battle of Khafji that the Iraqis do not have the resolve to stand up to a strong opponent. Gen. Myatt draws off combat battalions for EPW collection in order to allow rapid and unhindered attack.

Nearly 90 percent of U.S. Army Ready Reserve units called-up have reported to their mobilization stations. Results are better than ever thought possible. In merely a few days, soldiers who were thought to need weeks of training are ready. Some tank crews who have served in Germany qualify after a single live-fire battle test.

USS KIDD (DDG-993) and MOUNT HOOD (AE-29) begin participation in Operation Desert Storm.

An Iraqi patrol boat is attacked and left burning near Min-al-Bakr by a A-6E. At the Cor al-Amiya oil terminal, 15 EPWs are picked up by U.S. Navy helicopters.

U.S. Navy air unit HSL-34 (DET 5) begins participation in Operation Desert Storm.

After a B-52 bombing mission over the Kuwaiti "national forest", many enemy vehicles are observed fleeing. A-10 pilots report 20 tanks, 11 armored personnel carriers, 20 vehicles and three multiple rocket launchers destroyed. There have been five B-52 strikes and 19 tactical air strikes against the Republican Guard today (600 sorties).

U.S. Central Command sorties: USAF-1522, USN-447, USMC (fixed-wing)-238, Allied-398.

U.S. carriers launch 438 sorties today (combat and support). By this date, 278 Tomahawk cruise missiles have been launched. Coalition forces have flown over 34,000 sorties (2,500 today).

F-111s fly 19 A PGM strikes for a total of 19. NonPGM strikes number 12 A and eight MS for a total of 20.

F-117s fly seven CCC, three C, five MS, 15 RR, 11 SC, and four RG for a total of 45 strikes.

B-52 sorties today total 48 (all AI).

RAF Buccaneers' fly eight training sorties today for a total of eight sorties.

Canada flies a total of 10 air sorties today.

French aerial sorties today number two (both air interdiction).

Italian Tornados fly a total of seven air sorties today.

Total Saudi Arabian air sorties today number 167.

Total Kuwaiti air sorties today number 18 air interdiction.

By this date 80 percent of Operation Desert Storm expenses have been pledged by Coalition countries. This includes $ 9 billion from Germany ($ 3.5 billion paid and $ 5.5 billion pledged), $ 11 billion pledged from Japan, $ 21 billion pledged from Kuwait ($ 2.5 billion paid and $ 18.5 billion pledged), $ 14.6 billion ($ 1.6 billion paid and $ 13 billion pledged by Saudi Arabia (offer to pay for all food, water, petroleum and transportation for Coalition forces), $ 280 million ($ 60 million and $ 220 million pledged) by South Korea, $ 1.66 billion ($ 660 million paid and $ 1 billion pledged by the United Arab Emirates. The Netherlands has supplied $ 33 million dollars worth of ammunition.

2 February Tel Aviv, Israel, is attacked by two Scud missiles. One lands in Jordan, and the other impacts in the West Bank, causing no damage or injuries. Riyadh, Saudi Arabia, is targeted by a Scud missile, but is intercepted by a Patriot missile with resulting debris injuring 29 people.

Advanced elements of the 82nd Airborne Division's 3rd Brigade is transported by ten C-130 sorties.

One U.S. Marine (LCpl Eliseo C. Felix) is killed and two wounded by Marine cluster bombs dropped from a A-6E as they return from conducting an artillery mission. It has been decided that the 2nd Marine Division's attack will be led by the 6th Marines (Col. Lawrence H. Livingston) who has the most training in breaching operations. Division commander Maj. Gen. Keyes has served with Col. Livingston in Vietnam and has great confidence in the colonel.

USS BIDDLE (CG-34) commanded by Capt. Louis F. Harlow diverts the Saudi Arabian flagged MAWASHI AL-GASSEEM en route from Jeddah to Aqaba in the Northern Red Sea. The Bahamin ship CLYMENE is diverted by the SAMUEL B. ROBERTS in the Northern Red Sea en route from Houston to Aqaba. At the end of the day the SAMUEL B. ROBERTS (FFG-58) and the USS HALYBURTON (FFG-40) commanded by Cdr. Robert M. Hartling divert the Japanese flagged ARABIAN BREEZE en route from Jeddah to Aqaba.

U.S. Central Command sorties: USAF-1492, USN-398, USMC (fixed-wing)-263, Allied-

411.

U.S. carriers launch 311 sorties today (combat and support). Coalition forces have flown 37,000 sorties (2,600 today).

B-52 sorties today total 43 (39 AI, 4 OCA).

Capt. Gregory P. 'Dutch' Masters ("Rifle 01") flying F-15C 79-0074, 525th TFS/36th TFW destroys an IL-76 for kill Number 26.

Three Coalition aircraft are lost today. An A-6E (Lt. Cdr. Barry T. Cooke is missing in action and Lt. Patrick K. Conner is killed in action) and a USAF A-10 (Capt. Dale Storr) are shot down. A AH-1J Cobra (Maj. Eugene McCarthy USMC, and Capt. Jonathan R. Edwards USMC), is a noncombat loss. Capt. Storr becomes a POW.

U.S. Navy air unit VP-19 completes participation in Operation Desert Storm.

F-111s fly three C, 18 A, eight MS, and ten RR PGM strikes for a total of 39 and four SAD, eight C, eight MS, and eight SC for a total of 28 NonPGM strikes.

F-117s fly 12 A, two MS strikes for a total of 14.

British troops at *Keyes* observe large numbers of Coalition aircraft flying toward Iraq and Kuwait daily. Planes refueling high in the desert sky and then flying to attack increase morale, but nothing like veiwing the large B-52 bombers on their missions. When the B-52s are seen, the British are heartened to know that the Iraqis are being hit hard.

The French 6th Division is encamped at TAA (Tactical Assembly Area) *Olive* (Chief of Staff, Col. Jean-Francois Durand). French rations are viewed as superior to American MREs, and U.S. XVIII Airborne Corps soldiers barter heavily for them.

RAF Buccaneers' fly two air interdiction and two training sorties, for a total of four sorties.

Canada flies a total of 32 air sorties today.

French aerial sorties today number two (both air interdiction).

Total Saudi Arabian air sorties number 165.

Total Kuwaiti air sorties today number 15 air interdiction.

By this date 83 Iraqi Naval vessels have been sunk or disabled.

Today at the Al Kalia Naval Facility two EPGMs are attacked (one Exocet-capable) and disabled. One patrol boat is hit by two laser-guided bombs while the second is struck by twelve 500-pound bombs, some hitting a pier and producing secondary explosions. Helicopters from the NICHOLAS attack four patrol boats near Myeradam Island, destroying one patrol boat. A-6Es destroy a patrol boat in Kuwait harbor with two laser-guided bombs. All of Iraq's 143 missile boats have been damaged or destroyed by this date (except one that fled to Iran), and *Iraqi naval forces are now judged to be combat ineffective.*

Exercise *Sea Soldier IV* ends.

Twenty-six packages and six B-52 strikes pound the Republican Guard.

Iraq flies two helicopters over south-central Iraq.

3 February The U.S. Army's VII Corps (Lt. Gen. Fred Franks) has traveled west 330 miles and the XVIII Airborne Corps (Lt. Gen. Gary Luck) has traveled 500 miles to position themselves to begin the ground offensive.

The 2nd Marine Division's G-3 Col. Ronald G. Richard expands on the division's attack plan. The 1st Marine Division will lead the attack, breaching the Iraqi lines, and then taking the Al Jaber airfield. With the Iraqi's attention diverted, the 2nd Division will attack, and led by the 6th Marines, become the swordpoint of the U.S. Marines.

The battleship MISSOURI begins bombarding Iraqi prefabricated bunkers on the Kuwaiti coast. The bombardment of eight 1.25-ton 16-inch shells (18,000 pounds of high explosives) is the first combat bombardment of the USS MISSOURI since the Korean War and is the first time a Remotely Piloted Vehicle (RPV) is used for spotting gunfire in a conflict. USS NICHOLAS, equipped with a mine-detection device, guided the battleship into position off the heavily mined shore. Later, a sea mine explodes near the NICHOLAS but the shrapnel causes little damage.

A B-52G crashes into the sea by Diego Garcia and a U.S. Marine Corps UH-1N of HMLA-369 is a noncombat loss (Capt. David R. Herr, Jr. 28, of Fort Worth, Texas; Capt. James K. Thorp, 30, of Valley Station, Kentucky, Cpl. Albert G. Haddad, Jr., 22, of Denton, Texas and Cpl. Kurt A. Benz, 22, of Garden City, Michigan are killed in action). Three of the B-52 crewmen have been rescued by Naval Reservists of Helicopter Squadron-75, and three additional crewmen are missing in action.

U.S. Central Command sorties: USAF-1689, USN-379, USMC (fixed-wing)-301, Allied-407.

U.S. carriers today launch 325 sorties (combat and support). The resupply interdiction campaign has resulted in 25-35 major bridges being destroyed or damaged.

F-111s fly two CCC, one C, 29 A, and 12 RR PGM strikes for a total of 44 and seven A, eight E, and eight O for a total of 23 NonPGM strikes.

F-117s fly three CCC, one L, 25 C, three A, two RR, one SC for a total of 35 strikes.

B-52 sorties today total 42 (all AI).

RAF Buccaneers' do not fly today.

Canada flies a total of 32 air sorties today.

French aerial sorties today number two (both air interdiction).

Italian Tornados fly a total of seven air sorties today.

Total Saudi Arabian air sorties today number 167.

The Kuwait Air Force does not fly today.

Total Qatar air sorties today number four air interdiction. These are the first Qatar air sorties since 23 January.

4 February Three Scud missile sites are attacked. It is a rare day with no wind.

A U.S. Marine AV-8B Harrier destroys or damages 25 Iraqi tanks with Rockeye anti-tank bombs. It also attacks an Iraqi truck convoy at approximately 0400.

The battleship USS MISSOURI destroys an Iraqi communications bunker with seven 16-inch shells. It is operating with CURTS, NICHOLAS and two Royal Saudi Naval Force escorts.

U.S. Central Command sorties: USAF-1734, USN-420, USMC (fixed-wing)-266, Allied-397.

U.S. carriers launch 376 sorties today (combat and support). Over 44,000 sorties have been flown by Coalition forces (2,700 today).

Maj. Jim Rose flying an A-10 Warthog of the 504th TFS (Cajuns) is hit by an Iraqi heat-seeking missile under his left empennage. He is the first "Hogdriver" to make an emergency manual reversion under combat conditions.

F-111s fly eight C, 31 A, three MS, three RR, and eight PGM strikes for a total of 53, and fly four A, eight MS, four E, for a total of 16 NonPGM strikes.

F-117s fly eight CCC, 11 L, 28 C, one RR, and three SC for a total of 51 strikes.

B-52 sorties today total 41 (40 AI, one unknown).

At Incirlik, Turkey, six RF-4Cs of the 26th TRW arrives.

RAF Buccaneers' fly four training sorties today, for a total of four sorties.

Canada flies a total of 20 air sorties today.

French aerial sorties today number four (two air interdiction and two reconnaissance)

Italian Tornados fly a total of seven air sorties today.

Total Saudi Arabian air sorties today number 193.

The Kuwait Air Force does not fly today.

Republican Guard units have been hit by 250 sorties and six B-52 strikes within the last 24 hours.

5 February Lt. Col. Mark E. Swanstrom, 2nd Marine Division Engineer Officer leaves for Washington, D.C. He will meet with members of the Defense Intelligence Agency and Army Intelligence. After reviewing the division's Essential Elements of Information he will return with maps of the Iraqi lines (scale 1:12,500). These maps are distributed down to the company commander level.

U.S. Secretary of the Navy authorizes the involuntary call-up of up to 2,000 retired Marines (at least 20 years of active duty and under the age 60).

The battleship USS MISSOURI targets its 16-inch shells at an Iraqi artillery emplacement, utterly destroying it. MCINERNEY (FFG-8) commanded by Cdr. Michael O. Borns begins participation in Operation Desert Storm. She will remain in the area until 12 June.

The 3rd Marine Aircraft Wing (Maj. Gen. Royal N. Moore, Jr.) bombs and strafes a convoy of 25 Iraqi trucks generating multiple secondary explosions. The Marines also hit convoy traffic jams created at destroyed bridges between Baghdad and Basra.

U.S. Navy air unit HSL-42 (DET 8) begins participation in Operation Desert Storm.

U.S. Central Command sorties: USAF-1729, USN-231, USMC (fixed-wing)-234, Allied-472.

U.S. carriers launch 429 sorties today (combat and support). Silkworm anti-ship missile sites at Uum Qasabah are attacked by A-6s. It's two launchers and a number of control and support vehicles are struck. A total of 284 Tomahawk cruise missiles have been fired by today.

F-111s fly four CCC, 28 A, one MS, one RR, and two RG/GOB PGM strikes for a total of 36, and fly seven A, four E and eight O, NonPGM strikes for a total of 19. *For the first time the F-111s fly PGM strikes against Republican Guard tanks and artillery.*

F-117s fly two SAM, two CCC, two L, 21 C, ten A, ten MS, seven SC, and one RG for a total of 55 strikes.

B-52 sorties total 42 (all AI).

Coalition forces have flown 47,000 sorties by this date (2,800 today).

Republican Guard units have been attacked by 400 sorties and six B-52 strikes today.

There are now 800 Iraqi prisoners of war.

A F/A-18C (Lt. Robert J. Dwyer of Carrier Air Wing-8) is lost over the Northern Gulf as it is returning to its aircraft carrier. Dwyer is listed killed in action due to non-combat loss.

RAF Buccaneers' fly two air interdiction and two training sorties for a total of four sorties.

Canada flies a total of 20 air sorties today.

French aerial sorties today number two (both air interdiction).

Italian Tornados fly a total of seven air sorties today.

Total Saudi Arabian air sorties number 217.

Total Kuwait air sorties today number 19 air interdiction.

Total Qatar air sorties today number four air interdiction. These are the first Qatar air sorties since 3 February.

Thirty-three packages are flown against the Republican Guard.

6 February Last elements of U.S. Army VII Corps arrives in Saudi Arabia with the arrival of last of the 3rd Armored Division (Maj. Gen. Paul E. 'Butch' Funk).

The 5th Marine Expeditionary Brigade embarks from the USS GERMANTOWN (LSD-42) and 30 other amphibious vessels in the Persian Gulf. Embarking four air cushion landing craft (LCACs) for combat for the first time, GERMANTOWN makes U.S. Navy history.

The battleship WISCONSIN ("Whisky") relieves MISSOURI of its bombardment mission off the Kuwaiti coast. It begins firing Turret Two. It fires an eleven-round 16-inch salvo targeting an Iraqi artillery battery. Gun Captain GM3 Lawrence Tibayan commands Turret Two. Earlier in the day, MISSOURI destroyed four Iraqi artillery emplacements and a command bunker supporting the U.S. Marines. Next, it destroyed an Iraqi radar site with 28 16-inch shells. It has fired 112 16-inch shells and 12 5-inch shells since 4 February. *For the first time since the Korean War, the USS WISCONSIN has conducted a gunfire support mission.*

U.S. nuclear submarine USS LOUISVILLE is relieved by the USS CHICAGO (SSN-721) in the Red Sea.

The Coalition maritime interception campaign has challenged 7,100 merchantships, boarding 860, and diverting 40 by this date.

U.S. Air Force planners estimate that half of attack sorties against Iraq are diverted to alternative targets due to weather. Weather also impedes accuracy and bomb damage assessment.

U.S. Navy air units VP-40 begins participation in Operation Desert Storm.

U.S. Central Command sorties: USAF-1537, USN-167, USMC (fixed-wing)-125, Allied-445.

U.S. carriers launch 313 sorties today (combat and support). From the USS RANGER F-14A 162603 flown by Lt. Donald S. Broce and Cdr. Ron D. McElraft of VF-1 'Wolf Pack'/CVW-2 shoot down a Mi-8. This is kill number 32.

Coalition forces have flown over 49,000 sorties (2,500 today).

U.S. Marine and Navy aircraft have flown 11,000 sorties since the beginning of Operation Desert Storm. A Marine OV-10 calls for a fire mission on an Iraqi artillery emplacement from the USS WISCONSIN.

F-111s fly one SAM, one CCC, three A, two MS, seven RR and 143 RG/GOB PGM strikes for a total of 157, and fly no NonPGM strikes. This is the first day of tank plinking, with all strikes "masked." No Proven Force air units take part.

F-117s fly two SAD, five CCC, six L, 16 C, 26 A, two MS and two naval (N) for a total of 59.

B-52 sorties total 32 (all AI).

The Republican Guard campaign reaches a new height with the unit's being hit every three hours by A-6s, F-15s, F-16s, and B-52s, 24 hours a day.

Two Iraqi Su-25s and two MiG-21s are shot down by two F-15Cs of the USAF 36th Tactical Fighter Wing. MiG-21s are shot down by Capt. Thomas N. 'Vegas' Dietz flying 79-0078, 53rd TFS/36th TFW and Su-25s are shot down by 1st Lt. Robert W. 'Digs' Hehemann flying 84-0019, 53rd TFS/36th TFW. Capt. Robert R. Swain, Jr. flying A-10 77-0205, 706th TFS/926th TFG shoots down a BO 105 (this is the first ever aerial victory for an A-10). Capt. Dietz's victories are Kills 27 and 28, Lt. Hehemann's kills are numbers 29 and 30, and Capt. Swain's kill is number 31.

Lt. Gen. de la Billiere visits the British Division (Maj. Gen. Rupert Smith) in the *Keyes* concentration area north of Qaysumah. He voices his concern over the unreliability of British armored vehicles but is reassured by Maj. Gen. Smith.

British SAS commandos destroy a communications facility used by the Iraqis to control Scud missile operations. A heated firefight follows. After returning to Saudia Arabia with no casualties, two commandos find bullet holes in their smocks.

Three British relief ships HMS BRECON (M-29), HMS BROCKLESBY (M-33), and HMS BICESTER (M-36) are deployed.

RAF Buccaneers' do not fly today.

Canada flies a total of 26 air sorties today.

French aerial sorties today number two (both are reconnaissance).

Italian Tornados fly a total of seven air sorties today.

Total Saudi Arabian air sorties number 207.

Total Kuwait air sorties today number 15 air interdiction.

7 February Maj. Gen. Wayne Downing's Joint Special Operations Command is allowed to strengthen itself to approximately 400 men by an additional Delta Force squadron, a reinforced Ranger company, and a small SEAL Team-6 unit.

U.S. Special operations forces begin infiltrating into Iraq to attempt to inhibit or destroy

Scud missiles. They will target communication sites, mobile launchers, and missile facilities. On one occasion a Ranger platoon will destroy a 350-foot microwave tower and its communications site, before escaping safely.

As of this date there are 21 Patriot missile units in the theater (132 launchers).

Artillery of the VII Corps and 1st Cavalry Division begin a number of artillery raids near Wadi al-Batin (the wadi is a dry streambed paralleling the Kuwait-Iraq border and is a natural attack route towards King Khalid Military City or Riyahd). At 1400 artillery of the 1st Cavalry Division fires a 155mm howitzer with a laser-guided Copperhead projectile at a 40-foot Iraqi observation tower. The VII Corps artillery commander, Brig. Gen. Creighton Abrams, Jr. maintains his short range pieces well to the rear.

Iraqi artillery positions, naval and electronic-warfare sites are bombarded by the 16-inch guns of USS WISCONSIN. Piers at Khawr al-Mufattah Marina and 15 boats are destroyed using a remotely piloted vehicle (RPV) for spotting.

The USS BIDDLE diverts the German flagged RED SEA EUROPA en route from Greece to Aqaba. The U.S. nuclear submarine CHICAGO (SSN-721) begins participation in Operation Desert Storm.

A UH-1H is a noncombat loss to the US Army (one killed and four injured).

U.S. Central Command sorties: USAF-1543, USN-405, USMC-(fixed-wing)-308, Allied-434.

U.S. carriers launch 366 sorties today (combat and support). Near the Al Faw peninsula A-6s attack and heavily damage two Iraqi patrol boats. One F-18 is a non-combat loss over the Persian Gulf. Coalition forces have flown 52,000 sorties (2,600 today).

F-111s fly three SAD, one SAM, 13 A, 20 MS, and six SC for a total of 43 PGM strikes. They fly eight A, one MS, 25 O for a total of 34 NonPGM strikes.

F-117s fly eight SAD, ten CCC, three L, 31 C, and one SC strikes for a total of 53.

B-52 sorties total 41 (all AI).

RAF Buccaneers' fly six air interdiction sorties today for a total of six sorties.

Canada flies a total of 16 air sorties today.

French aerial sorties today number two (both air interdiction).

Italian Tornados fly a total of seven air sorties today.

Total Saudi Arabian air sorties number 159.

Total Kuwait air sorties today number 19 air interdiction.

Total Qatar air sorties today number five air interdiction.

Iraqi forces begin reinforcing the Wadi al-Batin with artillery and antitank weapons. An AT-12 battery of 100mm antitank guns dug into the walls of the wadi later ambush 1-5th Cavalry (Lt. Col. Michael Parker) killing three American soldiers and wounding nine. The Iraqis believe the main American attack will occur through the Wadi al-Batin.

Four Iraqi aircraft are shot down today: three Su-22s are shot down by two F-15Cs of the 33rd Tactical Fighter Wing attempting to flee to Iran (two by Capt. Anthony R. Murphy flying 85-0102, 58th TFS/33rd TFW and Col. Rick N. Parsons flying 85-0124, 58th TFS/33rd TFW). Maj. Randy W. May ("Killer 03") flying F-15C 80-0003, 525th TFS/36th TFW destroys a HIND or Mil Mi-8 HIP helicopter with an AIM-7.

Twenty packages (five B-52 strikes), and hundreds of other sorties hit the Republican Guard.

8 February Secretary Cheney and Gen. Colin Powell arrive in Saudia Arabia to discover if United States troops are prepared for ground combat. They are briefed by Lt. Gen. Fred Franks, Maj. Gen. Barry McCaffrey and the other military leaders.

Tel Aviv, Israel, is targeted by a Scud missile which is intercepted by a Patriot missile. The resulting debris, if the Patriot did strike the Iraqi missile, causes several injuries.

The battleship USS WISCONSIN supports a U.S. Marine Corps reconnaissance probe of southern Kuwait defenses. It bombards 12 Iraqi artillery positions with 36 rounds of 16-inch shells. Later, offshore of Khafji, Saudi Arabia, WISCONSIN bombards bunkers, troops and artillery positions. SPRUANCE (DD-963) begins participation in Operation Desert Storm.

At Al Hamra, United Arab Emirates, the U.S. Navy TF-156 is conducting maintenance, resupply and amphibious exercises.

U.S. Navy air unit HSL-48 (DET 1) begins participation in Operation Desert Storm.

U.S. Central Command sorties: USAF-1547, USN-379, USMC (fixed-wing)-275, Allied-475.

U.S. carriers launch 353 sorties today (combat and support). At Cor Al Zubayr A-6s damage or destroy an Iraqi training frigate, along with a TMC-45-Class patrol boat (Exocet-capable). Coalition forces have flown 55,000 sorties (over 2,500 today).

F-111s fly five C, 23 A, two SC, 94 RG/GOB for a total of 124 PGM strikes, and fly four A, four E, and eight O NonPGM strikes for a total of 16.

F-117s fly 26 C, six A, six MS, one RR, 23 SC for a total of 62 strikes.

B-52 sorties today total 44 (all AI).

RAF Buccaneers' fly eight air interdiction sorties today for a total of eight sorties.

Canada flies a total of 28 air sorties today.

French aerial sorties today number one (a reconnaissance sortie).

Italian Tornados fly a total of seven air sorties today.

Total Saudi Arabian air sorties today number 163.

Total Kuwait air sorties today number 19 air interdiction.

An Iraqi Alouette III is shot down by an A-10. Nine major bridges have been attacked within the last 24 hours to continue to interdict and isolate the Kuwaiti Theater of Operations (KTO).

RAF 31 Squadron Commander Jeremy Witts leads an eight-plane daylight attack on Al Kut oil refinery. Witts dive bombs the target despite heavy Iraqi fire.

Twelve packages, nine B-52 strikes hit Republican Guard related targets.

The Qatar Air Force does not fly today.

9 February General Schwarkopf recommends an attack between 21 and 25 February. President Bush approves.

West of Maradin Island U.S. Navy SEALs conduct an underwater reconnaissance. On land SEALs confirm Scud decoys.

In the Northern Red Sea the USS THOMAS C. HART (FF-1092) diverts the German flagged RED SEA ENERGY en route from Jeddah to Aqaba. PHILIPPINE SEA (CG-58) and HALEAKALA (AE-25) begin participation in Operation Desert Storm.

Marine Capt. Russell A. C. Sanforn flying an AV-8B Harrier from VMA-231 is shot down by an Iraqi heat-seeking missile and becomes a POW.

U.S. Central Command sorties: USAF-1619, USN-393, USMC-(fixed-wing)-266, Allied-455. USAF aircraft are 91.8 percent mission capable.

U.S. carriers launch 357 sorties today (combat and support). Near Faylaka Island an A-6E damages an Iraqi Zhuk patrol boat with a Rockeye missile. Later, a Silkworm antiship missile site is attacked by U.S. Navy aircraft. Coalition forces have flown 57,000 sorties (over 2,400 today).

U.S. Navy air unit VP-91 begins participation in Operation Desert Storm and HSL-46 (DET 7) completes participation in Operation Desert Storm.

F-111s fly ten A, four RR, 149 RG/GOB for a total of 163 PGM strikes and fly 12 O NonPGM strikes for a total of 12.

F-117s fly four SAD, six SAM, three CCC, three L, two C, 13 MS, five RR, nine SC for a total of 45 strikes.

B-52 sorties today total 50 (all AI). Eight packages, 11 B-52 strikes, hit the Republican Guard.

Due to illness, French Brig. Gen. Jean-Charles Mouscardes is relieved of command of *Division Daguet* by Brig. Gen. Bernard Janvier. In the midst of a sand storm the French soldiers meet their new commander.

RAF Buccaneers' fly four air interdiction sorties today, for a total of four sorties.

Canada flies a total of 20 air sorties today.

French air sorties today number two (both are air interdiction).

Total Saudi Arabian air sorties today number 190.

Total Kuwait air sorties today number 19 air interdiction.

South Korea becomes the 33rd Coalition partner in Operation Desert Storm.

Total Qatar air sorties today number four air interdiction.

10 February 5th Battalion, 11th Marines (Lt. Col. James L. Sachtleben) stands down from its artillery raid mission, and returns to the 1st Marine Division.

SIRIUS (TAFS-8) renews participation in Operation Desert Storm.

Over Southern Kuwait a Coalition AV-8B is shot down due to AAA.

In the northern Persian Gulf, two Iraqi patrol boats are sunk by A-6Es. U.S. Navy fighters also attack the Uum Qasr Naval Base.

U.S. Central Command sorties: USAF-1600, USN-430, USMC (fixed-wing)-305, Allied-450.

U.S. carriers launch 374 sorties today (combat and support). Coalition forces have flown 59,000 sorties (2,800 today).

U.S. Navy air units HC-6 (DET 7) begin participation in Operation Desert Storm.

Two B-52 strikes and hundreds of sorties are flown against the Republican Guard.

F-111s fly six C, one A, nine RR, three SC, 130 RG/GOB for a total of 149 PGM strikes, and 12 O NonPGM strikes for a total of 12.

F-117s fly ten SAD, 14 SAM, 14 CCC, three L, three C, 12 MS, two SC for a total of 58 strikes.

B-52 sorties today total 50 (all AI).

RAF Buccaneers' fly four air interdiction sorties today, for a total of four sorties.

Canada flies a total of 16 air sorties today.

French aerial sorties today number four (two air interdiction and two reconnaissance).

Italian Tornados fly a total of seven air sorties today.

Total Saudi Arabian air sorties number 171.

Total Kuwait air sorties today number 20 air interdiction.

The Qatar Air Force does not fly today.

11 February *Worldwide adverse publicity is created by Iraq after two U.S. laser-guided bombs strike Baghdad.* The U.S. believe their target is a camouflaged fortified command and control bunker. Iraq claims the site in the residential Al-Amerieh district is a bomb shelter filled with hundreds of civilians.

In excess of 50 oil field fires burn in Kuwait, mostly in the Al-Wafra area. The Iraqis hope to mask their troop movements by the smoke, and they are successful to small degree in complicating the Coalition air campaign.

U.S. Marines continue their patrolling and counter-reconnaissance movements. They continue to exchange cross border artillery fire with the Iraqis.

U.S. Central Command sorties: USAF-1543, USN-450, USMC (fixed-wing)-272, Allied-446. *With good weather Iraqi units are being attacked in the open.*

USS AMERICA carrier battle group transits the Strait of Hormuz, heading for the Persian Gulf (departing TF-155 for TF-154 or the Persian Gulf Battle Force). U.S. carriers launch 427 sorties today (combat and support).

An Iraqi helicopter is shot down by Sparrow missiles of F-15Cs of the USAF 36th Tactical Fighter Wing. Capt. Steven B. Dingee flying F-15C 79-0048, 525th TFS/36th TFW and Capt. Mark McKenzie flying F-15C 80-0012, 525th TFS/36th TFW destroys a Mi-8. This is kill number 37.

U.S. Navy aircraft help report on the extent and movement of the Persian Gulf oil spill. Coalition forces have flown 62,000 sorties (2,900 today).

Along the Saudi-Kuwait border bombs from a B-52 strike generate significant secondary explosions. In the evening's blackness, a flight turns on their lights as they return across the border, and thrill the French 6th Division with the spectacle.

F-111s fly one CCC, 14 MS, one RR, and 38 RG/GOB for a total of 54 PGM strikes, and four C, eight MS for a total of 12 NonPGM strikes.

F-117s fly five SAD, six CCC, 13 L, 25 C, eight MS, eight SC, one E for a total of 66 strikes. The 37th TFW flies 35 sorties. Ten F-117s hit "SAM's Town" with GBU-10s targeting radar vans.

B-52 sorties total 51 (47 AI, 4 OCA). A massive B-52 strike hits the Al-Taji military-industrial complex just north of Baghdad.

British troops are ordered to prepare for Exercise *Dibdibah Charge*. The Strafford Regiment advance west 60 kilometres across Wadi Al Batin to Forward Assembly Area Ray.

British minesweepers begin participation in Operation Desert Storm. They are commanded by Cdr. Jonathan Scoles from his command ship HMS HERALD.

With the arrival of 300 Afghan Mujahedeen soldiers, Coalition partners now number 34. U.S. troops alone number 510,000 (in excess of 90,000 Marines and 80,000 Navy).

Iraqi equipment confirmed destroyed by this date numbers 1,300 tanks, 800 armored vehicles, and 1,100 artillery pieces. This is approximately one-third of the Iraqi inventory.

Sixteen packages hit the Republican Guard, and eight packages and nine B-52 strikes pound Republican Guard logistic and ammunition sites.

RAF Buccaneers' fly eight air interdiction sorties and one training sortie for a total of nine sorties.

Canada flies a total of 16 air sorties today.

French aerial sorties today number four (two air interdiction and two reconnaissance).

Italian Tornados fly a total of seven air sorties today.

Total Saudi Arabian air sorties today number 177.

Total Kuwait air sorties today number 20 air interdiction.

The Qatar Air Force does not fly today.

12 February Col. Montgomery Meigs, USA, commander of the armor-heavy 2nd Brigade, 1st Armored Division, meets with battalion officers of 6-6 Infantry (6th Battalion, 6th Infantry) at 1400.

The U.S. 2nd Marine Division, led by the 2nd Light Armored Infantry Battalion, begins to move to its final staging position Al Khanjar for the coming ground war.

U.S. Navy air unit VPMAU begins participation in Operation Desert Storm.

U.S. Central Command sorties: USAF-1616, USN-299, USMC-(fixed-wing)-247, Allied-459.

U.S. carriers launch 334 sorties today (combat and support). Coalition forces have flown 65,000 sorties (2,600 today).

The Republican Guard continues to be heavily hit by B-52 strikes and hundreds of sorties.

F-111s fly two A, nine MS, nine RR, four SC and 183 RG/GOB for a total of 207 PGM strikes, and fly four SAD, four C, and four O for a total of 12 NonPGM strikes.

F-117s fly six SAD, one SAM, 14 CCC, 32 L, and three RR for a total of 56 strikes. Targets today in the vicinity of Baghdad include: Iraqi Air Force Headquarters; Radrel Sta; the Ministry of Defense; the Conference Center; Auto Exch-Radrel; Auto TP Exch; Maydan TP Exch; Iraqi Intelligence Service Headquarters; Radcom Xmtr-Revr; International Radcom Revr; Bath Party Headquarters; Al Firdos District Bunker; Headquarters, Director of General Internal Security; Director of Military Intelligence; Iraqi Internal Security Headquarters; the Presidental Bunker; and Aut Mpur-Radrel.

B-52 sorties total 44 (all AI).

British OBERON-Class submarines OPOSSUM (S-19) and OTUS (S-18) are on station in the Persian Gulf. Part of their mission is radio intelligence.

RAF Buccaneers' fly six air interdiction sorties today, for a total of six sorties.

Canada flies a total of 24 air sorties today.

French air sorties today number four (all reconnaissance).

Italian Tornados fly a total of seven air sorties today.

Total Saudi Arabian air sorties today number 190.

Total Kuwait air sorties today number 19 air interdiction.

The Qatar Air Force does not fly today.

13 February Coalition air attacks against Baghdad are reduced due to adverse publicity over the Al Firdos bunker. The Coalition has flown 170 sorties in the last 24 hours against Scuds.

VII Corps artillery raids continue with three MLRS batteries at 1815 (two batteries from the 42nd Field Artillery Brigade, one from the 1st Cavalry Division) attacking Iraqi artillery batteries. Attack is made by 27 launchers, each containing 216 rockets, spraying a total of 140,000 bomblets over the Iraqi artillerymen.

A major sand-table exercise is held for the 2nd Marine Division. The exercise includes a full-scale rehearsal of the 6th Marine's planned breach of the Iraqi defensive lines.

U.S. Central Command sorties: USAF-1542, USN-416, USMC (fixed-wing)-266, Allied-478.

U.S. carriers launch 359 sorties (combat and support). Coalition forces have flown 67,000 sorties (2,800 today). Due to oil field fires, especially in the Al-Wafra area, the Coalition air campaign is complicated.

USS MISSOURI fires 60 16-inch shells in nine naval gunfire support missions (one target is a command bunker and another an antenna complex). USS AMERICA (CV-66) Carrier Battle Group passes through the Strait of Hormuz heading toward the Persian Gulf. Task Forces 156 and 158 conduct training off the United Arab Emerates, and prepare an amphibious landing.

An Exocet-capable Frelon helicopter is shot down by U.S. Navy aircraft.

After attacking an SA-3 site near Al Qaim, Capt. Tim "TB" Bennett and Capt. Dan "Chewie" Bakke are the first pilots in USAF history to accomplish an air-to-air kill with a bomb. They accomplish the feat assisting the rescue of U.S. Special Forces soldiers by killing the target, an Iraqi helicopter. Shayka Mazhar AB, 15 miles south southeast of Baghdad is targeted by an eight-ship F-15E raid.

F-111s fly three C, eight A, 18 RR, and 176 RG/GOB for a total of 205 PGM strikes, and fly four CCC, four C, four MS four a total of 12 NonPGM strikes.

F-117s fly eight SAD, one SAM, 33 CCC, two L, four A, two SC, two RG for a total of 52 strikes.

B-52 sorties total 43 (36 AI, 7 OCA).

RAF Buccaneers' fly four air interdiction, and four offensive counter air sorties today for a total of eight sorties.

Canada flies a total of 24 air sorties today.

French air sorties today number four (all reconnaissance).

Italian Tornados fly seven sorties today.

Total Kuwait air sorties today number 20 air interdiction.

The Republican Guard units have been hit by 225 sorties, six B-52 strikes in the last 24 hours.

In early morning, nine enemy prisoners of war are captured.

Lt. Gen. de la Billiere visits British mine-hunters. He also visits the Flagship of Task Group commander Commodore Christopher Craig HMS LONDON (Capt. Ian Henderson) in the Persian Gulf.

German minehunters LINDAU-Class GOTTINGEN (M-1070) commanded by Lt. Cdr. Witter, KOBLENZ (M-1071 commanded by Lt. Cdr. Beckmann, and MARBURG (M-1080) commanded by Lt. Cdr. Fullner begin participation in Operation Desert Storm. The top German Navy commander is Capt. Jacobi.

Flight Lieutenant Edward David Smith RAF, though encountering intense anti-aircraft artillery fire over smoke-shrouded Republican Guard positions, and after vectoring U.S. aircraft to the area, destroys an Iraqi tank with a 500-pound bomb. By the war's end he will have earned the Distinguished Flying Cross.

A Royal Saudi Air Force F-5E, of No 17 Squadron is shot down over Southwest Iraq. The pilot is safe. Another Saudi F-15C, of No. 6 Squadron is a non-combat loss. Total Saudi

Arabian air sorties today number 217.

Total Qatar air sorties today number four air interdiction.

14 February U.S. Marine Gen. Boomer decides to shift the main point of his attack twenty miles to the west due to the level of Iraqi obstacles at his front. For the first time since 1971 Marine Corps active duty strength exceeds 200,000.

The 9,000 vehicle 1st Armored Division (Maj. Gen. Ron Griffith) moves toward TAA Garcia, the staging area south of the 2nd Armored Cavalry Regiment beginning at 0700. The 3rd Armored Division (Maj. Gen. Paul Funk) takes up its position west of the 1st Armored Division.

U.S. Central Command sorties: USAF-1468, USN-396, USMC (fixed-wing)-279, Allied-433.

USS AMERICA carrier battle group enters the Persian Gulf. U.S. carriers launch 355 sorties (combat and support). The Coalition has flown 70,000 sorties (2,800 today).

An F-15E 89-0487, flown by Capt. Richard T. Bennett and Capt. Daniel B. Blakke (WSO), 335th TFS/4th TFW shoots down a Hughes 500 helicopter.

F-111s fly three SAD, two MS, 13 RR, and 178 RG/GOB PGM strikes for a total of 196, and fly four C, four MS, and four SC for a total of 12 NonPGM strikes. PGM strikes are flown against the Medina and Hammurabi Republican Guard Divisions.

F-117s fly one SAD, three SAM, 19 CCC, 16 A, eight MS, four SC, two RG for a total of 53 strikes.

B-52 sorties total 46 (all AI).

The British Division begins to move to assembly area Ray for the coming attack.

Acting Petty Officer Marine Engineering Artificer Garry Paul Robins RN of HMS EXETER aids in the battle of an engine fire in dense, arid smoke. Marine Engineering Mechanic Leng later earns the Queen's Commendation For Brave Conduct for these actions.

Three Coalition aircraft are destroyed in combat (a EF-111A, F-5E, and Tornado). The USAF EF-111A crashes in Saudi Arabia with both its crewmembers killed. Tornado GR.Mk 1 ZD717, No. XV Squadron flown by Flight Lieutenant Rupert Clark, 31, (pilot) and Flight Lieutenant Stephen Hicks, 26, is shot down by two SA-2s over Al Taqaddum Airfield. Clark becomes a POW and Hicks is killed.

In Kuwait City Bay an Iraqi Osa patrol boat is sunk by A-6Es.

RAF Buccaneers' fly ten offensive counter air sorties today for a total of ten sorties.

Canada flies a total of 20 air sorties today.

French sorties today number four (all reconnaissance).

Italian Tornados fly seven air sorties today.

Total Saudi Arabian air sorties today number 176.

Total Kuwait air sorties today number 20 air interdiction.

The Qatar Air Force does not fly today.

Republican Guard units are hit by 200 sorties today.

15 February Gen. Schwarzkopf is briefed at 0900 on enemy prisoner of war interview results. The EPWs, most veterans of the Iran-Iraq War, are tired. They would surrender in larger numbers if there were no minefields, the Republican Guard, and threats to their families. All EPWs claim that if ground war begins, their brothers will surrender in great numbers. Central Command announces that 60 percent of enemy prisoners of war have willingly surrendered.

In the 65th Scud firing, a Scud missile targeted on Saudi Arabia disintegrates in flight, causing no injuries.

U.S. Marine Capt. Jonathan R. Edwards (Grand Rapids, Michigan) is the first Operation Desert Storm casualty buried in Arlington National Cemetery.

USS WORDEN (CG-18), SHIELDS (FF-1066), and VULCAN (AR-5) cease participation in Operation Desert Storm.

Two A-10s (Capt. Steve Phyllis and Capt. Rob Sweet) attacking Republican Guard Units are shot down by hand-held surface-to-air missiles. An A-6E is battle damaged and crashes, with its crew recovered safely. A-6E 155602 crashes on the deck of the USS AMERICA (CV-66) and is listed as a noncombat loss with its crew safe. Capt. Phyllis is killed in action and Capt. Sweet taken prisoner becoming a POW.

An Iraqi helicopter is shot down by an F-15 on an anti-Scud missile mission (records also state Capt. Todd K. Sheehy ("Springfield 27") flying A-10 81-0964, 511th TFS/10th TFW shoots down a Mi-8 'HIP'. This is kill number 38 and is the last of the Operation Desert Storm.

U.S. Central Command sorties: USAF-1543, USN-491, USMC (fixed-wing)-284, Allied-451.

U.S. carriers launch 395 sorties today (combat and support). The Coalition has flown 73,000 sorties against Iraq (2,600 today).

F-111s fly 38 A, ten RR, and 181 RG/GOB PGM strikes for a total of 229, and fly eight A, and four SC NonPGM strikes for a total of 12. PGM strikes target the Medina Division.

F-117s fly six SAM, six C, 18 MS, two RR, five SC, and 23 Breaching for a total of 60 strikes.

B-52 sorties total 50 (all AI).

The British 1st Armoured Division completes its movement to Forward Assembly Area Ray.

RAF Buccaneers' fly 12 offensive counter air sorties today, for a total of 12 sorties.

Canada flies a total of 12 air sorties today.

French air sorties today number four (all reconnaissance).

Italian Tornados fly seven air sorties today.

Total Saudi Arabian air sorties today number 160.

Total Kuwait air sorties today number 20 air interdiction.

Total Qatar air sorties today number four air interdiction.

Republican Guard units are hit by 100 sorties today. Coastal radars are more active (fear of amphibious assault?).

16 February A U.S. Bradley fighting vehicle and a M113 is hit by Hellfire missiles fired by a AH-64. Two Americans are killed, six wounded.

Two Scud missiles fail to hit Israel, impacting without effect.

To confuse Iraqi reconnaissance, U.S. Marines and other Coalition forces re-position. They continue their artillery duels with the Iraqi gunners.

Two Coalition aircraft (a UH-1 and F-16C 25 84-1379, 17th TFS flown by Capt. Dale Thomas Cormier, 30, of Crystal Lake, Illinois) are a noncombat loss. Cormier dies in the F-16 crash.

U.S. Central Command sorties: USAF-1382, USN-309, USMC (fixed-wing)-271, Allied-416.

U.S. carriers launch 281 sorties today (combat and support).

F-111s fly 12 RR and 91 RG/GOB PGM strikes for a total of 103, and no NonPGM strikes. The Medina and Hammurabi Divisions are targeted.

F-117s fly eight CCC, 13 C, four A, six RR, ten SC, for a total of 41.

B-52 sorties total 43 (all AI).

RAF Buccaneers' fly ten offensive counter air sorties today for a total of ten sorties.

Canada flies a total of 24 air sorties today.

French air sorties today number four (all reconnaissance).

Italian Tornados fly seven air sorties today.

Total Saudi Arabian air sorties today number 155.

Total Kuwait air sorties today number 20 air interdiction.

The Qatar Air Force does not fly today.

17 February An Apache team of the 2-229th Attack of the U.S. Army XVIII Airborne Corps attack an Iraqi bunker overlooking what will become MSR Newmarket, and take ten prisoners. In another engagement, a 2-229th Apache team supported by C Company, 3-502nd Infantry capture 30 more EPWs of the 2nd Battalion, 843rd Brigade, 45th Iraqi Infantry Division.

Beginning evening and continuing until early this morning, the biggest pre-G-Day artillery raid occurs today feinting a major attack. Five artillery battalions of the U.S. Army VII Corps destroy Iraqi air defenses, opening a 2-kilometer-square air corridor. Apache helicopters of 2-6th Cavalry, 11th Aviation Brigade (Lt. Col. Terry Branham) attack Iraqi towers and communication buildings. The raid is observed by Lt. Gen. Frederick Franks, Jr. and Brig. Gen. Creighton Abrams, Jr.

U.S. Marines participate in seven significant engagements with the Iraqis across the Kuwait border. Reconnaissance teams of the 2nd Marine Division advance to insertion points along the berm. Cut points and assembly areas are established by officers.

SYLVANIA (AFS-2) ceases participation in Operation Desert Storm.

U.S. Navy air unit HC-6/DET 4 completes participation in Operation Desert Storm.

U.S. Central Command sorties: USAF-1320, USN-397, USMC (fixed-wing)-146, Allied-280.

U.S. carriers launch 327 sorties (combat and support). Coalition forces have flown 78,000 sorties (2,600 today).

F-111s fly seven C, five A, seven MS, one RR, one SC, and 32 RG/GOB for a total of 53 PGM strikes. The fighters fly four C, and eight MS for a total of 12 NonPGM strikes. PGM strikes are directed against the Medina and Hammurabi Divisions.

F-117s fly three SAM, 15 C, five A, 17 MS, 13 SC, for a total of 56 strikes.

Each of three MC-130s drop one 15,000-lb., fuel/air BLU-82 bomb on Iraqi positions on Faylaka Island.

B-52 sorties total 50 (all AI).

POW Capt. Rob Sweet arrives in Baghdad and begins being tortured by the Iraqi Security Police. Capt. Dale Storr has already been tortured for 14 days.

RAF Buccaneers' fly two offensive counter air sorties today for a total of two sorties.

Canada flies a total of 12 air sorties today.

French air sorties today number one (a reconnaissance flight).

Italy flies no air sorties today.

Total Saudi Arabian air sorties today number 111.

Total Kuwait air sorties today number 12 air interdiction.

The Qatar Air Force does not fly today.

18 February At 0130 the 82nd Airborne Division begins armed reconnaissance missions in the area of the Iraqi 45th Infantry Division near main supply rout (MSR) Texas. Objective Rochambeau is attacked by 11 AH-64s, three UH-60s and one OH-58 of the 1-82nd Aviation. Objective White is hit by 12 AH-64s and three UH-60s of the 12th Aviation Brigade.

2nd Marine Division reconnaissance teams infiltrate into Kuwait to recon the Iraqi obstacles/minefields, and to discover any safe avenues of transit. Task Force "Troy", a deception force of 110 Reserve Marines begins engaging in a number of loud raids against Iraqi 5th Mechanized Division positions to convince them that the 2nd Division positions are still occupied.

USS TRIPOLI (LPH-10) and USS PRINCETON (CG-59) are mined. TRIPOLI strikes a moored contact mine blowing a 16 X 20-ft hole in her starboard bow. Within three hours PRINCETON activates a bottom-influence mine, badly damaging her aft. Four crew members of TRIPOLI and three crew members of PRINCETON are injured (one of them seriously).

USS PUGET SOUND (AD-38) begins participation in Operation Desert Storm.

An F-16 pilot is shot down 40 miles north of the Saudi Arabian border. He is later rescued by a MH-60 Blackhawks from the 3-160th Aviation flown by CWO Thomas Montgomery. Directed by Kuwaiti and U.S. Marine observers, Marine Corp helicopters attack six Iraqi armored personnel carriers (APC). Two are destroyed, the others flee.

U.S. carriers launch 456 sorties today (combat and support). Coalition forces have flown 80,000 sorties (2,400 today).

U.S. Central Command sorties: USAF-1718, USN-575, USMC (fixed-wing)-283, Allied-481.

F-111s fly three CCC, 11 C, 13 RR, and 104 RG/GOB for a total of 131 PGM strikes, and 12 MS NonPGM strikes are flown. The Medina and Hammurabi Divisions are targeted by the PGM strikes.

F-117s fly six L, four C, 37 A, four MS, two RR, and three SC, for a total of 56 strikes.

B-52 sorties total 50 (49 AI, one unknown).

RAF Buccaneers' fly 12 offensive counter air sorties today, for a total of 12 sorties.

Canada flies a total of 12 air sorties today.

French air sorties today number two (both reconnaissance).

Italian Tornados fly seven air sorties today.

Total Saudi Arabian air sorties today number 175.

Total Kuwait air sorties today number 20 air interdiction.

The Qatar Air Force does not fly today.

Republican Guards are struck by 100 sorties today.

19 February The 68th Iraqi Scud missile is launched at Israel, but it impacts without causing injuries.

The 1-5th Cavalry, (Lt. Col. Michael Parker) of the 1st Cavalry Division crosses the berm to probe for enemy mines. When they reach ten kilometers into the Wadi al-Batin, they engage an Iraqi battalion that includes tanks, BMPs, and artillery.

With the arrival of the 8th Marines (Col. Larry S. Schmidt), the entire 2nd Marine Division is now in place at Al Khanjar.

The aviation brigade of the 24th Infantry Division (Mechanized) attack various Iraqi positions across the border. Using a Copperhead round, B Battery, 4-41st Field Artillery, destroy an Iraqi border post.

USS BEAUFORT (ATS-2) and USS ADROIT (MSO-509) pass through an uncharted minefield to tow the cruiser PRINCETON to safety. A minefield of approximately 22 sea mines is located and marked off in the Northern Persian Gulf (153 mines have been found by this date). USS TRIPOLI is operationally mission-capable in the Northern Persian Gulf.

A OA-10 (Lt. Col. Jeff Fox) is shot down over Kuwait. A U.S. Navy A-6 destroys five camouflaged revetments in western Iraqi. Lt. Col. Fox becomes a POW.

U.S. carriers launch 460 sorties today (combat and support). Coalition forces have flown 83,000 sorties (2,800 today).

U.S. Central Command sorties: USAF-1655, USN-484, USMC (fixed-wing)-303, Allied-440.

F-111s fly 19 MS and 121 PGM strikes for a total of 140. Eight C and four RR NonPGM strikes are flown for a total of 12. The Medina and Hammurabi Divisions are targeted by PGM strikes.

F-117s fly six C, two MS, one RR, seven SC for a total of 16 strikes.

B-52 sorties today total 42 (all AI).

Spanish ships NUMANCIA, DIANA, and INFANTA CRISTINA complete participation in Operation Desert Storm.

German RHEIN-Class depot ship DONAU (A-69) commanded by Cdr. Nicolaisen begins participation in Operation Desert Storm.

Republican Guard Forces are hit by five packages, 100 sorties today.

British soldiers are informed that today is G-3: three days before G-day (ground attack day).

RAF Buccaneers' fly 12 offensive counter air sorties today, for a total of 12 sorties.

Canada flies a total of 12 air sorties today.

French sorties today number two (both reconnaissance).

Italian Tornados fly seven air sorties today.

Total Saudi Arabian air sorties today number 161.

Total Kuwait air sorties today number 20 air interdiction.

Total Qatar air sorties today number four air interdiction.

20 February Iraqi infantry, armor and artillery are engaged across the Kuwait border by U.S. forces. One hundred kilometers north, 300 revetted Iraqi vehicles are attacked, destroying 28 tanks and 28 other vehicles. One U.S. service member is killed and seven are wounded. In total 421 EPWs are captured today.

At 0810 Apaches of the 2-229th Attack and Cobras of the 3-101st Aviation attack near what will be MSR Newmarket, thus securing their MSR before the ground war begins. They take 406 EPWs.

The Iraqi 45th Infantry Division is hit by attacks of the 1-82nd Aviation and the 5-6th Cavalry, 82nd Airborne Division, supported by the 1-17th Cavalry. The 1-201st Field Artillery of the West Virginia National Guard, supports these attacks.

The 2nd Brigade, 1st Cavalry Division (Col. Randolph House) execute a reconnaissance-in-force maneuver into the Wadi al-Batin.

The U.S. VII Corps and XVIII Airborne Corps are in position to attack. Lt. Gen. Pagonis's logistics troops bring forward sufficient supplies to maintain the corps assault for 29 days. Fuel for 5.2 days is provided and ammunition for 45 days.

The 2nd Combat Engineer Battalion, 2nd Marine Division begins to prepare routes of attack on the berm, making 18 cuts though six will be used breaching the obstacles. Lance Corporal William E. Owens climbs an electrical pylon in full view of the enemy and draw sketches of the Iraqi minefield.

U.S. troop strength numbers 527,000.

USS ADROIT discovers a large minefield on sonar. They estimate that a lane will be clear for the battleship WISCONSIN in two to three days.

From the deck of USS AMERICA an S-3 Viking of Anti-submarine Squadron 32 bombs a high-speed Iraqi boat with three 500-pound bombs.

U.S. carriers launch 401 sorties today (combat and support). Coalition forces have flown 86,000 sorties (2,900 today).

To test napalms effectiveness in burning off oil, USMC aircraft drop napalm on three Iraqi oil trenches.

U.S. Central Command sorties: USAF-1399, USN-417, USMC (fixed-wing)-164, Allied-405.

Three U.S. aircraft are lost. While in combat, a U.S. Army helicopter crashes killing the pilot and co-pilot, and a U.S. Marine CH-46 helicopter and F-16 are a non-combat losses.

Two MC-130s drop a BLU-82 fuel/air bomb.

F-111s fly two C, 14 MS, and four RG/GOB for a total of 25 PGM strikes. They fly four L, four MS, four RR, and 13 RG/GOB for a total of 25 NonPGM strikes.

F-117s fly two CCC, eight C, 19 MS, two RR for a total of 31 strikes.

B-52 sorties today total 39 (all AI).

RAF Buccaneers' fly ten offensive counter air sorties today, for a total of ten sorties.

Canada flies a total of 20 air sorties today.

French air sorties today number two (both reconnaissance).

Italian Tornados fly seven air sorties today.

Total Saudi Arabian air sorties today number 171.

The Kuwait Air Force does not fly today.

The Qatar Air Force does not fly today.

For 10 days no Iraqi aircraft have flown. By this date, 42 Iraqi aircraft and six helicopters have been shot down.

Republican Guard units are hit by 100 sorties today.

21 February At the King Khalid Military City and on coastal Saudi Arabia four Scud missiles crash harmlessly.

Deep in Iraq, a U.S. Special Forces reconnaissance team call two F-15E Strike Eagles to destroy an Iraqi convoy. A MH-60 Black Hawk piloted by Capt. Charles Cooper and Chief Warrant Officer Michael Anderson crashes, killing the crew and the seven-man Delta Force team on board (including Sergeant Major Patrick Hurley, Master Sergeants Eloy Rodriguez and Otto Clark).

The 2nd Light Armored Infantry Battalion, 2nd Marine Division (Lt. Col. Keith T. Holcomb) begins screening actions to the division's front. The unit diverts the Iraqi's attention away from the division's breach site. They eventually engage Iraqi troops, artillery and tanks at least 17 times. They kill many Iraqis and destroy 12 tanks-an additional 35 with air strikes-and capture 120 EPWs. A Fire Support Plan of 193 targets is developed. They are arranged in programs for firing series, concentrations, and phases, as the division's attack progresses.

USS WISCONSIN fires 50 rounds of 16-inch high explosive shells at a command complex in Khafji, Saudi Arabia. More than 40 Iraqi mines have been discovered in the last 36 hours. USS NASSAU (LHA-4) launches U.S. Marine AV-8B jump jets for the first time in history for combat missions. Marine Attack Squadron 331 launches 243 AV-8B sorties.

U.S. Marines exchange fire with Iraqi troops, destroying Iraqi anti-aircraft equipment with small arms and rockets. The Kuwait border continues to increase in the numbers of engagements.

The USS SPRUANCE diverts the Panamanian flagged FRIO CARBIC in the Northern Red Sea. She is en route from Tampa to Aqaba.

Six Coalition aircraft are lost (CH-46 Sea Knight, F-16, SH-60 Seahawk, OH-58, MH-60 and UH-60). Only the OH-58 is lost due to combat. PO3 James F. Crockford dies in the Sea Knight launched from USS SEATTLE (AOE-3). The SH-60 helicopter's engine lost power taking off from the USS HALYBURTON (FFG-40). *These are the last U.S. Navy aircraft losses in Operation Desert Shield/Storm. Eleven total, 7 combat, 4 non-combat.*

U.S. Central Command sorties: USAF-1511, USN-435, USMC (fixed-wing)-257, Allied-424.

U.S. carriers launch 441 sorties today (combat and support). Coalition forces have flown 88,000 sorties (2,400 today).

At Incirlik four F-4Es of the 3rd TFW (PACAF) arrives. During the remainder of the war on classifed dates are the following Proven Force deployments: 21 B-52s of the 801st PBW to Moron, Spain, eight B-52s to Fairford, UK, 15 KC-135s 804th ARW, three E-3A of the 552nd AWACW, 11 C-130Hs of the 37th TAS, eight C-130Es of the 61st TAS and to Incirlik, 7 KC-10s to Malpensa, Italy, seven KC-10s and a KC-135 to Zaragoza, Spain, nine KC-135s to Mont De Marsen, nine KC-135s to Mildenhall, UK, one KC-135 to Andravida, Greece, seven KC-135s to Helenikon, Greece, and two RC-135s to Souda Bay.

F-111s fly four L, three MS, five RR and 141 RG/GOB for a total of PGM strikes. They fly 12 MS NonPGM strikes. The Medina and Hammurabi Divisions are hit, along with VIP bunkers.

F-117s fly 11 CCC, four L, 27 C, five RR, seven SC, for a total of 55 strikes. The 37th

TFW flies 37 sorties.

B-52 sorties today total 41 (all AI).

RAF Buccaneers' fly 12 offensive counter air sorties today for a total of 12 sorties.

Canada flies a total of 24 air sorties today.

French air sorties today number three (all reconnaissance).

Italian Tornados fly seven air sorties today.

Total Saudi Arabian air sorties today number 133.

Total Kuwait air sorties today number 12 air interdiction.

Total Qatar air sorties today number four air interdiction.

The U.S. Department of Defense authorizes the awarding of the National Defense Medal.

The Republican Guard is hit by 100 sorties.

22 February On a beach south of Kuwait City, U.S. Navy SEALs insert a team of CIA-trained Kuwaiti guerrillas. The Naval Special Warfare Task Group commanded by Capt. Ray Smith consists of 260 SEALs with their tactical operations center at Ras al Gar, 75 miles north of Dhahran, Saudi Arabia. SEAL missions have mostly consisted of observing Kuwaiti beaches through night vision equipment or swimming to the shore from their Zodiac rafts.

With a final artillery brigade joining VII Corps, all Coalition forces are now in position to attack.

A massive U.S. and British artillery bombardment of Iraqi artillery begins. During three separate Iraqi artillery attacks one U.S. Marine is killed and seven wounded. Eighteen Iraqi tanks and 15 vehicles are destroyed. U.S. Marines capture 87 EPWs.

The 2nd Combat Engineer Battalion, 2nd Marine Division (Lt. Col. John D. Winchester) completes passages through the berm. The 3rd Battalion, 23rd Marines (Lt. Col. Ray C. Dawson) advances into Kuwait to provide security for the division's artillery survey units.

Approximately 100 Kuwaiti oil wells have been destroyed. President George Bush announces that Iraq has *"launched a scorched-earth policy destroying the entire oil production system of Kuwait."*

In preparation for ground combat, the 3rd Marine Air Wing aircraft drop napalm on oil-filled Iraqi trenches to ignite the fuel.

USS JOHN F. KENNEDY (CV-67) has launched by this date over 800 sorties (80 direct bombing missile strike missions). U.S. carriers launch 393 sorties today (combat and support). Coalition forces have flown more than 91,000 sorties (over 2,700 today).

U.S. Central Command sorties: USAF-1614, USN-445, USMC (fixed-wing)-402, Allied-445. Due to good weather over 1300 sorties have been able to be flown against Iraqi forces.

F-111s fly three A, nine RR, and 228 RG/GOB PGM strikes for a total of 240, and fly 12 C for a total of 12 NonPGM strikes. The Tawakalna Division is targeted.

F-117s fly eight L, 22 C, five MS, for a total of 35 strikes.

B-52 sorties total 51 (all AI).

French organization of 2nd Foreign Legion Infantry Garrison is Corps Commander, Col. Derville; Assistant Commander, Lt. Col. Lecerf; Operations, Lt. Col. Germain; Reconnaissance, Maj. de Cockborne; 2nd Company, Capt. Chavancy; 3rd Company, Capt. Thiebault; 4th Company, Capt. deReviers; Service Company, Capt. Rouart.

RAF Buccaneers' fly 12 offensive counter air sorties, today for a total of 12 sorties.

Canada flies a total of eight air sorties.

French air sorties today number five (four air interdiction and one reconnaissance).

Italian Tornados fly seven air sorties today.

Total Saudi Arabian air sorties today number 144.

Total Kuwait air sorties today number 20 air interdiction.

The Qatar Air Force does not fly today.

British RFA ORANGELEAF completes participation in Operation Desert Storm.

The Republican Guard is hit by 100 sorties today. The Tawakalna is a new Republican Guard unit formed of veteran brigades of the Iran-Iraq War. The 55th Battalion, 9th Tank Brigade's mission is to defend Iraq and the KTO supply line, counterattacking if needed. 3rd Platoon, 1st Company (Lt. Saif ad-Din) is a typical platoon of three tanks and eight men.

23 February Iraq fails to comply with the Coalition deadline. At 2000 President George Bush addresses the nation on television. He reports that he has directed Commander-in-Chief, U.S. Central Command, Army Gen. H. Norman Schwartzkopf *"to use all forces available, including ground forces, to eject the Iraqi Army from Kuwait . . . The liberation of Kuwait has entered a final phase."*

The Secretary of Defense Dick Cheney announces that a *"large ground offensive"* has begun.

Two Scud missiles are fired (one targeted at Israel, the other at Saudi Arabia). Neither cause any damage.

At 2000 Sgt. Jeffrey Sims and his **5th Special Forces Group** A-Team, Operational Detachment Alpha 523 (Sgt. Roy Tabron and Sgt. Ron Torbett) land approximately six miles west of Qawam al Hamzah and Highway 8 in their MH-60 Black Hawk. Fifteen miles south, Capt. Christopher Conner, the commander of ODA-532, lands with his three-man team. About 1100, Sgt. Sim's hide site is spotted by a little girl and old man, which alert nearby villagers. After fighting over two hours against two bus loads of Iraqi soldiers a MH-60 Black Hawk of the "Night Stalkers" the 160th Regiment (flown by WO James "Monk" Crisafulli) rescues the team. Seven Green Beret hide sites south of the Euphrates river are never compromised. For five days they report that there are no large reinforcements on Highway 8.

At 0600 a 14-man **U.S. Navy SEAL team** (Task Unit Mike) in four naval special warfare speedboats commanded by Lt. Tom Deitz departs the staging base at Ras al Mishab, Saudi Arabia. They speed at 40 knots through mine infested waters to a position off a Kuwaiti beach. Their mission is to convince the Iraqi troops at Mina Saud, Kuwait, that an amphibious assault by 17,000 U.S. Marines is occurring by using explosives and machine guns. At 1930, the SEAL team arrives seven miles off Mina Saud. At 2200, three Zodiacs arrive 500 yards offshore, and Deitz observes the shore through a night vision scope for ten minutes. Approximately 2235, the six SEAL swimmers, including Lt. Deitz, are lying on the beach in two feet of water, 50 yards apart. At 2247, the SEALs pull detonation pins on their 20-lbs of C-4 explosive, set to explode at 0100. At 1230, the SEALs begin firing at the beach with .50-caliber machine guns and grenade launchers. At 0100 the 120 pounds of C-4 explosive detonates.

Under operational control of the French 6th Light Armored Division (Brig. Gen. Benard Janvier) the 2nd Brigade of the **82nd Airborne Division** seize a dominate position overlooking MSR Texas.

Six Apaches of the "Night Eagles", 3-1 Aviation, **1st Armored Division** (Lt. Col. William Hatch) fly a reconnaissance mission 60 kilometers north, covering a 25 kilometer division front with their Forward-Looking Infrared (FLIR) cameras.

Four artillery battalions of the **2nd Marine Division** advance into Kuwait. They move forward to be in position to provide fire support for the coming attack, due to Iraqi artillery's greater range.

The USS MISSOURI destroys targets on Faylaka Island.

Aircraft of Task Force 154 (MIDWAY, RANGER, ROOSEVELT, AMERICA) attack Faylaka Island. They target AAA positions, communication facility and bunkers.

Approximately 1900 a "friendly" aircraft launches an antiradiation missile. It hits the counterbattery radar of the 11th Marines, killing Sgt. Aaron A. Pack.

A USMC AV-8B is shot down near the Kuwaiti Ali Al Salem airfield. Capt. James N. Wilbourn is missing in action. A CH-46 from the USS SEATTLE is a noncombat loss.

F-111s fly ten CCC, 11 RR and 118 RG/GOB PGM strikes for a total of 139 PGM strikes. They fly 12 MS NonPGM strikes.

F-117s fly four CCC, nine L, 18 C, 12 MS, for a total of 43 strikes. The 37th TFW flies 37 sorties.

B-52 sorties total 43 (all AI).

HMS BRAZEN, and HMS CARDIFF complete participation in Operation Desert Storm.

Tally of 685 Iraqi tanks, 925 armored vehicles and 1,450 artillery pieces are confirmed destroyed by this date.

In Kuwait 450 of the countries oil wells are burning.

U.S. Central Command sorties: USAF-1643, USN-436, USMC (fixed-wing)-484, Allied-478.

U.S. carriers launch 384 sorties today (combat and support). Coalition forces have flown 94,000 sorties (2,900 today).

British Maj. John Rochelle, commander of C Company, Staffordshire Regiment, addresses his company. He reads from Shakespeare's Henry V, the night before Agincourt. A Company joins the Royal Scots Dragoon Guards and B Squadron, Scots Dragoon Guards. C Squadron, Queens Royal Irish Hussars in turn joins the Staffordshire Regiment.

RAF Buccaneers' fly 12 offensive counter air sorties today for a total of 12 sorties.

Canada flies a total of 32 air sorties today.

French air sorties today number four (all reconnaissance).

Italy flies no sorties today.

Total Saudi Arabian air sorties today number 164.

Total Kuwait air sorties today number 20 air interdiction.

The Qatar Air Force does not fly today.

24 February G-Day, ground attack day. At 0400 (240100Z) the Allied ground attack begins. Advance elements of the **101st Airborne Division** fly into Iraq and establishe an airhead (Objective Cobra). The U.S. **1st Marine Division** (with Kuwaiti and Saudis) attack along the coastal road. At 0530 the **2nd Marine Division** (led by the 6th Marines to the music of the Marine's Hymn blasting over psych/ops speakers) and Saudi Arabian troops attack through six breach lines toward Kuwait City. At 1500 the **24th Mechanized Infantry** begins its attack.

With electronic intelligence indicating that the 3rd and 4th Iraqi Corps are in confusion, Gen. Schwarzkopf calls Lt. Gen. Yeosock and Lt. Gen. Luck to ask if they can attack today rather than tomorrow. All units other than the **Joint Forces Command-North** agree to attack at 1500.

The U.S. Army **1st Infantry Division** spearheads the armored attack of the VII Corps, opening a hole for the corps to follow. The security zone of the Iraqi 26th and 48th Infantry Divisions is seized, preventing observation for intelligence or artillery fire direction.

At 0530, the 1st and 2nd Brigades advance through 20 holes in the berm army engineers have cut. At 0538, the 1st Brigade's (Col. Bert Maggart) Task Force 2-24th Armor and Task Force 5-16th Infantry advance left, while 2nd Brigade's (Col. Tony Moreno) Task Force 3-37th Armor and TF 2-16th Infantry (Lt. Col. Daniel Fake) advance right. By 0915, the battle is over with Iraqi resisters trapped in their bunkers and trenches when they are collapsed by 1st Infantry tanks. At 1430, 1st Infantry Artillery (Col. Mike Dotson) fire on the Iraqi 48th Infantry Division. Bombardment includes: 11,000 artillery rounds and 414 MLRS rockets (600,000 explosive bomblets over a 20 X 40-kilometer area) destroying all of the Iraqi's 83 guns. At 1500, TF 2-16th Infantry and TF 3-37th Armor begins lane clearing through minefields and Iraqi fortifications. With 4-37th Armor (Lt. Col. David Marlin) Col. Moreno's brigade has 76 Bradley's, 116 Abram tanks, and hundreds of artillery, engineer, air defense, maintenance, command and control and supply vehicles. A and D Tank Companies (Capt. Thomas Wock) lead the 2nd Brigade, arriving at Phase Line Colorado by 1800 (the day's limit of advance). The division has successfully breached the Iraqi line in 2 hours.

At 0727, 66 Blackhawk and 30 Chinook helicopters of the 1st Brigade, of the U.S. **101st Airborne Division (Air Assault)** commanded by Col. Tom Hill take off to seize a forward operating base 100 kilometers inside Iraq (FOB Cobra). Two minutes after landing, the 426th Supply and Transportation Battalion (Lt. Col. John Broderick) lands its first unit, and begins preparing refueling points. At 1000, A Company, 1-327th Infantry (Capt. John Russell) attacks a ridge 2 kilometers to the north, coordinated with aircraft and artillery, taking the dug-in position and 340 EPWs The 101st consists of 200 helicopters, nearly 1,000 vehicles, and in excess of 6,000 soldiers.

At dawn, the U.S. Army's **2nd Armored Cavalry Regiment**, VII Corp's lead scout is in position over the berm, on a 40-kilometer front. At 1430, an aerial picket of Cobra helicopters of the 4th Squadron lift off augmented by 18 Apaches, 13 OH-58s and 3 Blackhawks of 2-1st Aviation, **1st Armored Division**. As they identify targets, fighter bombers are directed to the targets by the regimental air liaison officer Capt. Chris Kupko, USAF. By 1630, lead squadrons are 40 kilometers within enemy terrain, fighting small engagements with Iraqi T-55 and BMPs, and have captured hundreds of EPWs. At 1700, two Chinooks of A Company, 5-159th Aviation led by Capt. Debra Davis fly a daring emergency aerial resupply mission, carrying tank ammunition.

By 2130 the U.S. **1st Armored Division** has formed a division wedge formation (1st Brigade forward and 2nd and 3rd Brigades to the left and right). The formation covers a 26-kilometer front.

At 0400, with two brigades abreast (at left, two Legion Regiments, 1st Hussars Airborne Regiment and C.R.A.P. commandos; at right with the U.S. 2nd of the 82nd is the French 4th Dragoon Regiment with engineers and artillery) the **French 6th Light Armored Division** (Brig. Gen. Benard Janvier) advances along MSR Texas toward as-Salman and the Euphrates Valley. The 2nd Brigade of the **82nd Airborne Division** follows in trucks. At 1100, an Iraqi brigade of the 45th Infantry Division on Objective Rochambeau is struck by MLRS and 155mm fire from the U.S. 18th Field Artillery Brigade. The 4th Regiment of Dragoons then assaults the objective and quickly captures it. By 1200, 30 kilometers south of as-Salman, the 6th Light Armored Division has destroyed a company of Iraqi T-55 tanks. A logjam on the supply route is minimized in the attack by priority of movement on the MSR being given to artillery, engineers, fuel and ammunition. After Objective White is enveloped by a simultaneous flanking attack, at 1410 the 6th Light Armored Division attack. By 1800, as-Salman and its airfield is surrounded by French Forces.

At 0400, the **1st Marine Division** begins to penetrate the two obstacle fields between the Umm Gudair and Al Wafrah oilfields. They attempt to infiltrate between the Iraqi 29th and 42nd Infantry Divisions. Task Force Grizzly (Col. Jim Fulks) and Task Force Taro (Col. John H. Admire) secure the flanks of the 1st Marine Division's main attack (Task Forces Ripper commanded by Col. Carlton W. Fulford Jr. and Task Force Papa Bear commanded by Col. Richard W. Hodory). By mid-afternoon, they breach the second barrier field and drive near the southwest corner of the burning Burqan Oilfield, seizing large numbers of EPWs. At 1753, Task Force Ripper consolidates its position near its objective Al Jaber Air Base. The I MEF has only 1,100 night vision goggles and is ill equipped to fight in the dark.

The Al Jaber airfield and Al Burqan oil field is taken by the **1st Marine Division**. An Iraqi armored unit attacking the **2nd Marine Division** from Kuwait City is destroyed. All the initial day's objectives are met within the first 12 hours. From 2nd Marine Division, one Marine and one soldier of the "Tiger Brigade" are killed, 12 wounded.

Early morning the **5th Marine Expeditionary Brigade** steam toward Mishab in their amphibious ships to act as the I MEF reserve. The units Marine Group 50 (Col. Randall L. "Grit" West) fly the brigade's heliborne assault unit to the area of Task Force Troy (south of Al Wafrah).

Tank strength of I MEF is 194 M60A1/A3s, 17 M60 W/M9s, 74 M1A1s, and 118 M1A1 (U.S. Army).

At 1500, the **U.S. Army VII Corps** crosses its line of departure begining Operation *Desert Saber.*

An Iraqis Silkworm anti-ship missile is fired at the WISCONSIN, while the battleship bombards Kuwait. The missile crashes into the water. Another Silkworm is destroyed by a Sea Dart missile fired from HMS GLOUCESTER (D-96), that is escorting the battleship. Carrier-based aircraft destroy the Iraqis missile battery.

Ground forces from the United States, United Kingdom, France, Saudi Arabia, United Arab Emirates, Bahrain, Qatar, Oman, Egypt, Syria and Kuwait attack.

USS SAMUEL B. ROBERTS intercepts the 100th ship in the maritime interception campaign. MACDONOUGH (DDG-39) and NICHOLAS (FFG-47) cease participation in Operation Desert Storm.

The 3rd Marine Aircraft Wing flies 671 sorties today (fixed wing aircraft averaging 2.36 sorties each). F/A-18 Hornets of Marine Aircraft Group 11 flying ground attack missions support the I MEF. Their Sparrow and Sidewinder missiles can quickly engage any Iraqi aircraft. Strength of the wing is: 38 AH-1J/Ws, 29 UH-1Ns, 59 CH-46Es, 26 CH-53Ds, six RH-53Ds, 24 CH-53Es, 63 AV-8Bs, 20 A-6Es, 12 EA-6Bs, 72 FA-18A/Cs, 12 FA-18Ds, 20 KC-130F/R/Ts, 19 OV-10A/Ds, and two UC-12Bs.

U.S. carriers launch 445 sorties today (combat and support). Aircraft of Task Force 154 (MIDWAY, RANGER, ROOSEVELT, AMERICA) continue to hit Faylaka Island in anticipation of a ground attack. Many targets the Navy must pass to the USAF due to their most numerous airframe, the F/A-18 lacking laser designators and therefore unable to deliver PGMs.

U.S. Navy air units HSL-44 (DET 8), and VPMAU complete participation in Operation Desert Storm.

U.S. Central Command sorties: USAF-1648, USN-442, USMC (fixed-wing)-436, Allied-536.

American B-52s fly around the clock, hitting frontline forces and breaching sites. In the following days they will hit Iraqi headquarters and staging areas south of the Euphrates River. In excess of 3,000 Coalition sorties are flown today.

B-52 sorties today total 47 (all AI).

F-111s fly eight RR, and 163 RG/GOB PGM strikes. They fly 14 MS NonPGM strikes. The Tawakalna Division is targeted by PGM strikes today.

F-117s fly 16 L, four C, 11 MS, 11 RR, for a total of 42 strikes.

French troops of the **6th Light Armored Division** assault Bordeaux Crossroads and its As Salman airfield. French units assaulting the Iraqis are: Group 1, 3rd Company, 2nd Foreign Infantry Regiment (Capt. Thiebault) with 1st of the Marine Mechanized Infantry (Capt. de Kersabiec); Group 2, 2/1st Foreign Cavalry Regiment (Capt. Yakovlev), 4/2nd Foreign Infantry Regiment (Capt. de Reviers); Group 3, 1/1st Foreign Cavalry Regiment (Capt. Dumont-Saint-Priest), 2/2nd Foreign Infantry Regiment (Capt. Chavancy).

After 1800, the **Joint Forces Command-North** attacks on MarCent's left flank, stopping just short of their breach for the night. The **Joint Forces Command-East** advances well until meeting the Iraqi 18th Infantry Division along the coast north of Raz az Zawr.

At 2130, Iraqi Col. Mohammed Ashad is ordered by the Iraqi 12th Armored Division commander to prepared positions as a forward screen for the Jihad Corps. With the Iraqi 37th Armored Brigade, Mohammed's 50th Armored Brigade is to orient itself southwest at their position west of the Wadi al-Batin. The 50th assumes positions 30 kilometers southeast of al-Busayyah. The Tawakalna Mechanized Division (Republican Guard) and the Adnan Infantry Division will back up the 12th Armored Division. On a low rise west of the wadi, Republican Guard commander Gen. Ayad Futayih al-Rawi prepares a rear slope tank ambush. Deploying Iraqi forces north to south are: the 29th Mechanized Brigade, the 9th Armored Brigade in the center and the 18th Mechanized Brigade to the south (Tawakalna). Moving to defend the Tawakalna's northern flank is the Adnan Infantry Division and to the division's rear is the Medina Division (Republican Guard).

According to the U.S. Air Force's *Gulf War Air Power Survey* Summary Report the strength of Iraqi Army on this date is approximately 200,000 to 222,000 personnel. The Iraqis possess approximately 800 fewer tanks, and 600 fewer artillery pieces than had been believed.

RAF Buccaneers' fly 12 offensive counter air sorties today, for a total of 12 sorties.

Canada flies a total of 46 air sorties today.

French air sorties today number two (both are air interdiction).

Italian Tornados fly seven air sorties today.

Total Saudi Arabian air sorties today number 204.

Total Kuwait air sorties today number 20 air interdiction.

The Qatar Air Force does not fly today.

25 February In early morning Brig. Gen. John Stewart, Jr. informs **VII Corps** commander Lt. Gen. Frederick Franks, Jr. that the Iraqis are not counterattacking. Schwarzkopf informs Franks that radio intercepts indicate that the Iraqi III Corps has ordered withdrawal and heavy tank transporters have been detected moving toward the Hammurabi assembly area. Schwarzkopf wants Franks to accelerate his attack to prevent the escape of the Republican Guard. JSTARS is concentrating on the 52nd Iraqi Armored, which with the Tawakalna has moved less than a brigade to Phase Line Smash (JSTARS has discovered the exact number of these tanks, and armored vehicles along with their location, speed and direction). In the afternoon, in nearly freezing weather pelted by muddy sand and rain, Franks selects contingency plan FRAGPLAN 7 for his VII Corps. It assumes that the Republican Guard when Desert Storm begins will not maneuver, but remain in position. His electronic mail order to his 145,000 soldiers is the most important in Operation Desert Storm. His three heavy divisions will turn clockwise, on-line, and destroy the Republican Guard.

Near Nasiriya along the Sahra al-Hajarah (The Desert of Stone) in the Euphrates Valley the **U.S. 24th Mechanized Infantry** wheels its 26,000 soldiers and 8,600 vehicles at 25 kilometers per hour east toward Basra. At 0300, at Objective Brown 140 kilometers north of the Saudi Border the **197th Infantry Brigade** (Col. Ted Reid) blocks the 24th Infantry Division's left while the 2nd Brigade (Col. Paul Kern) blocks to the right at Objective Gray The 1st Brigade (Col. John LeMoyne) attacks forward 50 kilometers beyond the Iraqi's first defense line. They now strike a rocky desert terrain, "the great dismal bog," which as the landscape begins its drop of 290-meters to the Euphrates, has become a quagmire from the constant rain. The divisional cavalry squadron 2-4th Cavalry (Lt. Col. Thomas Leney) begins to look for passable routes for the 197th Brigade. Attacking with the **U.S. 101st Airborne Division**, Objective Gold (a large enemy logistics center) is destroyed.

In rain and wind, scout platoon "Team Jerry" of the U.S. 3-187th Infantry, **101st Airborne Division** (1st Lt. Jerry Biller), is inserted in a very isolated landing zone, only a few kilometers south of the Euphrates River. After searching for a useable division size landing zone, at 1216 30 Chinooks of the 3rd Brigade (Col. Robert Clark) land at Landing Zone Sand 40 kilometers south of the Euphrates river. At 1508, combat-loaded Blackhawks with 14-16 soldiers in each land 500 air assault infantry directly next to the key Iraqi supply route of Highway 8. *In 31 hours using the largest U.S. air armada ever committed to an air assault operation, Maj. Gen. J.H. Binford Peay III has cut off Iraqi supply and reinforcement.*

Between 1220 and 1240, with its 4th Squadron leading, the **U.S. 2nd Armored Cavalry Regiment** engages T-55 tanks and APCs of the Iraqi 50th Armored Brigade of the 12th

Armored Division. The 2nd and 3rd Squadrons advance during the afternoon. They join with the 4th Squadron which with A-10s had destroyed the 50th Armored Brigade. In the evening, four soldiers are killed and four wounded when two of the regiment's M113 APCs are mistakenly attacked as enemy. By the end of the day, the regiment moves east to allow the **1st Armored Division's** cavalry squadron and the **1st and 3rd Armored Divisions** space to advance north toward Phase Line Smash.

Soon after the U.S. **1st Armored Division** begins advancing, its 1st Brigade strikes the southern sector of the Iraqi 806th Infantry Brigade, 26th Infantry Division 50 kilometers south of al-Busayyah (Objective Purple). With worsening weather, Gen. Griffith shifts the 1st Brigade west, in order to bypass the Iraqis and maintain the division's momentum. His trailing 3rd Brigade (Col. Dan Zanini) attacks the Iraqis and take many EPWs. Advancing toward Objective Purple, the 1st Brigade led by the 1-1st Cavalry makes contact with other elements of the Iraqi 26th Infantry, taking 300 EPWs. The 2-41st Field Artillery fires 1,500 artillery rounds and 350 MLRS rockets at al-Busayyah, during the coming night.

At 0400, movement of the Iraqi 3rd Armored Brigade and the 8th Mechanized Brigade is detected in the southern Burqan Oilfield. At 0415, the Iraqis encounter the left flank of the **1st Marine Division** while the main Iraqi attack blunders into the division's right flank. At 0555, at dawn, Company B, 4th Tank Battalion (Marine Reserves from Yakima, Washington, commanded by Capt. Ralph F. Parkison) detect a T-72 tank column. Without time to confirm with higher command, Capt. Parkison orders his M1A1s to attack, quickly destroying 34 of 35 enemy tanks. At 0835, T-72s 5,000 meters east of Brig. Gen. Myatt's Burqan Oilfield command post are detected with AH-1 Sea Cobras directed to attack the tanks. About 0925, the command group is surprised in the midst of the attack due to Myatt's belief that the oilfilds are inhospitable. By 1008, the command group's security force has destroyed several vehicles, the division's fight at close quarters due to the thick smoke. *This becomes the largest tank engagement in Marine Corps history.* By noon, both Marine divisions have reached Phase Line Red, preparations being made to attack the 1st Marine's objective, the Kuwait International Airport.

Objectives "Ice Cube" and "Ice Tray" are attacked through by the **2nd Marine Division**. The Marines battle the 39th Iraqi Infantry Brigade, 7th Iraqi Infantry Division, and the 116th Iraqi Brigade, 7th Iraqi Infantry Division. Both units finally surrender.

U.S. Army and U.S. Marine Corps troops capture 20 T-62 tanks, 40 APCs and engage 150 armored vehicles. Since the ground attack has begun, in excess of 270 Iraqi tanks have been destroyed. Elements of Marines approach Kuwait City.

At 2218, Lt. Gen. Boomer establishes his forward command post five kilometers southwest of "Ice Tray."

Elements of the **5th Marine Expeditionary Brigade** raid towards Al Wafrah, taking 13 prisoners. The remainder of the regimental team and its equipment lands in LCAC air-cushioned landing vehicles near Mishab. This is the first combat landing using these vehicles.

U.S. ground casualties are extremely light: 4 killed in action, 21 wounded.

The USS WISCONSIN and MISSOURI provide naval gunfire support for the ground offensive. MISSOURI fires 133 rounds of 16-inch high explosive shells (125 tons) on shore targets. Most are about the Kuwait International Airport.

U.S. carriers launch 524 sorties today (combat and support). Coalition forces have flown 97,000 sorties.

U.S. Central Command sorties: USAF-1518, USN-556, USMC (fixed-wing)-382, Allied-425.

Guarding the VII Corps southern flank the **British Division** attacks move forward through lanes cleared by the U.S. **1st Infantry Division** to attack the Iraqi 52nd Armored Division. Led by the **Queen's Royal Irish Hussars** (Maj. Vincent James Tobias Maddison) they pass phase line "New Jersey" Arthur Denaro calling over the radio "Move now! Tally-ho!" The British are to clear objectives Copper, Brass, Steel, Zinc, Platinum, and Tungsten respectively against Iraqi 7th Corps resistance. By 1515, the lead British 7th Brigade is assaulting east along the American divisional northern axis, and at 1930 the 4th Brigade is attacking along the southern axis. At 2230, the 4th Brigade begins its attack on Objective Bronze, destroying large logistics sites. Maj. Gen. Rupert Smith, when asked to send PSYOP loudspeakers forward to offer the Iraqis surrender, orders additional MLRS fire.

By the afternoon of 25 February, **Joint Forces Command-East** blasts through their opposition and advances up the coastal freeway.

Coalition minesweepers clear areas for battleship support.

Three U.S. Marine aircraft are shot down (a AH-64, AV-8B, and a OV-10D). Capt. J.S. Walsh flying a AV-8B Harrier of VMA-542 is shot down and rescued. Maj. Joseph J. Small and Capt. David M. Spellacy flying a OV-10 Bronco of Squadron VMO-1 is shot down. Maj. Small becomes a POW and Capt. Spellacy is KIA.

F-111s fly 32 A, four RR, and 74 RG/GOB PGM strikes for a total of 110 strikes, and four C, eight A, 53 RG/GOB NonPGM strikes for a total of 65.

All USAF F-117 flights are cancelled by CENTAF due to poor weather.

B-52 sorties total 47 (all AI).

Early morning in the Iraqi 7th Corps sector, the approximately 91 Chinese Type 59 tanks of Col. Mohammed Ashad's 50th Armored Brigade 30 kilometers southeast of al-Busayyah has yet to join the brigade's MTLB infantry carriers. At 1230, the U.S. Army 2-2nd ACR attacks, and within minutes, Col. Mohammed is their prisoner.

Exploding over Dhahran, Saudi Arabia, an Iraqi Scud scatters debris killing 27 U.S. Army Reserve personnel and wounding 100 more.

RAF Buccaneers' fly 12 offensive counter air sorties today, for a total of 12 sorties.

Canada flies a total of 34 air sorties today.

French air sorties today number four (all offensive counter air).

Italian Tornados fly seven air sorties today.

Total Saudi Arabian air sorties number 149.

Total Kuwait air sorties today number 22 air interdiction.

Total Qatar air sorties today number four air interdiction. The Qatar Air Force fly no more air sorties in Operation Desert Storm.

26 February Saddam Hussein announces on Baghdad Radio that Iraqi troops are withdrawing from Kuwait. President George Bush describes Hussein's announcement *"an outrage. He is not withdrawing. His defeated forces are retreating. The Coalition will continue to prosecute the war with undiminished intensity. The liberation of Kuwait is close at hand."*

Early morning Franks orders his **VII Corps** to destroy the Republican Guard no later than sunset on the 27th. By 1045, all major subordinate commands have received his order. By 1600, along an 80-kilometer front the VII Corps advances into the *largest tank battle since World War II.*

At 1200, the **U.S. 24th Infantry Division (Mech)** prepares to sever Highway 8 and seal off the Euphrates River Valley. At 1400, the **197th Infantry Brigade** (Col. Ted Reid) moves to attack Battle Position 101, the 2nd Brigade (Col. Paul Kern) to attack Battle Position 103 then wheel east to attack the Jalibah Airfield. The 1st Brigade (Col. John LeMoyne), the division's main attack, advances to attack Battle Position 102, cutting Highway 8. The 4-64th Armor (Lt. Col. John Craddock) charges across Highway 8 forcing a brigade of the Hammurabi Armored Division back toward Basrah. The fighting experienced with the Iraqi 47th and 49th Infantry and Republican Guard Commando is the most heated the 24th Infantry has experienced. At 2200, elements of the Republican Guard 3rd Commando Regiment springs an ambush on TF 1-18th Infantry's scout platoon (1st Lt. Lawrence Aikman), which Aikman quickly defeats.

At 0630, with Bradleys and Abrams on line, the 1st and 2nd Brigades of the **1st Armored Division** (Col. Jim Riley and Col. Montgomery Meigs) advance toward al-Busayyah. The 2nd Brigade with TF 6-6th Infantry and TF 2-70th Armor push toward the center of al-Busayyah, and the 1st Brigade moves through enemy positions south of the town. Little more than a skirmish, only the Iraqi 26th Infantry Commando Battalion attempts to stand up to the Americans. TF 6-6th Infantry (Lt. Col. Michael McGee) mops up, as the rest of the division continues the advance. During the afternoon, flying in his command and control Blackhawk Gen. Griffith, orders his 6,000 vehicle division to turn 90 degrees and head eastward, aligning directly with the Republican Guard. As one brigade holds its position, two other brigades separate and accelerate until the three brigades are joined and speed eastward. At 1312, "Snake 22" (CWO Gary Martin) a Cobra scout in a hunter killer team of the 1-1st Cavalry spots a tank column of 50 T-72s of the Tawakalna's 29th Mechanized Brigade. At 1500, TF 7-6th Infantry (Lt. Col. Ward Critz), and TF 1-37th Armor (Lt. Col. Ed Dyer) with TF 3-35th Armor (Lt. Col. Edward Kane) in reserve, move toward the Tawakalna. At 1900, the 1st Armored Division led by tanks of the TF 1-37th Armor, the only 1st Armored Division unit with their new turrets covered with depleted uranium shielding, advance forward against the Republican Guard. At the command "Dragon's Roar" the 1st Armored Division will go into online formation and strike the Republican Guard.

Tank D-24 (1st. Sgt. Anthony Steede, commander; Sgt. Dan Kugler, gunner; Spec. Brown, loader; Spec. Howerton, driver), the best tank crew in the U.S. Army is the center tank of the 1st Armored Division.

The **1st Armored Division's** 3-1st Aviation (Lt. Col. William Hatch) sends six A Company Apaches (Capt. Rick Stockhausen) against the Iraqi Adnan Infantry Division. Each Apache carrying eight Hellfire missiles and 38 2.75-inch rockets, A Company kills 38 T-72s, 14 BMPs, and approximately 70 trucks in the darkness.

The *Battle of Wadi Al-Batin* begins. At 1525, the **2nd Armored Cavalry Regiment** passes Phase Line Tangerine (65 Easting, the VII Corps final coordination line) with the 2nd Squadron in the north, the 3rd Squadron in the center and the 1st Squadron hitting in the south. At 1555, the 2nd Squadron begins to battle the Tawakalna Division's 18th Mechanized Brigade in the *Battle of 73 Easting*.

At the center of VII Corps, the **3rd Armored Division** covers 27 kilometers of battle front. At 1632, in the north, the 2nd Brigade (Col. Robert Higgins) strikes the southern end of the Tawakalna's 29th Mechanized and main fortifications of the 9th Armored. The 1st Brigade (Col. William Nash) pierces the Iraqi security zone to the south. With TF 4-32nd Armor (Lt. Col. John Kalb) in the north, TF 3-5th Cavalry (Lt. Col. John Brown) in the center and TF 4-34th Armor in the south the 1st Brigade draws first blood. Tank Charlie 1-1 (1st Lt. Marty Leners) 1st Platoon, C Company, of the 3-5th Cavalry destroys a T-72 tank. At 1920, scouts of TF 4-32nd Armor engage a T-72, but two Americans are killed and two seriously wounded by "friendly" 25mm fire. (later two 4-7th soldiers are killed also by friendly fire). With a dawn attack order already approved, and growing confusion in the darkness and inclement weather, Funk halts his division until sunrise. At 2300, Apaches destroy eight Tawakalna T-72s and 19 BMPs attempting to counterattack between the 1st and 3rd Armored Division.

At 1800, the **1st Infantry Division** prepares to pass through the **2nd Armored Cavalry Regiment** and attack the Republican Guard. At 2200, Rhame is in control of the battle, the VII Corps front now 80-kilometers consisting of nine heavy maneuver brigades. With the 1st Brigade (Col. Bert Maggart) and 3rd Brigade (Col. David Weisman) leading through the Iraqi obstacle belt, the 1st Infantry strikes the 18th Mechanized Brigade and the 37th Armored Brigade of the 12th Iraqi Armored Division. The Iraqi 18th Brigade, and various units of the 37th Brigade and 12th Armored Division are hit by the 1st Brigade, with two battalions abreast (TF 2-34th Armor commanded by Lt. Col. Gregory Fontenot to the left, 1-34th Armor commanded by Lt. Col. G. "Pat" Ritter to the right and TF 5-16th commanded by Lt. Col. Sidney "Skip" Baker following). With three battalion task forces on-line (TF 3-66th Armor to left, TF 2-66th Armor center and TF 1-41st Infantry to right) the 3rd Brigade (Col. David Weisman) hits the Iraqis at 2200.

At 0700, Task Force Ripper attacks east of Al Jaber Air Base, moving north toward the Sixth and Seventh Ring Road intersection. Due to thick smoke, close-in fire support by Sea Cobras seems impossible. With a jury-rigged laser designator, Col. Michael M. Kurth, commander of Marine Light Helicopter Attack Squadron 369 flies with his landing skids almost touching the ground, and under high tension wires, to bring Sea Cobra support to Task Force Ripper (Col. Kurth is later awarded the Navy Cross for his actions). By 0900, the **1st Marine Division** encounters vast numbers of surrendering Iraqi soldiers. At 1336, Task Forces Ripper, Papa Bear and Shepherd form a line of 14 kilometers south of the Sixth

Ring Road. Being led by eight Sea Cobras, Task Force Papa Bear wheels right, crossing the northwestern part of the Al Magwa Oilfield, aiming at the Kuwait International Airport. Ripper advances north to the Sixth and Seventh Ring Roads and Task Force Shepherd turns east to protect the division's flank. At 1647, Ripper begins a tank battle. At 2012 Brig. Gen. Myatt reports *"all of Kuwait City is in friendly hands, to include* (major supply routes), *police station, and airport."* though resistance had not ended. By 2040, Shepherd has occupied portions of the Kuwait International Airport.

By about 2210, the American Embassy is declared secure. Twelve Marines of the 2nd Force Reconnaissance unit are the first U.S. force to enter Kuwait City and retake the U.S. Embassy (1st. Lt. Brian G. Knowles commanding the 2nd Force Reconnaissance finds a tattered American flag still flying). The embassy is declared secure at about 2210. Marines sweep the streets for Iraqi pockets of resistance. Some units remaining in Kuwait city are Republican Guard.

At 0136, large numbers of Iraqi vehicles are detected moving near Kuwait City. Marine Harriers and Hornets attack Iraqi convoys with 500-and 1,000-pound bombs after they have been forced off the superhighway by aerially delivered mines. The attacks continue with Marine Aircraft Group 11 flying 298 sorties, at its height its commander, Col. Manfred A. "Fokker" Rietsch directing attacks from his F/A-18D. Thousands of vehicles are destroyed, damaged or abandoned on the highway nicknamed *"Highway to Hell"* Col. Rietsch's 66 combat missions was the highest number of any U.S. Marine during the war.

South of Kuwait City, the **13th Marine Expeditionary Unit** feints an attack.

The U.S. Army "Tiger Brigade" (Col. John B. Sylvester), 6th Marines, and the 8th Marines (Col. Larry S. Schmidt), **2nd Marine Division** commence attacking their final division objectives outside of Al Jahrah and Al Kuwait.

U.S. Army VII Corps, **11th Aviation Brigade** (Col. John Hitt) attack the Iraqi 10th Armored Division on Objective Minden and Varsity. Kill boxes are attacked by 18 Apaches of the 4-229th Attack commanded by Lt. Col. Roger McCauley (A Company is commanded by Capt. Greg Vallet, B Company is commanded by Capt. Ben Williams, and C Company is commanded by Capt. Steve Walters). They destroy 33 tanks, 22 armored personnel carriers and 37 other vehicles.

Battleships MISSOURI and WISCONSIN fire in excess of 1,000 16-inch high explosive shells supporting Coalition ground forces. From 11 nautical miles offshore, WISCONSIN supports the advancing Marines, with MISSOURI firing more than 1 million pounds of ordnance. Targets include: artillery, mortar and missile positions, storage sites and a Silkworm missile position.

U.S. Marine Light Attack Squadron-269 attacks Faylaka Island. Simultaneously Marine Medium Helicopter Squadron-263 and 365 and Marine Heavy Helicopter Squadron-461 simulate an vertical envelopment on Bubiyan Island.

U.S. Navy Attack Squadron 155 (VA-155) and U.S. Marine aircraft bomb fleeing Iraqi troops as they attempt to escape toward Basra from Kuwait City. Numerous tanks and vehicles of all types are destroyed. Today U.S. Navy and Marine aircraft will fly 3,000 sorties.

An American A-10 Thunderbolt mistakenly kills nine British Royal Engineers, and injures eleven, on Objective Steel.

Lt. Col. Seth G. Wilson and his wing man 1st Lt. Stephen Otto, USAF, flying two A-10 Warthogs, discover a Scud park at Al Qaim, near the Syrian border. Perhaps two dozen Scuds on mobile launchers await launching, a possible last-gasp attack reported by the CIA from a Baghdad operative. The A-10s attack with Maverick missiles and destroy three of the missiles.

F-111s fly one A, three RR, and five RG/GOB PGM strikes for a total of nine. They fly five SAM, four C, eight MS, 43 RR and two RG/GOB for a total of 62 NonPGM strikes.

F-117s fly two L, and four MS strikes for a total of six strikes.

B-52 sorties total 37 (all AI).

In the Northern Red Sea the USS BIDDLE commanded by Capt. Louis F. Harlow and Spanish SNS VENCEDORA commanded by Captain of Corvettes Nieto Manso diverts to Yanbu the Yugoslavian flagged LEDENICE en route from Port Sudan to Aquaba. CAPE COD (AD-43) begins participation in Operation Desert Storm.

At 0300, Challenger tank crews of the **Queen's Royal Irish Hussars** counter an Iraqi counterattack. At 2,500 meters the Hussars open up with the **Staffordshire Regiment** (Lt. Col. Charles Rogers). The battle lasts for ninety minutes, the British enjoying the outstanding advantage of thermal sights. Ten Iraqi vehicles are destroyed. At first light, Objective Zinc is cleared of 46 armored vehicles and 1,800 prisoners. In the afternoon, Platinum is taken along with many EPWs of the Iraqi 52nd Division. The British prepare to attack across the Wadi al-Batin into Kuwait.

The British **4th Armoured Brigade** (Brig. Christopher Hammerbeck) battles twenty Iraqi tanks for Objective Copper South. At 1400, Objective Brass, manned by an Iraqi armored brigade, is attacked destroying 30 tanks and 50 armored personnel carriers. The 1st Battalion of the **Royal Scots** and the 3rd Battalion of the **Royal Regiment of Fusiliers** dismount their Warriors and clear enemy trenches.

The British **Staffordshire Regiment** incur's three casualties assaulting Objective Zinc. Pvt. Andrew Kelly with minor shrapnel wounds in the legs, Pvt. 'Alfie' Roberts wounded by shrapnel in his thigh and Cpl. 'Angel' Heaven, the Staffordshire's most serious casualty with shrapnel wounds to his arms, legs and chest. Assaulting Platinum II, Capt. Toby Tennant is wounded in the legs while in his Warrior by friendly fire. Collecting prisoners, an Iraqi fires an RPG from behind a white flag killing Pvt. Carl 'Ted' Moult. Pvt. Sean Taylor has also been killed today.

Lt. Cdr. Peter Whitfield Nelson RAN, captain of a Sea King HC Mark 4, flies two British casualties in pelting rain and 30 knot winds to a field hospital. He earns the Air Force Cross for this action.

At 0700, the French **Division Daguet** begins Operation *Princess*, the final consolidation of Objective White and seizure of the town of As Salman. At 0930 the 1st Spahi Regiment links up with the U.S. **101st Airborne** on MSR Virginia. Two French soldiers of CRAP are killed and 25 wounded in the clearing of As Salman due to a mines, boobytraps or the large numbers of cluster bomb units (CBUs) on the ground. At 1645, two officers and five enlisted men of the U.S. 27th Engineers attached to the French 6th Division are also killed from the CBUs.

Egyptian troops advance steadily toward their objective of the Ali Al Salem Air Base. They are within 4,000 meters of it by 1955, but after a fight set in for the night.

U.S. carriers launch 598 sorties today (combat and support). Coalition forces have flown 100,000 sorties.

U.S. Central Command sorties: USAF-1673, USN-664, USMC (fixed-wing)-405, Allied-417.

RAF Buccaneers' fly six offensive counter air sorties today, for a total of six sorties.

Canada flies a total of 38 air sorties today.

French air sorties today number four (all are offensive counter air). France has flown a total of 92 sorties during Operation Desert Storm (36 air interdiction, eight offensive counter air, 44 reconnaissance, and four training).

Italian Tornados fly seven air sorties today.

Total Saudi Arabian air sorties today number 160.

Total Kuwait air sorties today number 20 air interdiction.

Coalition air sorties number 100,000. Because of poor weather, blowing sand and oil well fires, only Coalition helicopters can operate effectively.

27 February Engaging in a "classic tank battle" against approximately three divisions of Republican Guards, Coalition forces trap the Iraqi forces in the Euphrates Valley and destroy approximately 200 tanks, 50 armored vehicles and 20 artillery pieces. AH-64 Apaches catch Iraqi vehicles waiting to cross the Hawr al Hammar causeway.

At about 0400, a **Joint Forces Command-East** unit of troops from Saudi Arabia, the United Arab Emirates, Qatar, Oman, Bahrain and Free Kuwait (Gen. Sultan) advance through Task Force Shepherd's area east of the Kuwait International Airport.

To the south of TF 2-34th Armor, two Bradleys of the 1-34th scout platoon (1st Lt. Glenn Birnham) of the **1st Infantry Division** are destroyed by Iraqi fire, killing one American. In a diamond formation Ritter's battalion destroy tanks and BMPs. By 0600, TF 2-34th Armor and 1-34th Armor have destroyed over 100 Iraqi armored vehicles, TF 5-16th Infantry follows, taking prisoners and smashing a logistics support area. By dawn, Objective Norfolk has been taken. Six 3rd Brigade soldiers are killed, and five Abrams and five Bradleys are destroyed by "friendly" rounds.

At 0700, 4-32nd Armor (Col. John Kalb), **3rd Armored Division** destroys 15 T-72 tanks, and 25 armored and wheeled vehicles *in less than a minute*. The firing of his 43 tanks prevents the 29th Brigade, Tawakalna, from attacking into the 2nd Brigade's (Col. Robert Higgins) southern flank. At 1700, in wedge formation, reinforced tank battalion TF 4-8th Cavalry (Lt. Col. Beaufort Hallman) leads the 2nd Brigade. TF 4-18th Infantry is on the left, and TF 3-8th Cavalry is on the right. At 1722, TF 4-8th Cavalry's scout platoon "Spearhead" destroys an Iraqi squad with 25mm fire. At 1727, "Spearhead" sights four Republican Guard BMPs through their thermal sights. Hallman orders "Action front", and C Tank (Capt. Ernest Szabo) bounds its 1st Platoon forward. U.S. artillery blasts the Iraqi positions, and Apaches make repeated strikes. At 2247, the 3rd Platoon bounds forward 500 meters. Four hours follow of Bradleys and U.S. tanks destroying BMPs.

At 0001, the **3rd Armored Cavalry Regiment** turns east toward Objective Tim. In the early morning, they mistakenly kill one American soldier and wound another of the 54th Engineer Battalion, 1st Armored Division.

At 0800, the **101st Airborne Division** begins a mission to cut Highway 6, the Republican Guard's last escape route. Landing at Objective Tim at 0900, by 1400 it is converted into FOB Viper. At 1430, 64 Vipers prepare to subject engagement area (EA) Thomas north of Basrah to the fury of 64 Apaches. For four hours two battalions of the **12th Aviation Brigade** work over the north side of the EA, while the **101st Aviation Brigade** hit its southern side. Destroyed are: 14 personnel carriers, eight multiple rocket launchers, four antiaircraft guns, four grounded helicopters, 56 trucks and two radars. Of particular note is that the Apaches by observation during this operation control 160 X 380 kilometers of Iraq, or terrain approximately the size of Massachusetts.

At 0500, five battalions of the **24th Infantry Division (Mech)** artillery open fire on Jalibah Airfield. The 2nd Brigade's TF 1-64th Armor and TF 3-69th Armor (Lt. Col. Terry Stanger) fire on a T-55 battalion, demoralizing it. Tanks of C Company, 3-69th, later accidentally destroy three Bradleys of TF 3-15th, killing two soldiers and wounding eight others. By 1000, Jalibah Airfield is secure (the attack also destroys 14 MiG fighters in their hangers). At 40 MPH, Bradley and Abrams drivers move down Highway 8 encountering huge logistics and ammunition sites, and scattered elements of the al-Faw, Nebuchadnezzar and Hammurabi Republican Guard Divisions.

The U.S. **1st Marine Division** (Task Force Taro) clears the Kuwait International Airport, the Marines allowing the Kuwaitis to reclaim Kuwait City. Approximately 250 T-55/T-62 and 70 T-72 tanks are destroyed by the 1st Marines clearing the airport. The **2nd Marine Division** consolidates its positions outside of Al Jahrah and Al Kuwait, linking up with **Egyptian** and **Syrian** troops east of Ali Al Salem Air Base. The 1st and 2nd Marines ultimately claim 432 enemy artillery pieces, 608 armored personnel carriers and 1,040 enemy tanks destroyed.

President George Bush addresses the United States. He announces that *"Kuwait is liberated. Iraq's Army is defeated."* He further states that at 12 A.M. Eastern Standard Time *"all U. S. and Coalition forces will suspend further offensive combat operations."*

Iraq announces its intention to obey the U.N. cease-fire terms in a letter to the U.N.

The USS WISCONSIN detects two small boats by Remotely Piloted Vehicle fleeing Faylaka Island. The battleship contacts U.S. Navy A-6s to destroy the boats. It is believed they are carrying members of the Iraqi secret police. USS AVENGER (MCM-1) neutralizes a live bottom influence mine. YELLOWSTONE (AD-41) ceases participation in Operation Desert Storm.

USMC Capt. Reginald C. Underwood flying a AV-8B Harrier of VMA-331 is KIA. A Coalition OV-1D is shot down. By this date 103,000 Coalition sorties have been flown, with 3,000 this day alone. U.S. Marine and U.S. Navy pilots have flown in excess of 26,000 combat sorties.

Numerous AH-64s report that when they attack Iraqi armor, crews of the other tanks begin abandoning their vehicles.

The 3rd Marine Aircraft Wing has flown more than 18,000 combat sorties during Operation Desert Storm. The wing commander, Maj. Gen. Moore, has flown 12 missions.

U.S. carriers launch 577 sorties today (combat and support).

Lt. Col. Seth G. Wilson and his wing man 1st Lt. Stephen Otto USAF return in the morning to the Scud park at Al Qaim. They attack with their A-10 Warthogs destroying four Scuds with cluster bombs. Other A-10s arrive with U.S. Navy F/A-18 Hornets. The pilots together are credited with destroying 20 Scuds.

F-111s fly six CCC, seven RR PGM strikes for a total of 13. They fly 18 MS, seven RR, 12RG/GOB for a total of 37 NonPGM strikes. With the U.S. Navy lacking smart munitions, of the 7,400 tons of PGMs dropped during the war, the U.S. Air Force delivered approximately 90%.

F-117s fly 14 L, eight C, two A, seven MS, and 11 RR for a total of 42 strikes. Baghdad's Muthena airport, the Salmon Pak chemical-biological research facility, and most importantly, the Ba'th Party Headquarters is targeted by 20 'Black Jets' in the first wave. In the second wave, ten F-117s hit the Al-Musayyib rocket-motor test facility, the Al-Athir missile research, development, and production complex. *The Al-Athir site is the last F-117 target of the war.*

Capt. Rob Donaldson of the 37th TFW has flown the most air sorties in a Stealth Fighter during the Operation Desert Storm (23 sorties). Lt. Col. Ralph Getchell and Col. Alton Whitley have both flown 19 combat missions, with most F-117 pilots flying 20-21 combat missions. Of the 594 aircraft shelters spread all over Iraq, defending the world's sixth-largest air force, by the war's end 375 have been heavily damaged or destroyed ("plinked").

B-52 sorties total 29 (all AI). These are the last sorties flown by B-52s.

The British **4th Brigade** continues to attack Objective Tungsten, 26-27 February, destroying 76 guns.

The French **Division Daguet** fight at As Shabaka and at an observation post to the west, which is the last fighting by the French in the war. The 3rd Helicopter Regiment, flying as far north as 25 kilometers south of Sammawah, is *the most northernmost advance by the Coalition in Operation Desert Storm.*

RAF Buccaneers' fly 12 offensive counter air sorties today for a total of 12 sorties. These are the last sorties flown by the Buccaneers' in Operation Desert Storm.

The Canadian Air Force's 36 pilots have flown nearly 2,700 missions during the Operation Desert Storm, and 56 sorties during the 100-hour ground war. The CF-18 fighter pilots have dropped 15 tons of high explosives on Iraqi targets (tanks, artillery positions and truck convoys).

Canada flies a total of 32 air sorties today.

Italian Tornados fly seven air sorties today. They have flown 224 sorties during Operation Desert Storm.

Total Saudi Arabian air sorties today number 174.

Total Kuwait air sorties today number 19 air interdiction. Kuwait has flown exclusively air interdiction flights throughout the war, and the total number they have flown is 651.

Conditions at Basra and on the canal, prevent destruction like at Mutla Ridge or Hawr al Hammar. The area west of Basra is an area of farms and small towns, in which the Iraqi hide on neighborhood streets, mixing with the civilian population. Also, the area has a low weather ceiling for air attacks today.

U.S. Central Command sorties: USAF-1651, USN-671, USMC (fixed-wing)-147, Allied-471.

During the Operation Desert Storm, 88 Americans, 41 Kuwaitis, Egyptians, and Saudis, 29 British and two French service people are killed. Fratricide is a major cause of Coalition deaths, and by this date 15,000 simple infrared transmitters ("Bud lights") and 190 Anti-Fratricide Identification Devices (AFID) have been delivered to Coalition troops. Inverted "V" identification symbols have been used since the beginning of the war.

28 February The Iraqi Hammurabi Division is routed near Basra by the **U.S. 24th Infantry Division (Mech)** after a heavy artillery bombardment.

U.S. Army **1st Infantry Division** has battled across 260 kilometers, destroying in excess of 550 Iraqi tanks and 480 armored personnel carriers and capturing 11,400 EPWs (more than twice than any other unit). Eighteen 1st Infantry Division soldiers are killed in the war.

At 0300, TF 4-18th Infantry, **3rd Armored Division** is reinforced with a tank company. TF 4-18th Infantry has engaged enemy tanks and BMPs at ranges from 25 to 3,000 meters during the previous afternoon and night. The Republican Guard continues to mount counterattacks at the seam between the battalion and 4-8th Cavalry. At 0345, 2nd Brigade (Col. Robert Higgins) is ordered to pass the 3rd Brigade forward into battle, the 2nd becoming the division reserve.

After hearing President Bush's order to cease hostilities at 0800, Maj. Gen. Richard D. Hearney, Deputy Commanding General, I Marine Expeditionary Force, after confirming instructions from Gen. Schwarzkopf orders the U.S. Marines to: *"Cease all offensive operations effective 280500Z 0800C. Remain in current positions and assume defensive posture. Wartime rules of engagement remain in effect. Be prepared to resume offensive operations. Forces are allowed to defend themselves."*

The **2nd Marine Division** stays in position outside Al Jahrah and Al Kuwait as the ceasefire of 0800 arrives. With **I Marine Expeditionary Force** strength 92,990 the Operation Desert Storm is the *largest Marine Corps operation in history.*

USS AVENGER destroys an Italian Manta bottom influence mine in the area of the PRINCETON and TRIPOLI sea mine explosions.

According to the Department of Defence report, *Conduct of the Persian Gulf War*, during Operation Desert Storm Coalition air forces shot down 33 Iraqi fixed-wing aircraft (five MiG-29s, eight Mirage F-1s, two MiG-25s, eight MiG-23s, two Su-25s, four MiG-21s, three Su-7/17s and one IL-76) and five helicopters. More than forty percent of the Coalition's air victories were beyond visual range due to the pilot's confidence in the target being enemy from AWACS (Airborne Warning and Control System) information.

At 0600, on Phaseline Smash **British forces** advance towards Objective Cobalt astride the Basra road. By 0730, they are in position before the war ends. In Operation Desert Storm the British Division destroyed three Iraqi armored divisions, took more than 7,000 prisoners (including several senior commanders). The **4th Armoured Brigade** destroyed more than 60 main battle tanks, 90 armored personnel carriers and 37 artillery pieces while capturing 5,000 EPW.

U.S. carriers launch 282 sorties today (combat and support). During Operation Desert Storm the six American carriers launched 18,117 fixed-wing sorties. Of the total, 16,899 were combat (the 1,218 remaining included logistics flights, aircraft checkout flights for new pilots of repaired aircraft, and support activities).

During Operation Desert Storm, 288 Tomahawk cruise missiles were launched, USS FIFE (DD-991) firing the most with a grand total of 58.

U.S. Central Command sorties: USAF-575, USN-187, USMC (fixed-wing)-30, Allied-200.

During Operation Desert Storm six A-10 Warthogs are lost. Four are shot down over enemy territory (Capt. Dale Storr, Capt. Steve Phyllis, 1st Lt. Rob Sweet, and Lt. Col. Jeff Fox). Only Phylis died, all others becoming POWs. Though flying only 30 percent of the sorties, "Hogs" scored over half of confirmed bomb damage assessment, maintaining a mission capable rate of 95.7 percent.

Due to the war's end, no F-117 flights are flown, though 223 strikes have been flown during the war, including over 40 percent of the Coalition's sorties.

Sgt. 'Dixie' Oliver, **Staffordshire Regiment**, commands a burial party to help eleminate the health problem of the abundant Iraqi bodies lying in the desert. The British burial parties show the Iraqi remains respect, but do not say a prayer over their graves because they do not know the soldier's religion. They simply have a moment of silence for a fallen fellow soldier. Wallets, ID cards and passports are collected and passed up to Division.

Canada flies a total of two air sorties today. She has flown a total of 961 air sorties during all of Operation Desert Storm.

Total Saudi Arabian air sorties today number seven. During Operation Desert Storm the Royal Saudi Arabian Air Force has flown a total of 5,829 sorties.

Coalition has flown 110,000 sorties.

1 March At 0130, 300 Iraqi tracked and 700 wheeled vehicles are observed north of the Rumaila oil field. After the lead vehicle is destroyed by a Cobra helicopter firing a TOW missile, two battalions of U.S. armored fighting vehicles pass down the length of the convoy destroying them. In Operation Desert Storm there are 24 U.S. Marines killed in action, and 92 wounded in action (two soldiers of the Tiger Brigade died while serving with the Marines).

During 100 hours of combat U.S. Marines have captured, destroyed or damaged 1,060 tanks, 608 armored personnel carriers, 432 artillery pieces and two Scud launchers. They have also discovered an Iraqi bunker which contained chemical artillery shells.

The 3rd Marine Aircraft Wing stands-down for maintenance. Four F/A-18 Hornets remain on alert. Operation of the Kuwait International Airport is by Marine Air Control Group 38.

The AH-64A Apache Attack Helicopter during Operation Desert Storm destroyed: 837 tanks and armored vehicles and 501 wheeled vehicles, 12 grounded helicopters and fighters, 66 bunkers and radar sites, 120 artillery positions, 42 SAM and AAA positions. The helicopter assisted in the capture of 4,764 EPWs.

Lt. Gen. de la Billiere visits Kuwait City, and is astonished by the Iraqis' destruction.

In Kuwait City, the U.S., British, French and Canadian Embassies open and Kuwait International Airport becomes operational.

On Faylaka Island, hundreds of Iraqi soldiers surrender to the USS MISSOURI'S Remotely Piloted Vehicle (RVP).

Results of French *Operation Daguet*: the Iraqi 45 Division, destroyed; 2,900 EPW, captured; 20 T-55/T-62 destroyed, two T69 captured, 17 light armored vehicles destroyed; 120 trucks destroyed; 26 artillery pieces destroyed, 40 captured; 70 heavy mortars captured; 700 tons of explosives captured. French ordnance consumed: 290 105 mm artillery shells; 1,640 155 artillery shells; 22 Milan missiles; 560 120mm heavy mortar shells, 390 HOT missiles (Gazelle and Mephisto).

2 March The United Nations Security Council votes 11-to-1 approving Resolution 686 which provides the conditions Iraq must meet before a formal cease-fire can be established.

Two battalions of the Republican Guard are destroyed by the **U.S. 24th Division (Mech)** when they travel west on Highway 8 near Basra in defiance of the cease-fire agreement. 2-4th Cavalry helicopters assume aerial battle positions north of the causeway. Next, three M-109 self-propelled 155mm howitzer battalions, an 8-inch battalion, and a MLRS battalion fire scatterable mines and the Iraqi vehicles flee in all directions. After 0900, when 1-24th Aviation (Lt. Col. Tom Stewart) is reassigned to LeMoyne's control, 1-24th's 18 Apaches advance on-line from east to west and destroy 102 vehicles with 107 Hellfire missiles. Finally, 4-64th Armor (Lt. Col. John Craddock) sweeps up the road, attacking the

Hammurabi to its tip at the Fish Lake Causeway. Over 185 armored vehicles, 400 trucks, and 34 artillery pieces are destroyed.

U.S. Navy SEAL team 2 and 4 cease participation in Operation Desert Storm.

Top priority for the U.S. Navy is to sweep a mine lane to Ash Shaybah.

At 1100, Lt. Gen. Gary Luck arrives for an historic lunch with the French Division Daguet near As Salman. He is unexpectedly greeted by a Foreign Legion honor guard in immaculate white kepis.

Saudi Arabia agrees to begin processing EPWs.

3 March At Safwan Airfield, Iraq, General H. Norman Schwarzkopf and Prince Khalid bin Sultan bin Abdul Aziz meet for two hours with Iraqi Deputy Chief of Staff Lt. Gen. Sultan Hasheem Ahmad and seven Iraqi military officials. The Iraqis accept all demands put to them. They agree to the immediate release of some prisoners of war to show good faith, and safety precautions to make certain that hostilities will not accidentally flare up. They hold 17 American prisoners of war, 12 British, nine Saudi, two Italian and one Kuwaiti. The Iraqi have 14 other Coalition bodies to return.

The U.S. Army **1st Infantry Division** secures the area of peace negotiations, and provides a stark, overwhelming demonstration of force for the Iraqi delegation. The division colors will not return to Fort Riley, Kansas until 10 May. In the meanwhile, the division will assist in clearing enemy mines and equipment.

The US Army **1st Cavalry Division** has had 12 men killed in action during the war. They are: Spec. Steven D. Clark, Pvt. Ardon B. Cooper, Pvt. Michael L. Fitz, S/Sgt. Jimmy D. Haws, Spec. James P. Heyden, Spec. David C. Hollenbeck, Cpl. William Palmer, Sgt. Ronald M. Randazzo, Pvt. Roger E. Valentine, Pvt. David M. Wieczorek, Sgt. Scott L. Wittenburg, and Sgt. Harold P. Witzke, III.

On the USS OGDEN, 1,413 EPWs are prepared for transport to Saudi Arabian prisoner of war camps. An Iraqi prisoner of war and veteran of the Iran-Iraq War later remarks on the Coalition air campaign that his brigade received more damage in thirty minutes than in eight years in the previous conflict.

USS MCKEE (AS-41) begins participation in Operation Desert Storm.

According to the USAF *Gulf War Air Power Survey* the Iraqi Army suffered approximately seventy-six percent attrition in tanks, fifty-five percent in armored personnel carriers, and ninety percent in artillery by the war's end. The Republican Guard Tawakalna (Mechanized), Madinah, and Hammurabi Divisions suffered only about fifty percent attrition.

At Talil Airfield 20 Iraqi aircraft are captured (F-1s, MIG-21s, and eight helicopters) in their bunkers.

Four SAS British commandos have died during the war. They are: Cpl. David Denbury, 26; Sgt. Vince Phillips, 36; Cpl. Robert Consiglio, 24; and Cpl. Steven "Legs" Lane. Denbury was killed in action with Iraqi troops while all the others died from hypothermia.

4 March Maj. Gen. Myatt shifts the position of the 1st Marine Division's command post from the Kuwait International Airport, to the pre-ground war area at Manifah Bay (this is the first retrograde action of I MEF). The 5th Marine Expeditionary Brigade begins to reembark onto its ships.

Near the Jordanian border, ten prisoners of war are released by Iraq. They are later transferred to the hospital ship MERCY.

In an interview for the Air Force History Program Lt. Gen. Horner states that *"Anybody that does a campaign against transportation systems (had) better beware! It looks deceivingly easy. It is a tough nut to crack. (The Iraqis) were very ingenious and industrious in repairing them or bypassing them . . .I have never seen so many pontoon bridges. (When) the canals near Basra (were bombed), they just filled them in with dirt and drove across the dirt."*

F-15Es and other planes attempt to inspire the morale of Coalition troops they observe on the ground. The provide mini "airshows" flying acrobatics. They also "buzz" Saddam Hussein's statue in downtown Baghdad.

5 March Lt. Gen. Boomer shifts his command post from the "Police Station," to Jubayl.

An additional 35 POWs are released by Iraq. Approximately 22,308 Iraqi prisoners of war were taken by U.S. Marines.

In the Northern Red Sea the USS SAMUEL B. ROBERTS diverts the Romanian flagged SALAJ en route from Bulgaria to Aqaba to Port Suez. DENEBOLA (TAKR-289) ceases participation in Operation Desert Storm.

British SAS Sgt. Andy McNab is released from his Iraqi cell. Three commandos of his Scud hunting squad have died. Vince Phillips and Steve "Legs" Lane have died from exposure and Bob Consiglio has been shot in the head covering the escape of the SAS squad. One SAS commando escapes to Syria and four become POWs. The commandos are tortured acutely.

British Flying Officer Simon Burges, 23, and Squadron Leader Robert Ankerson, 40, are released from the Iraqis today.

Chief Petty Officer Philip John Hammond, RN, of Fleet Diving Unit A and B (RFA SIR GALAHAD) leads searches of oil tankers, bunkers and buildings for booby traps. He earns the Conspicuous Gallantry Medal. Acting Petty Officer Richard John Peake RN and Acting Petty Officer Andrew Seabrook RN of Fleet Diving Unit A had earned the Distinguished Service Medal earlier for countermining live enemy mines in rough seas.

Coalition forces have flown 114,000 sorties.

6 March In a prisoner exchange, 294 Iraqi EPWs are traded for 35 POWs. United States casualty results are: 124 KIAs, 102 noncombat fatalities, 357 WIAs.

The U.S. Marine 1st Division withdraws into defensive positions in Saudi Arabia from Kuwait. The 2nd Marine Division occupies the 1st's former positions.

USS DETROIT (AOE-4) ceases participation in Operation Desert Storm.

U.S. Navy air units HC-8/DET 2 completes participation in the Operation Desert Storm.

Prime Minister John Major speaks to the British troops.

British POW Flight Lieutenant Rupert Clark, 31, shot down 14 February is released by the Iraqis. After being captured by Iraqi farmers he was beaten on the feet, legs, hands, and lower body by heavy-duty electrical cable. A finger and one of his legs were broken.

By this date 116,000 sorties have been flown by Coalition aircraft. The United States has lost 57 aircraft. U.S. aircraft have operated out of twenty-three bases, eleven in Saudi Arabia.

7 March In the Northern Red Sea the USS MOOSBRUGGER diverts the Romanian flagged SALAJ en route from Bulgaria to Aqaba. Maritime interceptions to date are: 7,766 merchant ships challenged, 945 ships boarded, 48 diverted. The United States Navy has conducted 547 boardings.

At Jubail Lt. Gen. de la Billiere attends a ceremony as coffins, each draped with a Union Jack, are carried to a C-130.

U.S. nuclear submarine CHICAGO (SSN-721) ceases participation in Operation Desert Storm.

HMS BRAVE (Capt. R.M. Williams, MRF), HMS BRILLIANT (Capt. T. D. Elliot), HMS EXETER (Capt. N.R. Essenhigh), HMS MANCHESTER (Cdr. A. W. Forsyth), HMS HECLA (Cdr. H. P. May), RFA BAYLEAF (Capt. J. Summers), and RFA SIR GALAHAD (Capt. D.A. Reynolds) complete participation in Operation Desert Storm.

8 March Redeployment of U.S. Army units heading for the continental United States begins. The first group of 5,000 American servicemen depart Dhahran for the United States. The rate of 5,000 per day will continue. This and removing supplies, etc., is called Operation *Desert Farewell*.

After sweeping the harbor of Kuwait City for two weeks for mines, it is judged safe enough to reopen. USS NEW ORLEANS (LPH-11), and mine countermeasure ships from the United States, United Kingdom, Holland, and Belgium have cleared the harbor.

USS LEFTWICH (DD-984), and KILAUEA (TAE-26) cease participation in Operation Desert Storm.

Total Naval Reservists activated for the Operation Desert Storm number 21,109 (10,452 medical, 2,682 logistics support, 2,475 Seabees, 1,838 ship augment personnel, 961 cargo handlers, 469 Military Sealift Command, 387 combat intelligence, 354 mobile inshore undersea warfare personnel, 89 shipping control personnel, 88 minesweeper personnel, 28 combat search and rescue personnel, and 1,286 various ratings).

10 March At Andrews Air Force Base, Washington, D.C., 21 prisoners of war arrive.

R-Day, the first MEF units depart Saudi Arabia (7th Marine Expeditionary Brigade).

Antisurface Warfare results are: 143 Iraqi naval vessels destroyed/damaged; all Iraqi Naval Bases/Ports significantly damaged; all Northern Persian Gulf oil platforms searched and secured; no attacks by Iraqi surface vessels against Coalition forces.

USS BUNKER HILL (CG-52) ceases participation in Operation Desert Shield.

11 March USS SARATOGA (CV-60) and SPRUANCE (DD-963) cease participation in Operation Desert Storm. In the northern Red Sea, the 1,000th boarding of a freighter is completed. Air cover is provided by a helicopter of the USS BIDDLE (CG-34). After seven months of deployment, the USS COMFORT and MERCY are relieved of their duties as hospital ships.

USS THOMAS C. HART (FF-1092) and SEATTLE (AOE-3) cease participation in Operation Desert Storm.

U.S. Navy air units HC-8/DET 5, HS-3, HS-7, HSL-32/DET 7, HSL-48/DET 1, VA-35, VAQ-132, VAW-125, VF-103, VF-74, VFA-81, VFA-83, and VS-30 complete participation in the Operation Desert Storm.

Lt. Gen. Peter de la Billiere says farewell to the 7th Armored Brigade ("The Desert Rats"). An advance party of the Staffordshire Regiment returns to Germany.

12 March U.S. Navy SEAL team 1 ceases participation in Operation Desert Storm.

USS JOHN F. KENNEDY (CV-67), GATES (CG-51), SAN JACINTO (CG-56), PREBLE (DDG-46), HARRY W. HILL (DD-986), and ACADIA (AD-42) cease participation in Operation Desert Storm.

MISSISSIPPI (CGN-40) ceases participation in Operation Desert Storm. She has been in the area since mid-September.

The Kuwaiti port of Ash Shuaibah is reopened by command ship USS LASALLE (AGF-3), and HMS CATTISTOCK (M-31), followed by two tankers. The tankers carry water and supplies. LASALLE has been the Middle East Force flagship since 24 August 1972.

U.S. Navy air units HSL-42 (DET 1, DET 6), HSL-44 (DET 9), VA-46, VA-72, VA-75, VAQ-130, VAW-126, VF-14, VF-32, VS-22, cease participation in Operation Desert Storm.

Lt. Gen. Peter de la Billiere is made a Member of the Order of Bahrein, First Class, by Sheikh Isa, the Emir of Bahrein, in a ceremony in Bahrein.

13 March President George Bush establishes the Southwest Asia Service Medal for service personnel who served in Operations Desert Shield and Desert Storm.

As part of the ceasefire agreement, Iraq returns the remains of 13 Coalition service people (five United States, eight United Kingdom).

The 4th Marine Expeditionary Brigade departs the Persian Gulf. Approximately 60 percent of the U.S. Marine Corps' ammunition stocks ($200-$300 million) is in the theater at the end of the war.

USS WISCONSIN (BB-64), BIDDLE (CG-34), CAYUGA (LST-1186), DURHAM (LKA-114), FORT MCHENRY (LSD-43), OGDEN (LPD-5), OKINAWA (LPH-3), MOUNT HOOD (AE-29), SAN JOSE (AFS-7), and W.S. DIEHL (TAO-193) cease participation in Operation Desert Storm.

U.S. Navy air unit HSL-34/DET 1 completes participation in the Operation Desert Storm.

14 March The Sheikh Jaber Ahmad Al-Sabah, Emir of Kuwait returns from exile.

USS MIDWAY (CV-41), MOBILE BAY (CG-53), OLDENDORF (DD-972), CURTS (FFG-38), FIFE (DD-991), HALEAKALA (AE-25), HASSAYAMPA (TAO-145), KISKA (AE-35), PENSACOLA (LSD-38), RALEIGH (LPD-1), LA MOURE COUNTY (LST-1194), and SPICA (TAFS-9) cease participation in Operation Desert Storm.

U.S. Navy air units HC-11/DET 4, HS-12, HSL-37/DET 6, VA-115, VA-185, VAQ-136, VAW-115, VFA-151, VFA-192, and VFA-195 complete participation in the Operation Desert Storm.

HMS GLOUCESTER (Cdr. P.L. Wilcocks) and HMS LONDON (Capt I. R. Henderson) complete participation in the Operation Desert Storm.

16 March General Alfred M. Gray, Commandant of the Marine Corps, presents the Prisoner of War Medal to the five Marine POWs at Bethesda Naval Hospital.

PONCHATOULA (TAO-148) ceases participation in Operation Desert Storm.

17 March USS TRIPOLI is undergoing repairs in Bahrain from the mine attack of 18 February. Her crew is awarded the Combat Action Ribbon.

The British Forces Gulf newspaper publishes it's final issue. It carries the front page story of the Queen promoting Lt. Gen. Peter de la Billiere to General.

The British Royal Air Force has flown approximately 6,100 war sorties with Tornado strike and reconnaissance aircraft. The British Jaguar has flown over 600 daylight combat sorties or 10 percent of all RAF sorties.

18 March The first American ship that supported Desert Storm returns to her Norfolk home port. She is the USS SYLVANIA (AFS-2). In the Northern Red Sea, the USS NORMANDY diverts the Maltian flagged BRAHMS en route from Syria to Aqaba. Later, the USS NORMANDY and USS WILLIAM V. PRATT diverts the Cyprus flagged NOVMENCHU en route from Bremen to Aqaba. MERCURY (TAKR-10) ceases participation in Operation Desert Storm. She has been in the area since October 1990.

19 March Bodies of Wing Commander Nigel Elsdon and Flight Lieutenant Robert 'Max' Collier killed in action 18 January arrive in the United Kingdom.

Soldiers of the Staffordshire Regiment are driven to Al Jubail from Camp 4.

20 March An Iraqi Su-22 Fitter is shot down by a Sidewinder missile from a F-15C of the USAF 36th Tactical Fighter Wing near Takrit, Iraq.

British HMS HERALD (Cdr. P.H. Jones) completes participation in the Operation Desert Storm.

21 March MERCY (TAH-19) ceases participation in Operation Desert Storm.

French soldiers of Division Daguet and Americans of the XVIII Airborne Corps wash their flags in the Euphrates river in a age-old victory celebration. The flags will once again be washed on their return to France in the Seine.

22 March MARS (AFS-1) ceases participation in Operation Desert Storm.

Two Iraqi Su-22s are lost. One is shot down by a F-15C of the USAF 36th Tactical Fighter Wing and the second crashes as the F-15C approached. During the war 148 Iraqi aircraft were flown to Iran.

The French Division Daguet withdraws from the town of As Salman.

23 March The 1st Brigade (Tiger Brigade), 2nd Armored Division (Col. John B. Sylvester) returns to operational control of U.S. Army Central Command after serving with the 2nd Marine Division in Operation Desert Storm.

USS COMFORT (TAH-20), GUAM (LPH-9), GUNSTON HALL (LSD-44), IWO JIMA (LPH-7), NASSAU (LHA-4), MANITOWAC (LST-1180), PORTLAND (LSD-37), SAGINAW (LST-1188), SHREVEPORT (LPD-12), SPARTANBURG COUNTY (LST-1192), and TRENTON (LPD-14) cease participation in Operation Desert Storm.

Division Daguet withdraws all troops from Iraq except for helicopter regiments.

24 March USS MISSOURI (BB-63), FORD (FFG-54), and SACRAMENTO (AOE-1) cease participation in Operation Desert Storm. The two American battleships deployed during the war, the WISCONSIN and MISSOURI fired 80 16-inch gun missions (33 WISCONSIN, 47 MISSOURI). The battleships fired 1,083 16-inch rounds (324 WISCONSIN, 759 MISSOURI) for a total of 2,166,000 pounds of ordnance delivered. Ground forces called for 18% of missions, 82% of the missions pre-planned or self-determined. Targets for the *last deployment of American battleships in U.S. history* were: 17 artillery targets, 13 small boats in port, 10 AAA positions, 10 bunkers, eight firings on infantry in trenches, six ammunition storage sites, five rocket sites, five electronic targets (radar, communications etc.) four command or observation positions, four troops in the open, three logistics sites, three tanks, two buildings, two mine fields, one pier, and one truck. UAVs Unmanned Aerial Vehicles played an important role in the Operation Desert Storm. At least one UVA was airborne at all times during Desert Storm (522 sorties, 1641 flight hours). VC-6 for WISCONSIN 100 sorties were flown (342.9 hours) and for MISSOURI 64 sorties were flown (209.7 hours). Including U.S. Army and Marine Corps flights a total of 522 sorties were flown during the war.

U.S. Navy air unit DET 7 completes participation in the Operation Desert Storm.

Last elements of the Staffordshire Regiment returns to the United Kingdom.

25 March The crankshaft of the USS LEADER is cracked after the ship deliberately explodes a mine 600 yards away. She continues to sweep for mines, then heads toward port under her own power.

PASSUMPSIC (TAO-107) ceases participation in Operation Desert Storm.

26 March USS ALTAIR (TAKR-291) and BELLATRIX (TAKR-288) cease participation in Operation Desert Storm. They have been participating since September.

By this date there have been 8,379 Coalition maritime challenges, 1,055 boardings and 53 diversions. Of the 1,055 boardings, 571 were by the U.S. Navy.

U.S. Navy ship strength stands at 84: 28=Mediterranean, 8=Red Sea, 48=Persian Gulf/North Arabian Sea/Gulf of Oman.

British RFA ARGUS (Capt. D.E.W. Lench), RFA OLNA (Capt. A.F. Pitt, DSC) and RFA RESOURCE (unknown captain) completes participation in the Operation Desert Storm.

There are 411,500 U.S. troops in the Middle East (in excess of 43,000 Navy and 60,500 Marines).

27 March The first U.S. Navy air units return to the United States. CARRIER AIR WING 3: At Naval Air Station, Oceana, Virginia: Attack Squadron 75, Fighter Squadron 14, Fighter Squadron 32. At Naval Air Station, Norfolk, Virginia, Carrier Airborne Early Warning Squadron 126. At Naval Air Station Cecil Field, Florida: Attack Squadron 46 and 72 (Carrier Air Wing 3 has flown in excess off 11,000 sorties during its seven and a half-month deployment delivering 3.5 million pounds of ordnance). CARRIER AIR WING 17: Naval Air Station, Oceana, Virginia: Attack Squadron 35, Fighter Squadron 74, Fighter Squadron 103. Naval Air Station, Norfolk, Virginia, Carrier Airborne Early Warning Squadron 125. Naval Air Station, Cecil Field, Florida: Strike Fighter Squadron 81 and 83 (Carrier Air Wing 17 has flown 12,500 sorties in the Operation Desert Storm during its eight-month deployment delivering 4,047,000 pounds of ordnance).

28 March In the Al Jubail area of Saudi Arabia three U.S. Marines are wounded in a drive-by shooting.

USS JOHN F. KENNEDY and SARATOGA arrive at their east coast home ports.

30 March The 8th Marines (Col. Larry S. Schmidt), 2nd Marine Division remains in Kuwait under operational control of Marine Forces Southwest Asia. The 2nd Marine Division returns to Camp Lejeune, North Carolina, over the period of mid-April to mid-May. It will participate in the Washington, D.C. victory parade 8 June.

The crew of the USS PRINCETON is awarded the Combat Action Ribbon for the 18 February mine attack on their vessel.

KALAMAZOO (AOR-6) ceases participation in Operation Desert Storm.

31 March OPPORTUNE (ARS-41) ceases participation in Operation Desert Shield.

1 April By this date 165,000 U.S. troops have returned to the United States.

The USS MARVIN SHIELDS (FF-1066) arrives at San Diego. This is the first West Coast warship to return to her home port.

2 April Commander, Special Warfare Unit 2 ceases participation in Operation Desert Storm.

3 April U.S. Navy SEAL team 3 ceases participation in Operation Desert Storm along with Commander Special Boat Squadron 1, Special Boat Units 11, 12, and 13.

USS AMERICA (CV-66), VIRGINIA (CGN-38), NORMANDY (CG-60), PRATT (DDG-44), and SIRIUS (TAFS-8) cease participation in Operation Desert Storm.

U.S. Navy air units HC-6/DET 7, HS-11, HSL-44/DET 7, VA-85, VAQ-137, VAW-123, VF-102, VF-33, VFA-82, VFA-86, and VS-32 complete participation in the Operation Desert Storm.

4 April JASON (AR-8) ceases participation in Operation Desert Storm.

Maj. Gen. Royal N. Moore, Jr., 3rd Marine Aircraft Wing commander lands at the wing's home base of El Toro, California after personally flying his F/A-18 Hornet back from Bahrain. The last line units of the squadron will not return from Shaikh Isa Air Base, Bahrain until 17 May.

HMS CATTISTOCK (Lt. Cdr. M. P. Shrives), HMS ATHERSTONE (Lt. Cdr. P. N. M. Davies), and HMS HURWORTH (Lt. Cdr. R. J. Ibbotson) complete participation in the Operation Desert Storm.

6 April Iraq accepts the United Nations terms for a formal cease-fire.

SAN DIEGO (AFS-6) ceases participation in Operation Desert Storm.

U.S. Navy air unit HC-8/DET 4 completes participation in the Operation Desert Storm.

9 April The United Nations Security Council approves Resolution 689 which establishes an Observer Mission to monitor the permanent cease-fire.

USS HALYBURTON (FFG-40) and CURTISS (TAVB-4) cease participation in Operation Desert Shield.

U.S. Navy air unit HSL-44 (DET 6) completes participation in the Operation Desert Storm.

British RFA SIR PERCIVALE (Capt. I. F. Heslop) completes participation in Operation Desert Storm.

10 April NITRO (AE-32) ceases participation in Operation Desert Storm.

British Logistics Landing Ship RFA SIR TRISTRAM (Capt. S. Hodgson) completes participation in the Operation Desert Storm.

11 April The United Nations Security Council announces that the Operation Desert Storm is over.

USS LEFTWICH returns to her homeport of Pearl Harbor. She has served for 93 continuous days as a member of Middle East Force and Battle Force Zulu with COMDESRON 35 Capt. William L. Putnam embarked. Her crew has participated in 16 combat search and rescue (SAR) recoveries, two involving the capture of EPWs during the war.

British RFA SIR BELVEDERE (Capt. R. J. M. Wallace) completes participation in the Operation Desert Storm.

13 April PLATTE (AO-186) ceases participation in Operation Desert Storm.

16 April Major U.S. Marine Corps command changes occur today. Lt. Gen. Boomer departs Saudi Arabia. Maj. Gen. Myatt ceases command of the 1st Marine Division in the Operation Desert Storm. Maj. Gen. Keyes ceases command of the 2nd Marine Division in the Operation Desert Storm. Likewise Maj. Gen. Richard D. Hearney, Maj. Gen. John I Hopkins, Maj. Gen. Norman E. Ehlert, Maj. Gen. John J. Sheehan, Brig. Gen. James A. Brabham, Brig. Gen. Charles C. Krulak, Col. Michael V. Brock, Col. George E. Gorman, Lt.Col. Thomas A. Flaherty and Maj. Gleen Honeycutt cease wartime command of units.

17 April U.S. Navy SEAL team 8 ceases participation in Operation Desert Storm.

HMS DULVERTON (Lt. Cdr. C.G. Welborn), and HMS LEDBURY (Lt. Cdr. D. H. L MacDonald) completes participation in the Operation Desert Storm.

18 April Iraq reports that it retains 10,000 nerve-gas warheads, 1,000 tons of mustard and near gas, approximately 1,500 chemical weapons, and 30 Scud chemical warheads.

19 April USS RANGER (CV-61), VALLEY FORGE (CG-50), PAUL F. FOSTER (DD-964), and KANSAS CITY (AOR-3) cease participation in Operation Desert Storm.

U.S. Navy air units DET 8, HS-14, HSL-48/DET 2, VA-145, VA-155, VAQ-131, VAW-116, VF-1, VF-2, VS-38, and VRC-30 completes participation in Operation Desert Storm.

20 April USS THEODORE ROOSEVELT (CVN-71), HORNE (CG-30), RICHMOND K. TURNER (CG-20), JARRETT (FFG-33), and ALGOL (TAKR-287) cease participation in Operation Desert Storm. During the Persian Gulf War the six U.S. aircraft carriers deployed flew 18,117 fixed-wing aircraft sorties (16,899 combat, 1,218 logistics, checkout flights or indirect support sorties).

U.S. Navy air units HS-9, HSL-44/DET 5, VA-36, VA-65, VAQ-141, VAW-124, VF-41, VF-84, VFA-15, VFA-87, VS-24, and VRC-40 complete participation in Operation Desert Storm.

21 April USS HAMMOND (FF-1067) ceases participating in Operation Desert Storm.

Spanish ships REINA SOFIA (Capt. Abal Lopez-Valeiras) and ASTURIAS (Capt. De Benito Dorronzoro) arrive to assit in enforcing the peace.

23 April J. HUMPHREYS (TAO-188) ceases participation in Operation Desert Storm.

24 April Lt. Gen. Walter E. Boomer presents Silver Star Medals to Staff Sergeant Daniel A. Kur, Sergeant Gordon T. Gregory, and Corporals Bryan R. Freeman, Michael S. Kilpatrick and Bryan K. Zickefoose at Camp Pendleton. The I Marine Expeditionary Force is welcomed home.

PRINCETON (CG-59) ceases participation in Operation Desert Storm.

29 April SHASTA (AE-33) ceases participation in Operation Desert Storm.

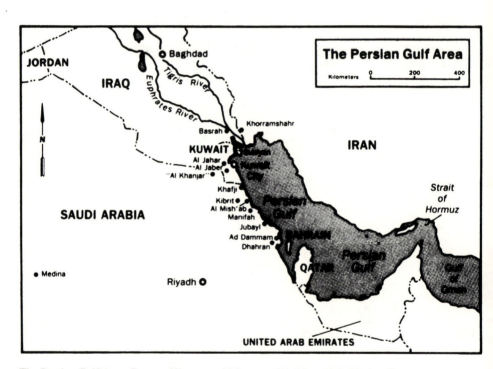

The Persian Gulf Area. Source: History and Museums Division, U.S. Marine Corps.

Gen. Colin Powell, USA. Chairman of the Joint Chiefs of Staff during Operation Desert Shield and Desert Storm. Photo courtesy of Gen. Powell.

Gen. H. Norman Schwarzkopf. Commander-in-Chief, Central Command, during Operation De
Shield and Desert Storm. Photo courtesy of Gen. Schwarzkopf.

IRAQI AIR SORTIES

(Incomplete through Sept. 1990)

Source: *Gulf War Air Power Survey.*

V. Adm. Stanley R. Arther, USN. Top U.S. Navy Commander in the Persian Gulf War. Shown here as Admiral, Arther commanded the largest U.S. Navy Task Force since World War II. Photo courtesy of the U.S. Navy.

R. Adm. Riley D. Mixson, USN. Commander, Carrier Group 2 and Commander, Naval Forces Red Sea. Photo courtesy of the U.S. Naval Institute.

Lt. Gen. Walter E. Boomer, USMC. Commander, 1st Marine Expeditionary Force. Shown here as General, Boomer was the top Marine Commander in the Persian Gulf War. Photo courtesy of the U.S. Marine Corps.

Coalition Air Sorties

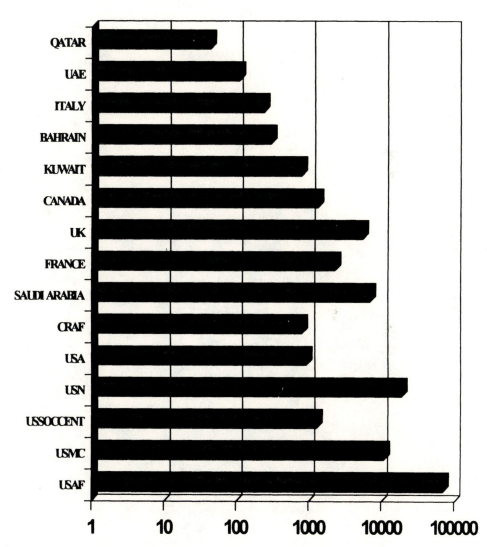

Source: *Gulf War Air Power Survey.*

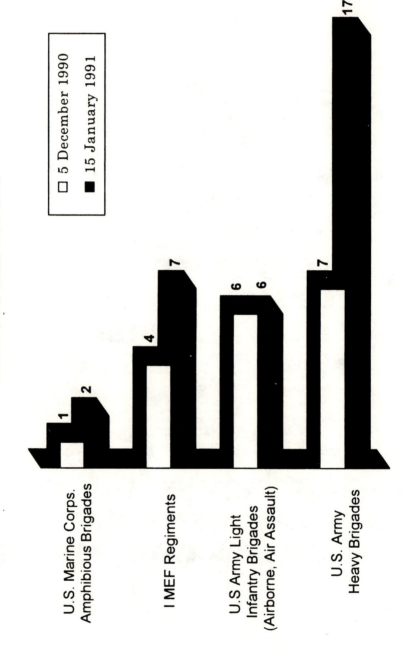

U.S. Ground Forces

Legend:
- □ 5 December 1990
- ■ 15 January 1991

U.S. Marine Corps. Amphibious Brigades
- 1
- 2

I MEF Regiments
- 4
- 7

U.S Army Light Infantry Brigades (Airborne, Air Assault)
- 6
- 6

U.S. Army Heavy Brigades
- 7
- 17

Source: *Conduct of the Persian Gulf War.*

Maj. Gen. James Myatt, USMC. Commander, 1st Marine Division. Shown here as Brigadier General, Myatt's division attacked directly into the Iraqi defensive trench system. Photo courtesy of the U.S. Naval Institute.

R. Adm. Raymond C. Smith, USN. Commanded U.S. Navy SEALS in the Persian Gulf War. The Command conducted 270 SEAL missions without a casualty. Photo courtesy of the U.S. Naval Institute.

Maj. Gen. William Keyes, USMC. Shown here as Lt. General, Keyes was Commander, 2nd Marine Division. Photo courtesy of Lt. Gen. Keyes.

Abrams M1A1 Tanks at USMC base, 29 Palms, California. Photo courtesy of General Dynamics Lands Systems Division.

Maj. Gen. Ronald Griffith, USA. Commander, 1st Armored Division. The 1st Armored Division was the center and spearpoint of the U.S. armored attack in Operation Desert Storm. Photo courtesy of the U.S. Army.

Brig. Gen. John Tilelli, USA. Commander, 1st Cavalry Division. Photo courtesy of the U.S. Army.

Maj. Gen. Paul Funk, USA. Commander, 3rd Armored Division. Photo courtesy of the U.S. Army.

Maj. Gen. Barry McCaffrey, USA. Commander, 24th Infantry Division. Gen. Schwarzkopf described McCaffrey as his "most aggressive and successful ground commander." Photo courtesy of the U.S. Army.

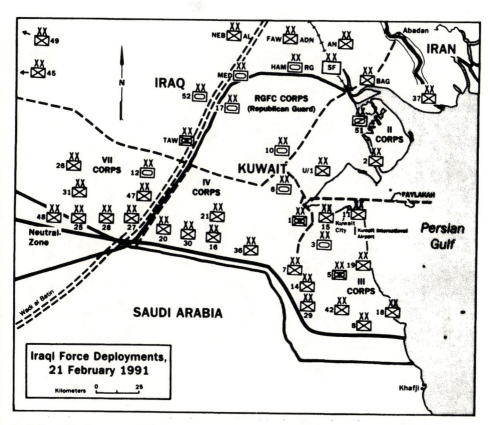

Iraqi Force Deployments, 21 February 1991. Source: History and Museums Division, U.S. Marine Corps.

Lt. Gen. Gary Luck, Commander of the U.S. Army 18th Airborne Corps (left) and Maj. Gen. J.H. Peay, III, Commander of the 101st Airborne Assault Division (right), just days before the commencing of Operation Desert Storm. Photo courtesy of the U.S. Army.

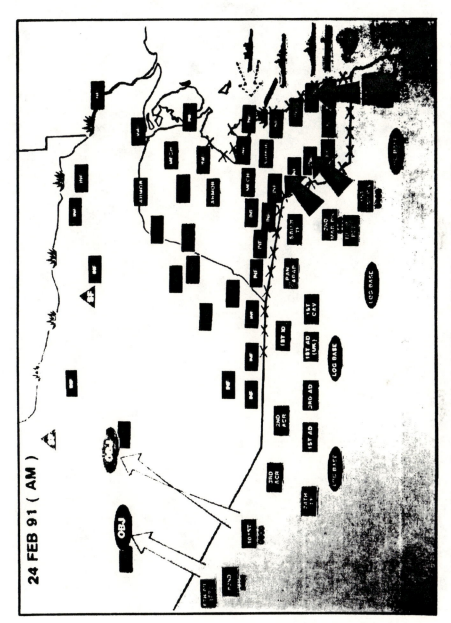

First stage of Operation Desert Storm ground attack, 24 February 1991. Source: History and Museums Division, U.S. Marine Corps.

Submarine USS Pittsburgh (SSN-720) fires a Tomahawk cruise missile at an Iraqi target. Photo courtesy of the U.S. Naval Institute.

Battleship USS Missouri (BB-63) fires on Iraqi positions in Kuwait, 12 February 1991. Photo courtesy of the U.S. Naval Institute.

GLOSSARY

A	Airfield.
AAA	Antiaircraft Artillery ("triple-A").
AB	Air Base.
A.B.C.	Arme blindee Cavalerie.
ABCC	A C-130 airborne command post for coordinating air strikes.
ACR	Armored Cavalry Regiment.
AD	Air Division or Armored Division.
ADA	Armored defense artillery.
AFB	Air Force Base.
AHB	Attack helicopter battalion.
AIM-7	Air-to-air missile, radar-guided ("Sparrow").
AIM-9	Air-to-air missile, infrared-guided ("Sidewinder").
ALARM	Air-Launched Anti-Radiation Missile.
Albino	Light colored F-15 aircraft.
Al Jouf	Saudi Arabian airfield approximately 300 miles northwest of KKMC and 545 miles northwest of King Fahd.
Al Khanjar	U.S. Marine support base 35 kilometers southwest of the heel of

Kuwait.   It contained a five-million-gallon fuel farm, a naval hospital with 14 operating rooms and the largest-ever supply point in Marine Corp history. It was built in 14 days by the 7th and 8th Engineer Support Battalions (Reinforced).

Amid	Iraqi Army/Air Force Brig. Gen. or Navy Commodore or Admiral.
AO	Area of operations.
APC	Armored personnel carrier.
Aqid	Iraqi Army/Air Force Col. or Navy Capt.
ArCent	United States Central Command, a subdivision of CentCom.
AREFS	Air Refueling Squadron.
Armco	Arabian-American Oil Company.
Armilla Patrol	British Naval patrol restricted to the Persian Gulf established in 1980.
ARW	Air Rescue Wing.
ASP	Ammunition supply point.
ATO	Air tasking order; order that describes what air missions are to be flown.
AWACS	Airborne Warning and Control System.
AWACW	Airborne Warning and Command Wing.
Bag	Aircraft auxiliary fuel tank (slang).
Baghdad Express	1st Force Service Support Group's supply operation from Jubayl and Mishab to Al Khanjar.
BAI	Battlefield air interdiction; air missions to attack enemy armor, artillery and support systems well behind enemy lines.
Barrage fire	Antiaircraft fire targeting an area of the sky rather than an individual aircraft.
BDA	Battle damage assessment.
BDE	Brigade.
BDU	Battle dress uniform.

Bedevilers   USN VF-74 Squadron.

Berm   A continuous wall 3-4 meters high of sand paralleling the Saudi-Kuwaiti border with police posts approximately every 15 kilometers.

BFV   Bradley Fighting Vehicle.

Big Red One   Nickname of the 1st Infantry Division (Mechanized).

Bimp   Slang for BMP.

Black Aces   USN VF-41 Squadron.

Black Knights   USN VF-154 Squadron.

BMP   Iraqi Army amphibious car manufactured by the Soviet Union.

BMS   Bombardment Squadron.

BN   Battalion.

Bounty Hunters   USN VF-2 Squadron.

BR   British or Breaching targets.

Bradley   M-2 infantry fighting vehicle/M-3 cavalry fighting vehicle.

BRDM   Soviet-designed armored wheeled reconnaissance vehicle.

Brown Side Out   Newssheet of I Marine Expeditionary Force.

BTR   Soviet-designed wheeled reconnaissance vehicle or tank destroyer.

Butt Camp   Slang name of Ab Qaiq.

BVR   Beyond Visual Range.

BW   Biological Warfare.

C   Nuclear/Biological/Chemical (targets).

CAB   Combat aviation brigade.

Cajuns   USAF 504th Tactical Fighter Squadron (Reserve A-10 squadron from New Orleans Naval Air Station).

CALCM   Conventual Air-Launched Cruise Missile.

CAP   Combat Air Patrol.

Capt.	Captain.
CAS	Close air support.
CAV	Cavalry.
CBU	Cluster Bomb Unit.
CCC	C3/Telecommunications.
CEM	Combined Effects Munition.
CD	Cavalry Division.
C-day	7 August 1990 (commencement of deployment).
Cement Factory	Large factory complex that dominated the 1st Marine Division's third defensive position.
CentCom	U.S. Forces Central Command. The responsibility of this joint force headquarters was Saudi Arabia and Kuwait with its subordinates ArCent, MarCent, and ComNavCent.
CEV	Combat engineer vehicle.
Chagul	British water container strapped to vehicles to cool water.
Chinook	CH-47 cargo helicopter.
Chobham	Bolt-on armor.
Clansmen	USN VA-45 Squadron.
Col.	Colonel.
Compo	British composite food rations.
ComUSCentAF	Commander, U.S. Air Force Component, Central Command.
ComUSNavCent	United States Naval Forces Central Command.
CONUS	Continental United States.
CP	Command post.
C.R.A.P.	Commando de Recherche et d'Action dans la Profondeur (French Special Operations Unit).
CSM	Command sergeant major.

CTA-50	Clothing and individual equipment.
CVBG	Aircraft Carrier Battle Group.
D.A.M.	Division aero-mobile.
D.B.	Division blindee.
DBDU	Desert battle dress uniform.
DCU	Desert camouflage uniform.
"Desert Cats"	Nickname of Canadian pilots in Persian Gulf War. Developed from badges of the two squadrons participating (416 Squadron of Cold Lake, Alberta wearing a lynx, 439 Squadron of Baden-Sollingen, Germany wearing a tiger).
"Desert Rats"	British 7th Armoured Brigade.
Dhobi	British slang for laundry.
DIA	Defense Intelligence Agency.
Diamondbacks	USN VF-102 Squadron.
D.I.Ma	Division d'Infanterie de Marine.
DivArty	Division artillery.
D.L.B.	Division legere blindee.
DMA	Defense Mapping Agency.
DMPI	Desired Mean Point of Impact.
DO	Deputy for Operations; USAF wing officer responsible for all flying.
D.P.	Division parachutiste.
DPICM	Dual-purpose improved conventional munitions.
Dragon City	XVIII Airborne Corps Headquarters (initially called Falcon Base).
DS	Direct support.
DSNET2	Defense System Network.
E	Electricity (target).

EA	Engagement area.
Eagles	USN VA-115 Squadron.
Easting	Eastward.
ECM	Electronic Countermeasures.
ECS	Electronic Combat Squadron.
EG	Egypt.
ELINT	Electronic intelligence.
EPAC	Eastern Province Area Command (Saudi Arabian Army). Command on eastern flank of MarCent.
EPW	Enemy Prisoner of War.
FA	Field artillery.
FAA	Forward assembly area.
FAC	Forward air controller.
Falcons	USAF 355th Tactical Fighter Squadron.
F.A.R.	Force d'Action Rapide (Rapid Deployment Force).
Fariq	Iraqi Army/Air Force Lt. Gen. or Navy V. Adm.
Fariq Awwal	Iraqi Army/Air Force Gen. or Navy Adm.
FEBA	Forward edge of the battle area.
FIBUA	Fighting in Built-Up Areas, i.e., urban warfare.
Firefinder	Countermorter/counterartillery radar.
First Team	Nickname for the 1st Cavalry Division.
FIST	Fire support team.
Fists of the Fleet	USN VFA-25 Squadron.
FISTV	Fire support team vehicle.
FLIR	Forward-looking infrared.
Flogger	MiG-23 fighter aircraft.

FLOT	Forward line of troops.
Flying Tigers	USAF 74th Tactical Fighter Squadron. This A-10 squadron is the direct descendant of Chennault's famous World War II unit.
FR	French.
Freelancers	USN VF-21 Squadron.
FSCL	Fire Support Coordination Line.
FSS	Fast sealift ship.
Fulcrum	MiG-29 fighter aircraft.
FUP	Forming Up Position, (British assembly area prior to attack).
G-Day	24 February, the beginning of ground combat.
Gen.	General.
Ghostriders	USN VF-142 Squadron.
"go-away brigade"	Iraqi 52nd Armored Brigade.
Gorilla package	Slang for a large body of aircraft.
GP	General purpose.
GPS	Global Positioning System (satellite navigation system).
Granby (Operation)	British codename for operation to assist the U.S. and Saudi Arabia after the Iraqi invasion of Kuwait.
GSR	Ground surveillance radar.
HAB	Hardened Aircraft Bunker.
Hail Mary	Code name: operation.
HAM	Hammurabi Republican Guard.
Hammer	Decision making officer on AWACS aircraft.
HARM	High-speed antiradiation missile.
HEAT	High-explosive antitank.
Hellfire	Laser-guided antitank missile.

HESH	High Explosive Squash Head, (British round fired by Challenger).
HET	Heavy equipment transporter.
HMMWV	High-mobility, multipurpose wheeled vehicle.
H-2	Major western Iraqi airfield.
ID	Infantry division.
IEW	Intelligence Electronic Warfare.
IFF	Identification Friend or Foe.
IN	Infantry.
IPB	Intelligence preparation of the battlefield.
Ironsides	Nickname of the 1st Armored Division.
ISA	Intermediate Staging Area.
Jayhawk	Nickname of VII Corps.
JFCN	Joint Forces Command North (Arab Coalition forces).
Jolly Rogers	USN VF-84 Squadron.
JSTARS	Joint Surveillance Target Attack Radar System.
KERO	Kuwait Emergency Recovery Organization.
KFIA	King Fahd International Airport.
Khanjar International	Two dirt airstrips next to Al Khanjar U.S. Marine support base.
KKMC	King Khalid Military City.
Knighthawks	USN VFA-136 Squadron.
KTF	Kuwaiti task force.
KTO	Kuwaiti theater of Operations.
KU	Kuwait.
L	Leadership (targets).
LAI	Light Armored Infantry.

LANDSAT	Land Satellite, NASA/NOAA Satellite Program.
LANTIRN	Low Altitude Navigation and targeting Infrared System for Night.
LD	Line of departure.
LGB	Laser-Guided Bomb.
Liwa	Iraqi Army/Air Force Maj. Gen. or Navy R. Adm.
Logbase	Supply depots (named Alpha, Bastogne, Bravo, Charlie, Echo, Hotel, November, Oscar, and Romeo) established to supply Coalition units and sustain the ground attack.
Lonesome Dove	Forward command post of the 3rd Marine Aircraft Wing a few kilometers west of Al Khanjar.
Lt. Col.	Lieutenant Colonel.
Lt. Gen.	Lieutenant General.
MAC	Military Airlift Command.
MAG	Marine Air Group.
Maj. Gen.	Major general.
Maqaddam	Iraqi Army/Air Force Lt. Col. or Navy Cdr.
MarCent	United States Marine Forces Central Command.
Mark-20	Aerial bomb containing bomblets and shaped charges mainly utilized against armored targets.
Mark-82	"Dumb" 500-pound general-purpose bomb (not laser guided).
Mark-84	"Dumb" 2,000-pound general-purpose bomb (not laser guided).
Maskirovka	Soviet term describing deception.
MBA	Main battle area.
MBT	Main battle tank.
MEB	Marine Expeditionary Brigade.
Mech	Mechanized.
MED	Medina Republican Guard.

MEDEVAC	Medical evacuation.
MEF	Marine Expeditionary Force. Capable of 60 days of combat without supply, this is the largest deployable Marine Formation.
MEL	Mobile Erector Launcher.
MEU	Marine Expeditionary Unit. The smallest U.S. Marine Air/ Ground Task Force.
MI	Military intelligence.
MICLIC	Mine-clearing line charges.
MIG	Soviet fighter plane.
MLRS	Multiple-Launch Rocket System.
MOPP	Mission oriented protective posture.
MPS	Maritime Prepositioning Squadron.
MR	Designation that air unit is "mission ready" or prepared to fly combat missions.
MRE	Meals, ready to eat (known to the troops as meals refused by Ethiopians).
MS	Military Support.
MSR Dodge	A paved road running from Dhahran, Saudi Arabia southwest to Riyadh then northwest to King Khalid Military City.
MTLB	Soviet-designed command or maintenance vehicle.
Mulazim	Iraqi Army/Air Force 2nd Lt. or Navy Ensign.
Mulazim Awwal	Iraqi Army/Air Force 1st Lt. or Navy Lieutenant Junior Grade.
Mushir	Iraqi General of the Army/Air Force or Navy Fleet Admiral.
N	Naval (target).
Naqib	Iraqi Army/Air Force Capt. or Navy Lt.
NBC	Nuclear, Biological, and Chemical.
NCO	Noncommissioned officer.
NEB	Nebuchadnezzar Republican Guard.

No-duff	British slang for a wartime event rather than one taking place in an exercise.
Nugget	New, inexperienced fighter pilot.
O	Oil (target).
OBJ	Objective.
OCA	Offensive Counter Air.
Pacific Wind	Planned mission to rescue American embassy personnel in Kuwait.
Panthers	USAF 353rd Tactical Fighter Squadron.
PB tablets	Nerve agent prophylactic.
PC	*Poste de Command* (Command Post).
PGM	Precision-Guided Munition.
Phase Line	An established map line used to control and coordinate the advance of troops (PL).
Pickle	Control in fighter aircraft used to release ordnance.
PSYOPS	Psychological Operations.
PTAS	Provisional Tactical Airlift Squadron.
Puckin' Dogs	USN VF-143 Squadron.
R.A.	Regiment d'artillerie.
RAF	Royal Air Force (U.K.).
R.A.Ma	Regiment d'artillerie de Marine.
R.A.P.	Regiment d'artillerie parachutiste.
Raid	Iraqi Army/Air Force Maj. or Navy Lt. Cdr.
Rainbow mission	Air attack mission with aircraft from different squadrons.
Rarden	British 30-mm cannon mounted on Warriors and Scimitars.
R.D.	Regiment de Dragons.
R.D.P.	Regiment de Dragons parachutistes.

Ready First	Nickname of the 1st Brigade, 3rd Armored Division.
R.E.C.	Regiment 'etranger de Cavalerie.
R.E.G.	Regiment 'etranger du Genie.
R.E.I.	Regiment 'etranger d'Infanterie.
R.E.P.	Regiment 'etranger parachutiste.
RG	Republican Guard.
RG/GOB	Republican Guard (target).
R.G.	Regiment du Genie.
RGFC	Republican Guard Forces Command.
R.G.P.	Regiment du Genie parachutiste.
R.H.P.	Regiment de Hussards parachutistes.
R.I.	Regiment d'Infanterie.
R.I.C.M.	Regiment d'Infanterie de chars de Marine.
R.I.Ma.	Regiment d'Infanterie de Marine.
Rivet Joint	RC-135 reconnaissance aircraft.
Roadrunner	Artillery operation.
Roland	French surface-to-air missile.
RPG	Rocket propelled grenade.
R.P.I.Ma.	Regiment parachutiste d'Infanterie de Marine.
RPV	Remotely piloted vehicle.
RR	Railroads/Bridges (targets).
RSAF	Royal Saudi Air Force.
RSLF	Royal Saudi Land Forces.
RW	Reconnaissance Wing.
S1	Adjutant officer.

S2	Intelligence officer.
S3	Operations and training officer.
S4	Supply officer.
SA	Saudi Arabia.
SA-2	Soviet radar-guided surface-to-air missile.
SA-3	Soviet radar-guided surface-to-air missile.
SA-6	Soviet radar-guided surface-to-air missile.
SA-8	Soviet radar-guided surface-to-air missile.
Sabkha	A low-lying coastal salt flat.
SABOT	Armor-piercing projectile.
SAD	Strategic Air Defenses.
Sagger	Soviet wire-guided antitank missile.
SAM	Surface-to-Air Missile.
Sam ring	Territory surrounding a SAM position where its missile may threaten aircraft.
SANG	Saudi Army National Guard.
Sappers	British Royal Engineers.
SAS	Special Air Service (British Special Forces).
SATCOM	Satellite communications.
SATNAV	Satellite navigation.
SC	Scud missiles (target).
Scimitar	British lightly armored reconnaissance vehicle.
SCUD	Ballistic missile.
SF	Special Forces.
Shamagh	Traditional Arab head-dress. Inspiration for derogatory term for Iraqis "Raghead".

Shamal	Seasonal windstorm of dust and rain.
SIGINT	Signals intelligence.
silver bullet	Nickname for SABOT antitank round.
Sledgehammers	Nickname of 197th Infantry Brigade.
Sluggers	USN VF-103 Squadron.
SO	Special Operations.
SOCCENT	Special Operations Command Central.
SOCOM	Special Operations Command.
SOF	Special Operations Forces.
SOG	Special Operations Group.
SOS	Special Operations Squadron.
Spearhead	Nickname of 3rd Armored Division.
SRW	Surveillance and Reconnaissance Wing.
Starfighters	USN VF-33 Squadron.
Stingers	USN VFA-113 Squadron.
Sultan Range	Weapons testing range near Ab Qaiq.
Sunday Punchers	USN VA-75 Squadron.
SWA	Southwest Asia.
Swordsmen	USN VF-32 Squadron.
SY	Syria.
T-72	Soviet main battle tank.
TAA	Tactical assembly area.
TAB	Target Acquisition Battery.
TAC	Tactical Air Command.
TACAIR	Tactical Air.

TACSAT	Tactical Satellite.
TAG	Tactical Airlift Group.
TAIRCW	Tactical Air Control Wing.
Tapline Road	Near the Kuwaiti and Iraqi borders the Tapline is a Saudi Arabian paved road paralleling one of the countries most important crude oil pipelines. It was a main supply route (MSR).
TAS	Tactical Airlift Squadron.
TAW	Tawakalna Republican Guard.
TF	Task Force.
TFP	Task Force Phoenix.
TFS	Tactical Fighter Squadron.
TFW	Tactical Fighter Wing.
TIALD	Thermal Imaging and Laser Designating.
Tiger Brigade	Nickname for 1st Brigade, 2nd Armored Division.
TIS	Tactical Intelligence Squadron.
TLAM	Tomahawk Land-Attack Missile.
TOGS	Thermal Observation Gunnery System--thermal imaging sights for British Challenger tanks.
Tophatters	USN VF-14 Squadron.
TOT	Time Over Target (air)/Time on Target (artillery).
TOW	Tube-launched, optically tracked, wire-guided antitank missile.
TRG	Tactical Reconnaissance Group.
TWMP	Track width mine plow.
UAV	Unmanned aerial vehicle (See RPV).
UBL	Unit basic load.
UK	United Kingdom/British.
UKLF	United Kingdom Land Forces.

USAF	United States Air Force.
USAFA	United States Air Force Academy, Colorado.
USCENTCOM	U.S. Central Command.
USMA	United States Military Academy, West Point.
USMC	United States Marine Corps.
USN	United States Navy.
USNA	United States Naval Academy, Annapolis, Maryland.
V	U.S. Navy designation for fixed-wing aircraft.
VA	Attack aircraft (wing, squadron).
VAB	Vehicule de l'Avant Blinde (French armored personnel carrier/command and communications vehicle).
Vanguards	USAF 76th Tactical Fighter Squadron.
VAQ	Reconnaissance aircraft (squadron, wing).
VAW	Airborne early warning.
VF	Fighter aircraft (squadron, wing).
Victory Division	24th Infantry Division.
Vigilantes	USN VFA-151 Squadron.
Viper	Slang term for F-16 Fighter aircraft.
VP	Patrol aircraft (squadron, wing).
VQ	Reconnaissance aircraft (squadron, wing).
VR	Transport aircraft (squadron, wing).
VS	Anti-submarine aircraft (squadron, wing).
Vultures	USAF 511th Tactical Fighter Squadron.
VW	Reconnaissance aircraft (squadron, wing).
Warrior	British infantry fighting vehicle.
WIA	Wounded in Action.

Wildcats	USN VFA-131 Squadron.
WIN	Intercomputer Network.
WINCS	WIN Communications Subsystem.
wog	Derogatory name for a Iraqi soldier.
Wolfpack	USN VF-1 Squadron.
WWMCCS	Worldwide Military Command and Control System.
XO	Executive officer.
ZA	Zone d'Action (area of combat operations).
Z.D.O.	Zone de deploiement operationnel.
Zeus	ZSU 23-4, radar-guided, four-barrel antiaircraft artillery.

COALITION PRISONERS OF WAR IN THE PERSIAN GULF WAR

American Forces
Capt. William F. Andrews USAF
Col. David W. Eberly USAF
Lt. Col. Jeffrey D. Fox USAF
Maj. Thomas E. Griffith Jr. USAF
Capt. Harry M. Roberts USAF
Capt. Richard D. Storr USAF
1st Lt. Robert J. Sweet USAF
Maj. Jeffrey S. Tice USAF

Maj. Rhonda Cornum USA
Spec. Troy Dunlap USA
Spec. David Lockett USA
Spec. Melissa Rathburn-Nealy USA
S/Sgt. Daniel Stamaris USA

Lt. Lawrence R. Slade USN
Lt. Robert Wetzel USN
Lt. Jeffrey N. Zaun USN

Lt. Col. Cliff M. Acree USMC
Capt. Michael C. Berryman USMC
CWO Guy Hunter USMC
Capt. Russel Sanborn USMC
Maj. Joseph J. Small USMC

British Forces
Squadron Leader Robert Ankerson
Flt. Lt. Simon Burges
Flt. Lt. Rupert Clark
Sgt Andy McNab (SAS)
Flt. Lt. Adrian Nichol
Flt. Lt. John Peters

Flt. Lt. Robert Stewart
Flt. Lt. David Waddington
(Three additional classified SAS prisoners of war).

Italian Forces
Flt. Capt. Mario Biehirloni

COALITION SERVICE PEOPLE
KILLED IN ACTION

United States Forces
L/Cpl. Thomas R. Adams, Jr., USMC
Spec. Andrew Alaniz, USA
Cpl. Frank C. Allen, USMC
S/Sgt.Michael R. Allen, USA
S/Sgt. David R. Ames, USA
CWO3 Michael F. Anderson, USA
S/Sgt. Anthony R. Applegate, USA
Capt. Jorge I. Arteaga, USAF
Spec. Steven E. Artherton, USA
Corp. Allen R. Auger, USMC
Private 1st Class Hans C.R. Avey, USA
S/Sgt. Russell F. Awalt, USA
Sgt. Stanley W. Bartusiak, USA
S/Sgt. Donald R. Bates, USA
Capt. Tommie W. Bates, USA
Spec. Cindy M. Beaudoin, USA
Sgt. Lee A. Belas, USA
AEM 3rd Class Michael L. Belliveau, USN
BT 2nd Clas Alan H. Benningfield, USN
Cpl. Stephen E. Bentzlin, USMC
Cpl. Stephen E. Bentzlin, USMC
Cpl. Kurt A. Benz, USMC
Sgt. Dennis W. Betz, USMC
Cpl. Scott F. Bianco, USMC
Capt. Thomas C. Bland Jr., USAF
S/Sgt. John P. Blessinger, USAF
Mr. James Blowe (Army Contractor)
Sgt. Tommy A. Blue, USA
Capt. Jeffrey J. Bnosky, USA
Spec. John A. Boliver, USA
Spec. Joseph P. Bongiorni, USA
Private 1st Class Tyrone Bowers, USA

Spec. Charles L. Bowman Jr., USA
Sgt. John T. Boxler, USA
Spec. William C. Brace, USA
Capt. Douglas L. Bradt, USAF
Private 1st Class Cindy D.J. Bridges, USA
Sgt. Roger P. Brilinski, Jr., USA
Sgt. Tracy D. Brogdon, USA
BT/F Tyrone M. Brooks, USN
Airman Ap. Christopher B. Brown, USN
Airman Ap. Darrel K. Brown, USN
Spec. James R. Brown, USA
Airman Ap. Steven A. Budzian, USN
Sen. M/Sgt. Paul G. Buege, USAF
S/Sgt. Ricky L. Bunch, USA
Sgt. Paul L. Burt, USA
Aviation Struct. Mech. 2nd. Class Michael R. Butch, USN
Spec. Thomas D. Butler, USA
Sgt. 1st Class William T. Butts, USA
Capt. Thomas R. Caldwell, USAF
Priv. 1st Class Kevin L. Calloway, USA
S/Sgt. John F. Campisi, USAF
Sgt. Jason C. Carr, USA
Lt. Col. Hector Carranza Jr., USA
Seaman Monray C. Carrington, USN
Spec. Clarence A. Cash, USA
Sgt. Christopher J. Chapman, USA
Capt. Michael L. Chinburg, USAF
Sgt. Barry M. Clark, USAF
Spec. Beverly S. Clark, USA
Airman Larry M. Clark, USN
M/Sgt. Otto F. Clark, USA
Spec. Steven D. Clark, USA
Mr. Samuel J. Clemente (Army Contractor)
L/Cpl. Edward M. Codispodo, USMC
Pfc. Gerald A. Cohen, USA
Pfc. Melford R. Collins, USA
Maj. Mark A. Connelly, USA
S/Sgt. Michael R. Conner Sr., USMC
Lt. Patrick K. Conner, USN
Lt. Cdr. Barry T. Cooke, USN
Cpl. Michael D. Cooke, USMC
Pfc. Ardon Bradley Cooper, USA
Capt. Charles W. Cooper, USA
Capt. Dale T. Cormier, USAF
Lt. William T. Costen, USN
Cpl. Ismael Cotto, USMC
Spec. Gary W. Crask, USA
Sgt. Alan B. Craver, USA
Aviation Stru. Mech/3rd James F. Crockford, USN
Capt. William D. Cronin Jr., USMC

Spec. Mark R. Cronquist, USA
Aeo. Mate/1st Shirley M. Cross, USN
Sgt. David R. Crumby, Jr., USA
Mr. George Cruz (Navy Contractor)
L/Cpl. James B. Cunningham, USMC
CWO/3rd John J. Curtin, USA
Pfc. Michael Dailey, USA
Spec. Roy T. Damian, Jr., USA
Pfc. Candace M. Daniel, USA
Spec. Michael D. Daniels, USA
Sgt. Donald C. Danielson, USA
Pfc. Robert L. Daugherty, USA
Spec. Manuel M. Davila, USA
Pfc. Marty R. Davis, USA
S/Sgt. Tatiana Dees, USA
Spec. Rolando A. Delagneau, USA
Signalman/3rd Class Delwin Delgado, USN
Sgt. Luis R. Delgado, USA
Sgt. Ross A. Dierking, USA
WO1 Thomas M. Diffenbaugh, USMC
Capt. Gary S. Dillon, USMC
Sgt. Young M. Dillon, USA
Capt. Kevin R. Dolvin, USMC
CWO2 Patrick A. Donaldson, USA
L/Cpl. Joseph D. Dougherty, III, USMC
Lt. Col. David A. Douthit, USA
Sgt. David Q. Douthit, USA
Sgt. Robert L. Durrell, USA
Lt. Robert J. Dwyer, USN
Capt. Jonathan R. Edwards, USMC
Capt. Paul R. Eichenlaub II, USAF
Private Dorothy L. Fails, USA
Capt. Mario Fajardo, USA
Spec. Steven P. Farnen, USA
LCpl. Eliseo Felix, USMC
Sgt. Douglas L. Fielder, USA
Aviation Mach. Mate/3rd Class George S. Finneral, USN
Pfc. Michael L. Fitz, USA
Aviation Ord. 3rd Class Anthony J. Fleming, USN
Private Joshua J. Fleming, USA
Aviation Storekeeper Airman Gilbert A. Fontaine, USN
Sgt. Ira L. Foreman, USA
Spec. John C. Fowler, USA
Capt. Arthur Galvan, USAF
S/Sgt. Mike A. Garrett, USA
CWO/4th Phillip H. Garvey, USA
L/Cpl. Arthur O. Garza, USMC
Pfc. Pamela Y. Gay, USA
S/Sgt. Kenneth B. Gentry, USA
Maj. John H. Gillespie, USA

Boiler Tech. 3rd Class David A. Gilliland, USN
CWO3 Robert G. Godfrey, USA
Sgt. Mark J. Gologram, USA
Capt. Daniel E. Graybeal, USA
LCpl. Troy L. Gregory, USMC
Capt. Walter D. Grimm, USAF
Airman Jorge L. Guerrero, USN
Cpl. Albert G. Haddad, USMC
1st Lt. Thomas J. Haggerty, USA
S/Sgt. Garland V. Hailey, USA
Sgt. Tracy Hampton, USA
Lt. Col.Joe H. Hancock, Jr., USA
S/Sgt. Steven M. Hansen, USA
S/Sgt. Michael A. Harris, Jr., USA
S/Sgt. Timothy R. Harrison, USAF
Spec. Adrian J. Hart, USA
S/Sgt. Raymond E. Hatcher, Jr., USA
S/Sgt. Jimmy D. Haws, USA
Sgt. James D. Hawthorne, USMC
Spec. Wade E. Hector, USA
1st Lt. Eric D. Hedeen, USAF
CWO2 Kerry P. Hein, USA
Sgt. Leroy E. Hein, Jr., USAF
Maj. Barry K. Henderson, USAF
Spec. Luis A. Henry-Garay, USA
Capt. David R. Herr, USMC
Spec. James P. Heyden, USA
Spec. David L. Heyman, USA
Spec. Timothy E. Hill, USA
Aviation Elect. Mate Kevin J. Hills, USN
L/Cpl. Adam T. Hoage, USMC
T/Sgt. Robert K. Hodges, USAF
Sgt. Larry G. Hogan, USMC
Lt. Col. Donnie R. Holland, USAF
Spec. Duane W. Hollen, Jr., USA
Spec. David C. Hollenbeck, USA
Aviation Elect. Tech. 3rd Class William A. Holt, USN
Damage Controlman 3rd Class Ron R. Holyfield, USN
Maj. Peter S. Hook, USAF
Mr. Trezzvant Hopson, Jr. (Navy Contractor)
Cpl. Raymond L. Horwath, Jr., USMC
PFc. Aaron Howard, USA
CWO3 Robert J. Hughes, USA
Sgt. Maj. Patrick R. Hurley, USA
Capt. William J. Hurley, USMC
Boiler Tech. Mark E. Hutchison, USN
Pfc. John Wesley Hutto, USA
Fireman Wilton L. Huyghue, USN
S/Sgt. Arthur Jackson, USA
Pfc. Kenneth J. Jackson, USA

Lt. Mark D. Jackson, USN
Fire Control Tech. 3rd Class Timothy J. Jackson, USN
Spec. Jimmy W. James, USA
Spec. Thomas R. Jarrel, USA
LCpl. Thomas A. Jenkins, USMC
Machinist's Mate Fireman Dale W. Jock, USN
Cpl. Daniel D. Joel, USMC
Airman Apprentice Alexander Jones, USN
Electrician's Mate 3rd Class Daniel M. Jones, USN
Spec. Glen D. Jones, USA
Cpl. Phillip J. Jones, USMC
S/Sgt. Jonathan H. Kamm, USA
S/Sgt. Damon V. Kanuha, USAF
Sgt. Kenneth T. Keller, USMC
2nd Lt. Shannon P. Kelly, USA
Mess Management Spec. Nathaniel H. Kemp, USN
Spec. Frank S. Keough, USA
Spec. Anthony W. Kidd, USA
S/Sgt. John R. Kilkus, USMC
Mr. Allen Kimbrell (Army Corps of Engineers)
Capt. Joseph G. Kime, III, USA
Pfc. Jerry L. King, USA
Pfc. Reuben G. Kirk, III, USA
Maj. Thomas F. Koritz, USAF
Pfc. David W. Kramer, USA
Sgt. Edwin B. Kutz, USA
Pfc. Dustin C. LaMoureux, USA
Cpl. Victor T. Lake, Jr., USMC
L/Cpl Brian L. Lane, USMC
L/Cpl. James M. Lang, USMC
Lt. Thomas S. Larson, USN
2nd Lt. Lorraine K. Lawton, USA
CWO3 Richard R. Lee, USA
LCpl. Michael E. Linderman, Jr., USMC
Sgt. J. Scott Lindsey, USA
Maj. William E. Long, USA
LCpl. James H. Lumpkins, USMC
Elect. Mate 2nd Class Daniel Lupatsky, USN
Spec. Anthony E. Madison, USA
Spec. Gary W. Mahan, USA
1st Lt. Joseph D. Maks, USA
WO George N. Malak, USA
Fireman Michael N. Manns, USN
WO Christopher A. Martin, USA
Spec. Steven G. Mason, USA
Sgt. Kelly L. Matthews, USA
Senior Master Sgt. James B. May, II, USAF
Spec. Christine I. Mayes, USA
Maj. Eugene T. McCarthy, USMC
Sgt. James R. McCoy, USA

Airman Brent A. McCreight, USN
Sgt. Melvin D. McDougle, USA
Boiler Tech. Fireman Daniel C. McKinsey, USN
Spec. Bobby L. McKnight, USA
Spec. Jeff T. Middleton, USA
Spec. James R. Miller, USA
Pfc. Mark A. Miller, USA
Spec. Michael W. Mills, USA
Sgt. Randall C. Mills, USA
Private Adrienne L. Mitchell, USA
Sgt. 1st Class Earnest F. Mitchem, USA
Spec. Phillip D. Mobley, USA
Sgt. Nels A. Moller, USA
Sgt. Garett A. Mongrella, USMC
1st Lt. Michael N. Monroe, USMC
S/Sgt. Lance M. Monsen, USMC
Sgt. Candelario Montalvo, Jr., USMC
S/Sgt. Thomas J. Moran, USMC
S/Sgt. Donald W. Morgan, USA
WO John K. Morgan, USA
S/Sgt. Jeffery E. Mullin, USA
Sgt. 1st Class Donald T. Murphy, USA
1st Sgt. Joe Murphy, USA
Spec. James C. Murray, Jr., USA
Spec. Donald R. Myers, USA
Mr. James F. Neberman (Army Material Command)
Airman Apprentice Randy L. Neel, USN
Airman 1st Class Rocky J. Nelson, USAF
Pfc. Shawnacee L. Noble, USA
Pfc. Michael A. Noline, USMC
Spec. Robert A. Noonan, USA
Sgt. Cheryl L. O'Brien, USA
T/Sgt. John L. Oelschlager, USAF
L/Cpl. Arthur D. Oliver, USMC
Capt. Jeffery J. Olson, USAF
1st Lt. Patrick B. Olson, USAF
S/Sgt. Patbouvier E. Ortiz, USA
Sgt. Aaron A. Pack, USMC
CWO4 John M. Paddock, USN
Spec. William F. Palmer, USA
Boiler Tech. Fred R. Parker, USN
Private Anthony T. Patterson, USA
Spec. Dale L. Paulson, USA
Spec. Kenneth J. Perry, USA
Spec. Kelly D. Phillips, USA
Capt. Stephen R. Phillis, USAF
WO David G. Plasch, USA
Aviation Boatswain's Mate Marvin J. Plummer, USN
1st Lt. Terry Plunk, USA
Senior Airman Ramono L. Poole, USAF

L/Cpl. Kip A. Poremba, USMC
L/Cpl. Christian J. Porter, USMC
Capt. James B. Poulet, USAF
Sgt. Dodge R. Powell, USA
Pfc. Norman R. Rainwater, USA
Sgt. Ronald M. Randazzo, USA
Pfc. Jeffrey D. Reel, USA
CWO Hal H. Reichle, USA
Capt. Fredrick A. Reid, USAF
Spec. Ronald D. Rennison, USA
Pfc. Todd C. Ritch, USA
Capt. Manuel Rivera, Jr., USMC
Sgt. Ernest Rivers, USMC
Sgt. Stephen R. Robinette, USA
S/Sgt. Michael R. Robson, USA
M/Sgt. Eloy A. Rodriguez, Jr., USA
Sgt. Jeffery A. Rollins, USA
Cpl. Timothy W. Romei, USMC
Maj. Marie T. Rossi, USA
Pfc. Scott A. Rush, USA
Sgt. Leonard A. Russ, USA
L/Cpl. Archimedes P. San Juan, USMC
1st Sgt. Henry J. Sanders, USA
Spec. Manuel B. Sapien, USA
Sgt. Baldwin L. Satchell, USA
Data Systems Tech. Matthew J. Schiedler, USN
S/Sgt. Mark J. Schmauss, USAF
Mr. Paul L. Schmidt, (Navy Contractor)
L/Cpl. Thomas J. Scholand, USMC
Lt. Col. Stephen G. Schramm, USAF
L/Cpl. Scott A. Schroeder, USMC
Sgt. Brian P. Scott, USA
Disbursing Clerk 3rd Class Timothy B. Seay, USN
Mess Management Spec. Jeffrey A. Settimi, USN
S/Sgt. David A. Shaw, USMC
Pfc. Timothy A. Shaw, USA
2nd Lt. Kathleen M. Sherry, USA
Fire Control Tech. Chief Jeffrey W. Shukers, USN
Spec. Stephen J. Siko, USA
Spec. Brian K. Simpson, USA
Machinist's Mate 3rd Class James A. Smith, Jr., USN
S/Sgt. James M. Smith, USA
Sgt. Michael S. Smith, USA
Sgt. Russell G. Smith, Jr., USA
LCpl. David T. Snyder, USMC
Lt. John M. Snyder, USN
Pfc. Jeffery W. Speicher, USA
Lt. Cdr. Michael S. Speicher, USN
Capt. David M. Spellacy, USMC
Spec. Otha B. Squires, USA

S/Sgt. Christopher H. Stephens, USA
Spec. John B. Stephens, USA
L/Cpl. Dion J. Stephenson, USMC
L/Cpl. Anthony D. Stewart, USMC
Raidoman Roderick T. Stewart, USN
Pfc. Adrian L. Stokes, USA
Spec. Thomas G. Stone, USA
Sgt. 1st Class Gary E. Streeter, USA
Sgt. William A. Strehlow, USA
Maj. Earl K. Stribling, USA
S/Sgt. Roy J. Sumerall, USA
Spec. Peter L. Swano, USA
CWO2 George R. Swartzendruber, USA
Cpl. James H. Sylvia, Jr., USMC
Pfc. Robert D. Talley, USA
Sgt. 1st Class David L. Tapley, USA
Spec. James D. Tatum, USA
Aviation Structural Mech. Phillip J. Thomas, USN
Capt. James K. Thorp, USMC
1st Lt. Donaldson P. Tillar, III, USA
L/Cpl. Thomas R. Tormanen, USMC
Spec. Steven R. Trautman, USA
Lt. Charles J. Turner, USN
Capt. Reginald C. Underwood, USMC
Lt.(jg) Craig E. Valentine, USN
Pfc. Roger E. Valentine, USA
Sgt. Mario Vega Velazquez, USA
Private Scott N. Vigrass, USA
Lt. Col. Carlos A. Viquez, USA
Boiler Tech. 1st Class Robert L. Volden, USN
Pfc. Robert C. Wade, USA
L/Cpl. James E. Waldron, USMC
Pfc. Charles S. Walker, USA
LCpl. Daniel B. Walker, USMC
Lt. Col. Michael C. Wallington, USA
Spec. Frank J. Walls, USA
Spec. Thomas E. Walrath, USA
Capt. Dixon L. Walters, USAF
Pfc. Patrick A. Wanke, USA
Spec. Bobby M. Ware, USA
Aviation Electrician 2nd Class Brian P. Weaver, USN
Maj. Paul J. Weaver, USAF
Spec. Troy M. Wedgewood, USA
Sgt. Lawrence N. Welch, USA
Aviation Structural Mechanic John D. West, USN
Sgt. Scotty L. Whittenburg, USA
Pfc. David M. Wieczorek, USA
Capt. James N. Wilbourn, III, USMC
Sgt. James Wilcher, USA
Mess Management Spec. Philip L. Wilkinson, USN

Cpl. Jonathan M. Williams, USA
Pfc. Corey L. Winkle, USA
CWO2 Bernard S. Winkley, USMC
Sgt. 1st Class Harold P. Witzke, III, USA
Spec. Richard V. Wolverton, USA
Spec. James E. Worthy, USA
Spec. Kevin E. Wright, USA
Spec. Carl W. Zabel, USA
Maj. Thomas C. M. Zeugner, USA

British Forces
Paul Peter Atkinson, Royal Fusiliers
David Clifford, Royal Military Police
Conrad Phillip Cole, Royal Fusiliers
Robert Consiglio, Special Air Service (SAS)
Stephen Richard Croft, Royal Corps of Transport
David Edwin Denbury, Royal Engineers
Neil Walker Duncan Donald, Queen's Own Highlanders
Michael James Dowling, Royal Electrical and Mechanical Engineers
Francis Carrington Evans, Royal Electrical and Mechanical Engineers
Alistair James Fogerty, Royal Ordnance Corps
Richard Gillespie, Royal Fusiliers
Thomas Haggerty, Royal Scots
Martin Ferguson, Queen's Own Highlanders
Terence William Hill, Royal Corps of Transport
Paul Patrick Keegan, Royal Artillery
James Scott Kingham, Royal Engineers
Donal James Kinnear, Royal Army Pay Corps
John William Lang, Queen's Own Highlanders
"Legs" Lane, Special Air Service (SAS)
Kevin Leech, Royal Fusiliers
Jason Patrick McFadden, Royal Corps of Transport
Carl Moult, Staffordshire Regiment
Vince Phillips, Special Air Service (SAS)
Robert Robbins, Royal Corps of Transport
Richard Allen Royle, Royal Engineers
Stephen Timothy Satchell, Royal Fusiliers
Shaun Patrick Taylor, Staffordshire Regiment
Lee James Thompson, Royal Fusiliers
Alastair John Wright, Royal Engineers

COALITION GROUND FORCES IN THE PERSIAN GULF WAR

British Forces, Lt. Gen. Peter de la Billiere
<u>1st Armoured Division</u>, Maj. Gen. Rupert Smith
7th Armoured Brigade ("Desert Rats"), Brig. Patrick Cordingley
The Royal Scots Dragoon Guards, Lt. Col. John Sharples
The Queen's Royal Irish Hussars, Lt. Col. Arthur Denaro
1st Battalion, The Queen's Dragoon Guards, Maj. Hamish MacDonald
1st Battalion, The Staffordshire Regiment, Lt. Col. Charles Rogers
40th Field Regiment, Royal Artillery, Lt. Col. R.R.H. Clayton, MBE
10th Air Defence Battery, Royal Artillery (unknown)
21st Engineer Regiment, Lt. Col. J. D. Moore-Bick
207th Signal Squadron, Royal Corps of Signals, Lt. Col. Neil Donaldson
654th Squadron, Army Air Corps, (unknown)
<u>4th Armoured Brigade</u> "Hell for Leather", Brig. Christopher Hammerbeck
14th/20th King's Hussars, Lt. Col. M. J. H. Vickery
3rd Battalion, Royal Regiment of Fusiliers, Lt. Col. A.L.D. de Hockepied
1st Battalion, The Royal Scots, Lt. Col. I. A. Johnstone
2nd Field Regiment, Royal Artillery, Lt. Col. J. Milne
46th Air Defence Battery, Royal Artillery
23rd Engineer Regiment, Lt. Col. D. J. Beaton
204th Signals Squadron
659th Squadron, Army Air Corps
<u>Divisonal Assets</u>
16th/5th, The Queen's Royal Lancers, Lt. Col. P. E. Scott
32nd Heavy Regiment, Royal Artillery, Lt. Col. P. H. Marwood
26th Field Regiment, Royal Artillery, Lt. Col. M. A. Corbet-Bucher
39th Heavy Regiment, Royal Artillery, Lt. Col. P. B. Williams
12th Air Defence Regiment, Royal Artillery, Lt. Col. P. C. Villalard
32nd Armoured Engineer Regiment, Royal Engineers, Lt. Col. Hutchinson
4th Regiment, Army Air Corps, Lt. Col. F. M. Wawn
1st Armoured Division Transport Regiment, Royal Corps of Transport, Lt. Col. G. J. Haig
4th Armoured Division Transport Regiment, Royal Corps of Transports, Lt. Col. T. M. Macartney
1st Armoured Division Field Ambulance, Royal Army Medical Corps

5th Armoured Division Field Ambulance
3rd Ordnance Battalion, Royal Army Ordnance Corps, Lt. Col. A. Taylor
7th Armoured Workshop, Royal Electrical and Mechanical Engineers
11th Armoured Workshop
Force Troops
205th General Hospital, Royal Army Medical Corps
24th Air Mobile Field Ambulance, Royal Army Medical Corps
22nd Field Hospital, Royal Army Medical Corps, Lt. Col. C. J. Town
32nd Field Hospital, Royal Army Medical Corps
33rd General Hospital, Royal Army Medical Corps
Elements of 30th Signals Regiment, Royal Corps of Signals, Lt. Col. S. Kidner
Forward Maintenance Area
6th Armoured Workshop, 7th Aircraft Workshop, 6th Ordnance Group
The Life Guards
9th/12th, Royal Lancers, (Prince of Wales's), Lt. Col. H. T. Dickens
17th/21st Royal Lancers, Lt. Col. R. D. S. Gordon
4th Royal Tank Regiment, Lt. Col. M. N. E. Speller
1st Battalion, The Grenadier Guards, Lt. Col. R. G. Cartwright
1st Battalion, Scots Guards, Lt. Col. J. J. Cargill
1st Battalion, The Devonshire and Dorset Regiment, Lt. Col. D. C. N. Shaw
1st Battalion, The Prince of Wales Own Regiment of Yorkshire, Lt. Col. J. C. L. King
.1st Battalion, Queen's Own Royal Highlanders, Lt. Col. H. B. H. E. Monro
1st Battalion, The Royal Green Jackets, Lt. Col. S. R. Stanford-Tuck
Arab-Islamic Force, Gen. Khalid bin Sultan
Royal Saudi Land Forces 5th Airborne Battalion
North Arab-Islamic Command
Syrian 45th Commando Brigade Maj. Gen. Habib (all Syrian Forces)
122nd Special Forces Battalion
183rd Special Forces Battalion
824th Special Forces Battalion
(Supported by one artillery and one antitank battalion)
126th Antiaircraft Artillery Brigade
39th Artillery Brigade
Reserve and Support Forces
Saudi Attack Aviation Battalion
RSLF 15th MLRS Battalion
RSLF 7th Target Acquisition
RSLF Antitank Company
RSLF 4th Airborne Battalion
Czechoslovakian NBC Defense Company
Kuwaiti "Haq" Brigade
Kuwaiti "Khulud" Brigade
Niger Infantry Battalion
Royal Saudi Land Forces 10th Mechanized Brigade
United Arab Emirates Mechanized Battalion
Northern Omani Brigade (Reinforced)
Othman Task Force
Royal Saudi Land Forces 8th Mechanized Brigade
Bahraini Motorized Infantry Company
Kuwaiti "Al Fatah" Brigade

Kuwaiti 2/15 Mechanized Battalion
Baker Task Force
Saudi Arabian National Guard 2nd Mechanized Brigade
Tariq Task Force
Royal Saudi Marine Battalion
Moroccan 6th Mechanized Battalion
Senegalese 1st Infantry Battalion
Reserve and Support Forces
RSLF 14th Field Artillery Battalion
RSLF 18th Missile Battalion
RSLF 2nd Antitank Company
RSLF 6th Target Acquisition Battery
Qatari Mechanized Battalion Task Force
1st East Bengal Infantry Battalion
South Korea Medical Unit
(including Czech, Dutch, Polish, and New Zealand Field Hospitals)
<u>U.S. 3rd Army</u>, Lt. Gen. Cal Waller
2nd Expeditionary Force
4th Marine Expeditionary Brigade, Maj. Gen. Harry W. Jenkins, Jr.
Headquarters and Service Company, 4th MEB
5th Marine Expeditionary Brigade, Brig. Gen. Peter J. Rowe
Headquarters and Service Company, 5th MEB
Surveillance, Reconnaissance, and Intelligence Support Group 5
13th Marine Expeditionary Unit (SOC), Col. John E. Rhodes
Battalion Landing Team 1/4
Marine Medium Helicopter Squadron 164 (HMM-164) (Reinforced)
MEU Service Support Group 13
<u>Forward Forces Command</u>
Saudi King Faisal Brigade (National Guard)
Pakistani 7th Armored Brigade
<u>Joint Forces Command East</u>, Maj. Gen. Sultan Adi (Al-Mutairi)(Salah).
Saudi 10th Mechanized Brigade
UAE Mechanized Battalion
North Oman Brigade
Task Force Othman
Saudi 8th Mechanized
Kuwaiti "Fatah" Brigades
Task Force Abu Bakar
Saudi 2nd National Guard Brigade
Task Force Tariq
Saudi Marine
Moroccan 6th Mechanized
Senegal Battalions
(Reserves: Qatari Mechanized Battalion and 1st East Bengal Infantry Battalion)
<u>1st Marine Expeditionary Force</u>
1st Marine Division, Maj. Gen. James M. Myatt
1st Marine Regiment, Col. Richard W. Hodory
1st Battalion, 1st Marines, Lt. Col. Michael O. Fallon
3rd Battalion, 9th Marines, Lt. Col. Michael H. Smith,
1st Tank Battalion, Lt. Col. Michael M. Kephart

3rd Marine Regiment, Col. John H. Admire
1st Battalion, 3rd Marines, Lt. Col. Michael V. Maloney
2nd Battalion, 3rd Marines, Lt. Col. Robert W. Blose, Jr.
3rd Battalion, 3rd Marines, Lt. Col. John C. Garret
4th Marine Regiment, Col. James A. Fulks
2nd Battalion, 7th Marines, Lt. Col. Roger J. Mauer
3rd Battalion, 7th Marines, Lt. Col. Timothy J. Hannigan
1st Battalion, 25th Marines, Lt. Col. Stephen M. McCartney
7th Marine Regiment, Col. Carlton W. Fulford
1st Battalion, 7th Marines, Lt. Col. James M. Mattis
1st Battalion, 5th Marines, Lt. Col. Christopher Cortez
3rd Tank Battalion, Lt. Col. Alphonso B. Diggs, Jr.
11th Marine Regiment (Artillery), Col. Patrick G. Howard
1st Battalion, 11th Marines, Lt. Col. John B. Sollis
2nd Battalion, 11th Marines, Lt. Col. Paul A. Gido
3rd Battalion, 11th Marines, Lt. Col. Mark W. Adams
5th Battalion, 11th Marines, Lt. Col. James L. Sachtleben
1st Battalion, 12th Marines, Lt. Col. Robert W. Rivers
3rd Battalion, 12th Marines, Lt. Col. Charles W. Adair
1st Combat Engineer Battalion, Lt. Col. Frank L. Kebelman III
1st Light Armored Infantry Battalion, Lt. Col. Clifford O. Myers III
1st Reconnaissance Battalion, Lt. Col. Michael L. Rapp
3rd Assault Amphibian Battalion, Lt. Col. Ronald S. Eluk
2nd Marine Division, Maj. Gen. William M. Keyes
6th Marine Regiment, Col. Lawrence H. Livingston
1st Battalion, 6th Marines, Lt. Col. Tom S. Jones
2nd Battalion, 2nd Marines, Lt. Col. Brian M. Youngs
3rd Battalion, 6th Marines, Lt. Col. Arnold Fields
8th Marine Regiment, Col. Larry S. Schmidt
1st Battalion, 8th Marines, Lt. Col. Bruce A. Gombar
2nd Battalion, 4th Marines, Lt. Col. Kevin A. Conry
3rd Battalion, 23rd Marines, Lt. Col. Ray C. Dawson
10th Marine Regiment, Col. Leslie M. Palm
2nd Battalion, 10th Marines, Lt. Col. Joseph R. Stewart
2nd Battalion, 12th Marines, Lt. Col. Michael J. Swords
3rd Battalion, 10th Marines, Lt. Col. Phillip E. Hughes
5th Battalion, 10th Marines, Lt. Col. Andrew F. Mazzara
1st Brigade, 2nd Armored Division, Col. John B. Sylvester, USA
1st Battalion, 67th Armored Regiment, Lt. Col. Michael T. Johnson, USA
3rd Battalion, 67th Armored Regiment, Lt. Col. Douglas L. Tystad, USA
3rd Battalion, 41st Mechanized Infantry Regiment, Lt. Col. Walter Wojdakowski, USA
1st Battalion, 3rd Field Artillery, Lt. Col. James R. Kerin, USA
502nd Forward Support Battalion, Lt. Col. Coy R. Scroggins, USA
142nd Signal Battalion, Lt. Col. Henry C. Cobb, Jr., USA
Battery A, 92nd Field Artillery (Multiple Launch Rocket System), Capt. Edward L. Hughes, USA
Company A, 17th Engineers, Capt. Craig Wells, USA
Company B, 4th Battalion, 5th A.D. Artillery, Capt. Charles D. Watt, USA
Headquarters Battalion, 2nd Marine Division, Col. Roger C. McElraft
2nd Assault Amphibian Battalion, Lt. Col. Robert L. Williams

2nd Combat Engineer Battalion, Lt. Col. John D. Winchester
2nd Light Armored Infantry Battalion, Lt. Col. Keith T. Holcomb
2nd Reconnaissance Battalion, Lt. Col. Scott W. McKenzie
2nd Tank Battalion, Lt. Col. Cesare Cardi
8th Tank Battalion, Lt. Col. Michael D. Cavallaro
Task Force Breach Alpha (2nd Marine Division)
Company B, 2nd Combat Engineer Battalion
Company D, 4th Combat Engineer Battalion
Provisional General Support Company, 4th Assault Amphibian Battalion
Detachment, 4th Tank Battalion
Task Force Vega (2nd Marine Division)
Company D, 4th Reconnaissance Battalion
Detachment, Antitank Company, 4th Tank Battalion
Detachent, 2nd Low Altitude Air Defense Battalion
Ground Combat Element
Regimental Landing Team 2
Headquarters Company, 2nd Marines
1st Battalion, 2nd Marines
3rd Battalion, 2nd Marines
1st Battalion, 10th Marines
2nd Light Armored Infantry Battalion
Company A, 2nd Assault Amphibian Battalion
Company A, 2nd Tank Battalion
Company A, 2nd Reconnaissance Battalion
Detachment, Truck Company, Headquarters Battalion, 2nd Marines Division
Air Combat Element
Marine Aircraft Group 40
Marine Attack Squadron 331 (VMA-331)
Marine Medium Helicopter Squadron 263 (HMM-263)
Marine Medium Helicopter Squadron 365 (HMM-365)
Marine Heavy Helicopter Squadron 461 (HMH-46)
Marine Light Attack Helicopter Squadron 299 (HMLA-269)
Marine Aviation Logistics Squadron 14 (MALS-14)
Headquarters and Headquarters Squadron 28 (H&HS-28)
Marine Air Control Squadron 6 (MAC-6)
Marine Wing Communications Squadron 28 (MWCS-28)
Detachment B, Marine Air Support Squadron 1 (MASS-1)
A Battery, 2nd Low Altitude Air Defense Battalion
Marine Wing Support Squadron 274 (MWSS-274)
Combat Service Support Element
Brigade Service Support Element 4
Ground Combat Element
Regimental Landing Team 5
Headquarters Company, 5th Marines
2nd Battalion, 5th Marines
3rd Battalion, 5th Marines
3rd Battalion, 1st Marines
2nd Battalion, 11th Marines (Reinforced)
Company D, 1st Light Armored Infantry Battalion
Company B, 1st Combat Engineer Battalion (Reinforced)

Company A, 4th Tank Battalion (Reinforced)
Antitank Platoon, 23rd Marines
Company A, 4th Assault Amphibian Battalion (Reinforced)
Company B, 1st Reconnaissance Battalion (Reinforced)
Air Combat Element
Marine Aircraft Group 50
Headquarters, Marine Aircraft Group 50
Detachment, Marine Air Control Group 38 (MACG-38)
Detachment Marine Air Control Squadron 7 (MACS-7)
Detachment C, Marine Air Support Squadron 6 (MASS-6) (Direct Air Support Center)
A Battery, 3rd Low Altitude Air Defense Battalion (Reinforced)
Detachment, Marine Aviation Logistics Squadron 16 (MALS-16)
Detachment, Marine Aviation Logistics Squadron 39 (MALS-39)
Detachment, Marine Aviation Logistics Squadron 13 (MALS-13)
Detachment, Marine Aviation Logistics Squadron 24 (MALS-24)
Detachment, Marine Wing Headquarters Squadron 3 (MWHS-3)
Detachment, Marine Wing Weapons Unit 3 (MWWU-3)
Detachment, Marine Wing Support Squadron (MWSS) (rotary wing)
Detachment, Marine Wing Support Squadron (MWSS) (fixed wing)
Marine Medium Helicopter Squadron 268 (HMM-268)
Marine Medium Helicopter Squadron 265 (HMM-265)
Detachment, Marine Heavy Helicopter Squadron 466 (HMH-466)
Marine Light Attack Helicopter Squadron 169 (HMLA-169)
Marine Attack Helicopter Squadron 773 (HMA-773)
Combat Service Support Element
Brigade Service Support Group 5
Detachment, Headquarters & Service Battalion, 1st FSSG
Detachment, 1st Landing Support Battalion (Reinforced)
Detachment, Communications Company
Detachment, 7th Motor Transport Battalion
Detachment, Medical Battalion (dental included)
Detachment, 7th Engineer Support Battalion
Detachment, 1st Supply Battalion
Detachment, 1st Maintenance Battalion
Joint Forces Command North, Gen. Alkami.
Syrian 4th Commando Brigade
Syrian 9th Armored Division
33rd Armored Brigade
52nd Brigade (Mechanized)
Muthana Task Force
Saudi 20th Brigade (Mechanized)
Kuwaiti 35th "Shid" Brigade (Mechanized)
Sa'ad Task Force
Saudi 4th Armored Brigade
Kuwaiti 15th Infantry Brigade
(Reserves: Kuwaiti "Haq" Brigade and Kuwaiti "Khulud" Brigade)
Egyptian II Corps
Egyptian 3rd Mechanized Division
23rd Armored Division
10th Brigade (Mechanized)

114th Brigade (Mechanized)
Egyptian 4th Armored Division
2nd Armored Brigade
3rd Armored Brigade
6th Brigade (Mechanized)
Egyptian 1st Ranger Regiment
US VII Corps, Lt. Gen. Fred Franks
1st Cavalry Division (Armored), John H. Tilelli, Jr.
1st "Ironhorse" Brigade, Col. George H. Harmeyer
2nd "Blackjack" Brigade, Col. Randolph W. House
4th Battalion, 5th Air Defense, Lt. Col. Randall D. Harris
8th Engineer Battalion, Lt. Col. Hans A. Van Winkle
Division Artillery, Col. James M. Gass
Aviation "Warriors" Brigade, Col. William D. McGill
Division "Wagonmasters" Support Command, Col. Richard J. Fousek
13th Signal, Lt. Col. Edgar W. Steele
312th Military Intelligence, Lt. Col. Richard N. Armstrong
1st Infantry Division (Mech) "Big Red One", Maj. Gen. Thomas G. Rhame
1st Brigade, Col. Lon E. Maggart
5th Battalion, 16th Infantry, Lt. Col. Sydney "Skip" Baker
1st Battalion, 34th Armor, Lt. Col. G. Patrick Ritter
2nd Battalion, 34th Armor, Lt. Col. Gregory Fontenot
2nd Brigade, Col. Anthony A. Moreno
2nd Battalion, 16th Infantry, Lt. Col. Daniel Fake
3rd Battalion, 37th Armor, Lt. Col. David Gross
4th Battalion, 37th Armor, Lt. Col. David Marlin
4th Brigade, Col. James Mowery
1st Squadron, 4th Cavalry, Lt. Col. Robert Wilson
1st Squadron, 1st Aviation, Lt. Col. Ronald Reichelsdorfer
4th Squadron, 1st Aviation, Lt. Col. Phillip L. Wilkerson, Jr.
Division Artillery, Lt. Col. Michael L. Dodson
1st Engineer Battalion, Lt. Col. Steven R. Hawkins
3rd Armored Division, "Spearhead", Maj. Gen. Paul E. "Butch" Funk
1st Brigade, Col. Bill Nash
2nd Brigade, Col. Bob Hughes
3rd Brigade, Col. Rob Goff
1st Armored Division, "Old Ironsides", Maj. Gen. Ronald Griffith
1st Brigade, Col. Jim Riley
1-7 IN, Lt. Col. Smith
4-7 IN, Lt. Col. Pat Egan
2nd Brigade, Col. Monty Meigs
6-6 IN, Lt. Col. Mike McGee
1-35 AR, Lt. Col. Jerry Wiedewitsch
2-70 AR, Lt. Col. Feyk
4-70 AR, Lt. Col. Steve Whitcomb
3rd Brigade, Col. Dan Zanini
7-6 IN, Lt. Col. Critz
1-37 AR, Lt. Col. Ed Dyer
3-35 AR, Lt. Col. Kane
4th Brigade, Col. Dan Petrosky

2-1 AVN, Lt. Col. John Ward
3-1 AVN, Lt. Col. Bill Hatch
TF Phoenix, Lt. Col. Travis
Division Artillery, Col. V.B. Corn
2-41 FA, Lt. Col. Leahy
2-1 FA, Lt. Col. Unterheseber
3-1FA, Lt. Col. Hahn
2nd Armored Cavalry Regiment, Col. L. Don Holder
42nd Field Artillery Brigade
72nd Field Artillery Brigade
142nd Field Artillery Brigade
210th Field Artillery Brigade
7th Engineer Brigade
11th Aviation Brigade
14th Military Police Brigade
US XVIII Airborne Corps, Lt. Gen. Gary Luck
24th Infantry Division (Mechanized), Maj. Gen. Barry McCaffrey
1st Brigade, Col. John LeMoyne
2nd Brigade, Col. Paul Kern
197th Infantry Brigade (Mechanized), Col. Ted Reid
Aviation Brigade, Col. Burt Tackaberry
Division Artillery, Col. Ron Townsend
Division Engineer Brigade, Col. Hank Miller
101st Air Assault Division, Maj. Gen. Binney Peay III
187th Air Assault Regiment, Col. John McDonald, Col. Bob Clark
1/187, Kinnison, C. Brian, Fahy, Priatko
2/187, Berdy, Lewis, McBride, Edwards
3/187, Greco, Carlson, Biller, Suchland, Woody
327th Air Assault Regiment
1st Brigade, Col. Tom Hill, Col. Jim Garity, Col. Bob Nicholas
1st Battalion/327, Lt. Col. Frank Hancock, Gill, Russell
2/327, Thomas
3/327, (unknown)
502nd Air Assault Regiment, Col. Greg Gile, Col. Ted Purdom, Col. Wood
1/502, (unknown)
2/502, Calvin, Greer
3/502, (unknown)
Aviation Brigade, Garrett
1/101, Cody, M. Davis, D. Gabram, Garcia
2/229, Brilinski, W. Bryan, Butts, Cornum, Dunlap, Godfrey, Pacheko, Stamaris
3/101, Curran
4/101, R. Johnson
5/101, Russ Adams
7/101, Willmoth, Fox, Pellitier
2/17, Hamlin, Kranz, Rister, Wyrick
Artillery Brigade, Anderson, P.Jones
French Forces, Lt. Gen. Michel Roquejeoffre
Division Daguet Brig. Gen. Benard Janvier
French 6th Light Armored Division, Reinforced
1st Foreign Legion Armored Regiment

1st Regiment de Spahis
2nd Foreign Legion Infantry Regiment
21st Marine Infantry Regiment
68th Marine Artillery Regiment
6th Foreign Legion Engineer Regiment
4th Airmobile Division
5th Combat Helicopter Regiment
1st Transport Helicopter Regiment
1st Infantry Regiment
9th Marine Division
2nd Marine Infantry Regiment
Detachment, 3rd Marine Infantry Regiment
11th Marine Artillery Regiment
10th Armored Division
4th Dragoon Regiment
82nd Airborne Division, Maj. Gen. Jim Johnson
1st Brigade, Col. Jack P. Nix, Jr.
2nd Brigade, Col. Ronald Roosz
3rd Brigade, Col. Glynn Hale
325th Parachute Regiment
504th Parachute Regiment
505th Parachute Regiment
1st Battalion, Lt. Col. John Schmader
3rd Armored Cavalry Regiment "Brave Rifles", Col. Doug H. Starr
18th Airborne Brigade
75th Field Artillery Brigade
196th Field Artillery Brigade
212th Field Artillery Brigade
214th Field Artillery Brigade
20th Engineer Brigade
12th Aviation Brigade
18th Aviation Brigade
16th Military Police Brigade
89th Military Police Brigade
800th Military Police Brigade
Delta Force, Maj. Gen. Wayne A. Downing

COALITION NAVAL FORCES IN THE PERSIAN GULF WAR

United States of America
BLUE RIDGE (BLUE RIDGE Class-LCC-19) Group
MIDWAY (MIDWAY-Class-CV-41) Carrier Battle Group
Carrier Air Wing 5
VFA-151 (F/A-18A), VFA-192 (F/A-18), VFA-195 (F/A-18), VA-185 (A-6E, KA-6D), VAW-115 (E-2C), VAQ-136 (EA-6B), HS-12 (SH-3H)
Destroyer Squadron 15
BUNKER HILL (TICONDEROGA-Class-CG-52), MOBILE BAY (TICONDEROGA-Class-CG-53), HEWITT (SPRUANCE-Class-DD-966), OLDENDORF (SPRUANCE-Class-DD-972), FIFE (SPRUANCE-Class-DD 991), CURTS (OLIVER HAZARD PERRY-Class-FFG-38)
SARATOGA (FORRESTAL-Class-CV-60) Carrier Battle Group
Carrier Air Wing 17
VF-74 (F-14A+), VFA-81 (F/A-18C), VFA-83 (F/A-18C), VA-35 (A-6E, KA-6D), VAW-125 (E-2C), VAQ-132 (EA-6B), VS-30 (S-3B) HS-3 (SH-3H)
Destroyer Squadron 24
PHILIPPINE SEA (TICONDEROGA-Class-CG-58, FLAGSHIP), SAMPSON (CHARLES F. ADAMS-Class-DDG-10), SPRUANCE (SPRUANCE-Class-DD-963), ELMER MONTGOMERY (KNOX-Class-FF-1082)
Cruiser-Destroyer Group 8
WISCONSIN (IOWA-Class-BB-64)
SOUTH CAROLINA (CALIFORNIA-Class-CGN-37), BIDDLE BELKNAP-Class-CG-34, THOMAS C. HART (KNOX-Class-FF-1092), DETROIT (SACRAMENTO-Class-AOE-4)
RANGER (FORRESTAL-Class-CV-61) Carrier Battle Group
Carrier Air Wing 2
VF-1 (F-14A), VF-2 (F-14A), VA-145 (A-6E), VA-155 (A-6E) VAW-116 (E-2C), VAQ-131 (EA-6B), VS-38 (S-3A), HS-14 (SH-3H)
Cruiser-Destroyer Group 5
VALLEY FORGE (TICONDEROGA-Class-CG-50), PRINCETON (PRINCETON-Class-CG-59), HORNE (BELNAP-Class-CG-30), HARRY W. HILL (SPRUANCE-Class-DD-986), PAUL F. FOSTER (SPRUANCE-Class-DD-964), JARRETT (OLIVER HAZARD PERRY-Class-FFG-33), FRANCIS HAMMOND (KNOX-Class-FF-1067),

KANSAS CITY (WICHITA-Class-AOR 3), SHASTA (KILAUEA-Class-AE 33)
INDEPENDENCE (FORRESTAL-Class-CF-62) Carrier Battle Group
Carrier Air Wing 14
VF-21 (F-14A), VF-154 (F-14A), VFA-25 (F/A-18C), VFA-113 (F/A-18C), VA-196
(A-6E, KA-6D), VAW-113 (E-2C), VAQ-139 (EA-6B), VS-37 (S-3A), HS-8 (SH-3H)
Cruiser-Destroyer Group 1
JOUETT (BELKNAP-Class-CG-29), ANIETAM (TICONDEROGA-Class-CG-54),
GOLDSBOROUGH (CHARLES F. ADAMS-Class-DDG-20), BREWTON (KNOX-
Class-FF-1086), REASONER (KNOX-Class-FF-1063), CIMARRON (CIMARRON-
Class AO-177), FLINT (KILAUEA-Class-AE 21)
AMERICA (KITTY HAWK-Class-CV-66) Carrier Battle Group
Carrier Air Wing 1
VF-33 (F-14A), VF-102 (F-14A), VFA-82 (F/A-18C), VFA-86 (F/A-18C), VA-85
(A-6E, KA-6D), VAW-123 (E-2C), VAQ-137 (EA-6B), VS-32 (S-3B) HS-11 (SH-3H)
Destroyer Squadron 22
NORMANDY (TICONDEROGA-Class-CG-60), VIRGINIA (VIRGINIA-Class-
CGN-38), PREBLE (COONTZ-Class-DDG-46), WIILIAM V. PRATT (COONTZ-
Class-DDG-44), HALYBURTON (OLIVER HAZARD PERRY-Class-FFG-40),
KALAMAZOO (WICHITA-Class-AOR-6), NITRO (NITRO-Class-AE-23)
JOHN F. KENNEDY (JOHN F. KENNEDY-Class-CV-67) Carrier Battle Group
Carrier Air Wing 3
VF-14 (F-14A), VF-32 (F14A), VA-46 (A-7E), VA-72 (A-7E), VA-75 (A-6E, KA-6D),
VAW-126 (E-2C)), VAQ-130 (EA-6B), VS-22 (S-3B), HS-7 (SH-3H)
Destroyer Squadron 36
THOMAS S. GATES (TICONDEROGA-Class-CG-51), SAN JACINTO
(TICONDEROGA-Class-CG-56), MISSISSIPPI (VIRGINIA-Class-CGN-40),
MOOSEBRUGGER (SPRUANCE-Class-DD-980), SAMUEL B. ROBERTS (OLIVER
HAZARD PERRY-Class-FFG-58), SEATTLE (SACRAMENTO-Class-AOE-3)
DWIGHT D. EISENHOWER (NIMITZ-Class-CVN-69) Carrier Battle Group
Carrier Air Group 7
VF-142 (F-14A+), VF-143 (F-14A+), VFA-131 (F/A-18), VFA-136 (F/A-18), VA-34
(A-6E, KA-6D), VAW-121 (E-2C), VAQ-140 (EA-6B) VS-31 (S-3B), HS-5 (SH-3H)
Cruiser-Destroyer Group 2
TICONDEROGA (TICONDEROGA-Class-CG-47), SCOTT (KIDD-Class-DDG-995),
TATTNALL (CHARLES F. ADAMS-Class-DDG-19), JOHN RODGERS
(SPRUANCE-Class-DD-983), JOHN L. HALL (OLIVER HAZARD PERRY-Class-
FFG-32), PAUL (KNOX-Class-FF-1080), SURIBACHI (SURIBACHI-Class-AE-21)
THEODORE ROOSEVELT (NIMITZ-Class-CVN-71) Carrier Battle Group
Carrier Air Wing 8
VF-41 (F-14A), VF-84 (F-14A), VFA-15 (F/A-18A), VFA-87 (F/A-18A), VA-36 (A-
6E), VA-65 (A-6E), VAW-124 (E-2C), VAQ-141 (EA-6B), VS-24 (S-3A), HS-9 (SH-
3H)
RICHMOND K. TURNER (LEAHY-Class-CG-20), LEYTE GULF (TICONDEROGA-
Class-CG-55), CARON (SPRUANCE-Class-DD-970), HAWES (OLIVER HAZARD
PERRY-Class-FFG-53), VREELAND (KNOX-Class-FF-1068), PLATTE
(CIMARRON-Class-AO-186), SANTA BARBARA (KILAUEA-Class-AE-28)
Battleship Battle Group
MISSOURI (IOWA-Class-BB-63) *(on station operated independently)*
Cruiser-Destroyer Group 3
HORNE (BELKNAP-Class-CG-30), KIDD (KIDD-Class-DD-993), JARRETT

(OLIVER HAZARD PERRY-Class-FFG-33), MCINERNEY (OLIVER HAZARD PERRY-Class-FFG-8), SACRAMENTO (SACRAMENTO-Class-AOE-1)

Amphibious Ready Group Alfa (Seventh Fleet)
13 Marine Expeditionary Unit
INCHON (IWO JIMA-Class-LPH-12), NASHVILLE (AUSTIN-Class-LPD-13), WHIDBEY ISLAND (WHIDBEY ISLAND-Class-LSD-41), NEWPORT (NEWPORT-Class-LST-1179), FAIRFAX COUNTY (NEWPORT-Class-LST-1193)

Amphibious Ready Group Bravo (Seventh Fleet, ComPhibRon 5)
OKINAWA (IWO JIMA-Class-LPH-3), OGDEN (AUSTIN-Class-LPD-5), DURHAM (CHARLESTON-Class-LKA-114), FORT MCHENRY (WHIDBEY ISLAND-Class-LSD-43), CAYUGA (NEWPORT-Class-LST-1186)

Amphibious Group 2 (ComPhibRon 12) R.Adm. John B. LaPlante
4th Marine Expeditionary Brigade
NASSAU (TARAWA-Class-LHA-4), GUAM (IWO JIMA-Class-LPH-9), IWO JIMA (IWO JIMA-Class-LPH-9), SHREVEPORT (AUSTIN-Class-LPD-12), RALEIGH (RALEIGH-Class-LPD-1), TRENTON (AUSTIN-Class-LPD-14), PENSACOLA (ANCHORAGE-Class-LSD-38), PORTLAND (ANCHORAGE-Class-LSD-37), GUNSTON HALL (WHIDBEY ISLAND-Class-LSD-44), SAGINAW (NEWPORT-Class-LST-1138), SPARTANBURG COUNTY (NEWPORT-Class-LST-1192), MANITOWAC (NEWPORT-Class-LST-1180), LAMOURE COUNTY (NEWPORT-Class-LST-1194)

Amphibious Group 3 (ComPhibRon 9)
5th Marine Expeditionary Brigade
TARAWA (TARAWA-Class-LHA-1), TRIPOLI (IWO JIMA-Class-LPH-10), NEW ORLEANS (IWO JIMA-Class-LPH-11), VANCOUVER (RALEIGH-Class-LPD-2), DENVER (AUSTIN-Class-LPD-9), JUNEAU (AUSTIN-Class-LPD-10), ANCHORAGE (ANCHORAGE-Class-LSD-36), GERMANTOWN (WHIDBEY ISLAND-Class-LSD-42), MOUNT VERNON (ANCHORAGE-Class-LSD-39), MOBILE (CHARLESTON-Class-LKA-115), BARBOUR COUNTY (NEWPORT-Class-LST-1195), FREDERICK (NEWPORT-Class-LST-1184), PEORIA (NEWPORT-Class-LST-1183)

Middle East Force *(Naval Flagship BLUE RIDGE attached)*
LASALLE (AGF-13, WORDEN (LEAHY-Class-CG-18), ENGLAND (LEAHY-Class-CG-22), MACDONOUGH (COONTZ-Class-DDG-39), DAVID R. RAY (SPRUANCE-Class-DD-971), LEFTWICH (SPRUANCE-Class-DD-984), REID (OLIVER HAZARD PERRY-Class-FFG-30), VANDEGRIFT (OLIVER HAZARD PERRY-Class-FFG-48), RENTZ (OLIVER HAZARD PERRY-Class-FFG-46), NICHOLAS (OLIVER HAZARD PERRY-Class-FFG-47), ROBERT G. BRADLEY (OLIVER HAZARD PERRY-Class-FFG-49), MARVIN SHIELDS (KNOX-Class-FF-1066), BARBEY (KNOX-Class-FF-1088)

Mine Countermeasures Force
AVENGER (AVENGER-Class-MCM-1), ADROIT (ACME-Class-MSO-509), IMPERVIOUS (AGGRESSIVE-Class-MSO-449), LEADER (AGGRESSIVE-Class-MSO-490), *(TRIPOLI of Amphibious Group Three acted as a mine countermeasures ship)*

Combat Logistics Force
MARS (MARS-Class-AFS-1), SYLVANIA (MARS-Class-AFS-2), NIAGARA FALLS (MARS-Class-AFS-3), WHITE PLAINS (MARS-Class-AFS-4), SAN DIEGO (MARS-Class-AFS-6), SAN JOSE (MARS-Class-AFS-7), HALEAKALA (NITRO-Class-AE-25), KISKA (KILAVEA-Class-AE-35), MOUNT HOOD (KILAVEA-Class-AE-29),

SIERRA (DIXIE-Class-AD-18), YELLOWSTONE (YELLOWSTONE-Class-AD-41), ACADIA (YELLOWSTONE-Class-AD-42), VULCAN (VULCAN-Class-AR-5), JASON (VULCAN-Class-AR-8), BEAUFORT (EDENTON-Class-ATS-2), COMFORT (T-AH-19), MERCY (T-AH-20)

Argentina

ALMIRANTE BROWN (MEKO-360-Class-D-10), SPIRO (4+2-MEKO-140-Class-F-43)

Australia

HMAS ADELAIDE (2-US-Class-FFG-7), HMAS DARWIN (2-US-ClassFFG-4), HMAS SUCCESS (DURANCE-Class-OR-304, HMAS WESTRALIA (LEAF-Class-AO-195), BRISBANE (Modified-US-DDG-2Class-D-41), SYDNEY (US-FFG-7-F-3)

Belgium

IRIS (TRIPARTITE-Class-M-920), MYOSOTIS (TRIPARTITE-M-922), ZINNIA (A-961), WIELINGEN (WIELINGEN-Class-F-910), WANDELAAR (WIELINGEN-Class-F-912)

Canada

ATHABASKAN (TRIBAL-Class-D-282), TERRA NOVA (IMPROVED RESTIGOUCHE-Class-F-259), PROTECTEUR (AOR-509)

Denmark

OLFERT FISHER (NIELS JUEL-Class-F-355)

France

CLEMENCEAU (CLEMENCEAU-Class-R-98), DUPLEIX (GEORGES LEYGUES-Class-D-641), MONTCALM (GEORGES LEYGUES-Class-D-642), CDT. BORY (COMMANDANT RIVIERE-Class-F-726), CDT. DUCUING (D'ESTIENNE D'ORVES-TYPE-A-69-Class-F-795), DOUDART DE LAGREE (COMMANDANT RIVIERE-Class-F-728), PROTET (COMMANDANT RIVIERE-Class-F-748), VAR (DURANCE-Class-A-608), DU CHAYLA (TYPE-T-47-D-630), JEANNE DE VIENNE (GEORGES LEYGUES-Class-D-643), LA MOTTE-PICQUET (GEORGES LEYGUES-Class-D-645), PREMIER MAITRE L'HER (D'ESTIENNE D'ORVES-TYPE-A-69-Class-F-792), DURANCE (DURANCE-Class-A-629), MARNE (DURANCE-Class-A-630), JULES VERNE (A-620), BUFFLE (A-696), RHIN (RHIN-Class-A-621), RANCE (RHIN-Class-A-618), FOUDRE (FOUDRE-Class-L-9011), BERRY (A-644) (also 2 TRIPARTITE minehunter/sweepers)

Germany (off the Suez Canal)

WERRA (RHEIN-Class-A-68), WESTERWALD (WESTERWALD-Class-A-1435), MARBURG (LINDAU-Class-M-1080), KOBLENZ (LINDAU-Class-M-1071), WETZLAR LINDAU-Class-M-1075), LABOE (HAMELN-Class-M-1097), UEBERHERRN (HAMELN-Class-M-1095)

Greece

LIMNOS (NETHERLANDS KORTENAER-Class-F-451), ELLI (NETHERLANDS KORTENAER-Class-F-450)

Italy

LIBECCIO (MAESTRALE-Class-F-572), ZEFFIRO (MAESTRALE-Class-F-577), ORSA (LUPO-Class-F-567), STROMBOLI (A-5327), AUDACE (AUDACE-Class-D-551), LUPO (LUPO-Class-F-564), SAGGITARIO (LUPO-Class-F-565), VESUVIO (A-5329), SAN MARCO (SAN GIORGIO-Class-L-9893)

Kuwait

ISTIQLAL (FPB-57-TYPE-P-5702), AL SANBOUK (TNC-45-TYPE-P-4505), SAWAHIL (unknown)

Netherlands

WITTE DE WITH (JACOB VAN HEEMSKERCK-Class-F-813), PIETER FLORISZ (KORTENAER-Class-F-826), JACOB VAN HEEMSKERCK (JACOB VAN HEEMSKERCK-Class-F-812), PHILIPS VAN ALMONDE (KORTENAER-Class-F-823), ZUIDERKRUIS (ZUIDERKRUIS-Class-A-832), ALKMAAR (ALKMAAR-Class-M-850), ZIERIKZEE (ALKMAAR-Class-M-862)

Norway
ANDENES (NORDKAPP-Class-W-320)

Poland
WODNIK (#251), PIAST (#281)

Portugal
SAO MIGUEL (#A-5208)

Spain
SANTA MARIA (SANTA MARIA-Class-F-81), DESCUBIERTA (DESCUBIERTA-Class), CAZADORA (DESCUBIERTA-Class-F-35), NUMANCIA (SANTA MARIA-Class-F-83), INFANTA ELENA (DESCUBIERTA-Class-F-33), VICTORIA (SANTA MARIA-Class-F-82), VENCEDORA (DESCUBIERTA-Class-F-36), DIANA (DESCUBIERTA-Class-F-32), INFANTA CRISTINA (DESCUBIERTA-Class-F-31)

United Kingdom
YORK (BATCH-3-Class-D-98), BATTLEAXE (BROADSWORD-Class-F-88), BRILLIANT (BROADSWORD-Class-F-90), BRAVE (BATCH-2-Class-F-94), BRECON (HUNT-Class-M-29), BROCKLESBY (HUNT-Class-M-33), BICESTER (HUNTER-Class-M-36), BAYLEAF (APPLELEAF-Class-A-109), JUPITER (BATCH-3A-Class-F-60), ORANGELEAF (APPLELEAF-Class-A-110), OLNA (OL-Class-A-123), FORT GRANGE (FORT GRANGE-Class-A-385), *(3 MINECOUNTERMEASURES SHIPS)*, DILIGENCE (STENA-Class-A-132), HERALD (IMPROVED-HECLA-Class-A-138), GLOUCESTER (BATCH-3-Class-D-96), CARDIFF (TYPE-42-Class-D-108), LONDON (BROADSWORD-TYPE-22-Class-F-95), BRAZEN BROADSWORD-TYPE-22-Class-F-91), ATHERSTONE (HUNT-Class-M-38), CATTISTOCK (HUNT-Class-M-31), HURWORTH (HUNT-M-39), HERALD HECLA-Class-138), HECLA (HECLA-Class-A-133), GALAHAD (L-3005), SIR PERCIVAL (L-3036), ARGUS (A-135), EXETER (TYPE-42-Class-D-89), DULVERTON (HUNT-Class-M-35), LEDBURY (HUNT-Class-M-30), SIR BEDIVERE (L-3004), SIR TRISTRAM (L-3505), RESOURCE (REGENT-Class-A-486), OPPOSUM (OBERON-Class-S-19), OTUS (OBERON-Class-S-18) *(Task Group 323.2 observing Libya=ARK ROYAL (R-07), MANCHESTER (BATCH-3-Class-D-95), CHARYBDIS (BATCH-3A-Class-F-75), SHEFFIELD (BROADSWORD-TYPE-22-Class-F-96*

USSR
ADMIRAL TRIBUTS *(plus a missile destroyer, frigate and an AMUR-Class repair ship.*

COALITION AIR FORCES IN THE PERSIAN GULF WAR

United States Air Force

1st Tactical Fighter Wing USAF, F-15C/D (at Dhrahran International Airport from Langley AFB, VA.)

27th Tactical Fighter Squadron

71st Tactical Fighter Squadron

53rd Tactical Fighter Squadron

33rd Tactical Fighter Wing, F-15C/D (at Tabuk and King Faisal AB from Eglin AFB, FL)

58th Tactical Fighter Sqaudron

4th Tactical Fighter Wing, F-15E (at Al Kharj, Thumrait and Al Kharj from Seymour Johnson AFB, NC)

335th Tactical Fighter Squadron

336th Tactical Fighter Squadron

67th TRW 12th TRS, RF-4C (at Sheikh Isa Bahrain from Bergstrom AFB, TX)

363rd Tactical Fighter Wing, F-16C/D (at Al Dhafra UAE from Shaw AFB, SC)

17th Tactical Fighter Squadron

33rd Tactical Fighter Squadron

388th Tactical Fighter Wing, F-16C/D (at Minhad UAE from Hill AFB, UT.)

4th Tactical Figher Squadron

347th Tactical Fighter Wing, F-16C/D (at Al Minhad UAE from Moody AFB, GA)

69th Tactical Fighter Squadron

345th Tactical Fighter Wing

353rd Tactical Fighter Squadron, 355th Tactical Fighter Squadron

356th Tactical Fighter Squadron

23rd Tactical Fighter Wing,

74th & 76th TFS, A-10A (at Damman and King Fahd Airport from England AFB)

354th Tactical Fighter Wing

353rd & 355th TFS A-10A (at Damman and King Fahd Airport from Myrtle Beach, AFB, SC)

366th TFW, 390th ECS, EF-111A (at Taif from Mountain Home AFB, ID)

37th Tactical Fighter Wing, F-117A (at Khamis Mushait AB from Tonopah TR,

NV)

415th Tactical Fighter Squadron

416th TFS

35th Tactical Fighter Wing, F-4G (at Sheikh Isa Bahrain from George AFB, CA)

561st TFS

552nd (Unknown) 963rd, 964th, E-3B/C (at Riyadh and Military City Airport from Tinker AFB, OK)

602nd (unknown) 23rd TASS, OA-10A (at Damman and King Fahd Airport from Davis Monthan AFB, AZ)

US Air Forces (Europe)

17th Tactical Fighter Wing

32rd TFG, 32nd TFS, F-15C/D (at unknown from Soesterberg AB, Netherlands)

26th TRW, 38th TRS, RF-4C (at Incirlik AB, Turkey from Zweibrucken AB, Germany)

36th TFW, 53rd TFS, F-15C/D (at Al Kharj from Bitburg AB, Germany)

48th Tactical Fighter Wing, 492nd, 493rd & 494th TFS, F-111F (at Taif from RAF Lakenheath, UK)

401st Tactical Fighter Wing, 612th TFS, F-16C/D (at Incirlik AB, Turkey from Torrejon AB, Spain), 614th Tactical Fighter Squadron (at Doha Qatar from Torrejon AB, Spain)

50th Tactical Fighter Wing, 10th TFS, F-16C/D (at Al Dhafra UAE from Hahn AB, Germany)

2nd Tactical Fighter Squadron

20th Tactical Fighter Wing, 79th TFS, F-111E (at Incirlik AB, Turkey from RAF Upper Heyford, UK, with rotations of 55th and 77th TFS)

10th Tactical Fighter Wing, A-10A (at Damman and King Fahd Airport from RAF Alconbury)

511th Tactical Fighter Squadron (Elements of the 366th Tactical Fighter Wing and the 552nd AEWCW)

66th ECW, 42nd ECS, EF-111A (at Incirlik AB, Turkey from RAF Upper Heyford, UK), 43rd ECS, EC-130H (at Incirlik AB, Turkey from Sembach AB, Germany)

417th Tactical Fighter Training Squadron

52nd Tactical Fighter Wing, 23rd TFS, F-4G (at Incirlik AB, Turkey from Spangdahlem AB, Germany)

Air Force Systems Command

4411th JSTARS Sqn flying E-8A (at Riyadh from Melborne, FL)

Military Airlift Command

314th TAW, 50th TAS flying C-130Es (at Bateen/Abu Dhabi)

61st TAS flying C-130E (at Incirlik AB, Turkey from Little Rock AFB)

317th TAW flying C-130E (at Masirah and Thumrait, then Damman/King Fahd Airport from Pope AFB, NC

374th TAW 21st TAS, C-130E (at Thumrait from Clark AFB, Philippines) 345th TAS C-130E at Thumrait from Yokota AB)

435th TAW 37th TAS, C-130E (at Al Ain, UAE, from Rhein Main AB, Germany)

463rd TAW 772nd TAS, C-130H (at Al Kharj AB, from Dyess AFB, TX), 773rd TAS, C-130H at Al Kharj AB

375th TAW 1401st MAS det 3 flying C-21As (at Riyadh and KKMC from Barksdale AFB, LA), 1401st MAS det 4 C-21A (at Riyadh and KKMC from Peterson AFB, CO), 1402nd MAS det 1, C-21A (at Riyadh/KKMC from Langley, AFB, VA), 1402nd MAS det 3 C-21A (at Riyadh/KKMC from Maxwell AFB, AL), 1402nd MAS det 4 C-21A (at Riyadh/KKMC from Eglin AFB, FL)

Special Operations Command

1st SOW, 8th SOS, flying MC-130Es (at Damman/King Fahd Airport from Hurlburt Field, FL), 9th SOS, flying HC-130N/P (at Damman/King Fahd Airport from Eglin AFB, FL), 16th SOS, flying AC-130H (at an unknown location from Hurlburt Field, Fl), 20th SOS, flying MH-60G (at unknown location from Eglin AFB, FL)

39th SOW, 21st SOS flying MH-53J at Batman and Incirlik ABs, Turkey from RAF Woodbridge, UK), 67th SOS, flying HC-130N/P (at Batman and Incirlik, Turkey from RAF Woodbrige UK)

Strategic Air Command (SAC Bombers and Reconnaissance)

9th SRW, 99th SRS, flying TR-1A/U-2R (at Taif from Beale AFB, CA), DET 3, flying TR-1A/U-2R (from RAF Akrotiri)

17th RW, 95th RS, flying TR-1A (at Taif from RAF Alconbury)

55th SRW, 343rd SRS, flying RC-135U (at Riyadh and KKMC from Offutt AFB, NE)

2nd BW, 62nd & 596th BS, flying B-52Gs at Jeddah and King Abdul Aziz International Airport)

42nd BW, 69th BS, flying B-52Gs (at Jeddah and King Abdul Aziz International Airport from Loring AFB, ME)

93rd BW, 328th BTS, flying B-52Gs (at Jeddah and King Abdul Aziz International Airport from Castle AFB, CA)

97th BW, 340th BS, B-52G (at Diego Garcia from Eaker AFB, AR)

379th BW, 524th BS, B-52G (at Jeddah and King Abul Aziz International Airport from Wurtsmith AFB, MI)

416th BW, 668th BS, B-52G (at Jeddah and King Abdul Aziz International Airport)

SAC Tankers

2nd BW, 32nd ARS, flying KC-10As (at Milan-Malpensa Airport, Italy and Zargoza AB, Spain from Barksdale AFB, LA), 71st ARS, KC-135A (at unknown location from Barksdale AFB, LA)

5th BW, 906th ARS, KC-135A (at unknown location from Minot AFB, ND).

7th BW, 7th ARS, KC-135A (at unknown location from Carswell AFB, TX).

9th SRW, 349th & 350th ARS, KC-135Qs (at Riyadh and KKMC from Beale AFB, CA)

19th ARW, 99th & 912th ARS, KC-135R (at Muscat-Seeb, Riyadh and King Khalid International Airport from Robins AFB, GA)

22nd ARW, 6th & 9th ARS, KC-10A (at Jeddah and King Abdul Aziz International Airport from March AFB, CA)

28th BW, 28th ARS, KC-135R (at Al Dhafra UAE and Muscat-Seeb from Ellsworth AFB, SD)

42nd BW, 42nd & 407th ARS, KC-135R (at unknown location from Loring AFB, ME)

68th ARW, 344th & 911th ARS, KC-10A (at Jeddah and King Abdul Aziz International Airport from Seymour Johnson AFB, NC)

92nd BW, 43rd & 92nd ARS, KC-135A/R (at unknown location from Fairchild AFB, WA)

93rd BW, 93rd & 924th ARS, KC-135A/R (at unknown location from Castle AFB, CA)

96th BW, 917th ARS, KC-135A (at Incirlik, Turkey from Dyess AFB, TX)

97th BW, 97th ARS, KC-135A (at Jeddah and King Abdul Aziz International Airport from Eaker AFB, AR)

301st ARW, KC-135R (at Muscat-Seeb from Malmstrom AFB, MT)

305th ARW, 70th & 305th ARS, KC-135R (at Riyadh and King Khalid International Airport from Grissom AFB, IN), EC-135Ls (at Riyadh and King Khalid International Airport)

319th BW, 905th ARS, KC-135R, (at Al Dhafra UAE, Muscat-Seeb, and Riyadh and King Khalid International Airport)

340th ARW, 11th & 306th ARS, KC-135R (at Al Dhfra, UAE, from Atlus AFB, OK)

376th SW, 909th ARS, KC-135A (at Riyadh and King Khalid International Airport from Kadena AB, Okinawa)

379th BW, 920th ARS, KC-135A, (at unknown location from Wurtsmith AFB, MI)

380th BW, 310th & 380th ARS, KC-135A/Q (at Riyadh and King Khalid International Airport from Plattsburgh, AFB, NY)

384th ARW, 384th ARS KC-135R (at Masirah from McConnell AFB, KS)

410th BW, 46th & 307th ARS KC-135A (at unknown location from K.I. Sawyer AFB, MI)

416th BW, 41st ARS KC-135R

Air Forces (Pacific)

3rd TFW, 3rd TFS, F-4E (at Incirlik AB, Turkey from Clark AFB, Philippines)

14 ADP(TAF) Air Division

1st TFW(P) 27 TFS,71 TFS, 682 ASOCS, 726 TCS, 1681 ALCS(P), all flying F-15C/D (24 27 TFS, 24 71 TFS) all at Dhaharan

4th TFW(P), 336 TFS 6 C-12s at Al Kharj, 335TFS, (24 F-15Es at Al Kharj, 157 TFS (24 F-15E), 138 TFS (24 F-16A), 4401 MMS(P) 18 F/A-16A), 1670 TAS (P) all above at Al Kharj.

33 TFW (P), 58 TFS (24 F15C/D) at Tabuk

37th TFW(P), 415 TFS (18 F15C/Ds at Khamis Mushait), 416 TFS (18 F15C/D), 417 TFS (6 F15C/D) all at Khamis Mushait

48th TFW(P) 492 TFS (22 F-111F) at Taif, 493 TFS (22 F-11F), 494 TFS (22 F-111F), 42 ECS, (5 EC-130(CC)390 ECS (1 EF-111), 1704 RECW(P) (5 TR-1), 1704 SRSP (6 U-2) all at Taif.

354th TFW(P), 353 TFS (24 A-10) at King Fahd, 355 TFS, (24 A-10), 74 TFS (24 A-10), 76 TFS (24 A-10), 23 TFS (12 OA-10)511 TFS (24 OA-10), 706 TFS (24 OA-10), 1682 ALCS(P), all at King Fahd.

363rd TFW, 17 TFS (24 F-16C/D), 33 TFS (24 F-16C/D), 10 TFS (24 F-16C/D), 1705 AREFS(P) KC-135R) all at Al Dhafra.

388th TFW(P), 69 TFS (72 F-16C/D), 4 TFS, 421 TFS, 125 TFS, 122 TFS, 185 TFS??, all at Al Minhad.

401th TFW(P), 614 TFS (24 F-16C/D) at Doha.

5 ADP, 35th TFW(P), 561 TFS (24 F-4G), 81 TFS (24 F-4G), 192 TRS (6 RF-4C), 12 TRS (6 RF-4C), 106 TRG (6 RF-4C), all at Shaikh Isa.

41st ECS(P), 41 ECS(CC) (6 EC-130H) at Bateen.

1610 ALDP TAW(P) 314 TAW (16 C-130E) at Bateen.

TAW(P), 435 TFW (40 C-130H) at Al Ain.

1612th MAS (P) (8 C-21), (7 C-12), (7 RU-21), at Riyadh.
1670th TAG(P) 1670 TAS(P) (16 C-130H), 1671 TAS(P), (763 TAS) at Al
    Kharj.
ALCS(P) at Riyadh.
ALCS(P) at Dhahran.
1683rd ALCS(P) at Al Jubail.
1690th WXGP(P) at Riyadh.
1640th, 1640 TAS(P) at Riyadh.
TAW(P), (317 TAW), (16 C-130E) at Masirah.
1707 AREFS(P) at Masirah.
1650th 1650 TAS(P) at Masirah.
TAW(P) ANG, (16 C-130), 1611 Aero Evac, SQ(P) at Sharjah.
TAW(P), 317 TAW (34 C-130E), 1661 TAS(P) (16 C-130E), 1662 TAS(P) at
    Thumrait
1675 TAS(P) at King Fahd.
AFSOC 719 SOS (5 AC-130A), AFSOC 16 SOS (3 AC-130H), AFSOC 850
    SOS (4 MC-130) all at King Fahd.
AFSOC 160 SOAR (8 MH-60), 160 SOAR (4 MH-47), at KKMC.
1700th
STRATW(P), 1700 SRS(P) (7RC-135V/W), 1704 SRS(P), U-2/TR-1, 1700
    ARS(P), (10 KC-135) all at Riyadh.
1701st
17 ADP, STRATW(P), 1708 BMW(P) (16 B-52) at Jeddah New.
(SAC) 807th ARS(P), (10 KC-135), 1709 ARS(P) (62 KC-135E/A, 1710
    ARS(P) (13 KC-10), 1711 ARS(P) all at Jeddah New.
ARW(P), 1702 ARS(P) (10 KC-10), 1702 ARS(P), (15 KC-135R), all at Seeb.
    1707 ARS(P) (10 KC-135) at Masirah.
ARW(P), 1703 AREFWP (20 KC-135A/Q, 26 KC-135R, 2 EC-135L) at King
    Khalid International Airport.
ARW(P) 1706 ARS(P) (15 KC-135E) at Cairo West.
ARW(P) 1712 ARS(P) (12 KC-135E) at Abu Dhuabi.
ARW(P) 1713 ARS(P) (12 KC-135E) at Dubai International.
BMW(P), 4300 BMS(P), (20 B-52G), 4300 ARS(P) (7 KC-10A), (5 KC-135R)
    at Diego Garcia.
801st BW(P), 801 BS(P), (22 B-52G), 801 ARS(P) (15 KC-135), at Moron.
7 AD, 802 nd ARW(P), flying KC-135 from Lajes Field, Azores
803rd ARS(P), 803 ARS(P) flying KC-135s from Hellinikon AB, Greece.
804th ARW(P), 804 ARS(P) flying KC-135s from Incirlik, Turkey.
808th ARS(P), 808 ARS(P), flying KC-135s from Malpensa, Italy.
809th ARS(P), 809 ARS(P) flying KC-135s from Andravida, Greece.
805 ARS(P), 805 at RAF Mildenhall.
805th ARS(P), (8 B-52Gs and an unknown # of KC-135s from RAF Fairford,
    UK.
525 TFS (24 F-15C), 612 TFS (37 F-16C) at Incirlik, Turkey.
Air National Guard
101st ARW, 132nd ARS KC-135E (at Jeddah and King Abdul Aziz International
    Airport from Bangor IAP, ME)
117th TRW, 106th TRS RF-4C (at Sheikh Isa Bahrain from Birmingham MAP,
    AL)
126th ARW, 108th ARS, KC-135E (at Jeddah and King Abdul Aziz International

Airport from Chicago-O'Hare Airport)

134th ARG, 151st ARS KC-135E (at Jeddah and King Abdul Aziz International Airport from McGhee Tyson Airport, Knoxville, TN)

136th TAW, 181st ARS KC-135E (at Al Ain UAE, Damman and King Fahd Airport from NAS Dallas, TX)

139th TAG 180th TAS C-130H (at Al Ain UAE from Rosecrans MAP, MO)

141st ARW, 116th ARS KC-135E (at Cairo West from Fairchild AFB, WA)

190th ARG, 117th ARS, KC-135E (at Jeddah and King Abdul Aziz International Airport from Forbes Field, KS)

128th ARG, 126th ARS, KC-135E (at Cairo West from Gen. Mitchell IAP, WI)

130th TAG, 130th TAS C-130H (at Al Ain UAE, Damman and King Fahd Airport from Yeager Airport Charelston, WV)

151st ARG, 191st ARS KC-135E (at Jeddah and King Abdul Aziz International Airport from Salt Lake City IAP, UT)

152nd TRG, 192nd TRS, RF-4C (at Sheikh Isa Bahrain from Reno-Cannon IAP, NV)

157th ARG, 133rd ARS, KC-135E (at Jeddah and King Abdul Aziz International Airport from Pease AFB, NH)

174th TFW, 138th TFS, F-16A/B (at Al Kharj from Hancock Field, Syracuse, NY)

166th TAG, 142nd TAS, C-130H (at Al Ain UAE, and Al Kharj from GTR Wilmington Airport, DE)

160th ARG, 145th ARS, KC-135E (at Jeddah and King Abdul Aziz International Airport and Dubai International Airport from Rickenbacker ANGB, OH)

161st ARG, 197th ARS, KC-135E (at unknown location from Phoenix IAP, AZ)

168th ARG, 168th ARS KC-135E (at Jeddah and King Abdul Aziz International Airport from Eielson AFB, AK)

169th TFG, 157th TFS, F-16A/B (at Al Kharj from McEntire ANGB, SC)

170th ARG, 150th ARS KC-135E (at unknown location from McGuire ANGB, NJ)

171st ARW, 147th ARS, KC-135E (at Jaddah and King Abdul Aziz International Airport, Dubai Intwernational Airport from GTR Pittsburgh IAP, PA)

193rd SOG, 193rd SOS, EC-130E (at Riyadh and Military City Airport from Harrisburgh IAP, PA)

106th Air National Guard, Alabama

192nd Tactical Fighter Squadron (Nevada Air National Guard)

138th Tactical Fighter Sqaudron, Syracuse, NY

157th Tactical Fighter Squadron, SC

Air Force Reserve

403rd TAW, 815th TAS, C-130H (at unknown location from Keesler AFB, MS)

434th ARW, 72nd ARS KC-135E (at Jeddah and King Abdul Aziz International Aiurport from Grissom AFB, IN)

452nd ARW 336th ARS, KC-135E (at Jeddah and King Abdul Aziz International Airport from March Field AFB, CA)

907th TAG, 356th TAS, C-130E (at unknown location from Rickenbacker ANGB, OH)

913th TAG, 327th TAS, C-130E (at unknown location from NAS Willow Grove, PA)

914th TAG, 328th TAS, C-130E (at unknown location from Niagra Falls IAP,

NY)

926th TFG, 706th TFS, A-10A (at Damman and King Fahd Airport from NAS New Orleans, LA)

927th TAG, 63rd TAS, C-130E (at Sharjah from Selfridge ANGB, MI)

939th ARW, 71st SOS, HH-3E (at unknown location from Davis Monthan AFB, AZ)

940th ARG, 314th ARS, KC-135E (at Jeddah and King Abdul Aziz International Airport from Mather AFB, CA)

706th Tactical Fighter Squadron, Louisiana

3rd Marine Corps Aircraft Wing

Marine Wing Headquarters Squadron 3 (MWHS-3) (-)

Marine Aircraft Group 11

Marine Aviation Logistics Squadron 121 (MALS-11) (Forward)

Marine All Weather Fighter Attack Squadron 121 (VMFA(AW)-121)

Marine Fighter Attack Squadron 212 (VMFA-212)

Marine Fighter Attack Squadron 232 (VMFA-232)

Marine Fighter Attack Squadron 235 (VMFA-235)

Marine Fighter Attack Squadron 314 (VMFA-314)

Marine Fighter Attack Squadron 451 (VMFA-451)

Marine All Weather Attack Squadron 224 (VMA(AW)-224)

Marine All Weather Attack Squadron 533 (VMA(AW)-533)

Marine Tactical Electronic Warfare Squadron 2 (VMAQ-2)

Marine Aerial Refueler Transport Squadron 252 (VMGR-252) (-)

Marine Aerial Refueler Transport Squadron 352 (VMGR-352) (-)

Detachment, Marine Aerial Refueler Transport Squadron 452 (VMGR-452)

Marine Aircraft Group 13

Marine Aviation Logistics Squadron 13 (MALS-13) (Forward)

Marine Attack Squadron 231 (VMA-231)

Marine Attack Squadron 311 (VMA-331)

Marine Attack Squadron 542 (VMA-542)

Detachment B, Marine Attack Squadron 513

Marine Obervation Squadron 1 (VMO-1)

Marine Observation Squadron 2 (VMO-2)

Marine Aircraft Group 16

Marine Aviation Logistics Squadron 16 (MALS-16) (Forward)

Marine Medium Helicopter Squadron 161 (HMM-161)

Marine Medium Helicopter Squadron 165 (HMM-165)

Marine Light Attack Helicopter Squadron 367 (HMLA-367)

Marine Light Attack Helicopter Squadron 369 (HMLA-369)

Marine Heavy Helicopter Squadron 462 (HMH-462)

Marine Heavy Helicopter Squadron 463 (HMH-463)

Marine Heavy Helicopter Squadron 465 (HMH-465)

Marine Heavy Helicopter Squadron 466 (HMH-466) (-)

Marine Aircraft Group 26

Marine Aviation Logistics Squadron 26 (MALS-26) (Forward)

Marine Medium Helicopter Squadron 261 (HMM-261)

Marine Medium Helicopter Squadron 266 (HMM-266)

Marine Medium Helicopter Squadron 774 (HMM-774)

Marine Heavy Helicopter Squadron 464 (HMH-464) (-)

Marine Heavy Helicopter Squadron 362 (HMH-362)

Detachment A, Marine Heavy Helicopter Squadron 772 (HMH-772)
Marine Attack Helicopter Squadron 775 (HMA-775)
Marine Light Helicopter Squadron 767 (HML-767)
Marine Air Control Group 38
Headquarters and Headquarters Squadron 38 (H&H-38)
Marine Air Control Squadron 2 (MACS-2)
Marine Air Traffic Control Squadron 38 (MATCS-38) (-)
Marine Air Support Squadron 3 (MASS-3)
Marine Wing Communications Squadron 38 (MWCS-38)(-)
2nd Light Antiaircraft Missile Battalion
3rd Light Antiaircraft Missile Battalion
2nd Low Altitude Air Defense Battalion (-)
3rd Low Altitude Air Defense Battalion (-)
Marine Wing Support Group 37
Headquarters and Headquarters Squadron 37 (H&HS-37)
Marine Wing Support Squadron 174 (MWSS-174)
Marine Wing Support Squadron 271 (MWSS-271)
Marine Wing Support Squadron 273 (MWSS-273)
Marine Wing Support Squadron 374 (MWSS-374)
US Navy squadrons/aircraft types and carrier air wings
HC-11, (Det 4)
Det 7
Det 8
Det 11
HC-1, (Det 6)
HC-6, (Det 1)
Det 4
Det 5
Det 7
HC-8, Det 1
Det 2
Det 5
Det 4
HM-14, Det 1 at Abu Dhabi
HSL-32, (Det7)
HSL-33, (Det 7)
Det 9
HSL-34, (Det 1)
Det 5
HSL-35, (Det 7)
HSL-36, (Det 8)
HSL-37, (Det 6)
HSL-42, (Det 1)
Det 3
Det 6
Det 7
Det 8
Det 9
HSL-43, Det 8
HSL-44, Det 5

Det 6
Det 7
Det 8
Det 9
HSL-46, Det 7
HSL-48, Det 1
Det 2
Det 3
VF-1, F-14A, CVW-2, USS RANGER (CV-41), NAS Miramar, CA
VF-2, F-14A, CVW-2, (CV-41), NAS Miramar, CA
VF-14, F-14A, CVW-3, (CV-67), NAS Oceana, VA
VF-21
VF-32, F-14A, CVW-3, CV-67, NAS Oceana, VA
VF-33, F-14A, CVW-1, CV-66, NAS Oceana, VA
VF-41, F-14A, CVW-8, CVN-71, NAS Oceana, VA
VF-74, F-14A+, CVW-17, CV-60, NAS Oceana, VA
VF-84, F-14A, CVW-8, CVN71, NAS Oceana, VA
VF-102, F-14A, CVW-1, CV-66, NAS OCEANA, VA
VF-103, F-14A+, CVW-17, CV-60, NAS Oceana, VA
VF-154
VA-46, A-7E, CVW-3, CV-67, NAS Cecil Field, FL
VA-72, A-7E, CVW-3, CV-67, NAS Cecil Field, FL
VFA-15, F/A-18A, CVW-8, CVN-71, NAS Cecil Field, FL
VFA-25
VFA-81, F/A-18C, CVW-17, CV-60, NAS Cecil Field, FL
VFA-82, F/A-18C, CVW-1, CV-66, NAS Cecil Field, FL
VFA-83, F/A-18C, CVW-17, CV-60, NAS Cecil Field, FL
VFA-86, F/A-18C, CVW-1, CV-66, NAS Cecil Field, FL
VFA-87, F/A-18A, CVW-8, CVN-71, NAS Cecil Field, FL
VFA-113
VFA-151, F/A-18A, CVW-5, CV-41, NAS Atsugi, Japan
VFA-192, F/A-18A, CVW-5, CV-41, NAS Atsugi, Japan
VFA-195, F/A-18A, CVW-5, CV-41, NAS Atsugi, Japan
VA-35, A-6E/KA-6D, CVW-17, CV-60, NAS Oceana, VA
VA-36, A-6E, CVW-8, CVN-71, NAS Oceana, VA
VA-65, A-6E/KA-6D, CVW-8, CVN-71, NAS Oceana, VA
VA-75, A-6E/KA-6D, CVW-3, CV-67, NAS Oceana, VA
VA-85, A-6E/KA-6D, CVW-1, CV-66, NASOceana, VA
VA-115, A-6E, CVW-5, CV-41, NAS Atsugi, Japan
VA-145, A-6E/KA-6D, CVW-2, CV-61, NAS Whidbey Island, WA
VA-155, A-6E, CVW-2, CV-61, NAS Whidbey Island, WA
VA-185, A-6E/KA-6D, CVW-5, CV-41, NAS Atsugi, Japan
VA-196
VAW-113
VAW-115, E-2C, CVW-5, CV-41, NAS Atsugi, Japan
VAW-116, E-2C, CVW-2, CV-61, NAS Miramar, CA
VAW-123, E-2C, CVW-1, CV-66, NAS Norfolk, VA
VAW-124, E-2C, CVW-8, CVN-71, NAS Norfolk, VA
VAW-125, E-2C, CVW-17, CV-60, NAS Norfolk, VA
VAW-126, E-2C, CVW-3, CV-67, NAS Norfolk, VA

VAQ-130, EA-6B, CVW-3, CV-67, NAS Whidbey Island, WA
VAQ-131, EA-6B, CVW-2, CV-61, NAS Whidbey Island, WA
VAQ-132, EA-6B, CVW-17, CV-60, NAS Whidbey Island, WA
VAQ-136, EA-6B, CVW-5, CV-41, NAS Atsugi, Japan
VAQ-137, EA-6B, CVW-1, CV-66, NAS Whidbey Island, WA
VAQ-139
VAQ-141, EA-6B, CVW-8, CVN-71, NAS Whidbey, Island, WA
VP-11
VP-19
VP-23
VP-4
VP-40
VP-46
VP-8
VP-91
VPMAU
VPU-1
VPU-2
VQ-1
VQ-2
VRC-30
VRC-40
VRC-50 (FUJAIRAH), Provide Detachment for Duration
VS-22, S-3B, CVW-3, CV-67, NAS Cecil Field, FL
VS-24, S-3A, CVW-8, CVN-71, NAS Cecil Field, FL
VS-30, S-3B, CVW-17, CV-60, NAS Cecil Field, FL
VS-32, S-3B, CVW-1, CV-66, NAS Cecil Field, FL
VS-37
VS-38, S-3A, CVW-2, CV-61, NAS North Island, CA
HS-3, SH-3H, CVW-17, CV-60, NAS Jacksonville, FL
HS-7, SH-3H, CVW-3, CV-67, NAS Jacksonville, FL
HS-9, SH-3H, CVW-8, CVN-71, NAS Jacksonville, FL
HS-11, SH-3H, CVW-1, CV-66, NAS Jackonville, FL
HS-12, SH-3H, CVW-5, CV-41, NAS Atsugi Japan
HS-14, SH-3H, CVW-2, CV-61, NAS North Island, CA
VMFA-232, -235, -312, 314, -333, -451
VMA-231, -311, -331, -542
VMAQ(AW)-224
VMAQ-2
VMO-1
VMO-2
VMGR-252, 352
Argentina
1 Boeing 707-320
2 C-130Hs PLUS Alounette IIIs on ship in the Red Sea.
Australia
AS 550B Ecureil helicopters (on ADELAIDE and DARWIN)
37 Squadron C-130E
Bahrain
12 F-16C/Ds and 12 F-5E/Fs

British Royal Air Force
(Elements of 17, 27, and 617 Squadrons
(Elements of 16 and 20 Squadrons)
(elements of 9 and 31 Squadrons)
2 Squadron
43 Squadron
6(C) Squadron
(Elements of 120, 201 and 206 Squadron)
Canadian Air Force
439 Tactical Fighter Squadron
416 Tactical Fighter Squadron
On HMCS ATHABASCAN and PROTECTOR
423 Squadron, Sea King CH-124A,
French Air Force
(Elements of)
5e escadrre de chasse, Mirage 2000C
12e escadre de chasse, Mirage F1C
11e escadre de chasse, Jaguar A
33e escadre de chasse
93e escadre de ravitaillement
1e escadron of the 54 escadre ("Dunkerque")
61e escadre de transport
61e escadre de transport
EE 54, C.160 Gabriel
EH67, SA 330B Puma
Italian Air Force
(Elements of 6 Stormo [Squadron], and 50 Stormo)
36 Stormo
Kuwait Air Force
9 & 25 Squadron A-4KU, TA-4KU
18 & 61 Squadron Mirage F1CK
New Zealand
40 Squadron
Qatar
14 Mirage F.1s and 6 Alpha Fighter-Interceptor-bombers
Royal Saudi Air Force
7 Squadron
13 Squadron
21 Squadron
29 Squadron
34 Squadron
37 Squadron
42 Squadron
66 Squadron
4 Squadron
6 Squadron
15 Squadron
16 Squadron
18 Squadron
17 Squadron

3 Squadron
5 Squadron
10 Squadron

IRAQI FORCES IN
THE PERSIAN GULF WAR

Republican Guard
Hammurabi 1st Republican Guard Armored Division
Medina 2nd Republican Guard Armored Division
(unknown reserve republican guard armored division)
Tawakalna 3rd Republican Guard Mechanized Division
Al Faw 4th Republican Guard Motorized Infantry Division
Nebuchadnezzar 6th Republican Guard Motorized Infantry Division
Adnan 7th Republican Guard Motorized Infantry Division
8th Republican Guard Special Forces Division
III Corps
7th Infantry Division
8th Infantry Division
14th Infantry Division
16th Infantry Division
18th Infantry Division
21st Infantry Division
26th Infantry Division
29th Infantry Division
30th Infantry Division
36th Infantry Division
IV Corps
2nd Infantry Division
11th Infantry Division
19th Infantry Division
(two unknown divisions)
42nd Reserve Infantry Division
(unknown reserve infantry division)
VII Corps
25th Infantry Division
27th Infantry Division
31st Infantry Division
47th Reserve Infantry Division
48th Reserve Infantry Division

12th Armored Division
VII Tank Corps
3rd Armored Division
6th Armored Division
10th Armored Division
5th Mechanized Division
51st Mechanized Division
IX Reserve Corps
26th Infantry Division
45th Reserve Infantry Division
49th Reserve Infantry Division

GROUND FORCES STRENGTH (Source: Gulf War Air Power Survey)

	1 Aug. 90	1 Jan.91	1 Feb.91	1 Apr. 91
Personnel	1,000,000	1,100,000	1,100,000	400,000
Divisions	63	66	66	30
(Infantry)	Classified			
(Mechanized Infantry)	Classified			
(Armored)	Classified			
Maneuver Brigades	275	270	270	135
Tanks	5,700	7,000	7,000	2,300
Armored Vehicles	10,000	11,200	11,200	3,100
(Infantry Fighting Vehicles)	Classified			
(Armored Personnel Carriers)	Classified			
(Reconnaissance)	Classified			
Artillery	100mm+ 3,400	3,800	3,800	1,250
(Self-propelled)	Classified			
(Towed)	Classified			
Mult.Rocket Launchers	300	340	340	60
SSM (Launchers)	80	110	105	

IRAQI AIR DEFENSE

Personnel	17,000	17,000	17,000	17,000
Air Defense Arty	7,500	7,600	7,600	5,850

(Self-Propelled)	Classified			
(Towed)	Classified			
SAM Batteries	120	120	200	85

IRAQI NAVY

1) Training frigate IBN MARJID (formerly IBN KHALDUM)
2) Five OSA II missile attack boats
3) Two OSA I missile attack boats
4) Three SO-1 submarine chasers
5) Six P6 fast attack torpedo boats
6) Five Zhuk patrol boats
7) Two Poluchat I patrol boats
8) PO2 coastal patrol craft
9) Two Bogomol coastal patrol craft
10) Nine PB 90 coastal patrol craft
11) Six Rotork Type 412 coastal patrol craft
12) Six WINCHESTER hovercraft
13) Two T-43 minesweepers
14) Three YEVGENYA minesweepers
15) Four NESTIN minesweepers
16) Three POLNOCNY-C landing ships
17) Three modified cargo ships
18) One SPASILAC salvage ship AKA
19) One military transport
20) One Yacht QADISSAYAH SADDAM
21) 14 various tugs and tenders

Personnel	5,000	5,000	5,000	3,000
Frigates	0	0	0	1
Missile Boats	9	13	3	1
Other Patrol Craft	50	50	50	4
Coastal Defense Missiles	50	50	50	4

IRAQI AIR FORCE (AL QUWWAT AL JAWWIYA AL IRAQIYA)

Personnel	18,000	18,000	18,000	18,000
Fighter/ F-Bombers	718	728	699	362
Bombers	15	15	9	7
Combat-capable trainers	370	400	400	252
Recon.	12	12	12	0
Transports	76	70	70	41
Helicopters (all types)	517	511	511	481
Attack	Classified			
Transport/Utility	Classified			
Civilian Aviation Trans.	59	60	60	42

KEY PERSONNEL IN
THE PERSIAN GULF WAR

Capt. Charles Stevenson Abbot, USN, Commander of THEODORE ROOSEVELT (CVN-71). Born 19 Jan.. 1945 in Florida. USNA 1966 (17th in class of 868). Meritorious Service Medal; Air Medal; Navy Commendation Medal; Navy Unit Commendation; Meritorious Unit Commendation. Naval Aviator; Nuclear Power Operational trained; test pilot. Feb. 1993, Deputy Director for Operations (Current Operations), J-33, Joint Staff.

Lt. Col. Bandar Bin Abdullah, RSAF, Commander, Saudi 13th Squadron.

Brig. Gen. Creighton Abrams, III, USA, Commander of VII Corps artillery. Born 1 Oct. 1940 in Winthrop, Massachusetts. Princeton University (AB, English); University of North Carolina (MA, English). Field Artillery School (Basic and Advanced); USA Command and General Staff College; USA War College. Commanded artillery battery in Vietnam. Son of the famous tank commander, Gen. Creighton W. Abrams, for which the M1A1 Abrams tank was named. Retired 31 Oct. 1993.

Cdr. James J. Adams, USNR, Commander of SPARTANBURG COUNTY (LST 1192). Born 27 Jan.. 1954 in New York. USNA, 1975.

Maj. Gen. John Admire, USMC, Commander of Task Force Taro. Born Tulsa, Oklahoma. Legion of Merit (Gold Star in lieu of 2nd award with Combat "V"); Bronze Star (Combat "V" and Gold Star in lieu of 2nd award); Purple Heart; Defense Meritorious Service Medal(Oak Leaf Cluster); Meritorious Service Medal; Combat Action Ribbon. General Admire has had an extensive university education including: University of Oklahoma (BA., Advertising, 1964; M.A. Journalism, 1965); Old Dominion University (M.A., Military History, 1982); Salve Regina Newport College (M.A. International Relations, 1988); and Naval War College (M.A. National Security and Strategic Studies, 1991). Commissioned 2nd Lt. 1965. Military education includes: The Basic School (1966); Advanced Infantry School (1968-69); Armed Forces Staff College (1981); and Naval War College (1984-85). Infantry Platoon Leader, Vietnam (1966-67); Infantry Company Commander, Camp Pendleton (1967-68); Infantry Battalion Advisor to Vietnamese Marine Corps, (1969-70); Infantry Company Commander, Camp Lejeune and Guantanamo Bay, Cuba (1973-74); Infantry Battalion and Battalion Landing Team S-3 (1974-75); 2nd Reconnaissance Battalion S-3 (1975-76); Marine Barracks Ceremonial Parade Commander and Senior White

House Military Social Aide for President Jimmy Carter; 1st Marine Aircraft Wing G-3 Plans Officer (1982-83); Commanding Officer, Third Reconnaissance Battalion, Okinawa Japan (1983-84); 3rd Marine Division G-3 (1987); Commander, Contingency MAGTF 3-88, Persian Gulf (1988); 1st Marine Expeditionary Brigade G-3 (1989-90); Commanding Officer, 3rd Marine Regiment, Kaneohe Bay, Hawaii (1990-91); Vice Director for Strategic Plans and Policy, J-5, Joint Staff, Washington, D.C. General Admire is married.

Cdr. Timothy Michael Ahern, USN, Commander of PAUL F. FOSTER (DD-964). Born 3 Mar. 1948 in Maryland. USNA, 1970. Navy Commendation Medal; Navy Achievement Medal; Combat Action Ribbon.

Lt. Col. Ahmed, RKA, Commander of 7th Armored Battalion, Kuwaiti 35th Armored Brigade. A graduate of the U.S. Army's Armor Advanced Course, the 7th Armored Battalion was involved with the hottest fighting with the Iraqis in Aug. 1990.

Maj. Gen. Mohammed Al-Dughastani, IA, Commander, Iraqi III Corps.

Lt. Col. Ali, RKA, Commander of 8th Armored Battalion, Kuwaiti 35th Armored Brigade. Graduate, U.S. Army Armor Advanced Course. Thoughtful, yet energetic officer, Ali is a national soccer champion and speaks English fluently.

Maj. Gen. Saleh Bin Ali Almohoyya, SRA, Saudi Commander of the Eastern Area Command (Arab Mechanized Division).

Lt. Gen. Sultan Hashim Ahmad Al-Jabburi, IA, Vice Chief of Staff of the Iraqi Army.

Capt. Eugene Alleman, BN, Belgium commander of WANDELAAR. Born in Roeselare, Belgium 3 Aug. 1944. Enlisted in Belgian Navy, Sept. 1964. Royal Military Academy; Royal Netherlands Naval Institute, 1969. Officer in the Order of the Crown; Officer in the Order of Leopold; Military Cross 1st Class; Military Merit Persian Gulf Operations; Kuwait Liberation Medal. Promoted to Captain of Corvette, 1984; XO of WIELINGEN; promoted to Captain of Frigate, 26 Sept. 1989. Married with no children, Capt. Alleman enjoys reading, gardening, and walking.

Col. Salam al-Masoud, RKA, Commander of Kuwaiti 35th Armored Brigade.
Graduate of Sandhurst. A massive black man and legend among the Kuwaitis. Commanding his unit, led entire Joint Forces Command-North's assault and was the first Kuwaiti unit to return to Kuwait City.

Capt. Ayhed Salah Al-Shamrani, RSAF, Saudi fighter pilot, 13th Squadron. Saudi air hero who shot down two Iraqi Mirage F1s 24 Jan.. Ten-year air force veteran closed to within 3,000 ft of Iraqis before firing AIM-9 Sidewinder missiles.

Brig. Gen. Abdulaziz Bin Khalid Al-Sudairi, RSAF, Royal Saudi Air Force Commander of King Khalid AB.

Col. Saber Al-Suwaidin, KAF, Commander, Kuwait Air Force.

Col. Marc Amberg, FAF, French Commander of Jaguars at Al Ahsa.

Lt. Col. Clint Ancker, USA, Executive Officer, 2nd Armored Division's Brigade Forward.

Col. Randall Anderson, USA, Commander, Division Artillery, 101st Airborne Division.

Capt. Bill Andrews, USAF, POW who earned one of only two Air Force Crosses given during the Persian Gulf War.

Cdr. Stuart D. Andrews, CAF, Canadian Commander of HMCS TERRA NOVA. Born in Toronto, Ontario. Enlisted in Canadian Forces, 1968 (cadet at College Militaire Royal, St-Jean, Quebec). Royal Military College, Kingston, Ontario. Service on HMCS MACKENZIE, and HMCS KOOTENAY. Promoted to lieutenant in 1976. Combat Control Officers Course, 1979; service on HMCS FRASER, 1981; Maritime Command Headquarters (computer/analyst and promotion to Lt.Cdr.); Canadian Forces Command and Staff College (Toronto); XO on HMCS ATHABASKAN; 12 July 1990 assumed command of HMCS TERRA NOVA.

V.Adm. Stanley R. Arther, USN, Commander, U.S. Seventh Fleet and Commander, U.S. Naval Forces Central Command. Born in 1936 in San Diego, California. Miami University, NROTC. Commissioned ensign June 1957. Naval Aviator, 1958. Naval Postgraduate School (B.S., Aeronautical Engineering). Navy Distinguished Service Medal (3X), legion of merit (4X, one with Combat "V"), Distinguished Flying Cross (11X), Meritorious Service Medal, Air Medal (4X), Strike/Flight Air Medal (47X), Navy Commendation Medal (2X, one with Combat "V"), Foreign decorations. Served on USS BENNINGTON (CVS 20), and USS HANCOCK (CVA 19) flying 500 Combat missions in a A-4 Skyhawk over Vietnam from her. George Washington University (Masters in Administration). Commanded USS SAN JOSE (AFS 7) and USS CORAL SEA (CV 43). In his biography Schwarzkopf called Arther "One of the most aggressive admirals I'd ever met" due to his willingness to place three aircraft carriers into the restrictive waters of the Persian Gulf. Adm. Arthur is married with four sons. Vice Chief of Naval Operations, 6 July, 1992.

Col. Mohammed Ashad, IA, Commander of the Iraqi 50th Armored Brigade, 12th Armored Division.

R.Adm. Bader, RSN, Senior Saudi Naval officer in Jubayl.

Lt. Col. Sidney "Skip" Baker, USA, Commander of TF 5-16th Infantry, 1st Brigade, 1st Infantry Division.

Cdr. Jean-Loup Bariller, FN, French Commander of MONTCALM.

Capt. Thomas Joseph Barnett, USN, Commander of HORNE (CG-30). Born 6 June 1942. USNA, 1964. Bronze Star; Navy Commendation Medal; Presidential Unit Citation; Legion of Merit; Navy Unit Citation; Joint Service Commendation Medal; Meritorious Service Medal; Navy Achievement Medal; Combat Action Ribbon; Meritorious Unit Commendation; Navy "E" Ribbon; Foreign Decorations.

Lt. Col. Raymond Barrett, USA, Commander, 3rd/15th Infantry, 24th Infantry Division.

Capt. Timothy Robert Beard, USN, Commander of SAN DIEGO (AFS-6). Born 12 Apr. 1944. USNA, 1966. Meritorious Service Medal; Air Medal (11X); Navy Commendation

Medal. Naval Aviator; Naval War College, Command and Staff, Junior Course.

Lt. Col. Andrew Beedy, USA, Commander, 2nd Battalion, 187th Infantry, 101st Airborne Division.

Capt. M.W. Bell, RAN, Australian Commander of HMAS DARWIN from 4 Feb. 1991 to 20 Oct. 1992. Capt. Bell joined the Navy 21 Feb. 1972.

Capt. Ronald V. Berg, USN, Commander of MOBILE (LKA-115).

Cdr. Wesley Allen Bergazzi, USN, Commander of DAVID R. RAY (DD 971). Born 16 Mar. 1949 in California. USNA, 1973.

Capt. David Spencer Bill, III, USN, Commander of battleship WISCONSIN (BB-64). Born 27 Aug. 1944 in Virginia. USNA, 1966. Bronze Star; Purple Heart; Meritorious Service Medal; Foreign Decorations. Royal College of Defense Studies. Director, Surface Combat Systems Division, June 1991; June 1993, Director for Operations and Plans, Commander in Chief, U.S. Atlantic Fleet. Father is retired captain and Naval Academy graduate.

1st Lt. Jerry Biller USA, Commanded Team Jerry, scout platoon of 3-187th Infantry, 101st Airborne which performed reconnaissance astride Highway 8.

Capt. Thomas E. Blount, USN, Commander of STERETT (CG-31). Born 9 Dec. 1943 in Florida. USNA, 1966.

Lt. Gen. Walt Boomer, USMC, Commander of I Marine Expeditionary Force. Born in Rich Square, North Carolina 22 Sept. 1938. Randolph Macon Academy, 1956; Duke University (cadet battalion commander in Naval Reserve Officer Training Corps, 1960). American University (Masters in Technology of Management) 1973. Commissioned 2nd Lt., 1960. The Basic School, Jan. 1961. Promoted 1st Lt., Dec. 1961; Capt., Apr. 1965. Earned two Silver Stars and two Bronze Stars during two tours, Vietnam (Rifle Company commander of Company H, 2nd Battalion, 4th Marines in 1966-67 and Vietnamese Marine Corps advisor, 1971). Legion of Merit; Navy Commendation Medal with Combat "V"; Combat Action Ribbon;Presidential Unit Citation with one bronze star; Navy Unit Commendation with two bronze stars; Meritorious Unit Commendation with two bronze stars; Marine Corps Expeditionary Medal; National Defense Medal with one bronze star; Armed Forces Expeditionary Medal; Vietnam Service Medal with bronze star; Southwest Asia Service Medal with three bronze stars; King Faisal Award, 2nd Class; "Order National du Meriate"; Republic of Vietnam Cross of Gallantry with silver and gold bars; Republic of Vietnam Meritorious Unit Citation (Gallantry Cross color with palm); Republic of Vietnam Meritorious Unit Citation (Civil Actions color); Republic of Vietnam Campaign Medal; Kuwait Liberation Medal. Promoted to Major, May 1968. USNA instructor of management, 1974-76. Promoted to Lt. Col. Sept. 1976. XO, 3rd Marines, 1st Marine Brigade, then Commanding Officer, 2nd Battalion, 3rd Marines in Hawaii, July 1977-June 1980. Naval War College (graduating with distinction), June 1981. Promoted to Col. 1 Nov. 1981. Director, 4th Marine Corps District, 17 June 1983. Commanding Officer, Marine Security Guard Battalion, Quantico, 1985-86. Promoted to Brig. Gen.2 June 1986. Commanding General, 4th Marine Division (Rein), FMF 27 May 1988. Promoted to Maj. Gen. 14 Mar. 1989 and Lt. Gen. 8 Aug. 1990. Commanding General, U.S. Marines Central Command/I Marine Expeditionary Force, 15 Aug. 1990. Promoted to General, 1 Sept. 1992 assuming position of Assistant Commandant of the Marine Corps, Aug. 1992. General Boomer is married with two daughters and one son. He enjoys reading military history, outdoor activities, especially hunting. A good listener.

Cdr. Michael Oscar Borns, USN, Commander of MCINERNEY (FFG-8). Born 13 Mar. 1948 in Virginia. USNA, 1970. Navy Commendation Medal; Navy Achievement Medal; Meritorious Unit Commendation. Naval War College, Command and Staff Junior Course.

Brig. Gen. James A. Brabham Jr., USMC, Commander of 1st Force Service Group (Reinforced). Born in Pennsylvania in 1939. Cornell University (Civil-Engineering), 1962. Two tours in Vietnam (Commanded Shore Party battalion and Engineer Advisor to Vietnamese Marine Corps). USNA, instructor. Commander Marine Corps Systems Command.

Capt. Douglas J. Bradt, USN, Commander of NEW ORLEANS (LPH-11).

Cdr. Thomas L. Breitinger, USN, Commander of WHIDBEY ISLAND (LSD-41).

Lt. Col. Gary Bridges, USA, Commander, 3rd Battalion, 327th Infantry Regiment, 101st Airborne Division.

Wing Commander John Anthony Broadbent, RAF, Flew 21 operational missions during the war in his Tornado and was awarded the Distinguished Service Order.

Lt. Col. John Broderick, USA, Commander of 426th Supply and Transportation Battalion.

Lt. Col. John Brown, USA, Commander of TF 3-5th Cavalry, 1st Brigade, 3rd Armored Division.

Maj. Gen. Lester P. Brown, USAF, Acting Ninth Air Force Commander. Born 7 Feb. 1939 in Norfolk, Va. Virginia Polytechnic Institute (two years then enlisted USAF in 1959); University of Nebraska (bachelor's in history) 1965; Golden Gate University (Masters in Public Administration), 1978. USAF commission, Aviation Cadet Program, Sept. 1960. USAF Squadron Officer School, 1969; Air Command and Staff College, 1976; Industrial College of the Armed Forces, 1978; Air War College, 1980. Distinguished Service Medal; Legion of Merit (Oak Leaf Cluster); Distinguished Flying Cross; Meritorious Service Medal; Air Medal (11 Oak Leaf Clusters); Air Force Commendation Medal; Presidential Unit Citation (2 Oak Leaf Clusters); Air Force Outstanding Unit ("V" device/4 Oak Leaf Clusters); National Defense Service Medal (Service Star); Armed Forces Expeditionary Medal; Vietnam Service Medal (3 Service Stars); Small Arms Expert Marksmanship Ribbon; Republic of Vietnam Gallantry Cross (with Palm); Republic of Vietnam Campaign Medal. Sept. 1960-Nov. 1961, Bombardier-navigator training; Nov. 1961-Dec. 1964, Royal Air Force Station Alconbury, England; Sept. 1965-Sept. 1966, Pilot training, Moody AFB; Apr. 1969-Apr. 1970, flew 184 combat missions over Southeast Asia with 34th and 469th TFS, Korat Royal Thai AFB, Thailand; July 1972 Chief of Standardization/evaluation, 52nd TFW then Operations Officer, 81st TFS (F-4C Wild Weasel); June 1977 assumed command of the 63rd TFS; June 1982 assumes command of the 40th Tactical Group; Mar. 1984-Mar. 1986, Commander, 81st TFW, Royal Air Force Station, Bentwaters, England; June 1987-July 1988 Vice Commander, 12th Air Force; (Promoted to Maj. Gen. 1 May 1989); July 1988-Aug. 1990, Commander, 24th Air Division; Aug. 1990 Sept. 1990 Deputy Commander, HQ,

9th Air Force; Sept. 1990-May 1991, Commander, 9th Air Force (Rear); May 1991-Sept. 1991, Commander, USAF Air Defense Weapons Center; Sept. 1991-present Commander, 1st Air Force, Tactical Air Command/Commander, Continental U.S. North American Aerospace Defense Region. Gen. Brown is married and has four children.

Cdr. Randall R. Brown, USN, Commander of VREELAND (FF-1068).

Lt. Col. William Bryan, USA, Commander 2nd Battalion, 229th Aviation Regiment.

Capt. Clarence W. Burck, USN, Commander of VANCOUVER (LPD-2).

Capt. James L. Burke, USN, Commander of RICHMOND K. TURNER (CG-20).

Cdr. Cyrus Hugh Butt IV, USN, Commander of OLDENDORF (DD-972). Born 30 Mar. 1949 in Rhode Island. USNA, 1971. Navy "E" Ribbon (3X); Navy Commendation Medal; Meritorious Service Medal.

Capt. Patrick Anthony Callahan, USN, Commander of PHILIPPINE SEA (CG-58). Born 18 Dec. 1943 in Illinois. USNA, 1966.

Capt. Dominic Joseph Caraccilo, USA, Commander, Headquarters Company, 2nd Brigade, 82nd Airborne Division. USMA, 1984; Cornell University (Engineering). Bronze Star; Combat Infantryman's Badge; RANGER Tab; Senior Parachutist Wings; Air Assault Badge. Infantry Officer Basic & Advanced Course. Married, Capt. Caraccilo has one son and is the author of *The Ready Brigade of the 82nd Airborne in Desert Storm*.

Capt. Arthur K. Cebrowski, USN, Commander of MIDWAY (CV-41). Oct. 1992, Commander Carrier Group Six; Apr. 1994, Director, Space and Electronic Warfare, Office of the Chief of Naval Operations.

Capt. Ernest Edward Christenson, Jr., USN, Commander of RANGER (CV-61). Born 6 July 1942 in Maryland. USNA, 1964. Distinguished Flying Cross (3X). Naval War College, Advanced Study in Strategy and Sea Power. Deputy Director for Operations, June 1992; Sept. 1993, Commander, Fleet Air, Caribbean.

R.Adm. Stephen S. Clarey, USN, Commander of Amphibious Group THREE.

Col. Robert Clark, USA, Commander, 3rd Brigade, 101st Airborne Division.

Capt. Stephen R. Cleal, USN, Commander of VULCAN (AR-5).

Lt. Col. Richard Cody, USA, Commander of Task Force Normandy, 1 Battalion, 101st Aviation Brigade.

Lt. Col. Tom Coleman, USAF, Squadron Commander, 504th Tactical Fighter Squadron, (Cajuns).

Cdr. Giles Combarieu, FN, French Commander of DUPLEIX.

Capt. Rapallo Comendador, SN, Spanish Commander of the Naval Group of Spain in the

Persian Gulf War.

Wing Commander Jerome Connolly, RAF, Awarded Air Force Cross for service.

Capt. Mayo Consentino, SN, Spanish Commander of CAZADORA.

Cdr. James D. Cope, USN, Commander of AVENGER (MCM-1).

Wing Commander William Cope, RAF, Commanded unit made up of crews from Nos. 12 and 208 Squadrons (plus No. 237 OCU).

Brig. Patrick Cordingley, BA, Commander of British 7th Armoured Brigade (The "Desert Rats"). Described as friendly and direct. Greatly enjoyed working with the United States Marine Corps. Commanded war from a Challenger tank.

Capt. L.G. Cordner, RAN, Australian Commander of HMAS SYDNEY from 12 Oct. 1990 to 29 Apr. 1992. Capt. Cordner joined the Navy 3 Jan. 1968.

Col. David E. Cormack, USAF, Commander 1703rd Air Refueling Wing (Provisional).

Col. V.B. Corn, USA, Commander, Division Artillery, 1st Armored Division.

Cdr. Kevin J. Cosgriff, USN, Commander of ROBERT G. BRADLEY (FFG-49).

Lt. Col. John Craddock, USA, Commander of 4-64th Armor, 24th Infantry Division.

Commo. Christopher Craig, RN, Senior British Royal Navy Commander in Persian Gulf. Naval helicopter pilot and instructor. Earned DSC as commander of HMS ALACRITY (F 174) during the Falklands War. An aggressive leader he is a dark, large, solid man.

Lt. Col. Ward Critz, USA, Commander of TF 7-6th Infantry, 3rd Brigade, 1st Armored Division.

Capt.(N) C. Dennis E. Cronk, CAF, Canadian Commander of HMCS PROTECTEUR. Born in Vancouver, B.C. Enlisted in Royal Canadian Navy (Cadet, Royal Roads Military College), 1961; BSc Degree, Royal Military College, 1965; service on West Coast destroyers; Promoted Lt. Cdr., May 72; Canadian Forces Command and Staff College, Toronto; Combat Officer, HMCS ATHABASKAN; XO, HMCS HURON; promoted to Cdr., 1977; assumed command of HMCS GATINEAU, July 79; promoted to Capt. (N), 1984; assumed command of HMCS PRESERVER, Aug. 89; assumed command of HMCS PROTECTEUR, 9 Jan. 91. Capt. (N) Cronk is married and has a son and daughter.

Lt. Col. Mark Curran, USA, Commander, 3rd Battalion, 101st Aviation Brigade.

Capt. James A. Curtis, USN, Commander of TRENTON (LPD-14).

Lt. Col. Dell Lee Dailey, USA, Commander of 3-160th Special Operations Aviation Regiment. Born 27 July 1949 in South Dakota. USMA, 1971. 21/61 Infantry (1972-74); 2nd Aviation Brigade, Korea (1974-75); Fort Stewart (1976); 24th Division (1978); 1/75th Infantry (1978-79); 11th Armored Cavalry Regiment, Germany (1979).

Col. John Kneeland Davidson, USA, VII Corps Intelligence Officer. Born 17 Jan. 1938 in Illinois. USMA, 1960.

Capt. Deborah Davis, USA, Executive Officer of A Company, 5-159th Aviation, 2nd Armored Cavalry Regiment. Led determined emergency aerial resupply, 24 Feb..

Cdr. Dennis R. Dean, USN, Commander of WILLIAM V. PRATT (DDG-44).

Capt. Gilbert DeCock, BN, Belgian commander of WIELINGEN. Born in Sint-Gilles-Wass, 8 Mar. 1945. Royal Naval Institute, 1964-69. Military Cross (2nd Class); Officer in the Order of King Leopold; Officer in the Order of the Crown; Kuwait Liberation Medal. Capt. DeCock is married with two children. He enjoys tennis and wood sculpture.

Cdr. Benoit Chomel de Jarnieu, FN, French Commander of PREMIER MAITRE L'HER.

Gen. Peter de la Billiere, BA, Commander of British Forces. Born 29 Apr. 1934. Harrow School; Staff College; Royal College of Defense Studies. Korean War veteran. Twenty years with SAS group beginning in 1956 (commander, 22 SAS Regiment, 1972-74). SAS commander in Falkland Islands War. At time of Gulf War of his 39 years of service, nearly eight had been in the Middle East. Fluent in colloquial Arabic. Most decorated officer of British armed forces. Enjoys sailing, squash and farming.

Cdr. Mauric Demoisson, FN, French commander of PROTET.

Lt. Col. Arthur Denaro, BA, British commander of The Queen's Royal Irish Hussars. Described as cheerful and resolute he was greatly concerned with his men's morale. Well known to Prince Charles and a close friend of Lt. Gen. de la Billiere.

Lt. Col. David Deptula, USAF, Deputy in charge of the strategic air campaign under Glosson.

Lt. Col. James Donald, USA, Commander, 1st Battalion, 502nd Infantry Regiment, 2nd Brigade, 101st Airborne Division.

Capt. DeBenito Dorronzoro, SN, Spanish Commander of ASTURIAS.

Col. Michael Dotson, USA, Commander of Artillery, 1st Infantry Division. Born 14 June 1949 in North Carolina. USMA, 1974. 2/60 Air Defense Artillery, Germany (1975).

Capt. W.A. Dover, RAN, Australian Commander of HMAS ADELAIDE from 3 Apr. 1989 to 2 Jan. 1991. Capt. Dovers joined the Navy 19 Jan. 1970.

Capt. John I. Dow, USN, Commander of NASSAU (LHA-4).

Gen. Wayne Allan Downing, USA, Commander of Delta Force and the Joint Special Operations Task Force. Born 10 May 1940 in Peoria, Illinois. USMA, 1962. Tulane University, Masters in Business Administration. Silver Star (2X); Legion of Merit; Distinguished Flying Cross (2X); Bronze Star Medal (Combat "V"); Air Medal (10X); Purple Heart; Meritorious Service Medal. Ranger School, Sept. 1962-Feb. 1963; 503rd Airborne Infantry Regiment and Aide-de-Camp of Commanding General 173rd Airborne

Brigade (1963-65); 1/503rd Airborne Infantry Regiment, Vietnam (1965-66); 25th Division, Vietnam (1968-70); Armed Forces Staff College (1972); 1/75th Infantry executive officer (1975-76); 2/75th Infantry (1977-79); Air War College (1980). Commanded all special operations forces of U.S. military services in Operation Just Cause (Panama). Commanding General, US Army Special Operations Command, Ft. Bragg, N.C. beginning Aug. 1991. Promoted to General, 1993 and appointed Commander-in-Chief, Special Operations Command.

Capt. Raymond A. Duffy, USN, Commander of LAMOURE COUNTY (LST-1194).

Lt. Col. Edward Dyer, USA, Commander of TF 1-37th Armor, 3rd Brigade, 1st Armored Division. Born 23 Feb. 1950. USMA, 1972. 1/32 Armor, Germany (1974-78); Fort Knox (1978).

Lt. Col. Pat Eagan, USA, Commander, 4-7 Infantry, 3rd Brigade, 3rd Infantry Division (attached to 1st Armored Division).

Capt. Paul W. Ecker, USN, Commander of SAN JACINTO (CG-56).

Capt. Ectors, BN, Belgian commander of MYOSOTIS (Aug 90-Nov 90).

Capt. Lawrence E. Eddingfield, USN, Commander of ANTIETAM (CG-54).

Capt. Michael B. Edwards, USN, Commander of DETROIT (AOE-4).

Col. Robert Efferson, USAF, Group Commander, 504th Tactical Fighter Squadron (Cajuns) at Al Jouf (primary missions to seek out Scuds targeting Israel). Flew Thuds in Vietnam.

Cdr.(s.g.) Henrik M. Elbro, DN, Commander, Danish corvette OLFERT FISCHER (to 11 Dec.). Born 28 Feb. 1944. Knight of the Order of Dannebrog; Navy Long Service Medal; Medal of Merit of the Defence Forces; Kuwait Liberation Medal. 1 Nov. 1968 Lieutenant; 1 Nov. 1973 Lieutenant Commander; 1978-1979, Standing Naval Force Atlantic, Operation Officer; 1 Aug. 1979, Commander; 1981-1982, Staff course;1983-1988, Admiral Danish Fleet, Staff Officer; 1988-1989 Executive Officer, corvettes; 1989-1991 Commanding Officer, corvettes; 16 Feb. 1990, Commander (s.g.); 1991-1993 Commanding Officer Danish Action Information School; 1993-1994, Admiral Danish Fleet, ACOS Plans.

Capt. Robert Lee Ellis, Jr., USN, Commander of INDEPENDENCE (CV-62). Born 29 Apr. 1944 in Virginia. USNA, 1966. Distinguished Flying Cross; Air Medal(12 X); Navy Commendation Medal (3X); Navy Unit Commendation; Meritorious Service Medal (2X). Apr. 1992, Director, East Asia and Pacific Region, Office of the Assistant Secretary of Defense (International Security Affairs).

Cdr. David R. Ellison, USN, Commander of KIDD (DDG-993). Born 30 May 1947 in Massachusetts. USNA, 1970. Meritorious Service Medal; Navy Commendation Medal; Meritorious Unit Commendation;

Col. Faisal Eurwailli, RSAF, Saudi Flying Wing Commander at King Khalid, AB.

Lt. Col. Daniel Fake, USA, Commanded TF 2-16th Infantry, 1st Infantry Division.

Cdr. Mark Steven Falkey, USN, Commander of PORTLAND (LSD-37). Born 29 July 1950 in Florida. USNA, 1972. Navy Commendation Medal.

Cdr. Mark Fitzgerald, USN, From the KENNEDY led the first A-7 package against Iraq as the war began.

Capt. Thomas Arthur Fitzgibbons, USN, Commander of JUNEAU (LPD-10). Born 24 Mar. 1943 in Massachusetts. USNA, 1966.

Capt. Wirt R. Fladd, USN, Commander of TARAWA (LHA-1).

Capt. Vasilio Flokos, GN, Greek Commander of ELLI. Born in 1950 at Piraeus, Attica. Speaks English and French. Married with two children.

Lt. Col. Gregory Fontenot, USA, Commander of TF 2-34th Armor, 1st Brigade, 1st Infantry Division.

Capt. George T. Forbes, USN, Commander, Destroyer Squadron 7 on PAUL F. FOSTER (DD-964). He commanded 12 ships and 18 helicopters.

Capt. Marco Franco, SN, Spanish Commander of NUMANCIA.

Lt. Gen. Frederick Melvin Franks, Jr. USA, Commander of VII Corps. Born 1 Nov. 1936. USMA, 1959. Silver Star; Distinguished Flying Cross; Bronze Star Medal (Combat "V"); Air Medal (43X); Purple Heart (2X). 11th Armored Cavalry Regiment (1960-63); Columbia University, Masters (1966) and Columbia University, Masters (1975). USMA English Dept. (1966-69); Vietnam 1969-1970 (11th Armored Cavalry Regiment). Armed Forces Staff College (1972); 1/3rd Armored Cavalry Regiment (1975-76); National War College (1977); Commanding General, 1st Armored Division. Schwarzkopf described Franks as his "most aggressive and successful ground commander" during the Persian Gulf War. Has artificial leg from Vietnam. Small and quiet he became Commanding General, U.S. Army Training and Doctrine Command at Ft. Monroe, Virginia in Aug. 1991.

Capt. William E. Franson, USN, Commander of KANSAS CITY (AOR-3).

Cdr. Michael Frimenko, Jr., USN, Commander of SANTA BARBARA (AE-28).

Cdr. Thomas W. Frohlich, USN, Commander of PREBLE (DDG-46).

Col. James A. Fulks, USMC, Commander of Task Force Grizzly.

Maj. Gen. Paul Edward "Butch" Funk, USA, Commander, 3rd Armored Division. Born 10 Mar. 1940, Roundup Montana. Montana State University (BS in Agriculture, MA in Psychological Counseling, EdD in Education Administration). ROTC commission 2nd Lt. 5 June 1961. Distinguished Service Medal; Distinguished Flying Cross; Legion of Merit (with Oak Leaf Cluster); Bronze Star (with Oak Leaf Cluster); Meritorious Service Medal (with 2 Oak Leaf Clusters); Air Medals with "V" Device; Army Commendation Medal with "V" Device (with 4 Oak Leaf Clusters). Armor School (Basic and Advanced); Armed Forces Staff College; U.S. Army War College. Jan. 62-Mar. 62 Student, Armor Officer Basic Course; Mar. 62-Feb. 63 Platoon Leader, Company C, 2nd Battalion, 13th Armor, 1st

Armored Division; Feb. 63-Jan. 64 Platoon Leader (later S-1) HQ, 2nd Battalion, 13th Armor, 1st Armored Division; 27 Nov. promoted to 1st Lt.; May 65-Oct. 65 Platoon Leader, Company A, 1st Battalion, 33rd Armor, 3rd Armor Division, USA(Europe); Nov. 65-Apr. 67 Commander, Company A, 1st Battalion, 33rd Armor, 3rd Armor Division, USA (Europe); 10 June 66 promoted to Capt.; Apr. 67-July 67 XO, HQ Company, 1st Battalion, 2nd Brigade, USA Training Center, Fort Lewis, Washington; July 67-June 68 Student, Armor Officer Advanced Course, USA Armor Center; June 68-Oct. 68 Student, Officer Rotary Wing Aviator Course, USA Primary Helicopter School; Oct. 68-Feb. 69 Student, Officer Rotary Wing Aviator Course, USA Aviation School; Feb. 69-Dec. 69 XO, Troop A, 1st Squadron (Airmobile), 9th Cavalry, 1st Cavalry Division, USA, Vietnam; Dec. 69-May 70 Commander, Troop A, 1st Squadron (Airmobile), 9th Cavalry, 1st Cavalry Division (Airmobile), USA, Vietnam; 3 June 70 promoted to Major; Apr. 73-Jan. 74 Commander, Troop D, 4th Squadron, 7th Cavalry, 2nd Infantry Division, USA, Korea; June 74-Jan. 75 Student, Armed Forces Staff College; 7 Aug 77, promoted to Lt. Col. Sept. 77-Apr. 79 Commander, 5th Battalion, 33rd Armor, 194th Armored Brigade, USA Armor Center; Apr 79-July 79 XO, 194th Armored Brigade, USA Armor Center; Aug. 79-June 80 Student, USA War College; 1 Nov. 82 promoted to Col.; July 80-June 84 Assistant Chief of Staff, G-3 (Operations), 1st Cavalry Division (later Deputy G-3 of training), III Corps and later Chief of Staff, 1st Cavalry Division; July 84-Aug. 85 Commander, 194th Armored Brigade, US Armor Center; 1 July 87, promoted to Brig. Gen.; Sept. 85-Nov. 87 Assistant Commandant, USA Armor School; Nov. 87-Sept. 88 Assistant Division Commander, 9th Infantry Division (Motorized); Sept. 88-Oct. 89 Commanding General, National Training Center and Fort Irwin, California; 1 July 90, promoted to Maj. Gen.; Oct. 89-Apr. 91 Commanding General, 3rd Armored Division, USA Europe and 7th Army; Dec. 90-Apr. 91 Commanding General, 3rd Armored Division; May 91-July 92 Vice Director, J-3, The Joint Staff, Washington, DC.

Cdr. Daniel E. Gabe, USN, Commander of SHASTA (AE-33).

Cdr. Patrick M. Garrett, USN, Commander of LEFTWICH (DD-984).

Col. Thomas Garrett, USA, Commander, Aviation Brigade, 101st Airborne Division.

Capt. John P. Gay, USN, Commander of JOHN F. KENNEDY (CV-67).

R.Adm. Nick Gee, USN, Commander of Cruiser-Destroyer Group 8. Commander, Joint Task Force Four, July 1991.

Capt. Alan M. Gemmill, USN, Commander of SAN JOSE (AFS-7).

Lt. Col. Robert "Nail 01" George, USAF, Squadron Commander, 23rd Tactical Air Support Squadron, (Nail FACs).

Col. Ralph Getchell, USAF, Commander of the 415th TFW.

Col. Emmitt Edison Gibson, USA, Commander, 12th Aviation Brigade. Born 7 Feb. 1944 in North Carolina. USMA, 1966. Bronze Star Medal, Combat Infantryman's Badge, Meritorious Service Medal (3X). 325th Infantry, 82nd Airborne Division (1966-67); Military Assistance Command, Vietnam (1967-68); 11th Infantry (1969-70); Aviation School (1971); 82nd Airborne Division (1972-77); Executive Officer, 223rd Aviation Brigade, Germany

(1977); Commanding Officer, 48th Aviation Company (1978-80).

Capt. Henry C. Giffin, III, USN, Commander of THOMAS S. GATES (CG-51). Born 16 Nov. 1945 in New York. USNA, 1967. Navy Commendation Medal; Foreign Decorations. June 1992, Assistant Chief of Logistics, Headquarters, Allied Forces South.

Col. Greg Gile, USA, Commander, 2nd Brigade, 101st Airborne Division.

Lt. Gen. Buster C. Glosson, USAF, Commander, 14th Air Division. North Carolina State University (B.S. Electrical Engineering) 1965; Armed Forces Staff College; National War College, 1981. Commissioned 2nd Lt. 23 Jan. 1965. Distinguished Service Medal; Defense Superior Service Medal; Legion of Merit (2 Oak Leaf Clusters); Distinguished Flying Cross; Defense Meritorious Service Medal; Meritorious Service Medal (2 Oak Leaf Clusters); Air Medal (3 Oak Leaf Clusters); Air Force Commendation Medal; Presidential Unit Citation; AF Outstanding Unit (with "V" and 2 Oak Leaf Clusters); National Defense Service Medal (service Star); Vietnam Service Gallantry Cross with Palm; Republic of Vietnam Campaign Medal; Kuwait Liberation Medal. July 1966-Dec. 1967, instructor pilot, T-38, 3500th Pilot Training Squadron; (Promoted to 1st Lt. 6 Sept. 1966 and Capt. 25 May 1968); Dec. 1967-Sept. 1971, T-38 instructor, 3250th Fighter Training Squadron; Sept. 1971-Apr. 1972, Student USAF Operational Training Course, F-4, 4435th Tactical Fighter Squadron; Apr. 1972-Sept. 1972, Commander, F-4E, 4th Tactical Fighter Squadron, Pacific Air Forces, Takhli Royal Thai Air Force Base, Thailand; Sept. 1972-Apr. 1973, Air Operations Officer, 366th Tactical Fighter Wing, Pacific Air Forces, Takhli Royal Thai Air Force Base; Apr. 1973-Sept. 1974, Chief, Fighter and Forward Air Controller, HQ, 13th Air Force, Pacific Air Forces, Clark Air Base, Philippines; (1 Aug. 1976); July 1977-Jan. 1978, Student, Armed Forces Staff College; Jan. 1978-Aug. 1978, Student, USAF Operational Training Course, F-4D, 307th TFS; Aug. 1978-Aug. 1979, Chief, Standardization and Evaluation Division, 56th TFW, Tactical Air Command; (Promoted to Lt. Col. 1 Dec. 1979); Aug. 1979-June 1980, XO to Commander, USAF TFWC; June 1980-Aug. 1980, Chief, Standardization and Evaluation Division, 414th Fighter Weapons Squadron; Aug. 1980-July 1981, Commander, 414th Fighter Weapons Squadron; July 1981-June 1982, Student, National War College; (Promoted to Col. 1 Oct. 1982); June 1982-July 1983, Chief, Tactical Forces Division, Deputy Director for Forces, HQ, USAF; July 1983-Aug. 1984, Chief, Programs Division, Deputy Director for Resources, HQ, USAF; Aug. 1984-July 1986, Vice Commander, the Commander, 347th TFW; July 1986-June 1987, Commander, 1st TFW, HQ, Tactical Air Command; (Promoted to Brig. Gen. 1 July 1988); June 1987-Sept. 1988, Deputy Chief of Staff, Plans and Programs, HQ, USAF, Europe; Sept. 1988-July 1990, Deputy Assistant Secretary of Defense (Legislative Affairs); July 1990-Aug. 1990, Deputy Commander, Joint Task Force Middle East, USCENTCOM; Aug. 1990-May 1991, CENTAF Director of Campaign Plans, USCENTCOM, and Commander, 14th AD (Provisional); (Promoted to Maj. Gen. 1 June 1991); May 1991-May 1992, Director, Legislative Liaison, and Director, AF Issues Team; Promoted to Lt. Gen. 1 June 1992; June 1992- to present, Deputy Chief of Staff for Plans and Operations, Washington. Commander of all U.S. Air Force Wings in the Persian Gulf War and Horner's director of campaign plans. Rated a Command Pilot with more than 3,600 hours he has flown F-4s, F-5s, F-15Cs, F-15Es and T-38s. Glosson is married with a son and daughter.

Cdr. Grey A. Glover, USN, Commander of MACDONOUGH (DDG-39).

Capt. Goddyn, BN, Belgian commander of MYOSOTIS (Dec 90-Apr 91).

Lt. Col. Gregory T. "Greg" Gonyea, USAF, Commander of the 416th TFS "Ghost Riders".

Capt. Oscar Adolfo Gonzalez, AN, Argentinean Captain of the Corvette A.R.A. SPIRO. Born 3 July 1944 in Zarate, Province of Buenos Aires. Enlisted in Argentina Navy in Cadet preparatory course 4 Feb. 1963. Midshipman, 29 Dec. 1967; Corvette Lieutenant, 31 Dec. 1969; Frigate Lieutenant, 31 Dec. 1972; Ship Lieutenant, 31 Dec. 1974; Corvette Captain, 31 Dec. 1980; Frigate Captain, 31 Dec. 1986; Ship Captain 31 Dec. 1992.

Cdr. Brent B. Gooding, USN, Commander of CARON (DD-970).

Gen. Alfred M. "Al" Gray, USMC, Commandant of the U.S. Marine Corps. Born in Rahway, New Jersey in 1929. Enlisted in Marine Corps, 1950 reaching rank of Sergeant. Commissioned 2nd Lt., Apr. 1952. Artillery officer, 1st Marine Division, Korean War. Two tours, Vietnam (as Col. commanded Ground Combat Element, 9th Marine Amphibious Brigade in evacuation of Saigon, 1975). Commanding General, 2nd Marine Division, 1981. Promoted to Lt. Gen. 29 Aug. 1984 Commanding General, Fleet Marine Force, Atlantic. Commanding General, II Marine Amphibious Force. Promoted to General and became Commandant of the Marine Corps, 1 July 1987. Married with no children, he is of stocky build, and chews tobacco. Retired 30 June 1991.

Brig. Gen. George A. Gray III, USAF, Commander, 1st (16th) Special Operations Wing. Born 12 Apr. 1945 in Childress, Texas. The Citadel (BA) 1967; Webster University (Master's), 1976; Air War College, 1987. Defense Superior Service Medal; Legion of Merit (Oak Leaf Cluster); Distinguished Flying Cross; Bronze Star Medal; Meritorious Service Medal (2 Oak Leaf Clusters); Air Medal (6 Oak Leaf Clusters); Joint Service Commendation Medal; Air Force Commendation Medal (3 Oak Leaf Clusters). C-130 pilot, 50th Tactical Airlift Squadron, Ching Chuan Kang AB, Taiwan flying combat missions into South Vietnam; 1981, Director of Operations, 40th TAS, 317th TAW (participated in first development of the C-130 Special Operations Low-Level II program supporting operational requirements of the Joint Special Operations Command; 1983, Commander, 39th TAS (Operation Urgent Fury); 1985, Director of Combat Operations/Commander, 1701st Mobility Support Squadron; 1986-87, Air War College; 1987-June 1989, Director of Plans and Policy, Joint Special Operations Command, Fort Bragg, NC; June 1989, Commander, 1st Special Operations Wing (Operation Just Cause); Aug. 1992-present, Commander, 438th Airlift Wing at McGuire, Air Force Base, New Jersey. Gen. Gray is married and has a daughter and three sons.

Lt. Col. Jim Green, USAF, Squadron Commander, 74th Tactical Fighter Squadron (Flying Tigers). Former F-4 and aggressor pilot at Air Force Fighter Weapons Wing. Flew 38 missions as a "Hog Driver" flying A-10 Warthogs during Persian Gulf War.

Cdr. Kevin Patrick Green, USN, Commander of TAYLOR (FFG-50). Born 28 Aug. 1949 in California. USNA, 1971. Navy Commendation Medal; Meritorious Service Medal; Navy Achievement Medal.

Capt. James Grier, USAF, Air Liaison Officer for 20th Saudi Mechanized Infantry Brigade.

David J. Grieve, USN, Commanded Mine Countermeasures Force.

Maj. Gen. Ronald Houston Griffith, USA, Commander of 1st Armored Division. Born 16

Mar. 1936 in LaFayette, Georgia. Champion high school baseball player. University of Georgia (BS-Physical Education) 1961; Shippensburg State College (MS-Public Administration). Commissioned 2nd Lt. 28 Dec. 60. USA Medical Field Service School (Officer Basic Course); Armor School (Advanced Course); USA Command and General Staff College; USA War College. Distinguished Service Medal; Legion of Merit (2 Oak Leaf Clusters); Bronze Star (with "V" Device); Bronze Star (with 5 Oak Leaf Clusters); Purple Heart; Meritorious Service Medal (Oak Leaf Cluster); Air Medals; Joint Service Commendation Medal; Army Commendation Medal (2 Oak Leaf Clusters); Combat Infantryman Badge; Army Staff Identification Badge. Jan. 61-Mar. 61 Student Medical Service Corps Officer Basic Course; Mar. 61-May 62 Medical Platoon Leader; June 62-July 63 Assistant Sports Officer; 28 Dec. 63 promoted to 1st Lt.; Nov. 63-July 64 XO (later S-4), HQ Company, 4th Battalion, 37th Armor; Sept. 64-Dec. 64 Student, Defense Language Institute; Dec. 64-Nov. 65 Assistant Sub-Sector Advisor, 275th Regional Force Company, USMAC, Vietnam; Feb. 66-Jan. 66 Student, Armor Officer Advanced Course; July 66-July 67 Commander, 502nd Administrative Company, 2nd Armored Division; 28 Dec. 67 promoted to Capt.; July 67-June 69 Assistant Professor of Military Science, U. of California; June 69-June 70 Assistant G-4, 4th Infantry Division (later XO), 2nd Battalion (Mechanized), 8th Infantry, 4th Infantry Division, Vietnam; Aug. 71-June 72 Student, USA Command and General Staff College; 28 Dec. 74 promoted to Major; June 72-Sept. 75 Staff Officer, War Plans and Forces Division; 10 May 76 promoted to Lt. Col.; Sept. 75-July 76 Operations Research Analyst, Manpower and Force Programs Analysis Team; Nov. 76-Nov. 78 Commander, 1st Battalion, 32nd Armor, 3rd Armored Division, USA Europe; June 79-June 80 Student, USA War College; Sept. 80-May 81 Force Analyst, Manpower and Force Programs Analysis Division; May 81-Apr. 82 Chief, War Plans Division, Strategy, Plans and Policy Directorate, Office of the Deputy Chief of Staff for Operations and Plans; 1 July 82 promoted to Col.; Aug. 82-Aug. 83 Commander, 1st Brigade, 2nd Infantry Division, Korea; Sept. 83-July 84 Chief, Combat Arms Division, Officer Personnel Management Directorate; July 84-Jan. 86 Chief of Staff, 1st Cavalry Division, III Corps; Jan. 86-Apr. 87 Executive to the Deputy Chief of Staff for Operations and Plans; 1 Dec. 87 promoted to Brig. Gen.; Apr. 87-Sept. 88 Deputy Director for Operations, Readiness and Mobilization; Sept. 88-July 89 Assistant Division Commander, 1st Cavalry Division; July 89-Oct. 89 Special Assistant to the Commander-in-Chief, USA Europe and 7th Army; 1 Oct. 90 promoted to Maj. Gen.; Dec. 90-May 91 Commanding General, 1st Armored Division

Cdr. Frank B. Guest III, USN, Commander of MOOSBRUGGER (DD-980).

Maj. Gen. Habib, SA, Commander of all Syrian Forces.

Cdr. David W. Hagstrom, USN, Commander of CAYUGA (LST-1186).

Col. Glynn Hale, USA, 3rd Brigade, 82nd Airborne.

Capt. David A. Halla, USAF, Air Liaison Officer, Kuwaiti Liberation Brigade.

Lt. Col. Beaufort Hallman, USA, Commander of TF 4-8th Cavalry, 2nd Brigade, 3rd Armored Division.

Lt. Col. Hamid, RKA, 2nd Mechanized Battalion commander, Kuwaiti 35th Armored Brigade. Once the commander of the Kuwaiti armor school, Hamid is described as nervous and aggressive.

Brig. Christopher Hammerbeck, BA, British commander of the 4th Armoured Brigade ("Hell for Leather"). Parachute Regiment. Armor Warfare expert.Lt. Gen. de la Billiere describes him as an "exceptional military thinker." Commanded war from a Challenger tank. Friend of Rupert Smith.

Capt. Louis F. Harlow, USN, Commander of BIDDLE (CG-34).

Cdr. Robert Michael Hartling, USN, Commander of HALYBURTON (FFG-40). Born 9 June 1951 in New York. USNA, 1973. Navy Achievement Medal.

Gen. Muzahim Saab Hassan, IA, Commander, Iraqi Air Force.

Lt. Col. William John Hatch, USA, Commander of 3-1st Aviation, 1st Armored Division. Born 21 Nov. 1950 in Arizona. USMA, 1972. 1/77 Armor, Fort Carson (1973); 10th Cavalry (1974-75); Aviation School, Fort Rucker (1976); 417th Cavalry, Korea (1976-77); 2/10 Cavalry, Fort Ord (1978).

Cdr. James A. Hayes, USN, Commander of FORT MCHENRY, (LSD-43).

Cdr. Hebrard, FN, French Commander of DU CHAYLA.

Col. David Heebner, USA, Commander, 10th Air Defense Brigade. Commanded Patriot brigade from Darmstadt, Germany, in Israel.

Group Captain David Henderson, RAF, Commanding British Air at Muharraq International Airport.

Capt. Joseph K. Henderson, USN, Commander of BLUE RIDGE (LCC-19).

Cdr. Ronald E. Hewitt, USN, Commander of KISKA (AE-35).

Cdr. William F. Hickman, USN, Commanded JOHN A. MOORE (FFG-19).

Col. Robert Higgins, USA, Commander, 2nd Brigade, 3rd Armored Division.

Cdr. Robert A. Higgins, USN, Commander of ELMER MONTGOMERY (FF-1082).

Col. James Thomas Hill, USA, Commander, 1st Brigade, 101st Airborne Division (Air Assault).

Capt. James B. Hinkle, USN, Commander, Destroyer Squadron 24. He coordinated air defense of the Mediterranean theater of operations. Apr. 1992, Executive Assistant to the Vice Chief of Naval Operations, Office of the Chief of Naval Operations.

Col. John Hitt, USA, Commander, 11th Aviation Brigade.

Cdr. Mark Allan Hoke, USN, Commander of FAIRFAX COUNTY (LST 1193). Born 13 Dec. 1947 in Indiana. USNA, 1970.

Lt. Col. Keith T. Holcomb, USMC, Commanded 2nd Light Armored Infantry Battalion, 2nd

Marine Division. 1978-79 UN observer in Lebanon of the Palestine Liberation Organization and Israeli Army. Naval Post-Graduate School (Masters of Arts, National Security Affairs, Mideast), Commandant of the Marine Corps Fellow in Center for Strategic and International Studies, Defense Language Institute (Syrian dialect of Arabic).

Col. Don Holder, USA, Commander, 2nd Armored Cavalry Regiment.

Capt. Edward Brigham Hontz, USN, Commander of PRINCETON (CG-59). Born 1 Mar. 1945 in Pennsylvania. USNA, 1967.

Cdr. Roger Keith Hope, USN, Commander of PLATTE (AO-186). Born 7 June 1949 in Ohio. USNA, 1971.

Maj. Gen. John I. Hopkins, USMC. Commander of 7th Marine Expeditionary Brigade. Born in Brooklyn, New York in 1932. USNA, 1956. University of Southern California (Masters Degree). Earned Silver Star in Vietnam. Retired, 1 Feb. 1993.

Col. Hal Hornburg, USAF, Commander, 4th Tactical Fighter Wing (Provisional).

Lt. Gen. Charles A. Horner, USAF. Born in 19 Oct. 1936 in Davenport, Iowa. University of Iowa (B.A.) 1958; College of William and Mary (Master's, Business Administration), 1972. ROTC commission 1959. Distinguished Service Medal; Silver Star (Oak Leaf Cluster); Legion of Merit; Distinguished Flying Cross; Meritorious Service Medal (2 Oak Leaf Clusters); Air Medal (2 Oak Leaf Clusters); Air Force Commendation Medal (3 Oak Leaf Clusters); Presidential Unit Citation (Oak Leaf Cluster); Air Force Outstanding Unit Award (3 Oak Leaf Clusters); Combat Readiness Medal; National Defense Service Medal; Armed Forces Expeditionary Medal (Service Star); Vietnam Service Medal (Service Star); Small Arms Expert Marksmanship Ribbon; Republic of Vietnam Campaign Medal; Kuwait Liberation Medal. Nov. 1960, F-110 training; (F-100 pilot, 492nd TFS, Lakenheath, England; Dec. 1963-Dec. 1965, F-105 pilot, 4th TFW; June 1965-Dec. 1965 flew 41 combat missions over North Vietnam in F-105s, 388th TFW from Korat Royal Thai AFB, Thailand (returned May 1967-Sept. 1967 flying 70 additional combat missions over North Vietnam); Sept. 1967-Nov. 1968, F-105 instructor, Fighter Weapons School; Oct. 1969-Jan. 1971, Air Operations Officer, HQ, Tactical Air Command; Jan. 1971-Jan. 1972 Armed Forces Staff College; June 1976; graduated, National War College, June 1976; Mar. 1979-Aug. 1979, Vice Commander, 58th Tactical Training Wing (then Commander); May 1980-Aug. 1981, Commander, 474th TFW; Aug. 1981-May 1983, Commander, 833rd Air Division; May 1983-Oct. 1983, Commander, 23rd North American Aerospace Defense Command Region /Tactical Air Command Air Division; Oct. 1983-May 1985, Commander USAF Air Defense Weapons Center; promoted to Lt. Gen. 1 May 1987. Ninth Air Force AND USCENTAF air forces and a Middle East expert. Married to a church organist and has two daughters and a son. He hunts quail and regularly golfs. British general de la Billiere describes him as having a slouching posture, often swearing but an excellent officer.

Col. Randolph House, USA, Commander, 2nd Brigade, 1st Cavalry Division.

Capt. Robert E. Houser, USN, Commander of NIAGARA FALLS (AFS-3).

Capt. William Baile Hunt, USN, Commander of WORDEN (CG-18). Born 10 Sept. 1943 in Washington, D.C. USNA, 1965. Meritorious Service Medal; Navy Commendation

Medal (2X); Meritorious Unit Commendation. Naval War College, Command and Staff Junior Course.

Cdr. Richard Jeffrey Ibbotson, RN, Commanding Officer of HMS HURWORTH. Received Distinguished Service Cross for service during Operation Granby.

Capt. Dennis Wayne Irelan, USN, Commander of SACRAMENTO (AOE-1). Born 17 Feb. 1946 in Missouri. USNA, 1968. Navy Commendation Medal, Meritorious Service Medal, Navy Achievement Medal.

Lt. Cdr. Darlene Iskara, USN, Commander of OPPORTUNE (ARS-41). She is the first woman to ever command a U.S. Navy ship. Graduate of San Francisco State University, 1974. Commissioned U.S. Navy officer after Officer Candidate School, 1979. Naval School of Diving and Salvage; Surface Warfare Officer (Basic) School.

Lt. Cdr. David Moore Jackson, USN, Commander of IMPERIOUS (MSO-449). Born 5 Aug. 1956. Navy Achievement Medal, Navy Commendation Medal, Navy Achievement Medal, Meritorious Unit Commendation.

Maj. Gen. James L. Jamerson, USAF, Commander, Proven Force (USAF Task Force operating out of Incirlik, Turkey.

Brig. Gen. Benard Janvier, FA, French commander assuming command 9 Feb..

Maj. Gen. Harry W. Jenkins, Jr., USMC, Commander of 4th Marine Expeditionary Brigade. Born 29 Nov. 1938 in Oakland, California. Graduate of San Jose State College (B.A., 1960) and University of Wisconsin (Masters, 1972). Commissioned, 2nd Lt., 1960. Legion of Merit; Bronze Star (Combat "V", three gold stars); Defense Meritorious Service Medal; Naval Commendation Medal (Combat "V"); Combat Action Ribbon; Presidential Unit Citation (two bronze stars); Navy Unit Commendation; Meritorious Unit Commendation; National Defense Service Medal(one bronze star); Vietnam Service Medal (one silver star); Southwest Asia service Medal (two bronze stars); Sea Service Deployment Ribbon (one bronze star); Arctic Service Ribbon; Republic of Vietnam Cross of Gallantry(one bronze star); Kuwait Liberation Medal. Graduated Basic School, Jan. 1961; promoted 1st Lieutenant Jan. 1962; Jan. 1965-Feb. 1967, Marine Corps Mountain Warfare Training Center, Bridgeport, California (Senior Instructor in the Survival School, Assistant Operations Officer of the Training Center); promoted to captain, June 1965; 1967, Amphibious Warfare School; Jan. 1968 transferred to Republic of Vietnam, (Rifle Company Commander, Operations Officer, and XO, 3rd Battalion, 26th Marines); promoted to major, Nov. 1968; assigned as Civil Affairs Officer, 1st Marine Division, Jan. 1969; Apr. 1969-June 1972 NROTC, University of Wisconsin; Aug. 1975- June 1976 Marine Corps Command and Staff College; Regimental Operations Officer, 9th Marines; promoted to lieutenant colonel July 1977; Aug. 1979-June 1980, Naval War College; July, 1982 promoted to colonel; Aug. 1983, 2nd Marine Division G-3; May 1984, Commanding Officer, 2nd Marine Regiment, 2nd Marine Division; June 1986, Chief of Staff, 2nd Marine Division; 1 Oct. 1987; 22 Aug. 1989, Commanding General, 4th Marine Expeditionary Brigade; promoted to major general 1 Aug. 1990; Assistant Chief of Staff/Director Intelligence Division, HQUSMC, 15 July 1991; 16 Apr. 1993, Director, Expeditionary Warfare Division (staff of Chief of Naval Operations). Major General Jenkins is married and has a daughter and son.

Cdr. Christopher H. Johnson, USN, Commander of VANDEGRIFT (FFG-48).

Lt. Gen. James Houston Johnson, Jr., USA, Commander of 82nd Airborne Division. Born 16 Dec. 1937 in Tuscaloosa, Alabama. USMA, 1960; Shippensburg State College (MA, Public Administration). Infantry School (Basic); Ranger School; Armor School (Advanced); Armed Forces Staff College; US Army War College. Served with the 101st Airborne Division in Vietnam. Retired 31 Oct. 1993.

Col. Jesse Johnson, USA, Commander of 5th Special Forces.

Lt. Col. Robert Johnson, USA, Commander, 4th Battalion, 101st Airborne Division.

Lt. Gen. Robert B. Johnston, USMC. Gen. Schwarzkopf's Marine Chief of Staff. Born in Edinburgh, Scotland 6 Oct. 1937. San Diego State College (B.A., English) and commissioned 2nd Lt., Dec. 1961. United States International University (Master's, Business Administration). Promoted to 1st lieutenant, June 1963; two tours, Vietnam (May 1965, Assistant Regimental S-3, 1st Marine Brigade, 1967-1968, Rifle Company Commander, 3rd Battalion, 9th Marines and as Assistant G-2, 3rd Marine Division); promoted to captain Sept. 1965; Amphibious Warfare School, July 1968; promoted to major Oct. 1971; 1972-1973, Joint U.S. Military Advisory Group, Korea; promoted to lieutenant colonel Mar. 1978; Aug. 1978-June 1979, National War College; July 1981-Feb. 1983, 2nd Battalion, 8th Marine Regiment, 2nd Marine Division; Feb. 1983-May 1984, Commander, 8th Marine Regiment; May 1984, Commander, Officer Candidate School, 21 Aug. 1987 promoted to brigadier general; Sept. 1987, Assistant Division Commander, 3rd Marine Division; Nov. 1987, Commanding General, 9th Marine Amphibious Brigade; 4 May 1990 promoted to major general; 15 June 1990, United States Central Command; May 1991, Deputy Commander in Chief and Chief of Staff, U.S. Central Command; 27 Aug. 1991 promoted to lieutenant general; 6 Sept. 1991 Commanding General I Marine Expeditionary Force/Commanding General Marine Corps Base Camp Pendleton, California; 19 June 1992 relinquished command of Marine Corps Base, Camp Pendleton; Commanding General, I Marine Expeditionary Force until 8 July 1993 (Commander, United Task Force, Operation Restore Hope, Somalia, 9 Dec. 1992-4 May 1993; 19 July 1993, Deputy Chief of Staff for Manpower and Reserve Affairs. Lieutenant General Johnston is married with two sons.

Cdr. Charlie A. Jones, USN, Commander of BREWTON (FF-1086).

Maj. Chris J. Joynson, BA, British Commander of B Company, Staffordshire Regiment. Was honored by being "Mentioned in Despatches" during the Persian Gulf War.

Capt. Albert L. Kaiss, USN, Commander of MISSOURI (BB-63).

Lt. Col. John Kalb, USA, Commander of TF 4-32nd Armor, 1st Brigade, 3rd Armored Division.

Cdr. Curtis Allen Kemp, USN, Commander of FIFE (DD-991). Born 4 Dec. 1949 in California. USNA, 1972.

Cdr. Craig Kennedy, USN, Commander of BREWTON (FF-1086).

Col. Paul Kern, USA, Commander, 2nd Brigade, 24th Infantry Division.

Cdr. Paul K. Kessler, USN, Commander of SAGINAW (LST-1188).

Maj. Gen. William Keys, USMC, Commander of 2nd Marine Division. Born in Fredericktown, Pa. USNA, 1960, Navy Cross, Silver Star, Legion of Merit with "V", Bronze Star ("V"), Republic of Vietnam Cross of Gallantry with Palm and Silver Star, Armed Forces Honor Medal(1st Class), Staff Service Honor Medal (1st Class). 2nd Lt., June 60. Two tours Vietnam, 3rd Battalion, 5th Marines and 6th Marines, Commander. Assistant Commander of 2nd Marine Division, Maj. Gen. 14 Mar. 1989, Commander, 2nd Marine Division, 27 Sept. 1989. Commanding General Fleet Marine Force Atlantic/Commanding General II Marine Expeditionary Force/Commander Striking Force Atlantic/Commanding General Fleet Marine Force Europe, July 1991.

Lt. Col. Abdallah bin Khalid, RSAF, A Saudi prince and Tornado fighter pilot.

Capt. Larry L. King, USN, Commander of ARCADIA (AD-42).

Lt. Col. Henry Lee "Hank" Kinnison, IV, USA, 1st Battalion, 187th Infantry Regiment, 101st Airborne Division. Born 8 Dec. 1948 in New Mexico. USMA, 1972. 101st Airborne Division (1974-77); The Infantry School (1977).

Lt. Col. Don Kline, USAF, Commander, 27th TFS/1st TFW.

Maj. Simon Knapper, BA, British Commander of A Company, Staffordshire Regiment. Earned the Military Cross for service during the Persian Gulf War.

Lt. Col. Michael Kobbe, USA, Commander, 2nd Squadron, 2nd Armored Cavalry Regiment. Born 1 Oct. 1950 in Texas. USMA, 1972. 1/81 Armor (1973); 2/5th Cavalry (1974-75); 3/11 Armored Cavalry Regiment XO, Germany (1975);

Cdr. Timothy Alan Kok, USN, Commander of NEWPORT (LST-1179). Born 13 Feb. 1948 in Michigan. USNA, 1970. Navy Commendation Medal (3X); Navy Achievement Medal; Navy Unit Citation; Meritorious Unit Citation (2X).

Capt. Charles M. Kraft, USN, Commander of DURHAM (LKA-114)

Lt. Gen. Charles C. Krulak, USMC, Commander, Direct Support Group. Born 4 Mar. 1942 in Quantico, Virginia. USNA, 1964 (B.S. Engineering); George Washington University (M.S. in Labor Relations, 1973). Defense Distinguished Service Medal; Distinguished Service Medal; Silver Star; Bronze Star (Combat "V" with two gold stars); Purple Heart (gold star); Meritorious Service Medal; Navy Commendation Medal; Combat Action Ribbon; Presidential Unit Citation (bronze star); National Defense Service Medal (bronze star); Vietnam Service Medal (silver star and two bronze stars); Southwest Asia Service Medal (two bronze stars); Sea Service Deployment Ribbon; Republic of Vietnam Cross of Gallantry; Republic of Vietnam Meritorious Unit Citation (Gallantry Cross Color); Republic of Vietnam Meritorious Unit Citation; Republic of Vietnam Campaign Medal; Kuwait Liberation Medal. Amphibious Warfare School (1968); Army Command and General Staff College (1976); National War College (1982). Two tours in the Republic of Vietnam (platoon and rifle company commander); Commanding Officer, Special Training Branch, and Recruit Series, MCRD, San Diego, California (1966-1968); Commanding Officer, Counter-Guerilla Warfare School, Okinawa (1970); Company Officer, USNA (1970-1973);

Commanding Officer, Marine Barracks, Naval Air Station, North Island, California (1973-1976); Commanding Officer, 3rd Battalion, 3rd Marines (1983-1985); 5 June 1989 promoted to brigadier general; 1 June 1990, Commanding General, 2nd Force Service Group/Commanding General 6th Marine Expeditionary Brigade; 20 Mar. 1992 promoted to major general; 24 Aug. 1992 Commanding General, Marine Corps Combat Development Command. Lieutenant General Krulak is married and has two sons.

Cdr. Jean-Michel L'Henaff, FN, French Commander of COMMANDANT DUCUING.

Cdr. Terrence P. Labrecque, USN, Commander of ANCHORAGE (LSD-36).

Lt. Col. William J. Lake, USAF, Commander of the 415th TFS "Nightstalkers".

Col. Romeo Lalonde, CAF, Commander of all Royal Canadian Air Force Units. Born in 1941. Native of Penetanguishene, Ontario. A 28-year air force veteran at the time of the war he is the oldest son of an automobile repair shop owner and one of 13 children.

Gen. Vincent Lanata, FAF, Commander of French Air Force. Joined air force in Oct. 1957. Certified pilot, 1958. Promoted to General d'Armee Aerienne, Aug. 1989. Promoted to air force commander, Dec. 1991.

Brig. Gen. John Landry, USA, VII Corps Chief of Staff.

R.Adm. John B. LaPlante, USN, Commander of Task Force 156.

Lt. Cdr. Steven E. Lehr, USN, Commander of LEADER (MSO-490).

Col. John LeMoyne, USA, Commander, 1st Brigade, 24th Infantry Division.

Lt. Col. Thomas Leney, USA, Commander of 2-4th Cavalry, 24th Infantry Division.

Cdr. Robert David Liggett, USN, Commander of HAWES (FFG-53). Born 9 May 1949 in Pennsylvania. USNA, 1972.

Brig. Gen. Lawrence H. Livingston, USMC, Commanded 6th Marines, 2nd Marine Division. Born 5 Nov. 1940, in Defiance Ohio. Chapman College, (B.A. in both Economics and Business Administration). Enlisted in Marine Corps in 1960. Navy Cross; Silver Star; Legion of Merit; Bronze Star (with Combat "V" and three gold stars); Purple Heart (four gold stars); Navy Commendation Medal (Combat "V"); Combat Action Ribbon (gold star); Good Conduct Medal; Republic of Vietnam Honor Medal (1st Class); Republic of Vietnam Cross of Gallantry (two silver stars, and one bronze star). 1966, Vietnam (squad leader, platoon sergeant, platoon commander, company gunnery sergeant); Officer Candidates School (Meritorious NCO program), Basic School, 1968; Platoon Commander, 5th Marine Division, 5th MEB & 3rd Marine Division; 1970, Basic Infantry Battalion (Mortar Platoon Commander, Company Commander, Battalion Operations Officer, Battalion XO); promoted to Captain, Apr. 1971; 2nd Vietnam tour, Infantry Advisor (1st Battalion, Vietnamese Marine Corps); June 1973, Amphibious Warfare School; 1976, 5th Marine Regiment, 1st Marine Division (Company Commander, Battalion Operations Officer, Battalion XO); promoted to major July 1978; 1980, Armed Forces Staff College; promoted to Lt. Col. Oct. 1983; 1986-1987, National War College; promoted to colonel, Sept. 1989; 1990,

Commanding Officer, 6th Marines; 6 Apr. 1992, promoted to Brig. Gen. Commanding General, Marine Corps Base, Camp Lejeune. Brigadier General Livingston is married and has two sons and a daughter.

Lt. Cdr. David Lionel Harold Livingstone, RN, Flight Commander on HMS GLOUCESTER. Flew 360 hours supporting naval operations in the war and received the Distinguished Service Cross.

Capt. Palencia Luaces, SN, Spanish Commander of CRISTINA.

Capt. Lucarelli, BN, Belgian Commander of IRIS (Aug 90-Dec 90) and WANDELAAR (Jan. 91).

Gen. Gary Luck, USA, Commander of XVIII Airborne Corps. Born 5 Aug. 1937, Alma, Michigan. Kansas State University (BS-Industrial Engineering); Florida State University (MBA-ORSA/Information Technology); George Washington University (PhD-ORSA/Information Technology). USA Armor School (Basic and Advanced); Armed Forces Staff College; USA War College. Defense Distinguished Service; Distinguished Service (with Oak Leaf Cluster); Legion of Merit (Oak Leaf Cluster); Distinguished Flying Cross(2 Oak Leaf Clusters); Bronze Star (Oak Leaf Cluster); Purple Heart; Meritorious Service Medal; Air Medals; Army Commendation Medal; Humanitarian Service Medal; Combat Infantryman Badge; Master Parachutist Badge; Army Aviator Badge; Air Assault Badge, RANGER. 25 May 60 ROTC commissioned 2nd Lt.; May 60-Aug. 60 Platoon Leader, HQ Troop, 1st Reconnaissance Squadron, 4th Cavalry; Aug. 60-Oct. 60 Student, Armor Officer Basic Course, USA Armor School; Oct. 60-Aug. 62 Platoon Leader, Company C (later Company D and HQ Company, 3rd Medium Tank Battalion (Patton), 69th Armor, 25th Infantry Division. USA Pacific Command, Hawaii; Aug. 62-Mar. 63 Commander, Company B, 3rd Medium Tank Battalion (Patton); (25 May 63 promoted to 1st Lt.); Mar. 63-Nov. 63 Maintenance Officer, HQ Company, 1st Battalion, 69th Armor, 25th Infantry Division; Dec. 63-Mar. 64 Commander, Special Forces "A" Detachment, Company D, 7th Special Forces Group (Airborne), 1st Special Forces, Fort Bragg; Mar. 64-Aug. 64 Assistant Group S-4 (Logistics), 3rd Special Forces Group (Airborne), 1st Special Forces, Fort Bragg; Aug. 64-Aug 65 Adjutant, Special Forces "C" Team, Company D, 5th Special Forces Group (Airborne), 1st Special Forces, USA Vietnam; Aug. 65-Nov. 65 Commander, Detachment "A", Company D, 5th Special Forces Group (Airborne), 1st Special Forces, USA Vietnam; Nov. 65-Mar. 66 S-3 (Operations), 4th Squadron, 12th Cavalry, 5th Infantry Division (Mechanized); Mar. 66-July 66 Student, Officer Rotary Wing Aviator Course, USA Primary Helicopter School, Fort Wolters; July 66-Nov. 66 Student, Officer Rotary Wing Aviator Course, USA Aviation School, Fort Rucker; Nov. 66-Apr. 67 Student, Armor Officer Advanced Course; (25 May 67 promoted to Capt.); Apr. 67-Sept. 67 Platoon Leader, Troop B, 3rd Squadron, 17th Air Cavalry; Oct. 67-Aug. 68 Commander, C Troop (later S-1, 3rd Squadron, 17th Cavalry, 12th Combat Aviation Group, 1st Aviation Brigade, USA, Vietnam; Aug. 68-Apr. 69 Operations Officer, Office of S-3 (Operations) Simmons Army Aviation Command, XVIII Airborne Corps; Aug. 69-June 71 Student, Florida State University; Aug. 71-Jan. 72 Student, Armed Forces Staff College; Jan. 72-May 73 Personnel Staff Officer, Analysis Branch, Capabilities and Analysis Division; (25 May 74 promoted to Major); May 73-May 75 Assistant Chief, Procurement, Education, Research and Training Division; May 75-Dec. 76 Commander, 2nd Squadron, 17th Cavalry, 101st Airborne Division (Air Assault); Dec. 76-Aug. 77 Assistant Chief of Staff, G-3 (Operations), 101st Airborne Division (Air Assault); Aug. 77-June 78 Student, USA War College; June 78-June

79 Chief, Force Modernization Division, Office, Deputy Chief of Staff for Operations, USA Europe; June 79-June 81 Commander, 2nd Brigade, 8th Infantry Division (Mechanized), USA Europe; (25 May 81 promoted to Lt. Col.) June 81-Sept. 82 Chief of Staff, 8th Infantry Division (Mechanized), USA Europe; (15 Mar. 82 promoted to Col.); Sept. 82-June 84 Director of Force Programs, Office of the Deputy Chief of Staff for Operations and Plans, USA, Washington, DC; (1 Aug. 83 promoted to Brig. Gen.); June 84-Aug. 85 Assistant Division Commander, 101st Airborne Division; Aug. 85-Dec. 86 Commanding General, 2nd Infantry Division, 8th USA, Korea; (1 Sept 86 promoted to Maj. Gen.); Dec. 86-Dec. 89 Commanding General, Joint Special Operations Command; 1 Dec. 89 promoted to Lt. Gen.; Dec. 89-June 90 Commanding General, USA Special Operations Command; Aug. 90-Apr. 91 Commanding General, XVIII Airborne Corps; Apr. 91-May 93 Commanding General, XVIII Airborne Corps and Fort Bragg, North Carolina; June 1993 Commander-in-Chief, United Nations Command/Combined Forces Command/Commander, US Forces, Korea. Speaks German.

Maj. Julian Lyme-Perkis, BA, British Commander, Royal Artillery, Staffordshire Regiment.

Maj. Hamish MacDonald, BA, Commander of British 1st Battalion. The Queen's Dragoon Guards.

Col. Bert Maggart, USA, Commander of 1st Brigade, 1st Infantry Division.

Lt. Col. Robert J. "B" Maher, USAF, Commander of the 417th TFTS.

Capt. Nieto Manso, SN, Spanish Commander of VENCEDORA.

Capt. Thomas Fletcher Marfiak, USN, Commander of BUNKER HILL (CG-52). Born 2 Feb. 1944 in Connecticut. USNA, 1966. Defense Distinguished Service Medal; Meritorious Service Medal; Navy Commendation Medal; Navy Achievement Medal, Navy Unit Commendation. Mar. 1992, Director, Surface Warfare Plans/Programs/Requirements Division, Office of the Chief of Naval Operations.

Lt. Col. David Marlin, USA, Commanded 4-37th Armor, 2nd Brigade, 1st Infantry Division.

Cdr. William J. Marshall III, USN, Commanded by GERMANTOWN (LSD-42).

Capt. Marsiam, BN, Belgian commander of DIANTHUS.

Capt. Michael F. Martus, USN, Commander, Destroyer Squadron 14. He commanded the maritime interdiction force and Red Sea surface action group as well as coordinating French and Greek navy units with U.S.

Cdr. Richard B. Marvin, USN, Commander of REASONER (FF-1063).

Andrew Massey, Commander of British Special Forces.

Capt. John J. Mazach, USN, Commander of AMERICA (CV-66). June 1993, Commander Carrier Group Two.

Col. John McBroom, USAF, Commander, 1st Tactical Fighter Wing.

Maj. Gen. Barry Richard McCaffrey, USA, Commander of 24th Infantry Division (Mechanized). Born 17 Nov. 1942 in Taunton, Massachusetts. USMA, 1964; American University, Masters in Government (1970). Silver Star (2X); Bronze Star Medal (3X); Purple Heart (3X), Distinguished Service Cross (2X); Combat Infantry's Badge. 2/325th Infantry, 82nd Airborne Division (1964-66); Military Assistance Command, Vietnam (1966-67); 2/7 Cavalry, 1st Cavalry Division, Vietnam (1968-69); Department of Social Science, USMA (1972-75); Command and General Staff College (1976); XO 2/30th Infantry Division, Germany (1977), Commanding Officer, 2/30th Infantry Division; Army War College (1982). Speaks Spanish.

Capt. Richard J. McCarthy, USN, Commander of RALEIGH (LPD-1).

Lt. Col. Roger McCauley, USA, Commander of 4-229th Attack, 11th Aviation Brigade.

Capt. Doug McClean, CAF, Canadian Commander of PROTECTEUR.

Lt. Col. Richard McDow, USAF, Squadron Commander, 355th Tactical Fighter Squadron. Vietnam Veteran and former Hanoi POW.

Capt. G. Bruce McEwen, USN, Commander of TRIPOLI (LPH-10).

Lt. Col. Mike McGee USA, Commander, 6-6 Infantry, 1st Armored Division. Born in 1950 in Texas. Texas Tech. Commissioned 2nd Lt. 1973. Six foot five inches and 220 pounds.

Lt. Col. Scott W. McKenzie, USMC, Commanded 2nd Reconnaissance Battalion, 2nd Marine Division.

Col. Montgomery Meigs, USA, Commander, 2nd Brigade, 1st Armored Division. USMA. Great-great-grandfather was Quartermaster General of the Union Army in the Civil War. Father killed in action in WW II leading his tank battalion against German troops.

Cdr. Richard Melnick, CAF, Canadian Commander HURON.

Capt.(N) Duncan E. Miller, CAF, Commander, Canadian Task Group 302.3. Enlisted Royal Canadian Navy, 1965; Bishop's University and Sub-Lieutenant, 1968; ASW Air Controller and Navigating Officer, HMCS MARGAREE, 1968-1972; Promoted to Lieutenant and Combat Control Officers Course, 1972, Combat Officer/Class 'A' Air Controller on HMCS SKEENA, 1973; Promoted to Lt. Cdr. 1975; Commander, minesweeper HMCS COWICHAN, 1977; Commander, Second Canadian Training Division, 1978; Royal Naval Staff College, 1978; Executive Assistant to Commander, Maritime Forces Pacific, 1979; XO, HMCS GATINEAU, 1981; Promoted to Cdr., June 84; Commander, HMCS NIPIGON, July 86-Sept. 87; Promoted to Captain, Sept. 87; Commanding Officer, Canadian Forces Maritime Warfare Center from Sept. 87; Deputy Chief of Staff Operational Test Evaluation for Maritime Command, Sept. 88-Aug. 89; Commander, Fist Canadian Destroyer Squadron, Sept. 90. Capt.(N) Miller is married and has three children.

Capt. A.E. Mitchell, USN, Commander of SOUTH CAROLINA (CGN-37).

R.Adm. Riley D. Mixson, USN, Commander of Carrier Group 2 and Commander Naval

Forces Red Sea. Flew 250 combat missions over Vietnam. Director Air Warfare Division, July 1991. Retired 1 Mar. 1994.

Capt. Joseph Scott Mobley, USN, Commander of SARATOGA (CV-60). Born 16 Oct. 1941 in Indiana. USNA, 1966. Legion of Merit; Distinguished Flying Cross; Bronze Star; Air Medal; Purple Heart; Navy Commendation Medal; Executive Assistant to the Deputy Chief of Naval Operations, Aug. 1992; Nov. 1993, Director, Aviation Manpower and Training Branch, Office of the Chief of Naval Operations.

Col. (Prince) Bandar A. Bin Mohammed, RSAF, Commander, 13th Squadron.

Capt. David J. Montgomery, USN, Commander of SHREVEPORT (LPD-12).

Cdr. Glenn Harold Montgomery, USN, Commander of CURTS (FFG-38). Born 18 June 1949 in New York. USNA, 1971; National University (MBA). Navy Commendation Medal; Meritorious Service Medal (2X).

Capt. J.S. Moore, RAN, Australian Commander of WESTRALIA from 9 Oct. 1989 to 9 June 1991. Capt. Moore began his naval career in the British Royal Navy 15 Sept. 1982.

Maj. Gen. Royal N. Moore Jr., USMC, Commander of 3rd Marine Aircraft Wing. Born in Pasadena, California in 1935. Commissioned 2nd Lt., June 1958 (Naval Aviation Cadet program). Graduate, Chapman College (Economics/Business Administration) June 1971. Distinguished Flying Cross and Air Medal with 18 bronze. Fixed wing/helicopter pilot. During the Vietnam War Moore flew 287 combat missions. Retired 1 July 1992.

Col. Anthony Moreno, USA, Commander, 2nd Brigade, 1st Infantry Division.

Cdr. Dennis Gilbert Morral, USN, Commander of NICHOLAS (FFG-47). Born 15 Sept. 1950 in Pennsylvania. USNA, 1972. Navy Commendation Medal (2X).

Wing Commander Richard Vaughan Morris, RAF, Awarded Air Force Cross for Gulf War service.

Brig. Gen. Jean-Charles Mouscardes, FA, French commander relieved 9 Feb..

Cdr. Craig H. Murray, USN, Commander of REID (FFG-30)

Cdr.(s.g.) Henrik Muusfeldt, RDN, Born 8 Mar. 1946. Knight of the Order of Dannebrog; Navy Long Service Medal; Medal of Merit of the Defence Forces; Member of the British Empire; Kuwait Liberation Medal. 1 Nov. 1969, Lieutenant; 1 Nov. 1974 Lieutenant Commander; 1972-1978 Commanding Officer, Danish Fast Patrol Boat; 1978-1982, Chief of Defence, Staff Officer; 1 Feb. 1981, Commander; 1982-1983 Staff course; 1983-1985 Staff Officer; 1985-1986 Executive Officer, corvettes; 1986-1989 Chief of Defence, Staff Officer; 1989-1990 Naval Command College, Newport R.I.; 1990-1991 Commanding Officer, HDMS HVIDBJORNEN; 1 Feb. 1992, Commander (s.g.) 1991-1994 Commanding Officer of corvettes.

Maj. Gen. James Mike Myatt, USMC, Commander of 1st Marine Division. Born in San Francisco, California. Enlisted in Marine Corps Reserve; 2nd Lieutenant May 1963;

Graduate of Sam Houston State University (Physics). Naval Postgraduate School (Masters in Engineering Electronics); Naval War College, Command and Staff Course; Norwegian National Defense College. Distinguished Service Medal, Silver Star, Defense Superior Service Medal, Legion of Merit, Bronze Star Medal (with Combat "V"), Meritorious Service Medal (Gold Star), Joint Service Commendation Medal, Combat Action Ribbon, Vietnamese Honor Medal 1st Class. Two combat tours in Vietnam (platoon commander, S-4 officer, company commander and Vietnamese Marine Corps advisor). Instructor at USNA; XO 3rd Battalion, 2nd Marines; S-4 of 2nd Marines; Assist. Chief of Staff G-5 and Operations Officer, 4th Marines Amphibious Brigade; 17 July 1985-10 Sept. 1987, Commander, 26th Marine Expeditionary Unit; Brig. Gen. 27 June 1988; Aug. 1990, Commanding General, 1st Marine Division, Camp Pendleton; deployed to Saudi Arabia for Persian Gulf War; 15 Jan. 1991, Maj. Gen. 5 Aug. 1992, Assistant Chief of Staff, U.S. Forces, Korea. Maj. Gen. Myatt is married and has two daughters.

Cdr. David E. Myers, USN, Commander of MOUNT VERNON (LSD-39).

Capt. Zarco Narvarro, SN, Spanish Commander of SANTA MARIA.

Col. William Lafayette Nash, USA, Commander 1st Brigade, 3rd Armored Division. Born 10 Aug. 1943 in Arizona. USMA, 1968. Silver Star, Bronze Star Medal (2X, Combat "V"), Purple Heart. 3/3 Armored Cavalry Regiment (1969); 1/11th Armored Cavalry Regiment, Vietnam (1969-70); 82nd Airborne Division (1970-73); Aviation School (1973); 11th Armored Cavalry Regiment, Germany (1975-77); Command and General Staff College (1978).

Brig. Gen. Turki Bin Nasir, SA, Saudi general.

Capt. John Bernard Nathman, USN, Commander of LA SALLE (AGF-3). Born 11 Apr. 1948 in Texas. USNA, 1970. Navy test pilot.

Wing Commander Andrew Ernest Neal, RAF, Awarded Air Force Cross for flying more operational sorties than any of his pilots or captains.

Cdr. Danny C. Nelms, USN, Commander of PENSACOLA (LSD-38)

Cdr.(s.g.) Thor B. Nielsen, RDN, Commander, Danish corvette OLFERT FISCHER. Born 27 Aug. 1943. Knight of the Order of Dannebrog; Navy Long Service Medal; Medal of Merit of the Defence Forces; Kuwait Liberation Medal. 1 Nov. 1968, Lieutenant; 1 Nov. 1973, Lieutenant Commander; 1974-1978 Admiral Danish Fleet, Staff Officer; 1978-1979 Staff course USA/Denmark; 1 Aug. 1979, Commander; 1980-1985 Admiral Danish Fleet, Staff Officer; 1985-1986 Executive Officer and Commanding Officer, corvettes; 1989-1992 Commanding Officer, corvettes; 1 Feb. 1992, Commander (s.g.); 1992-1994, Admiral Danish Fleet, ACOS Operations.

Capt. Konstantinos Nikitiadis, GN, Greek Commander of LIMNOS. Born in 1949 in Athens, Attica. Speaks English and French. He is married with one child.

Col. Anthony Normand, USA, Commander of 4th Psychological Operations Group (POG). Used 117 themes to confuse and "Win hearts and minds" of Iraqi soldiers and civilians.

Lt. Col. Mike O'Connor, USAF, Squadron Commander, 511th Tactical Fighter Squadron (Vultures)

Capt. Michael S. O'Hearn, USN, Commander of IWO JIMA (LPH-2).

Capt. James W. Orvis, USN, Commander of ENGLAND (CG-22).

Lt. Gen. William G. Pagonis, USA, Logistics Commander of the 22nd Support Command. Born 30 Apr. 1941 in Pennsylvania. Pennsylvania State University, 1964 (Commissioned, ROTC), MBA in Business Logistics and Operations Research, 1969. Distinguished Service Medal, Legion of Merit, Silver Star, Bronze Star. Germany 1965. South Vietnam, 1097th Transportation Company (Medium Boat) 1967-1968. South Vietnam, 1970-1971. Command and General Staff College, 1972. Congressional liaison officer, 1975. 10th Transportation Battalion, Fort Eustis, 1977. Naval War College, 1979. Panama, 193rd Infantry Brigade, Commander of Logistics Support Command 1980-1981. Division Support Command, 4th Infantry Division, 1982. 21st Support Command, 1985. June 1988, selected for Major General. Commanding General, 21st Theater Army Area Command, U.S. Army Europe and 7th Army.

Brig. Gen. Leslie M. Palm, USMC, Commanded 10th Marines, 2nd Marine Division. Born 14 Oct. 1944 in Marysville, California. University of Oregon, 1966; Army Command and General Staff College (Master's, Military Arts and Sciences, 1980); Naval War College (M.A. National Security and Strategic Studies). Legion of Merit (Combat "V", gold star); Meritorious Service Medal; Navy Commendation Medal (Combat "V", two gold stars). Commissioned 2nd lieutenant, 1 Nov. 1966; Field Artillery Officer's Basic Course graduate, Nov. 1967; Dec. 1967-Dec. 1968 Vietnam (Forward Observer and Fire Direction Officer, 1st Battalion, 13th Marines at Khe Sahn and commanded a 155mm gun platoon and 8" platoon, 5th 155mm Gun Battery); promoted to captain, 1 Dec. 1970; Jan. 1972, Commander, "D" Battery, 2nd Battalion, 12th Marines, 3rd Marine Division; promoted to major 1 July 1977; July 1977-June 1979 S-3 Officer, 1st Battalion, 10th Marines, 2nd Marine Division; June 1980, graduated Army Command General Staff College; 1 July 1982, promoted to lieutenant colonel; Oct. 1983-July 1985 Commander, 4th Battalion (redesignated 5th Battalion), 11th Marines; June 1986 graduated Naval War College; 1 Oct. 1988 promoted to colonel; 16 Aug. 1990 Commander 10th Marines, 2nd Marine Division; 1 May 1992 promoted to brigadier general; Assistant Deputy Chief of Staff for Manpower and Reserve Affairs, HQUSMC. Brigadier General Palm is married and has two children.

Lt. Col. Michael Parker, USA, Commander of 1-5th Cavalry.

Capt. Nigel E. Parkhurst, USN, Commander of DENVER (LPD-9).

Capt. Bernard W. Patton, USN, Commander of WHITE PLAINS (AFS-4).

Capt. Bob Riley Patton, Jr., USN, Commander of LEYTE GULF (CG-55). Born 10 Jan. 1944 in Kentucky. USNA, 1967. Meritorious Service Medal (2X); Navy Commendation Medal (2X); Navy Achievement Medal.

Gen. James Henry Binney Peay III, USA, Commander of 101st Airborne Assault Division. Born 10 May 1940 in Richmond, Virginia. Virginia Military Institute (BS, Civil Engineering); George Washington University. Field Artillery School (Basic and Advanced);

USA Command and General Staff College; US Army War College. Aug. 1994, Commander in Chief, U.S. Central Command.

Capt. Perez Perez, SN, Spanish Commander of I. ELENA.

Capt. Joseph W. Perrotta, Jr., USN, Commander of NORMANDY (CG-60).

Col. Dan Petrosky, USA, 4th Brigade, 1st Armored Division (Aviation Brigade).

Capt. Braden James Phillips, USN, Commander of OGDEN (LPD-5). Born 23 July 1946 in New York. USNA, 1968. Navy pilot. Meritorious Service Medal(3X); Navy Unit Commendation; Combat Action Ribbon; Meritorious Unit Commendation.

Capt. William W. Pickavance, USN, Commander of MARS (AFS-1).

Cdr. K. John Pickford, CAF, Canadian Commander of HMCS ATHABASKAN. Born in Halifax. Enlisted in Royal Canadian Navy/ commissioned sub-lieutenant, 1973. Duty on various East Coast destroyers; Navigating Officer, HMCS ANNAPOLIS/promoted lieutenant, 1977; Combat Officer, HMCS ALGONQUIN/promoted Lt. Cdr., 1981; XO, HMCS PROTECTEUR, Dec. 88; Commander, HMCS ATHABASKAN, July 90. Cdr. Pickford is married and has two daughters.

Capt. Curiel Pina, SN, Spanish Commander of DIANA.

Capt. Dana Pittard, USA, Commander, "D" Company, 1-37 Armor, 1st Armored Division. USMA. U.S. Army Airborne and Ranger Schools. MacArthur Award. Married.

Wing Commander George William Pixton, RAF, Commanded Jaguar Detachment at Muharraq, Bahrain (first British Air elements to arrive after invasion). Awarded Distinguished Flying Cross.

Capt. Don P. Pollard, USN, Commander of MISSISSIPPI (CGN-40).

Gen. Colin Powell, USA, Born Apr. 5, 1937 in Harlem, New York. Graduated Morris High School, N.Y. 1954. City College of New York (Geology Major, Reserve Officers' Training Corps cadet Col.) 1958. Purple Heart, Bronze Star Legion of Merit. Military Adviser, South Vietnam 1962-63, 1968-69. George Washington University, (Master's of Business Administration), 1971. White House Fellow, 1972. Korea, Battalion Commander, 1973. 101st Airborne Division, 2nd Brigade commander 1975. National War College, 1976. 4th Infantry Division, 1981-83. Senior Military Assistant, Secretary of Defense, 1983-86. V Corps, commander 1986. Chairman, Joint Chiefs of Staff. Six feet tall, 200 lbs., Powell is married and has three children. Religion is Episcopalian and his favorite hobby is repairing Volvos.

Capt. Edmund Lee Pratt, Jr., USN, Commander of YELLOWSTONE (AD-41). Born 5 Sept. 1943 in Florida.

Capt. M.L. Proctor, RAN, Australian Commander of ADELAIDE from 3 Jan. 1991 to 4 Nov. 1992. Capt. Proctor joined the Navy 19 Jan. 1970.

Col. Theodore Purdom, USA, Commander, 2nd Brigade, 101st Airborne Division.

Capt. D.J. Ramsay, RAN, Australian Commander of HMAS SUCCESS from 15 Mar. 1991 to 8 June 1993. Capt. Ramsay joined the Navy 29 Jan. 1963.

Maj. Austin Ramsden, BA, British Commander of B Squadron, Staffordshire Regiment.

Cdr. Dale A. Rauch, USN, Commander of MANITOWOC (LST-1180).

Capt. Eddie Stephen Ray, USMC, Commander, Company B, 1st Battalion, 1st Marines. Born in Los Angeles. University of Washington. Earned Navy Cross for his company's defending the division command post by the Al Burqan Oilfield (the most important battle of the 1st Marine Division in Desert Storm).

Capt. James Armstrong Reid, USN, Commander of GOLDSBOROUGH (DDG-20). Born 12 July 1947 in Massachusetts. USNA, 1969; University of Colorado (M.S.) 1973. Meritorious Service Medal; Navy Commendation Medal.

Lt. Col. Gene Renuart, USAF, Squadron Commander, 76th Tactical Fighter Squadron (Vanguards).

Maj. Gen. Thomas G. Rhame, USA, Born 27 Jan. 1941, Winnfield, Louisiana. Louisiana State University, 1963 (Accounting). ROTC, commissioned 1963. Syracuse University, Master of Business Administration. Infantry Basic and Advanced courses, Airborne School, Armed Forces Staff College, U.S. Army War College. Distinguished Service Medal, Silver Star (with Oak Leaf cluster), Legion of Merit, Bronze Star with "V" Device (with two Oak Leaf clusters), the Meritorious Service Medal(with two Oak Leaf clusters), the Air Medal, Army Commendation Medal with "V" device, Combat Infantry Badge, General Staff Identification Badge. Platoon and Company Commander 1st Battalion, 87th Infantry (Baumholder, Germany. Two tours in Vietnam (Commanded B Company, 1st Battalion, 12th Cavalry in 1967, District Senior Advisor, USAMACV, 1971). Has served as Assistant Chief of Staff for Personnel, Commander, 2nd Brigade, 3rd Infantry Division (Kitzingen, Germany. Chief of Staff, 3rd Armored Division (Frankfurt, Germany, Commander of 1st Infantry Division. Married with two children.

Col. John E. Rhodes, USMC, Commander of 13th Marine Expeditionary Unit (Special Operations Capable). Born in California. San Jose State University, 1966 (B.S. in Business and Industrial Management). University of Southern California, Systems Management, 1973. Silver Star (2X); Distinguished Flying Cross (4X); Air Medal; Combat "V"; Purple Heart; Combat Action Ribbon. USMC Officers Candidates School, 1967; Naval Aviator, Aug. 1968; HML-367/1st Marine Aircraft Wing, Phu Bai, Republic of Vietnam (flying CH-46s), 1969; 3rd Marine Aircraft Wing (1970, 1976); Command and Staff College, 1978; Commanding Officer, Air Base Squadron 36, 1st Marine Aircraft Wing; Commanding Officer, HMM-163, 3rd Marine Aircraft Wing; Army War College; Logistics Officer, 1st Marine Division, 1987; Assistant Chief of Staff, G-4, 5th MEB, 1988-89; Commanding Officer, MEU, 26 July 1989.

Col. Jim Riley, USA, Commander, 1st Brigade, 1st Armored Division.

Capt. Munoz-Delgado Diaz Del Rio, SN, Spanish Commander of DESCUBIERTA.

Commo. C.A. Ritchie, RAN, Australian Commander of HMAS BRISBANE from 25 June 1990 to 29 Oct. 1991. He joined the Navy 25 Jan. 1965.

Lt. Col. G. "Pat" Ritter, USA, Commander of 1-34th Armor, 1st Brigade, 1st Infantry Division.

Cdr. Jean-Paul Robyns, BN, Belgian commander of IRIS. Born in Menen, Belgium 13 May 1952. Royal Athenaum College (Latin-Greek). Speaks Dutch, French, English, and German. Married, he has two sons and enjoys long distance running (3 hours is his best time in the marathon) and reading history books.

Maj. John M. Rochelle, BA, British Commander of C Company, Staffordshire Regiment. Earned Military Cross during the Persian Gulf War.

Lt. Col. Charles T. Rogers, BA, British commander of 1st Battalion, The Staffordshire Regiment. Earned OBE for service during Persian Gulf War.

Col. Ronald Rokosz, USA, Commander, 2nd Brigade, 82nd Airborne Division.

Cdr. David C. Rollins, USN, Commander of THOMAS C. HART (FF-1092).

Lt. Gen. Michel Roquejeoffre, FA, Commander of French Forces.

Cdr. Rossignol, FN, French Commander of DOUDART DE LAGREE.

Brig. Gen. Peter J. Rowe, USMC, Commander of 5th Marine Expeditionary Brigade. Born in Connecticut in 1938. Xavier University, 1962. Commissioned 2nd Lt., 1962. San Diego State University (Masters). Vietnamese Language. During battles for Hue City and Khe Sanh, South Vietnam commanded an interrogation-translation team. Assistant Commander, 1st Marine Division. Retired, 1 Sept. 1992.

Capt. John Russell, USA, Commander of A Company, 1-327th Infantry, 101st Airborne. Maneuvered unit to attack Iraqi bunkers near FOB Cobra.

Capt. Charles R. Saffell, Jr., USN, Commander of GUAM (LPH-9). July 1993, Deputy Director for Unified and Specified Command, Joint Chiefs of Staff.

Lt. Col. Saeed, RSAF, Commander 7th Squadron.

Capt. Saille, BN, Belgian commander of ZINNIA (Jan. 91-Apr 91).

Col. David Sawyer, USAF, Wing Commander, 76th Tactical Fighter Squadron (Vanguards).

Lt. Col. John Schmader, USA, Commander, 1st Battalion, 505th Parachute Infantry Regiment, 82nd Airborne Division.

Col. Larry S. Schmidt, USMC, commanded 8th Marines, 2nd Marine Division.

Gen. H. Norman Schwarzkopf, USA, Born Aug. 22, 1934 in Trenton, New Jersey. Educated in Iran, Switzerland, Germany and Italy, 1946-51. USMA, 1956 (43rd in class of

480. Purple Heart (2X), Silver Star (3X), Bronze Star (3X), Distinguished Service Medal. 101st Airborne Division, 1957-59. Berlin, Germany, 1959-1961. Univ. of Southern California (Guided Missile Engineering, Masters) 1964. USMA, Instructor, 1964-65. Adviser, South Vietnam, 1965-66. USMA, Mechanical Engineering Instructor, 1966-68. Command & General Staff College, 1968-69. 1st Battalion, 6th Infantry, 198th Infantry Brigade, Americal Division, commander, 1969-70. 172nd Infantry Brigade, 1974-76. 1st Brigade, 9th Infantry Division, commander, 1976-78. U.S. Pacific Command (Deputy Director, 1978-80. 8th Mechanized Infantry Division (assistant commander) 1980-82. Grenada Operation, Deputy Commander Joint Task Force, 1983. 24th Mechanized Infantry Division, 1983-85 (Commander). Assistant Deputy Army Chief of Staff, 1985-86. I Corps, (Commander), 1986-87. Deputy Army Chief of Staff, 1987-88. U.S. Central Command, 1988-91. Six feet three inches tall, 240 lbs., Schwarzkopf is married with three children (two daughters and a son), and enjoys fishing, skeet shooting and tennis.

Capt. R.E. Shalders, RAN, Australian Commander of HMAS DARWIN from 11 Aug. 1990 to 3 Feb. 1991. Capt. Shalders joined the Navy 23 Jan. 1967.

Col. Sandy Sharpe, USAF, Wing Commander, 355th Tactical Fighter Squadron (Falcons).

Lt. Col. Rick Shatzel, USAF, Squadron Commander, 353rd Tactical Fighter Squadron (Panthers).

Cdr. Eric B. Shaver, USN, Commander of CIMARRON (AO-177).

Maj. Pat Shull, USA, Commander of TF Shull, 24th Infantry Division.

Capt. John Fleet Sigler, USN, Commander of BELKNAP (CG-26). Born 2 Sept. 1943 in Virginia. USNA, 1966 (22 in class of 868); Stanford University. July 1993, Commander, Amphibious Group One.

Capt. Edward J. Simmons, USN, Commander of SYLVANIA (AFS-2).

Cdr. Michael Doyle Simpson, USN, Commander of MARVIN SHIELDS (FF-1066). Born 20 Feb. 1951 in Kentucky. USNA, 1973.

Lt. Cdr. Kemp L. Skudin, USN, Commander of BEAUFORT (ATS-2).

Commo. Graham V. Sloper, RAN, Australian Commander of HMAS SUCCESS from 19 Dec. 1988 to 14 Mar. 1991. Commo. Sloper joined the Navy 28 Jan. 1958.

Cdr. Douglas Arthur Smartt, USN, Commander of FRANCIS HAMMOND (FF-1067). Born 20 July 1949 in Tennessee. USNA, 1971. Combat Action Ribbon; Defense Meritorious Service Medal (3X); Navy Commendation Medal (2X); Meritorious Unit Commendation.

Wing Commander Ian Travers Smith, RAF, Led first operational mission from Tabuk and by the end of the war had flown a total of 20 operational sorties for which he was awarded the Distinguished Service Order.

R.Adm. Raymond Charles Smith, Jr., USN, Commander Naval Special Warfare Group.

Born 6 July 1943 in California. 1967 USNA. Bronze Star, Navy Commendation Medal. Meritorious Service Medal. Underwater Demolition Team platoon commander, Vietnam. Commanded SEAL Delivery Team ONE, and Naval Special Warfare School, Coronado, California. Command conducted 270 SEAL missions during Persian Gulf War without a casualty. June 1992, Commander, Naval Special Warfare Command.

Maj. Gen. Rupert Smith, BA, Commander of 1st Armoured Division, British Army. Lt. Gen. de la Billiere describes him as being refreshingly unorthodox in his ideas. Dark and handsome with grey streaks in his hair Smith has a logical mind.

Cdr. Thomas E. Snyder, USN, Commander of HARRY W. HILL (DD-986).

Cdr. William L. Snyder, USN, Commander of JARRETT (FFG-33).

Cdr. William W. Spotts, USN, Commander of FORD (FFG-54).

Lt. Col. Terry Stanger, USA, Commander of TF 3-69th Armor, 24th Infantry Division.

Col. Doug Starr, USA, Commander of 3rd Armored Cavalry Regiment

Capt. Gonzalez Aller Suevos, SN, Spanish Commander of VICTORIA.

Maj. Suleiman, RKA, Operations officer of the Kuwaiti 35th Armored Brigade. Graduate, Jordanian Army Staff College.

Cdr. William D. Sullivan, USN, Commander of SAMPSON (DDG-10).

Gen. Prince Khalid bin Sultan, Saudi prince and commander of Arab-Islamic Force. Sandhurst, Auburn University (master's degree in political science) U.S. Air Force Air War College. Described as burly and genial.

Commo. Kenneth J. Summers, CAF, Canadian Theater Commander, Bahrain and Chief of Staff Operations, Maritime Command Headquarters, and Commander, Canadian Fleet. Officer Cadet, Royal Roads Military College, 1963; Graduate, Royal Military College, Kingston, 1967; Long Operations Course, 1972; XO, HMCS ATHABASKAN; CO HMCS ALGONQUIN; Canadian Forces Command and Staff College; promoted to Captain July 1985; Commander, Second Canadian Destroyer Squadron, 1988; promoted to Commodore, 1989. Resides in Halifax with his wife, son and daughter. Eldest son is a naval officer-cadet at RRMC, Victoria, B.C.

Col. John B. Sylvester, USA, Commanded 1st Brigade (Tiger Brigade), 2nd Armored Division attached to the 2nd Marine Division.

R.Adm. Raynor Andrew K. Taylor, USN, Commander of Middle East Force (Flagship, LASALLE (AGF-13). Born 22 Dec. 1935 in Massachusetts. USNA, 1960 (61 in class of 797). Legion of Merit (3X); Navy Commendation Medal; Meritorious Service Medal; Meritorious Unit Citation. (Special Assistant to Commander Naval Surface Force, U.S. Atlantic Fleet, Dec., 1992. Retired 1 May 1993.

Capt. Ernest Francis Tedeschi, Jr., USN, Commander of VALLEY FORGE (CG-50). Born

28 Mar. 1942 in Connecticut. USNA, 1965. Meritorious Service Medal; Navy Commendation Medal (2X); Oct. 1993, Commander, Naval Base San Francisco/Commander Logistics Group One.

Cdr. Thomas W. Thiesse, USN, Commander of FREDERICK (LST-1184).

Capt. Mack A. Thomas, USN, Commander of OKINAWA (LPH-3).

Lt. Col. Jerry Thompson, USA, Commander, 1st Battalion, 5th Special Forces Group.

Cdr. Alan Douglas Thomson, USN, Commander of FLINT (AE-32). Born 7 June 1950 in Florida. USNA, 1972.

Lt. Cdr. Steven E. Thorton, USN, Commander of ADROIT (MSO-509).

Capt. Harold J. Tickle, USN, Commander of INCHON (LPH-12).

Capt. Alejandro Jose Tierno, AN, Argentinean Captain of destroyer A.R.A. HERCULES. Born 12 Jan. 1945 in Buenos Aires. Enlisted in Argentina Navy 1 Feb. 1961. Midshipman, 30 Dec. 1966; Corvette Lieutenant, 31 Dec. 1968; Frigate Lieutenant, 31 Dec. 1971; Ship Lieutenant, 31 Dec. 1973; Corvette Captain, 31 Dec. 1979; Frigate Captain, 31 Dec. 1985; Ship Captain, 31 Dec. 1990.

Gen. John Harold Tilelli, Jr., USA Commander of the 1st Cavalry Division. Born 2 Oct. 1941, Brooklyn, New York. Pennsylvania Military College (BS-Economics); Lehigh University (MA-Education Administration). ROTC commissioned 2 June 1963. USA Armor School (Basic and Advanced); USMC Command and Staff College; USA War College. Distinguished Service Medal (Oak Leaf Cluster); Legion of Merit; Bronze Star (with "V" Device); Bronze Star (with Oak Leaf Cluster); Meritorious Service Medal (3 Oak Leaf Clusters); Air Medal; Army Commendation Medal (2 Oak Leaf Clusters); Combat Infantryman Badge; Parachutist Badge; Army Staff Identification Badge. Aug. 63-Oct. 63 Student, Armor Officer Basic Course; Oct. 63-Nov. 64 Platoon Leader (later XO, HQ Company), 3rd Battalion, 77th Armor; Nov. 64-Feb. 65 S-3 (Air), 3rd Battalion, 77th Armor; Mar. 65-Jan. 66 XO, Troop C, Reconnaissance Squadron, 2nd Armored Cavalry Regiment, USA Europe; (2 June 66 promoted to 1st Lt.) Jan. 66-July 66 Liaison Officer (later Assistant Adjutant, and later Adjutant) 2nd Reconnaissance Squadron, 2nd Armored Cavalry Regiment, USA Europe; July 66-Sept. 66 Commander, Troop E, 2nd Reconnaissance Squadron, 2nd Armored Cavalry Regiment, USA Europe; Sept. 66-Oct. 67 Commander, Headquarters Company, 18th Engineer Brigade, USA Vietnam; Jan 68-Sept. 68 Student, Armor Officer Advanced Course, USA Armor School; (2 June 70 promoted to Capt.); Sept. 68-Nov. 71 Assistant Professor of Military Science, Lafayette College; Nov. 71-Mar. 72 Student, Vietnam Training Center, Foreign Service Institute, Washington, DC; Mar. 72-Jan. 73 District Senior Advisor, Advisory Team 84, USMACV, Vietnam; Jan. 73-Aug. 73 Operations Officer, Electronics Command, USA Material Command; Aug. 73-Jan. 74 Student, Marine Corps Command and Staff College; June 74-Aug. 75 S-3, 1st Squadron, 11th Armored Cavalry Regiment, USA Europe; Aug. 75-June 77 XO, 1st Squadron, 11th Armored Cavalry Regiment (later S-3), 11th Armored Cavalry Regiment, USA Europe; (2 June 77 promoted to Major, 2 Aug. 77 promoted to Lt. Col.); July 77-Apr. 78 Chief, Platoon Tactical Division, Command and Staff, USA Armor School; Apr. 78-Nov. 79 Commander, 2nd Squadron, 6th Cavalry, USA Armor School; Nov. 79-June 81 Armor

Force Integration Staff Officer; June 81-July 82 Assistant Director of the Army Staff; Aug. 82-June 83 Student USA War College; (1 Sept. 83 promoted to Col.); June 83-Nov. 83 Chief, Ground Combat Systems Division; Nov. 83-Aug. 85 Chief of Staff, 1st Armored Division, USA Europe; Aug. 85-May 87 Commander, 2nd Armored Cavalry Regiment, USA Europe; May 87-Apr. 88 Chief of Staff, VII Corps, USA Europe; 1 Aug. 88 promoted to Brig. Gen.; (1 Oct. 91 promoted to Maj. Gen.) July 90-Aug. 92 Commanding General, 1st Cavalry Division; Aug. 92-Mar. 93 Assistant Deputy Chief of Staff for Operations and Plans, Washington. Speaks German.

Cdr. Terry W. Tilton, USN, Commander of PEORIA (LST-1183).

Capt. Roy W. Tobin, USN, Commander of JASON (AR-8).

Wing Commander Glenn Lester Torpy, RAF, Regularly led missions, often alone and was awarded the Distinguished Service Order for his *"selfless leadership and devotion to duty."*

Cdr. John W. Townes III, USN, Commander of SAMUEL B. ROBERTS (FFG-58).

Capt. Wilbur Cobb Trafton, USN, Commander of SEATTLE (AOE-3). Born 31 Jan. 1944 in Florida. USNA, 1966. Meritorious Service Medal; Navy Commendation Medal; Air Medal; Navy Unit Citation.

Lt. Col. William Tucker, USA, Commander, 1st Battalion, 82nd Aviation Regiment, 82nd Airborne Division.

V.Adm. Jerry L. Unruh, USN, Commander of INDEPENDENCE (CF-62), Commander, Third Fleet, Apr., 1991.

Capt. Abal Lopez-Valeiras, SN, Spanish Commander of REINA SOFIA.

Lt. Col. Robert VanAntwerp, USA, 326th Engineer Battalion, 101st Airborne Division.

Capt. VanDyck, BN, Belgian Commander of ZINNIA (Aug 90-Dec 90).

Cdr. Joseph M. Volpe, USN, Commander of HEWITT (DD-966).

Capt. Gary Martin Voorheis, USN, Commander of VIRGINIA (CGN-38). Born 6 Oct. 1945 in New York. Meritorious Service Medal; Navy Commendation Medal.

Lt. Gen. Cal Waller, USA, Commander of 3rd Army after 15 Feb.

Col. George Walton, USAF, Commander, 35th TFW.

Lt. Col. John Ward, USA, Commander, 2-1 Aviation, 1st Armored Division

Cdr. William H. Ward, USN, Commander of NITRO (AE-23).

Lt. Col. Charles C. Ware, USA, Commander, 2nd Battalion, 7th Infantry Regiment, 24th Infantry Division.

Cdr. Christopher Edward Weaver, USN, Commander of SPRUANCE (DD-963). Born 4 July 1949 in Missouri. USNA, 1971. Navy Commendation Medal (3X); Combat Action Ribbon.

Capt. Floyston A. Weeks, USN, Commander of JOUETT (CG-29).

Col. David Weisman, USA, Commander, 3rd Brigade, 1st Infantry Division.

Cdr. G.A. Wellham, RAN, Australian Commander of HMAS WESTRALIA from 10 June 1991 to 25 Nov. 1992. Cdr. Wellham joined the Navy 20 Jan. 1969.

Capt. Mark D. Wessman, USN, Commander of MOUNT HOOD (AE-29).

Col. Al Whitley, USAF, Commander of the 37th TFW.

Lt. Col. Jerry Wiedewitsch, USA, Commander, 1-35 Armor, 2nd Brigade, 1st Armored Division.

Cdr. Philip Lawrence Wilcocks, RN, Commanding Officer, HMS GLOUCESTER. Received Distinguished Service Cross for his service.

Capt. Jean Wild, FN, French Commander, of CLEMENCEAU.

Cdr. Joseph B. Wilkinson, Jr., USN, Commander of BARBOUR COUNTY (LST-1195).

Cdr. Thomas J. Wilson, USN, Commander of BARBEY (FF-1088).

Capt. Timothy Paul Winters, USN, Commander of KALAMAZOO (AOR-6). Born 22 Dec. 1942 in New Jersey. USNA, 1967.

Wing Commander Jeremy John Witts, RAF, Awarded the Distinguished Service Order for key missions including the attacks on Mudaysis Airfield and Al Kut Petroleum Production Facility.

Capt. Thomas Wock, USA, Commanded D Tank Company, 4-37th Armor, 2nd Brigade, 1st Infantry Division.

Capt. Stephen Russell Woodall, USN, Commander of MOBILE BAY (CG-53). Born 6 Oct. 1945 in Washington, D.C. USNA, 1967. Naval War College, Command and Staff, Junior Course. Bronze Star; Combat Action Ribbon; Navy Commendation Medal; Navy Unit Commendation.

Cdr. Dennis Lee Worley, USN, Commander of HALEAKALA (AE-25). Born 9 Nov. 1950 in Virginia. USNA, 1972. Navy Commendation Medal (2X); Navy Unit Commendation; Meritorious Unit Commendation.

Air Vice-Marshal William Wratten, RAF, British Royal Air Force commander. Former fighter pilot. Royal College of Defense Studies. Falklands Islands veteran. Described as stocky and balding with common sense and sincerity. Air warfare expert.

Lt. Col. Bruce Wright, USAF, Commanded 614th Tactical Fighter Squadron.

Lt. Gen. John Yeosock, USA, Commander of 3rd Army, relieved 15 Feb. Born 18 Mar. 1937 in Wilkes-Barre, Pennsylvania. Pennsylvania State University, (BS-Industrial Engineering) US Naval Post Graduate School (MS-Operations Research and Systems Analysis); University of Pittsburgh (Advanced Management Program for Executives). US Armor School (Basic); USMC Amphibious Warfare School; Armed Forces Staff College; National War College. ROTC Commission, 28 Aug. 1959. Sept. 59-Nov. 59 Student, Armor Officer Basic Course; Nov. 59-June 61 Platoon Leader (later XO, later Commander) Troop L, 3rd Reconnaissance Squad, 3rd Armored Cavalry Regiment; June 61-Aug. 62 Platoon Leader, Combat Support Company, 2nd Battle Group, 1st Infantry, 2nd Infantry Division; 28 Aug. 62, promoted to 1st Lt.; Sept. 62-Nov. 62 Student, Armor Communication Class, USA Army School; Dec. 62-June 64 Liaison Officer, HQ and HQ Troop (later Commander) Troop K, 3rd Reconnaissance Squadron, 3rd Armored Cavalry Regiment, USA Europe; July 65-Jan. 66 Student, Amphibious Warfare School, USMC; (Promoted 28 Aug. 66 to Capt.); Jan. 66-May 67 Subsector Advisor, Advisory Team 93, USMACV, Vietnam; May 67-Oct. 69 Student, Operations Research/Systems Analysis, Naval Postgraduate School; Oct. 69-June 70 Student, Armed Forces Staff College; July 70-Mar. 72 Operations Research Analyst, Office of the Assistant Vice Chief of Staff, Army, Washington, DC; Mar. 72-June 73 Analyst, Office of the Project Manager for Reorganization of the Army, Office of the Chief of Staff; (Promoted 28 Aug. 73 to Maj.); June 73-June 75 Commander, 3rd Squadron (later Special Assistant to the Commander) 3rd Armored Cavalry Regiment; Aug. 75-June 76 Student, National War College; July 76-July 78 Chief, Force Development Branch, Office, Assistant Chief of Staff, Operations, J-3, United Nations Command/US Forces Korea/Eighth USA, Korea; Sept. 78-Feb. 80 Commander, 194th Armored Brigade; (Promoted 28 Aug. 80 to Lt. Col.); Feb. 80-June 81 Chief of Staff, 1st Cavalry Division; (Promoted to Brig. Gen. 22 Jan. 82); June 81-June 83 Project Manager, Saudi Arabian National Guard Modernization, Saudi Arabia; June 83-Jan. 84 Assistant Division Commander, 1st Cavalry Division; (Promoted to Maj. Gen. 1 Oct. 84); Jan. 84-June 86 Deputy Chief of Staff for Operations, USA Forces Command; June 86-May 88 Commanding General, 1st Cavalry Division; May 88-Mar. 89 Assistant Deputy Chief of Staff for Operations and Plans, Office of the Deputy Chief of Staff for Operations and Plans, USA, Washington, DC; (Promoted to Lt. Gen. 16 Mar. 89); Mar. 89-Aug. 90 Deputy Commanding General, Forces Command/Commanding General, 3rd USA; Aug. 90-Apr. 91 Commander, ARCENT, Persian Gulf War; Apr. 91-Jul 92 Deputy Commanding General, Forces Command/Commanding General, 3rd USA; 6 feet tall and thin he smokes cigars.

Col. Daniel Zanini, USA, Commander, 3rd Brigade, 1st Armored Division.

Maj. Gen. Mahammad Bin Zayed, Commander, Armed Forces of the United Arab Emirates.

V.Adm. Ronald J. Zlatoper, USN, Commander Carrier Group 7. Born in Cleveland, Ohio. Rensselaer Polytechnic Institute (B.S. in mathematics), 1963. George Washington University (Masters in Data Systems); Massachusetts Institute of Technology (Masters in management). Naval War College (William S. Sims Award). Commissioned in 1963 through Rensselaer's Naval ROTC program. Defense Distinguished Service Medal, Navy Distinguished Service Medal, Legion of Merit, Distinguished Flying Cross, Meritorious Service Medal, Air Medal, Navy Commendation Medal (with Combat "V"). 1965-68 flew an A-6 "Intruder" over North Vietnam with Attack Squadron 65. 1975-77, Air-to-Surface Guided Missile Program Coordinator/F/A-18 Coordinator, office of Chief of Naval

Operations. 1978-80 Executive Officer and Commanding Officer of Attack Squadron 85. 1982-83 , Commander, Carrier Air Wing 1. 1983-85 Military Assistant, Secretary of Defense. 1986-87, Senior Air Wing Commander, Carrier Air Wing 15. 1987-88, Chief of Staff for Commander 7th Fleet on Blue Ridge (LCC-19). Promoted R.Adm. 1988. Commanding Carrier Group 7 in the Persian Gulf War he was the Anti-Surface Warfare Commander in the Arabian Gulf responsible for the destruction of the Iraqi Navy. His battle group ships and aircraft participated in the first aircraft and cruise missile attacks on Iraqi forces. Zlatoper is married with a daughter and son. Chief of Naval Personnel/Deputy Chief of Naval Operations, Manpower & Personnel, 7 Nov. 1991.

BIBLIOGRAPHY

PUBLISHED WORKS

Abu-Mansoor, Fauad. Al-Sbooh Al-Araby (Newspaper), August 13, 1990.

Adkins, Ronald A. "Iron Sappers Lead the Way: The 16th Engineer Battalion's Support of the 1st Armored Division in Southwest Asia." Army War College paper. March 1993. 77 p.

Admire, Brig Gen. John H. Admire. "The Third Marines in Desert Shield." *Marine Corps Gazette*, August 1991, pp.81-84.

_____. "The Third Marines in Desert Storm." *Marine Corps Gazette*, September 1991, pp. 67-71.

Al-Nakhi, Brig. Gen. Ibrahim M. "The Gulf War: U.A. E. Participation in the War." Army War College paper, April 1993, 40 p.

Armstrong, Lt. Col. Charles L. "Early Observations on Desert Shield." *Marine Corps Gazette*, January 1991, pp. 34-36.

"Army's Patriot:High-Tech Superstar of Desert Storm." *Army.* March 1991, pp.40-42.

Arntz, Stephen J. "Roadrunner Operations in Desert Storm.", *Field Artillery*, June 1991, pp.35-39.

Arthur, V. Adm. Stanley R. "Desert Storm at Sea." *U.S. Naval Institute Proceedings*, May 1991, pp. 82-87.

Association of the United States Army. *Operations Desert Shield and Desert Storm: The Logistics Perspective*. Arlington, Virginia, 1991.

_____.*Personal Perspectives on the Gulf War.*1993.

_____.*U.S. Army in Operation Desert Storm: An Overview.* 1991.

Australia's Gulf War. Victoria: Melbourne University Press, 1992.

Baker, R. Adm. Brent. "Desert Shield/Storm; the War of Words and Images." *Naval War College Review*, Autumn 1991, pp. 59-65.

Barna, Capt. Tom D. "MPF Offload: No Longer a Paper Tiger." *Marine Corps Gazette*, November 1991, pp. 40-41.

Benson, Nicholas. *Rats' Tales: The Staffordshire Regiment at War in the Gulf.* London: Brassey's, 1994.

Bergot, Erwin, with Alain Gandy. *Operation Daguet.* Paris: Presses de la Cite, 1991.

Billiere, Gen. Sir Peter de la. "The Gulf Conflict: Planning and Execution." *Military Science: RUSI Journal.* Winter 1991, pp.7-12.

_____. *Storm Command: A Personal Account of the Gulf War.* London: HarperCollins, 1992.

Bird, Julie, and Tom Donnelly. "Friendly Fire." *Army Times.* September 19, 1991, pp. 3-4,11.

Boomer, Lt. Gen. Walter E. "Special Trust and Confidence Among the Trailbreakers." *U.S. Naval Institute Proceedings*, November 1991, pp. 47-50.

Boomer, Lt. Gen. Walter E. "Words of Encouragement." *Marine Corps Gazette*, November 1991, pp. 66.

Boyd, Morris J. & Mitchell, Randall A. "Focusing Combat Power-The Role of the FA Brigade." *Field

Artillery, February 1992, pp. 46-52.

Brabham, Brig. Gen. James A. "Training, Education Were the Keys." *U.S. Naval Institute Proceedings*, November 1991, pp. 51-54.

Brame, William L. "From Garrison to Desert Offensive in 97 Days." *Army*, February 1992, pp. 28-31, 34-35.

Braunbeck, Cdr. Michael C. "Front Line Lessons." *U.S. Naval Institute Proceedings*, May 1991, pp. 90-91.

Braybrook, Roy. *Air Power: The Coalition and Iraqi Air Forces.* London: Osprey Publishing, 1991.

Burba, Gen. Edwin H., Jr. "Training, Quality, Decisive Factors in Desert Victory." *Army*. October 1991, pp. 63-69.

Canadian Forces in the Persian Gulf/ Forces Canadiennes dans le Golfe Persique. Canadian Media Liaison Office, 1991.

Canan, James W. "Airpower Opens the Fight." *Air Force Magazine*, March 1991, p. 17.

_____. "The Electronic Storm." Air Force Magazine 74, no. 6. June 1991, p. 26.

Cancian, Lt. Col. Mark F. "Marine Corps Reserve Forces in Southwest Asia." *Marine Corps Gazette*, September 1991, pp. 35-36.

Caporale, Louis G. "Marine Corps Historical Notes from the Gulf War." *Marine Corps Gazette*, December 1991, pp. 44-46.

Caraccilo, Dominic J. *Ready Brigade of the 82nd Airborne in Desert Storm: A Combat Memoir by the Headquarters Company Commander.* Jefferson, North Carolina: McFarland & Co., 1993.

Carhart, Tom. *Iron Soldiers.* New York: Pocket Books, 1994.

Carr, Col. John J. "Logistics Planning for Desert Storm." *Army Logistician.* September-October 1991, pp. 23-25.

Certain Victory: The American Army in the Gulf War. U.S. Army Special Study Group. Washington, February 1993.

Conduct of the Persian Gulf War: An Interim Report to Congress. U.S. Department of Defense. Washington, July 1991.

Conduct of the Persian Gulf War. U.S. Department of Defense. Washington, April 1992.

Cooke, James J. *100 Miles from Baghdad: With the French in Desert Storm.* Westport, Connecticut: Praeger, 1993.

Cordingley, Brig. Patrick. 7th Armoured Brigade: Commander's Diary-Part II." *Army Quarterly* 123 July 1993, pp. 287-95.

Cornum, Rhonda, told to Peter Copeland. *She Went to War: The Rhonda Cornum Story.* Novato, California: Presidio, 1992.

Coyne, James P. *Airpower in the Gulf.* Washington: Air Force Association, 1992.

Cushman, Lt. Gen. John H. "Command and Control in the Coalition." *U.S. Naval Institute Proceedings*, May 1991, pp. 74-80.

Danis, Aaron. "Iraqi Army: Operations and Doctrine." *Military Intelligence*, April-June 1991, pp. 6-12.

"Defense for a New Era: Lessons of the Persian Gulf War." House Armed Services Committee. Washington: U.S. Government Printing Office, 1992.

Donnelly, Michael. "Groping through G-Day in a Dust Storm." *Army Times*, 15 April 1991, pp. 16, 18.

Dunn, V. Adm. Robert F. "Early Gulf War Lessons." *U.S. Naval Institute Proceedings*, March 1991, pp. 25.

Edmond, Maj. Rick J., and Capt. Kermit E. Steck. "M1A1 NETT in Southwest Asia." *Armor.* March-April 1991, pp. 14-15.

Eshel, David. "Fighting Under Desert Conditions." *Marine Corps Gazette*, November 1990, pp. 40-44.

Evans, Lt. Col. David. "With the Army and the Air Force." *U.S. Naval Institute Proceedings*, June 1991, pp. 62-64.

Evans, Cdr. Frank. "Princeton Leaves the War." *U.S. Naval Institute Proceedings*, July 1991, pp. 70-72.

Ewers, Col. Norman G. "A Conversation with Lt. Gen. Royal N. Moore, Jr." *Marine Corps Gazette*, October 1991, pp. 44-49.

Flanagan, Lt. Gen. (Ret.) Edward. *Lightning: The 101st in the Gulf War*. London: Brassey's, 1994.
_____."100-Hour War." *Army*. April 1991, pp.18, 21-26.
_____."Special Operations-Hostile Territory Was Their AO in Desert Storm." *Army*. September 1991.
Floris, John P. "1-41 FA in Desert Storm: A Test Bed for Doctrine and Equipment." *Field Artillery*, December 1991, pp. 37-42.
Foley, Maj. Gen. Thomas. "Desert Shield Deployment Rivals Patton's Rush to the Bulge." *Armor*. January-February 1991.
Fontenot, Gregory. "Fright Night: Task Force 2/34 Armor." *Military Review* 73, January 1993, pp.38-52.
Fowler, Donald E., II. "The 141st Signal Battalion Experience in Operations Desert Shield, Desert Storm: Combat was Different from Training and Doctrine." Army War College paper, March 1993. 50 p.
Franks, Gen. Frederick, Jr. "After the OPFOR, the Medina Ain't Nothin'." *Army*. October 1991, pp. 73-77.
Franks, Tommy R., & Hollis, Patricia S. "Deception, Firepower and Movement." *Field Artillery*, June 1991, pp. 31-34.
Friedman, Norman. The Air Campaign." *U.S. Naval Institute Proceedings*, April 1991, pp. 49-50.
_____. *Desert Victory: The War for Kuwait*. Annapolis: Naval Institute Press, 1991.
Fulgham, David. "Lack of Opposition Puzzles Pilots Who Flew First Mission." *Aviation Week and Space Technology*. January 21, 1991, p. 23.
_____."U.S. Mounts Swift Response to Iraq's Invasion of Kuwait." *Aviation Week and Space Technology*. August 13, 1990, pp. 18-22.
_____."U.S. Special Forces Advisors Integrate Armies from Arab Nations." *Aviation Week & Space Technology*. February 25, 1991.
Gallantry in the Gulf." *Army Quarterly*, July 1991, pp. 269-78.
Gass, Col. James M. "1st Cav Div Arty." *Field Artillery*. February 1991, pp. 26-27.
Gibson, Col. Emmitt E. "Insights of Commander, 12th Aviation Brigade." *Aviation Commander*. April 6, 1992.
Godden, John. *Shield and Storm: Personal Recollections of the Air War in the Gulf*. London: Brassey's, 1994.
Gingrich, John R. "Battle for Safwan, Iraq." Army War College paper, April 1992.
Gross, David F. "The Breach of Sadam's Defensive Line: Recollections of a Desert Storm Task Force Commander." Army War College paper, April 1993, 104p.
Guere Eclair dans le Gulfe, editions Jean-Claude Lattes et Addim. 1991.
Gulf Logistics. London: Brassey's, 1994.
Gulf War Air Power Survey, U.S. Air Force summary report, May 1993.
Gulf War: An Airman's Perspective. Washington: Armed Forces Journal International, 1993.
Hallion, Richard P. *Storm Over Iraq: Air Power and the Gulf War*. Washington: Smithsonian Institution Press, 1992.
Harris, G. Chesley. "Operation Desert Storm: Insights From a Brigade Perspective." *Infantry*, November-December 1992, pp. 20-25.
Hellen, 1st Lt. John. "2nd Armored Cavalry: the Campaign to Liberate Kuwait." *Armor*. July-August 1991, pp. 8-12.
Hillman, James L. "Task Force 1-41 Infantry: Fratricide Experience in Southwest Asia." Army War College paper, April 1993, 48 p.
Hogg, Adm. James R. "Judging Our Success." *U.S. Naval Institute Proceedings*, May 1991, pp. 100.
Holcomb, Capt. Grant K. "Why We Fought." *Marine Corps Gazeette*, April 1991, pp. 44-51.
Hopkins, Maj. Gen. John I. "This Was No Drill." *U.S. Naval Institute Proceedings*, November 1991, pp. 58-62.
Horne, R. Adm. Charles F., III. "Mine Warfare Is With Us And Will Be With Us." *U.S. Naval Institute Proceedings*, July 1991, pp. 63.
Hothus, Michael D. "Myths and Lessons of Iraqi Artillery.", *Field Artillery*, October 1991, pp. 7-9.
Huddleston, Maj. Craig S. "Commentary on Desert Shield." *Marine Corps Gazette*, January 1991, pp. 32-33.
Huddleston, Maj. Craig. "The Opening of Desert Storm: From the Front Lines." *Marine Corps*

Gazette, April 1991, pp. 52-53.

"Iraqi MiG-29 Shot Down Partner." *Aviation Week and Space Technology*, February 18, 1991 p. 63.

Jacobson, Michael R. "Iraqi Infantry." *Infantry*, January-February 1991, pp. 33-37.

Jensen, Mark S. "MLRS in Operation Desert Storm." *Field Artillery*, August 1991, pp. 30-34.

Jupa, Richard & Dineman, James. "The Iraqi Republican Guards: Just How Elite Were They?" *Command*, November-December 1991, pp. 44-50.

Kamiya, Maj. Jason K. *A History of the 24th Mechanized Infantry Division Combat Team During Operation Desert Storm.* Fort Stewart, Georgia, 1991.

Kelly, Orr. *Brave Men--Dark Waters: The Untold Story of the Navy Seals.* Novato, California: Presidio, 1992.

Keys, Lt. Gen. William M. "Rolling With the 2d Marine Division." *U.S. Naval Institute Proceedings*, November 1991, pp. 77-80.

Kindsvatter, Peter S. "VII Corps in the Gulf War: Ground Offensive." *Military Review*, February 1992, pp. 16-37.

Kirkpatrick, Charles E. *The Land Warfare Papers #9: Building the Army for Desert Storm.* Washington, DC: The Institute for Land Warfare, Association of the U.S. Army, November 1991.

Knight, Kenneth R. et al. "Movement-to-Contact: 'Red Dragons' in Operation Desert Shield." Field Artillery, June 1991, pp. 42-45.

Krause, Michael D. *"The Battle of 73 Easting, 26 February 1991: A Historical Introduction to a Simulation.* Study, U.S. Army Center of Military History and Defense Advance Research Projects Agency, August 1991. 61p.

Krulak, Brig. Gen. Charles C. "A War of Logistics." *U.S. Naval Institute Proceedings*, November 1991, pp. 55-57.

"Kuwaiti Mirage F-1s Fly Missions against Targets in Occupied Homeland." *Aviation Week and Space Technology*. February 18, 1991, p.61.

Langford, Capt. Gary D. "Iron Rain: MLRS Storms Onto the Battlefield." *Field Artillery*. December 1991, pp. 50-54.

Lenorovitz, Jeffrey M. "French Air Force Mirage F1CRs Join Attacks on Iraqi Targets." *Aviation Week and Space Technology*, February 4, 1991, pp. 65-66.

_____."French Use Jaguar Fighter/Bombers to Strike Desert Storm Targets." *Aviation Week and Space Technology*. January 28, 1991, pp. 22-23.

Lionetti, Mag. Gen. Donald M. "Air Defense: No Road To Basrah." *Army.* July 1991, pp. 16-26.

Mackenzie, Richard. "Apache Attack." *Air Force Magazine* 74, no.10. October 1991, pp. 54-60.

_____."A Conversation with Chuck Horner." *Air Force Magazine.* 74, no. 6. June 1991, p. 58.

Martin, Capt. James M. "We Still Haven't Learned." *U.S. Naval Institute Proceedings*, July 1991, pp. 64-68.

Mazzara, Lt. Col. Andrew F. "Artillery in the Desert, 1991, Report #1." *Marine Corps Gazette*, April 1991, pp. 53-55.

Mazzara, Lt. Col. Andrew F. "Supporting Arms in the Storm." *U.S. Naval Institute Proceedings*, November 1991, pp. 41-45.

McIntire, Katherine. "Speed Bumps: 82nd Airborne's Shaky Line in the Sand." *Army Times*, 21 October 1991, pp. 12-14, 18, 76-77.

McNab, Sgt. Andy. *Bravo Two Zero.* New York: Island Books, 1993.

Merritt, Gen. (Ret.) Jack N. *Special Report: Operation Desert Shield/Desert Storm: The Logistics Perspective.* Washington, D.C.: Institute of Land Warfare, September 1991.

"Mid-East Carrier War." *The Hook* 19, no. 1. Spring 1991, p. 50.

Mixson, R. Adm. Riley D. "Where We Must Do Better." *U.S. Naval Institute Proceedings*, August 1991, pp. 38-39.

Moore, Molly. *A Woman at War: Storming Kuwait with the U.S. Marines.* New York: Scribner's, 1993.

Moore, Lt. Gen. Royal N., Jr. "Marine Air: There When Needed." *U.S. Naval Institute Proceedings*, November 1991, pp. 63-70.

Morse, Stan, ed. *Gulf Air War Debrief.* Westport, Connecticut: Airtime Publishing, 1991.

Myatt, Maj. Gen. J. M. "The 1st Marine Division in the Attack." *U.S. Naval Institute Proceedings*,

November 1991, pp. 71-76.

Naylor, Sean D. "Flight of Eagles: 101st Airborne Division's Raids into Iraq." *Army Times*, 22 July 1991, pp. 8-12, 15.

_____."Home of the Brave." *Army Times*, 27 January 1992, pp. 8, 12-14, 16, 58.

Nordwall, Bruce. "US Relies on Combination of Aircraft, Satellites, UAVs for Damage Assessment." *Aviation & Space Technology*. February 4, 1991.

O'Ballance, Edgar. *The Gulf War*. London: Brassey's, 1991.

O'Donovan, Lt. Col. John A. "Combat Service Support During Desert Shield and Desert Storm: From Kibrit to Kuwait." *Marine Corps Gazette*, October 1991, pp. 26-31.

Oliveri, Frank. "Conventional ALCM Revealed." *Air Force Magazine* 75, no.3. March 1992, p.17.

Pagonis, Lt. Gen. William G. *Moving Mountains: Lessons in Leadership and Logistics from the Gulf War*. Boston: Harvard Business School Press, 1992.

Palmer, Michael A. "The Navy Did its Job." *U.S. Naval Institute Proceedings*, May 1991, pp. 88-93.

Pardew, James W., Jr. "The Iraqi Army's Defeat in Kuwait." *Parameters* 21, Winter 1991-1992, pp.17-23.

"Patriot Missile Defense: Software Problem Led to System Failure at Dhahran, Saudi Arabia." U.S. General Accounting Office, February 1992.

Petrosky, Daniel J., & Hillard, Marshall T. "An Aviation Brigade Goes to War." *Aviation Digest*, September-October 1991: pp.44-65.

Phillips, Jeffrey E. *America's First Team in the Gulf*. Dallas: Taylor Publishing Co., 1992.

Pope, Col. John R. "U.S. Marines in Operation Desert Storm." *Marine Corps Gazette*, July 1991, pp. 63-69.

Postal, Theodore A. Lessons of the Gulf War Experience with Patriot." *International Security*, Winter 1991-2.

Primakov, Yevgeni. "The Inside Story of Moscow's Quest for a Deal." *Time*, April 4, 1991.

_____. "My Final Visit with Saddam Hussein." *Time*, April 11, 1991.

Puryear, Capt. A.A., and Lt. Gerald R. Haywood, II. "Ar-Rumaylah Airfield Succumbs to Hasty Attack." *Armor*. September-October 1991, pp.16-20.

"Redlegs in the Gulf." *Field Artillery*. October 1991.

Reischl, Timothy J. "Crossing the Line in the Sand: 4th Battalion, 67th Armor in Southwest Asia." Army War College paper, April 1993. 80 p.

Ripley, Tim. *Land Power: The Coalition and Iraqi Armies*. London: Osprey Publishing, 1991.

Rolston, David A."Victory Artillery in Operation Desert Shield." *Field Artillery*, April 1991, pp.23-25.

Sack, John. *Company C: The Real War in Iraq*. New York: Morrow, 1995.

Scales, Col. Robert H., Jr. "Accuracy Defeated Range in Artillery Duel." *International Defense Review*. May 1991, pp. 473-481.

_____.*Certain Victory: The U.S. Army in the Gulf War*. U.S. Army Desert Storm Study Project, 1993.

Schemmer, Ben F. "Special Ops Teams Found 29 Scuds Ready to Barrage Israel 24 Hours Before Cease-Fire." *Armed Forces Journal International*, July 1991, p. 36.

_____."USAF MH-53J Pave Lows Led Army Apaches Knocking Out Iraqi Radars to Open Air War." *Armed Forces Journal International*. July 1991.

Schubert, Frank N., and Theresa L. Kraus, eds. *Whirlwind War: The United States Army in Operations Desert Shield and Desert Storm*. Washington, D.C. U.S. Army Center of Military History, January 31, 1992.

Schwarzkopf, H. Norman, with Peter Petre. *It Doesn't Take a Hero*. New York: Bantam, 1992.

Scicchitano, J. Paul. "Eye of the Tiger." *Army Times*, 10 June 1991, pp. 12-13, 16, 18, 61.

_____."Night Strikes: The Secret War of the 1st Cavalry Division." *Army Times*. September 23, 1991, pp.8, 14-16.

Shanahan, Michael K. "Doctrine or Not? XVIII Airborne Corps Movement During Operation Desert Storm." Army War College paper, March 1992.

Simmons, Brig. Gen. Edwin H. "Getting Marines to the Gulf." *U.S. Naval Institute Proceedings*, May 1991, pp. 50-64.

_____."Getting the Job Done." *U.S. Naval Institute Proceedings*, May 1991, pp. 94-96.

Smallwood, William L. *Strike Eagle: Flying the F-15E in the Gulf War*. London: Brassey's, 1994.

_____.*Warthog: Flying the A-10 in the Gulf War*. 1993.

Smith, Jean Edward. *George Bush's War*. New York: Henry Holt, 1992.

Smith, Stephen S. "The 1st Battalion, 7th Infantry in the Gulf War." Army War College, March 1993, 53 p.

Steele, Dennis. "155 Miles into Iraq: The 101st Strikes Deep." *Army*, August 1991, p. 30.

_____."Tanks and Men: Desert Storm from the Hatches." *Army*, June 1991, pp. 28-34.

Stein, Janice Gross. "Deterrence and Compliance in the Gulf." *International Security*. Fall 1992.

Stein, Robert M. "Patriot Experience in the Gulf." *International Security*, Summer 1992.

Stewart, John F., Jr. *Operation Desert Storm: The Military Intelligence Story*. 3rd U.S. Army, April 1992.

Summers, Harry G., Jr. *On Strategy II: A Critical Analysis of the Gulf War*. New York: Dell, 1992.

Tanner, J.K. "The British Soldier in the Gulf." *Military Illustrated*, October 1991, pp. 10-18.

The 3rd Armored Division Fought Saddam's Toughest Troops Through Rain and Wind." *Armor*. March-April 1991.

"U.K. in the Gulf." *Aircraft Illustrated* 24, no. 4. April 1991, pp. 177-79, 184-85.

U.S. Army. *1st Infantry Division, 1st Brigade*. Desert Shield/Storm History. Fort Riley, Kansas, 1992. 450p. #05-1-1992.

U.S. Army. *2nd Battalion, 29th Field Artillery*. Desert Storm: Combat Historical Summary, 15 January-16 April 1991.

U.S. Army. 702nd Transportation Battalion (Provisional). *"Battalion Operations Diary, Saudi Arabia, 1990-1991."* 41 p.

U.S. News & World Report. *Triumph Without Victory: The Unreported History of the Persian Gulf War*. Times Books, New York, 1992.

Vallance, Group Capt. Andrew "Andy". "Air Power in the Gulf War: The RAF Contribution." *Air Clues: The Royal Air Force Magazine* 45, no. 7. July 1991, pp. 251-54.

Vogel, Steve. "Fast and Hard: The Big Red One's Race Through Iraq." *Army Times*, 25 March 1991, pp. 12-13.

_____. "Hell Night--For the 2nd Armored Division (Forward) It Was No Clean War." *Army Times*. October 7, 1991, pp. 8, 14-15, 18, 24, 69.

_____. "A Swift Kick." *Army Times* 5 August 1991, pp.10-14, 18, 28, 30, 61.

_____. "The Tip of the Spear." *Army*, 13 January 1992, pp. 8, 10, 12-13, 16, 54.

_____. "VII Corps Soldiers Describe Incidents." *Army Times*. September 19, 1991, p. 3.

Wilson, Jeffery S. "Desert Storm: A Look Back." *Ordnance* February 1992, pp. 26-31.

Yeosock, Lt. Gen. John J. "Army Operations in the Gulf Theater." *Military Review*. September 1991, pp. 2-15.

OFFICIAL DOCUMENTS

British Ministry of Defence, Inspector General, Doctrine and Training. *"Operation Granby: An Account of the Gulf Crisis of 1990-91 and the British Army's Contribution to the Liberation of Kuwait."* UK, 1991.

Cureton, Lt. Col. Charles H., *U.S. Marines in the Persian Gulf, 1990-1991: With the 1st Marine Division in Desert Shield and Desert Storm*. Washington: U.S. Government Printing Office, 1993.

Melson, Maj. Charles D. *U.S. Marines in the Persian Gulf, 1990-1991: Anthology and Annotated Bibliography*. Washington: U.S. Government Printing Office, 1992.

Mroczkowski, Lt. Col. Dennis P. *U.S. Marines in the Persian Gulf, 1990-1991: With the 2d Marine Division in Desert Shield and Desert Storm*. Washington: U.S. Government Printing Office, 1993.

Quilter, Col. Charles J., II. *U.S. Marines in the Persian Gulf, 1990-1991: With the I Marine Expeditionary Force in Desert Shield and Desert Storm*. Washington: U.S. Government Printing Office, 1993.

U.S. Air Force Analysis of Air Operations during Desert Shield/Desert Storm. (USAF Studies and Analysis Agency), 1991.

U.S. Air Force. *Nighthawks over Iraq: A Chronology of the F-117A Stealth Fighter in Operations*

Desert Shield and Desert Storm. Special Study 37FW/HO-91-1. Tonoph, Nev.: Office of History, HQ 37th Fighter Wing, January 9, 1992 (written by Harold P. Myers and Vincent C. Breslin).

U.S. Army Headquarters, 1st Brigade, 2nd Armored Division. *"Actions of the 'Tiger' Brigade during Operation Desert Shield/Desert Storm, August 10, 1990-March 1, 1991."* Fort Hood, TX, undated.

U.S. Army, Headquarters, *1st Infantry Division. Operations Desert Shield and Desert Storm Command Report.* Saudi Arabia, 19 April 1991.

U.S. Army Headquarters, *3rd Armored Division.* Briefing. Saudi Arabia, undated.

U.S. Army Headquarters, *5th Special Forces Group. Collection of Operational Orders and Reports, January 17-February 28, 1991.* Fort Bragg, NC.

U.S. Army Headquarters, *11th Air Defense Brigade. Desert Shield/Desert Storm After-Action Report.* Fort Bliss, TX, undated.

U.S. Army Headquarters, *101st Airborne Division (Air Assault). Lessons Learned from Operations Desert Shield and Desert Storm.* Fort Campbell, KY, June 27, 1991.

U.S. Army Headquarters, *VII Corps. After-Action Review. Saudi Arabia, March 11, 1991.*

U.S. Army Headquarters, *XVIII Airborne Corps. After-Action Brief for Operation Desert Shield and Desert Storm (Updated).* Fort Bragg, NC, 25 September 1991.

U.S. Army Armor Center. *Desert Shield and Desert Storm Emerging Observations.* Fort Knox, KY, October 7, 1991.

U.S. Army Central Command Military Intelligence History (A three-volume, 13-chapter history).

U.S. Army National Guard Bureau After-Action Review Briefing. Undated.

U.S. National Guard Bureau After-Action Report:Operation Desert Shield and Operation Desert Storm Executive Summary. Arlington, VA: October 1991.

U.S. Navy. *"The United States Navy in Desert Shield/Desert Storm."* Washington: Department of the Navy, May 1991.

INDEX

Abbot, Capt. Charles S., USN, 59, 66;
  biography of, 211
Abrams, Brig. Gen. Creighton, III, USA,
  101, 112; biography of, 211
Adams, Cdr. James J., USNR, 22; biography
  of, 211
Ad Dammam, 10-11
ADELAIDE, 17, 35. *See also* Australian
  Navy
Admire, Maj. Gen. John, USMC, 123;
  biography of, 211; lack of Iraqi resolve,
  93
ADROIT, 20, 33; discovers large minefield,
  116; tows PRINCETON, 114. *See also*
  U.S. Navy
Afghanistani troops (Mujahedeen), 106
Ahern, Cdr. Timothy M., USN, 66;
  biography of, 212
Ahmad, Lt. Gen. Sultan Hasheem IA, 138,
  212
A. J. HIGGINS, 7. *See also* U.S. Navy
Al Ain, UAE, 20
Al Batin, Wadi. *See* Wadi Al-Batin
Al Dhafra, UAE, airfield, 8-9, 14, 26, 28;
  first Italian aircraft arrive, 31
Al Jouf, 10, 21, 23, 26; Desert Storm
  launched from, 71
Al Jubayl, 1, 9, 11, 14, 22, 24, 72; arrival of
  Staffordshire Regiment, 39
Al Kalia Naval Facility, 96
Al Khafji, See Khafji, Battle of
Al Kharj, 8, 59, 61
Al Mindad, UAE, 20
Al-Rawi, Lt. Gen. Ayad Futayih, 1, 124-25
ALTAIR, 13
AMERICA, 59, 67-68, 72, 105, 108-10,

116, 120, 145. *See also* U.S. Navy
Amphibious Ready Group Alpha, 24
Amphibious Ready Group Bravo, 24, 26
ANCHORAGE, 51, 65. *See also* U.S. Navy
Andersonville (Initial Staging Area), 57
ANTIETAM, 4, 43. *See* U.S. Navy
Arabian Gulf Exercise, 8
Argentina Navy, 31, 80. *See* biographies of
  individual commanders
Armilla Patrol, 3. *See* British Royal Navy
Arther, V.Adm. Stanley R., USN, 51;
  biography of, 213
Assembly Area Horse, 41
Assembly Area Thompson, 60, 62
ATHABASKAN, 18, 64. *See also* Canadian
  Navy
ATHERSTONE, 3, 10, 24, 145-46. *See also*
  British Royal Navy
AUDACE, 15. *See also* Italian Navy
Australian Navy, 17, 80
AVENGER 134, 136. *See also* U.S. Navy
AWACS, 7, 9, 43, 136. *See also* U.S. Air
  Force
Aziz, Brig. Gen. Turki Bin Nasser Abdul,
  SA, 138

B-52 (bombers), 7, 9, 12, 14-15, 18, 27, 30,
  69; attack front lines and breaching sites,
  124; attempt to kill Saddam Hussein, 83;
  combat sorties, 73, 76-78, 80-82, 84, 86-
  87, 89, 92, 94-98, 100-04, 107; crash off
  Diego Garcia, 96; generates significant
  secondary explosions, 106; low-level
  sorties, 31; war record, 68; pounds
  Republican Guard, 88, 90-92, 96, 98,
  106, 108. *See also* U.S. Air Force

ISBN 0-313-29606-5

90000>

EAN

9 780313 296062

HARDCOVER BAR CODE